The Legalistic Organization

Sim B Sitkin
Robert J. Bies

editors

SAGE Publications
International Educational and Professional Publisher
Thousand Oaks   London   New Delhi

For information address:

SAGE Publications, Inc.
2455 Teller Road
Thousand Oaks, California 91320

SAGE Publications Ltd.
6 Bonhill Street
London EC2A 4PU
United Kingdom

SAGE Publications India Pvt. Ltd.
M-32 Market
Greater Kailash I
New Delhi 110 048 India

Library of Congress Cataloging-in-Publication Data

Main entry under title:

The legalistic organization / edited by Sim B Sitkin, Robert J. Bies
      p. cm.
      ISBN 0-8039-4863-8 (cl.)   —   ISBN 0-8039-4864-6 (pbk.)
      Includes bibliographical references and index.
      1. Organizational behavior. 2. Decision-making. 3. Sociological
jurisprudence. 4. Associations, institutions, etc.—Law and
legislation.   5. Juristic persons—Psychological aspects. I. Sitkin,
Sim B . II. Bies, Robert J.
HD58.7.L447   1994
302.3'5—dc20   93-41636

94 95 96 97 98 10 9 8 7 6 5 4 3 2 1

Sage Production Editor: Rebecca Holland

Contents

Introduction

People often ask us how we came to be interested in the topic, the legalistic organization. In a nutshell, it was luck. But a more complete answer is that at about the same time—1986—both of us began our interest serendipitously, while conducting field research on very different topics: for Sim, how professionals handled issues of secrecy and confidentiality, and for Bob, how managers deliver bad news. What we found was that the professionals and managers, in our separate studies, were both manifesting "litigiphobia," that is, the fear of being sued by employees, customers, and regulators. Further, they reported that these concerns were beginning to influence heavily (a) how they made decisions; (b) which words they would choose when communicating to employees, customers, and regulators; (c) their patterns of interactions and relationships; and (d) the structure and design of their organizations.

Our shared interest in the legalistic organization led us to put together symposia on this topic at the Academy of Management Meetings in 1987, 1989, and 1991. At these symposia, other scholars reported that they, too, were finding evidence of the legalization of organizational processes and structure. It became clear that there was an emerging group of scholars interested in this phenomenon who were also conducting empirical research on it. Some of their work appeared in special issues (which we edited) of *Organizational Science* and the *Employee Responsibilities and Rights Journal*, both of which were published in 1993.

This book takes the next exciting steps beyond those issues and includes state-of-the-art conceptual essays and empirical research on the legalistic organization. The authors in this book represent a wide range of disciplinary perspectives, empirical methodologies, and organizational contexts. Indeed, the authors make clear that the phenomenon of the legalistic organization can be studied fruitfully, both theoretically and empirically. More specifically, the authors illustrate and analyze what we have identified as the key dimensions of the legalistic organization: formal rules and procedures, adversarial relations, legalistic rhetoric, and inordinate attention given to legal sanctions and criteria in decision making.

But beyond the definitions and dimensions of the legalistic organization, chapters in this book highlight the dilemmas and paradoxes associated with this phenomenon. Not only do the chapters illustrate the negative, dysfunctional—even sinister—aspects of the legalistic organization, they also correctly point out the positive, functional aspects of the legalistic organization (e.g., ensuring justice and fairness). In other words, the legalistic organization is not a phenomenon that is easily understood in simplistic either-or terms; rather, it is a complex, very real phenomenon that affects our lives on a daily basis.

In putting together this book, our debt of gratitude is great and to many. First, we owe an intellectual debt to a variety of scholars who pioneered work in this area (e.g., Max Weber—remember, he did call it *legal*-rational mode of authority; Philip Selznick—in his 1969 book, *Law, Justice, and Industrial Society,* is absolutely brilliant and insightful, and must reading for all; John Meyer and Mark Yudof—for their independent insights on the legalization process in educational institutions). Second, we are thankful for being able to work with the authors in this book, as they brought us new and fresh insights concerning the legalistic organization and the legalization process. Their patience with us as active editors was appreciated as well. Third, we are grateful to have had the opportunity to work with Harry Briggs. He is a first-rate editor who "managed" us well (and who also has great taste in book topics).

And, finally, words cannot capture the gratitude and thanks due to our respective families, who put up with us in the process of putting this book together. So, from our hearts, we dedicate this book to them. To Susan, Kelly, Vivian, Leah, and Jared. For without whom.

Robert J. Bies
Sim B Sitkin

Preface

There are many principles of social ordering. The great jurisprudent, Lon Fuller, who was one of the preeminent contracts scholars of the 20th century, once divided this terrain into nine categories: coordination that arises tacitly through interaction (customary law and standard practice, with or without judicial enforcement), contract, property, officially declared law, adjudication, managerial decision, voting, mediation, and deliberate resort to chance. Fuller made no claim that his list was exhaustive. If the concept of social ordering is expanded to include decision making more generally, one might create a taxonomy, based on the work of Charles Lindblom, that distinguishes among political, market, and socialization mechanisms for allocative and other decisions. So, too, the implementation theorists tell us that there is a wide variety of options in terms of gaining compliance with decisions, for example, judicial enforcement of rules, persuasion, co-optation, empowerment, and so forth.

In the realm of social ordering, it is no great epiphany to discover that law and the coercive powers of the state are not the only game in town, though doubtless jingoistic lawyers sometimes forget. It is also true, as the organizational theory and compliance literatures suggest, that we should be self-conscious about how decisions are made (or should be made) and implemented. Different modes of decision making involve varying costs in different settings in terms of time, efficiency, predictability, and fairness. One job of social science, amply carried out in the essays that follow, is to enrich our understanding of the symbolic and real consequences of relying on different decision-making options.

But what many sometimes forget is that each vessel of social ordering is not hermetically sealed, that there is a mixing of the categories and, indeed, leakage from one to another. And, most critically, the method or methods of decision making themselves may transform the social order or the organizational milieu within which the decisions are made. That is the critical contribution of this excellent volume, edited by Professors Sitkin and Bies. To be sure, the authors of the essays are concerned with the costs and benefits of resorting to law to make decisions and resolve disputes. But they also confront the more global issues: What is the impact of law, including legal reasoning, legal institutions, rules, procedures, and the culture of law, on complex organizations? What is their impact on other modes of social ordering? How does the law-saturated organization redefine its ostensibly nonlegal decision-making processes? What emerges is a path-breaking consideration of The Legalistic Organization.

A major question posed by Scott, Sitkin, Bies, Pfeffer, and others in their research is whether legalization of complex organizations is in itself destructive or, indeed, pathological. I would answer this question in the negative. I view myself as having good credentials to proffer this answer. I often have worried about the impact of rules and formal procedures on complex organizations. More than a decade ago, I expressed the fear that the legalization of dispute resolution within public schools might undermine the learning environment and the trusting relationship between students and teachers that facilitates learning. I noted how the revolution in rights, the diminished respect for experts and administrators, and the decline of public trust in public institutions had produced legalization. Yet legalization itself threatened to create more distrust, the very condition it was designed to overcome. No matter where one looked—prisons, psychiatric facilities, schools, private corporations, welfare agencies, police forces—the distrust/legalization spiral was much in evidence.

The essays in this volume are a strong antidote to the suppositions that law is always essential to social ordering; that formal rationality is always superior to informality and cooperation; and that legal analysis is necessarily coincident with common sense, efficiency, and fairness. But, whatever our concerns about the excesses, costs, and rigidities of legalization, scholars should never lose sight of the fundamental role of law in controlling discretion; protecting entitlements and rights; and securing fairness, equal treatment, and predictability. Certainly, the peoples of Eastern Europe, now clamoring for the rule of the law, well understand this. There may be other means of controlling discretion in particular cultures or contexts, as Professor Smitka's essay on Japan illustrates, but this does not diminish the importance of law. If some believe that modern regulation of the workplace goes too far, unnecessarily undermines efficiency, and distorts corporate decision making, this does not mean that legal rules forbidding racial discrimination in employment practices, sexual harassment on the job, and unsafe working conditions should be repealed. Although Americans may believe that the legalization of dispute resolution within families is generally a bad idea (e.g., children suing parents for breaking their social promises), we may nonetheless continue to promulgate and enforce rules on child abuse and neglect and interspousal battery.

My point, I suppose, is that there is nothing inherently good or evil about discretion or legal constraints on discretion. Just as there can be too much law, there can be too much discretion. Just as there can be too little law, there can be too little discretion left in the system. Much depends on the context, objectives, the costs. I always enjoyed Edmund Burke's rendering of this problem: "[If] the effect of liberty to individuals is, that they may do what they please: we ought see what it will please them to do, before we risk congratulations. . . . " One may be a strong adherent of free enterprise and economic efficiency, and yet believe that employers should not be permitted to fire whistle-blowers.

In closing, I would only make two suggestions to those who study complex organizations and the impact of legalization. First, they should be careful not to caricature law. Sometimes there is a tendency for those outside the legal system to view the law in mechanistic terms, as consisting of rigid and self-evident rules, which leave little room for interpretation and for blending with the varying factual circumstances that arise. The legal realists, however, have demonstrated that legal rules are not so inflexible, that there is discretion in their formulation and application, that judges can take account of the human features of a dispute. Indeed, it is somewhat ironic that the exponential growth in research on legalization takes place at a time when critical legal scholars, feminist law theorists, and others debate whether legal rules are inherently indeterminant, whether there is such a thing as genuine rule of law rather than rule by men and women. Indeed, one fertile area for research is to look at who interprets legal rules within a complex organization and how the requirements of the law are transmitted within the organization. Is there a tendency to simplify and to remove ambiguity for operational reasons? Do lay managers view law differently than judges and lawyers?

Second, there is always temptation to romanticize what life would be like without law, lawyers, judges, "technicalities," red tape, and lawsuits. This reflects a perceived loss of community in the modern (or postmodern) state and a yearning for a future based on trust, cooperation, and mutual respect. Recall the words of Grant Gilmore:

The better the society, the less law there will be. In Heaven there will be no law, and the lion will lie down with the lamb. . . . The worse the society, the more law there will be. In Hell there will be nothing but law, and due process will be meticulously observed.

But, Gilmore to the contrary, just as there is genuine impulse toward community and substantive justice, there is an equally human impulse to equal treatment and formal justice. Both impulses are good and distinctly human in a world that has characteristics of both heaven and hell.

Mark G. Yudof

For permission to reprint the following, the editors gratefully acknowledge:

From "Poindexter-Iran-Contra," AP story tag, by J. Drinkard, 1987, DIALOG. Copyright © 1987 by Associated Press. Reprinted with permission.

From "Minority Report: Iran-Contra Hearings," by C. Hitchens, The Nation magazine. Copyright © 1987, The Nation Company, Inc. Reprinted with permission.

From "Reagan's Shadow CIA: How the White House Ran the Secret 'Contra' War," by R. Parry and B. Barger, 1986 (November), New Republic, p. 23. Copyright © 1986 New Republic. Reprinted with permission.

From "Iranarms-Byrd," UPI story tag, by S. Gerstel, 1987, DATELINE: WASHINGTON, United Press International. Copyright © 1987 by UPI. Reprinted with the permission of United Press International.

From E. Alterman, 1987 (July), Washington Monthly, p. 19. Reprinted with permission from The Washington Monthly. Copyright © 1987 by The Washington Monthly Company, 1611 Connecticut Avenue, NW, Washington, D.C. 20009. (202) 462-0128.

Introduction and Theoretical Context

1

Law and Organizations

W. Richard Scott

A lthough the godfather of organization theory, Max Weber, pointed to the close association of law and organizations nearly a century ago, the great bulk of theory and research on organizations has failed to honor or build on this legacy. Only occasionally have analysts sought to link organizational and legal scholarship, and until quite recently, such efforts have not been regarded as mainstream but as marginal. The present volume contributes to recent efforts to rekindle interest in Weber's agenda.

I attempt to provide a conceptual frame for locating the work reported here by identifying three broad classes of scholarship relating law and organizations. The first two are only briefly described and illustrated; the third, which incorporates the type of work collected in this volume, is discussed at greater length. The categories I propose are: (1) the organization of legal systems and services; (2) crime and organizations; and (3) the legal environment of organizations. The first emphasizes the effects of organizations on the law; the second examines the ways in which organizations are involved—both as perpetrators and victims —in behaviors defined as problematic by the law; and the third emphasizes the effects of law, including legal systems and legal culture, on the structure and functioning of organizations.

■ The Organization of Legal Systems and Services

No doubt the most conventional treatment of law and organizations— and the lion's share of scholarly work conducted to date relating these two topics—is that which treats lawyers and legal activity, criminals and criminal acts, as simply another kind of social behavior, which, like all behavior, is subject to bureaucratization. Lawyers increasingly work in and for organizations; the court system is a complex bureaucratic apparatus; police and prisons are highly organized; criminals often operate as a part of "organized crime"; and even the victims of crime seek help from service organizations and increasingly mobilize to advance or protect their interests in social movement organizations.

As a part of a generation of sociologists who examined the impact of bureaucratization on professions, Smigel (1964) carried out the first systematic study showing the increasing importance of law firms as a basis for legal practice. The examination of organizational effects on professional autonomy and careers continues up to the present (e.g., Galanter, 1991; Heinz & Laumann, 1982; Nelson, 1988). Lawyers have been employed, of course, for an even longer time in staffing a wide variety of federal and state agencies, but these organizational settings have received less research attention than they deserve. (However, for useful discussions of the effects of lawyers on administrative agencies and vice versa, see Kelman, 1981; Mendeloff, 1979; Skowronek, 1982; Weaver, 1977; Wilson, 1980.)

An interesting analysis of the federal court system in the United States, as a complex bureaucratic structure subject to overload and gridlock, is provided by Heydebrand (1990). Cicourel (1968) has examined the organization of juvenile justice systems. Prison systems were among the first organizations studied by sociologists (see, e.g., Clemmer, 1940; Cloward, Cressey, Grosser, McCleery, Ohlin, Sykes, & Messinger, 1960; Sykes, 1958; not to forget the classic discussion by Goffman, 1961, of total institutions). More recently, Foucault (1979) has examined the development of prisons and the changes over time in their technologies of discipline as a homologue for the increasing regulation of social life as knowledge, power, the control of the body, and the control of space are mobilized in ever more efficient and impersonal forms.

The organization of the police has also received considerable attention (see Bittner, 1990; Ericson, Baranek, & Chan 1991; Manning, 1977; Manning & Van Maanen, 1978; Wilson, 1968). Indeed, police organizations have provided the site for some of the most compelling studies by ethnomethodologists and phenomenologists, such as Bittner and Van Maanen, who dissect the ways in which social order is constructed in day-to-day encounters. Criminals also take advantage of the benefits of organizing (see Ianni, 1972; Kelly, 1986). These systems, both of lawkeepers and lawbreakers, and their interaction represent interesting situations for organization theory—and difficult problems for their leaders—because they are organized in opposition to each other. Police confront organized gangs and criminal syndicates; prison officials, large number of concentrated inmates. The usual incentives (e.g., monetary or solidarity rewards) available to organizations are largely missing; and liberal societies constrain the exercise of excessive force. How to maintain some semblance of control in such circumstances is the problem confronted by law enforcement agencies.

Finally, the victims of crimes increasingly seek help from existing organizations in the form of protection or therapy, or they create new organizations to obtain mutual assistance or to seek redress and reform (see, e.g., Knudsen & Miller, 1991; McCarthy, Wolfson, Baker, & Mosakowski, 1988).

This first category of work focuses on a distinctive sector of society: one in which the organizations and roles are seen to be a part of the legal/social control subsystem of the wider society. This sector, like all societal sectors, is permeated by organizations, and its work is substantially modified because it takes place within organizational contexts.

■ Crime and Organizations

Categories two and three focus attention on the relation between law and organizations, not for that subset of organizations specializing in law enforcement or law-breaking activities, but for the full range of organizations. Category two incorporates studies which recognize that all organizations are capable of engaging in illegal activity and, conversely, that any organization may become the target of illegal acts. Organizations confront the law both as violators and as victims.

The simpler cases of crime in organizations involve rogue individuals—participants who abuse their power or position for their own gain. Crimes such as embezzlement or grand theft are committed by individuals within organizations. Given the interdependence of tasks and individuals in organizations, such cases may involve multiple conspirators and even entire subunits or departments. The victim of such deviant activities is often the employing organization. Organizations can also be targeted for criminal attacks by nonmembers, for example, when products such as drugs are tampered with or when equipment is sabotaged (see Mitroff & Kilmann, 1984).

Much more interesting and significant, however, are those deviant acts that are committed by the organization itself. Sherman (1982, p. 4) clarifies the distinction:

> It is important to distinguish deviance committed *by* organizations from deviance committed *in* organizations. Deviance committed by an organization is collective rule-breaking action that helps achieve organizational goals. Deviance committed in an organization is individual or collective rule-break actions that does not help to achieve organizational goals, or that is harmful to those goals.

The catalogue of organizational crimes is long, and the number of organizations involved can sometime stagger comprehension. Price-fixing, insider trading, false and misleading advertising, corruption of public officials, illegal surveillance, violation of patents and copyrights, tax fraud, illegal disposal of hazardous wastes—these are some of the more common crimes committed by corporations and governmental units. Sutherland (1949) provided the first major discussion of criminal behavior by organizations, but this subject has now spawned a large literature, both academic and popular (see, e.g., Clinard & Yeager, 1980; Ermann & Lundman, 1982a; Herling, 1962; Vaughan, 1983; Weisburd, Wheeler, Waring, & Bode, 1991). The scope of such problems is graphically illustrated by the recent Savings and Loan industry scandals in the United States, the illegal network of bribery and corruption linking the Italian government and dozens of major corporations, and the fraudulent practices surrounding the Bank of Credit & Commerce International (BCCI) (see, e.g, Beaty & Gwynne, 1993; Day, 1993; Pizzo, Fricher, & Muolo, 1991; Stewart, 1991).

Ermann and Lundman (1982b, p. 7) suggest that deviant actions by organizations can come about in three ways:

> First, the limited information and responsibility characteristics of positions within large organizations can produce a situation where no individual has been deviant but the combinations of their work-related actions produces deviance. Second, organizational elites can indirectly initiate deviant actions by establishing particular norms, rewards and punishments for people occupying lower-level positions. Third, elites at or near the top of an organization can consciously initiate a deviant action and explicitly use hierarchically linked positions to implement it.

Such a discussion illustrates the difficulty faced by legal bodies in determining who is to be held responsible for organizational misdeeds.

The classic analysis of these issues is by Stone (1975), who also describes the poverty and ineffectiveness of sanctions available to the courts when corporate wrongdoing is uncovered. (For an interesting examination of the distinctions between corporate and individual rights and responsibilities, see Dan-Cohen, 1986.) The conditions under which insiders attempt to call attention to deviant actions by organizations—becoming whistle-blowers—has also been studied by organizational researchers (see Near & Miceli, 1987).

■ The Legal Environment of Organizations

The third and, to my mind, most interesting arena of work relating law and organizations is also the least developed. It is this area to which Weber made his most important intellectual contributions, but it is also this area that was so long neglected by organizational analysts. Only recently, and particularly with the development of the new institutional theory in organizations, have scholars begun to recognize the importance of legal environments for organizations.

Organizational theorists recognized during the 1960s that organizations are open systems, dependent on and greatly influenced by the environments in which they operate. However, for many years primary attention was given by researchers to the technical aspects of environments: to the exchange of resources and task-related information necessary for the production of goods and services. It was not until the late 1970s that organizational theorists called attention to the institutional facets of environments. (For an extended review of these developments, see Scott, 1992.)

The institutional environment consists of the symbolic systems that we as social beings develop to impute meaning to our world, the cultural rules we employ to construct frameworks that permit common understandings and support collaborative actions. Institutional systems contain both cognitive and normative elements. Earlier institutional theorists, such as Parsons (1951) and Selznick (1957), accorded primacy to normative elements, including role expectations and enforcement mechanisms; more recent analysts, such as Berger and Luckmann (1967) and Meyer and Rowan (1977) emphasize the importance of cognitive constructions, including framing assumptions and constitutive rules (see DiMaggio & Powell, 1991; Scott, 1987). Both are important components of institutions, and legal systems are an important creator and carrier of these processes in modern societies.

Suchman (1993) has proposed that legal environments can be partitioned into three components: the regulatory, the interactional, and the definitional. I follow his suggestion and discuss each.

Regulatory Environments

The regulation of organizational behavior, typically by the state, is the most widely recognized facet of the legal environment. Many of the chapters in the present volume deal with the effects of the regulatory environment on organizations. All organizations are subject to regulation by the state, although the nature and degree of these controls vary widely across societies and sectors. The regulatory efforts of the state create distinctive governance regimes at the level of the sector or organizational field, a critical intermediate unit that connects the study of individual organization structure and functioning on the one hand to societal-level processes on the other. As DiMaggio (1986, p. 337) asserts: "The organization field has emerged as a critical unit bridging the organizational and societal levels in the study of social and community change."

Both organizational sociologists and political scientists have begun to devote attention to examining the types of governance systems that develop at the field level (see, e.g., Campbell, Hollingsworth, & Lindberg, 1991; Schmitter, 1990; Streeck & Schmitter, 1985; and for a review, see Scott, forthcoming); the effects of these differing regulatory systems on the "structuration" of the field of organizations (see, e.g., Carroll, Delacroix, & Goodstein, 1988; DiMaggio, 1983; DiMaggio & Powell, 1983; Fligstein, 1990); as well as the effects of these rules and interorganizational systems on the structure and functioning of individual organizations (see Carroll et al., 1988; Meyer, 1983; Scott & Meyer, 1983, 1991). For example, fields vary greatly in their governance mechanisms, from market controls through mutually enforced industry norms to highly centralized state controls. (See, for example, the chapter by Smitka, this volume, on the different types of institutions for managing contracts.) And fields vary in their structuration, from low awareness of boundaries and low levels of interaction and order to well-recognized boundaries and taut networks of ordered relations. Finally, organizational forms vary in their degree of specialization, the clarity of their role in the field division of labor, and their administrative and technical coherence. Theorizing the nature of these relations among regime, structuration, and organizational variables is an important task on which work has just begun.

There exists a large literature on the effects of regulatory systems on sector performance, but this literature is (a) largely economic or political in focus and (b) tends to be associated with politically conservative assumptions about the evils of government interference in "free" market mechanisms. Only a few studies emphasize the effects on organizations of regulatory systems, and the response by organizations to these control attempts (see, e.g., Alexander & Scott, 1984; Johnson, 1979; Noll, 1985; Sproull, 1981; Tamuz & Sitkin, 1991; Weaver, 1978).

Interactional Environments

A second component of the legal environment as viewed by Suchman (1993) emphasizes how legal institutions and legal culture influence the ways in which societal actors construct problems and the techniques and procedures for dealing with them. We come, at last, to the major focus of this volume: how the legal environment functions to transform—to *legalize*—social processes for handling problems and disputes.

In their introductory essay to this volume, Sitkin and Bies define legalization as "a process which encompasses the diffusion of legalistic reasoning, procedures, and structures as a means of sustaining or enhancing the legitimacy of the organization (or an organizational sub-unit) with critical internal or external constituencies."

I prefer to adopt only the first half of this sentence (ending with the word *structures*) as the definition of legalization, so that one could treat the remaining phrase as one among several testable explanations for the observed phenomenon. Indeed, some types of legalization appear to undermine the legitimacy of organizations in the eyes of some constituencies, for example, economists who give primacy to efficiency and cost-benefit criteria.

In an earlier discussion of legalization within education, Meyer (1983, pp. 218-219) defines legalization as: "the disorderly introduction of legal authority into the educational order—instances of the exercise of authority that violate the routinized order and chain of command, that introduce new rules without their integration into the established set."

While this approach does highlight important problems associated with the elaboration of legal requirements, I think it is a mistake to restrict the meaning of the term legalization to the pathological aspects of the process, just as I object to definitions of bureaucratization which render it an epithet (see Scott, 1992, p. 39). Sitkin and Bies (this volume) assume a stance similar to my own in this respect, recognizing that legalism can be overplayed but is not inherently pathological. By embracing a neutral definition of the concept, analysts are freed to examine the conditions under which legalization leads to more or less beneficial effects. Embracing a neutral position also helps the analyst recognize that different constituencies will make different assessments of the same process, for as Friedman (1975, p. 247) observes: "[legalization is] a subjective judgment: one man's legalism is another man's idealism."

While many of the essays collected in the present volume stress the problems associated with legalization processes (e.g., Browning & Folger; Culnan, Smith, & Bies; Roth, Sitkin, & House; Randall & Baker), Selznick (1969) views these developments as involving the introduction into organizations, viewed as private governments, of some of the vital protections developed within public governance systems to protect the rights of citizens from the inappropriate use of power. One woman's red tape is another woman's due process. (A similar theme is apparent in the chapters by Kesner & Kaufmann; Shapiro & Kolb; Van Maanen & Pentland.) I believe that it is accurate to say that much of the work represented in this volume is heavily indebted to Selznick's pioneering work. It was he who refocused our attention on the legal aspects of organizations and called attention to legalization processes within organizations as fundamentally transforming relations, both within the organization and between the organization and its environment.

Much attention in the present volume is given to the recognition that legal institutions privilege process controls, stressing procedures over outcomes (see, e.g., Feldman & Levy; Sitkin & Bies). This insight derives from Weber's analysis of *rational-legal* administrative systems that obtain their legitimacy from conformity to a set of rules promulgated by a properly constituted authority. Albrow (1970, p. 65) elaborates this conception:

> At the heart of Weber's idea of formal rationality was the idea of correct calculation, in either numerical terms, as with the accountant, or in logical terms, as with the lawyer. . . . Each of the propositions involved in his pure type of bureaucracy referred to a procedure where either legal norms or monetary calculation were involved, and where impersonality and expert knowledge were necessary. Any such procedure was for Weber intrinsically rational, irrespective of its relation to organizational objectives. In

short, he was not offering a theory of efficiency, but a statement of the formal procedures which were prevalent in modern administration.

Weber's conception of formal rationality was, thus, at variance with the contemporary notion of economic or technical rationality, which stresses the efficient utilization of means to attain ends (although Weber's discussion is somewhat ambiguous and sometimes conflates these two definitions).

The new institutional theory has attempted to revive this distinction. For example, Meyer and I distinguish between institutional and technical environments in terms of whether the controls imposed on organizations are primarily based on conformity to established processes or on efficiency in producing outcomes (Scott & Meyer, 1983, 1991). DiMaggio and Powell (1983, p. 147) point to the growing importance of institutional pressures that "make organizations more similar without necessarily making them more efficient." Weber's work established the foundation for contemporary arguments that there is more than one variety of rationality.

Alexander (1983) asserts that Weber was ambivalent about the extent to which legal rational structures supported normative and voluntaristic behavior. While some of his analysis emphasized the contrast between traditional and modern structures, insisting that in the latter "men enacted their own rules in order to rise above the received exigencies established by the traditional authority of their time" (p. 98), other passages from Weber stress the impersonal and deterministic character of bureaucracy: "The content of discipline is nothing but the consistently rationalized, methodically prepared and exact execution of the received order, in which all criticism is unconditionally suspended and the actor is unswervingly and exclusively set for carrying out the command" (Weber, 1946, p. 253). Alexander (1983, p. 101) paraphrases this view: "Order is received, not enacted; the actor is passive, not critical." The iron cage of excessive legalism has descended.

But other analysts, neo-institutionalists, suggest a different conception of rule following, one closer to Weber's more optimistic vision. Thus, March and Olsen (1989, pp. 22, 24) observe:

To say that behavior is governed by rules is not to say that it is either trivial or unreasoned. Rule-bound behavior is, or can be, carefully considered. Rules can reflect subtle lessons of cumulative experience, and the process by which appropriate rules are determined and applied is a process

involving high levels of human intelligence, discourse, and deliberation
. . . [Moreover] the number and variety of alternative rules assure that
one of the primary factors affecting behavior is the process by which some
of those rules, rather than others, are evoked in a particular situation.

In sum, legalization imposes rules on behavior, but whether the
rules result in mindless conformity and passivity or support mindful
intelligence and activism should be determined by empirical observation, not by theoretical presumption.

Definitional Environments

The third component of legal environments identified by Suchman
stresses the role played by law in constituting social actors and relationships, a theme also found in the chapters in this volume by
Feldman and Levy; Shapiro and Kolb; Stutman and Putnam; and Van
Maanen and Pentland. In contrast to a behaviorial perspective, institutionalists insist that social actors are not "real" primordial crea-
tures, but are social constructions, defined and given meaning by
social institutions (see Meyer, Boli, & Thomas, 1987). Who and what
a "citizen" is, for example, is not a matter of "natural rights" but a
creation of specific constitutional systems. Krasner (1988) specifies
four component elements entailed in the social construction of an actor:
endowments (e.g., property rights), utilities (preferences), capabilities
(capacity to act, resources), and self-identity (internalized definition
of social position or role). Much of the regularity we observe in social
behavior is explained by the institutional definition of social identities (see Berger & Luckmann, 1967).

Not only individual actors but collective actors also are socially
constructed. A number of social scientists have examined the social
and political processes giving rise to the limited liability corporation as a new legal entity (see Coleman, 1974, 1990; Creighton, 1990;
Seavoy, 1982). This and other organizational forms (for example, co-
operatives, partnerships, nonprofit associations, unions) are the products of socially constituted, legally defined and enforced rules. In
the modern world, law does not merely regulate organizations; it
constructs them.

By constructing and allocating rights among organizations, law also
has a major impact on the relations among organizations. Campbell and

Lindberg (1990) detail the ways in which, by defining and enforcing property rights, the state influences the economic behavior of organizations in differing sectors. Property rights are the "rules that determine the conditions of ownership and control of the means of production" (p. 635), and include labor laws defining the power of workers to organize, antitrust laws that limit ties between competitors, and patent laws that limit access to new technologies. Such rules not only specify the relation between actors and property but, necessarily, affect the relations among the actors themselves. Campbell and Lindberg (1990, p. 637) conclude:

> [T]he state provides the legal framework within which contracts are written and enforced. . . . The state's influence, quite apart from sporadic interventions, is always present in the economy insofar as it provides an institutional and legal framework that influences the selection of different governance regimes and thereby permanently shapes the economy.

While recognizing the importance of legal environments in constituting and constraining organizations, it is important that we also recognize the power of actors to shape institutional rules. Numerous observers, including Feldman and Levy, and Van Maanen and Pentland, in this volume, have noted that the complexity of law is such that actors have some leeway to select, to interpret, to challenge one or another requirement. Institutional environments are not so uniform or oppressive as early accounts suggested; there is ample room within them for organizational participants to maneuver and engage in strategic behavior (see Oliver, 1991).

Organizational actors also directly shape the law. As is well known, many engage in lobbying and, in various other ways, attempt to influence the content of the law. Some powerful organizations and their trade associations are in a position to draft legislation and virtually dictate the laws governing practice in their arenas. Sometimes the process is more interactive. Dobbin and associates (Dobbin, Sutton, Meyer, & Scott, 1993) describe the ways in which personnel officials in companies subject to affirmative action legislation explored a number of alternative practices before the courts determined which approach was to be regarded as consistent with the law. Only after this interactive process was a standard model established that diffused through the organizational field.

■ Concluding Comments

I have attempted in this introductory chapter to provide a brief overview of the ways in which scholars have framed and examined the relation between law and organizations. I have suggested that most organizational researchers have focused on the organization of legal systems—for example, law firms, the judicial system, and the organization of police and prisons. Considerable attention has also been paid, particularly in recent years, to the ways in which organizations become implicated in criminal activities, both as perpetrators and as victims. But, up to the present time, there has been relative neglect of the ways in which the legal environment affects organizations.

The chapters brought together in this volume explore two important facets of the legal environments of organizations: regulatory systems and legalization processes. Employing a variety of theoretical perspectives and empirical techniques, they provide us with a much more elaborate picture of both the ways in which organizations respond to wider societal rules and regulatory frameworks and the ways in which they themselves create law-like rules and procedures— to effect control, to protect rights, to delay settlements, to enhance legitimacy, and for many other reasons.

Legalization is one of several important processes that organization theorists have just begun to explore. There are others that are pointed to by the new institutionism, especially the way in which law operates to constitute organizations and interorganizational relations.

There are no more important issues for analysts to understand than the ways in which organizations are shaped by legal rules and processes. At the same time, however, it is vital that our models recognize the possibilities available to individuals and organizations to shape the law. We create our iron cages, but we can also create the keys to unlock them.

■ References

Albrow, M. (1970). *Bureaucracy*. New York: Praeger.

Alexander, J. (1983). *Theoretical logic in sociology: The classical attempt at theoretical synthesis: Max Weber* (Vol. 3). Berkeley: University of California Press.

Alexander, J., & Scott, W. R. (1984, May/June). The impact of regulation on the administrative structure of hospitals. *Hospitals and Health Services Administration, 29,* 71-85.

Beaty, J., & Gwynne, S. C. (1993). *The outlaw bank: A wild ride into the secret heart of BCCI.* New York: Random House.

Berger, P. L., & Luckmann, T. (1967). *The social construction of reality.* New York: Doubleday.

Bittner, E. (1990). *Aspects of police work.* Boston: Northeastern University Press.

Campbell, J. L., Hollingsworth, J. R., & Lindberg, L. N. (Eds.). (1991). *Governance of the American economy.* New York: Cambridge University Press.

Campbell, J. L., & Lindberg, L. N. (1990). Property rights and the organization of economic activity by the state. *American Sociological Review, 55,* 634-647.

Carroll, G. R., Delacroix, J., & Goodstein, J. (1988). The political environment of organizations. In B. M. Staw & L. L. Cummings (Eds.), *Research in organizational behavior* (Vol. 11, pp. 359-392). Greenwich, CT: JAI Press.

Cicourel, A. (1968). *The social organization of juvenile justice.* New York: John Wiley.

Clemmer, D. (1940). *The prison community.* Boston: Christopher.

Clinard, M. B., & Yeager, P. C. (1980). *Corporate crime.* New York: Free Press.

Cloward, R. A., Cressey, D. R., Grosser, G. H., McCleery, R., Ohlin, L. E., Sykes, G. M., & Messinger, S. L. (1960). *Theoretical studies in the social organization of the prison.* New York: Social Science Research Council.

Coleman, J. S. (1974). *Power and the structure of society.* New York: Norton.

Coleman, J. S. (1990). *Foundations of social theory.* Cambridge, MA: Belknap Press of Harvard University Press.

Creighton, A. L. (1990). *The emergence of incorporation as a legal form for organizations.* Unpublished doctoral dissertation, Stanford University.

Dan-Cohen, M. (1986). *Rights, persons, and organizations: A legal theory for bureaucratic society.* Berkeley: University of California Press.

Day, K. (1993). *S & L hell: The people and the politics behind the one trillion dollar savings and loan scandal.* New York: Norton.

DiMaggio, P. J. (1983). State expansion and organizational fields. In R. H. Hall & R. E. Quinn (Eds.), *Organizational theory and public policy* (pp. 147-161). Beverly Hills, CA: Sage.

DiMaggio, P. J. (1986). Structural analysis of organizational fields: a blockmodel approach. In B. M. Staw & L. L. Cummings (Eds.), *Research in organizational behavior* (Vol. 8, pp. 355-370). Greenwich, CT: JAI Press.

DiMaggio, P. J., & Powell, W. W. (1983). The iron cage revisited: Institutional isomorphism and collective rationality in organizational fields. *American Sociological Review, 48,* 147-160.

DiMaggio, P. J., & Powell, W. W. (1991). Introduction. In W. W. Powell & P. J. DiMaggio (Eds.), *The new institutionalism in organizational analysis* (pp. 1-38). Chicago: University of Chicago Press.

Dobbin, F. R., Sutton, J. R., Meyer, J. W., & Scott, W. R. (1993). Equal opportunity law and the construction of internal labor markets. *American Journal of Sociology, 99,* 396-427.

Ericson, R. V., Baranek, P., & Chan, J. (1991). *Representing order.* Toronto: University of Toronto Press.

Ermann, M. D., & Lundman, R. J. (1982a). *Corporate deviance.* New York: Holt, Rinehart & Winston.

Ermann, M. D., & Lundman, R. J. (1982b). Overview. In M. D. Ermann & R. J. Lundman (Eds.), *Corporate and governmental deviance* (2nd ed.). New York: Oxford University Press.

Fligstein, N. (1990). *The transformation of corporate control*. Cambridge, MA: Harvard University Press.

Foucault, M. (1979). *Discipline and punish: The birth of the prison* (A. Sheridan, Trans.). New York: Vintage/Random House.

Friedman, L. M. (1975). *The legal system: A social science perspective*. New York: Russell Sage.

Galanter, M. (1991). *Tournament of lawyers*. Chicago: University of Chicago Press.

Goffman, E. (1961). *Asylums*. Garden City, NY: Doubleday/Anchor.

Heinz, J. P., & Laumann, E. (1982). *Chicago lawyers: The social structure of the bar*. New York: Russell Sage.

Herling, J. (1962). *The great price conspiracy*. Washington, DC: Robert B. Luce.

Heydebrand, W. V. (1990). *Rationalizing justice*. Albany: State University of New York Press.

Ianni, F.A.J. (1972). *A family business: Kinship and social control in organized crime*. New York: Russell Sage.

Johnson, C. A. (1979). Judicial decisions and organization change: Some theoretical and empirical notes on state court decisions and state administrative agencies. *Law and Social Science Review, 14*, 17-56.

Kelly, R. J. (Ed.). (1986). *Organized crime: A global perspective*. Totowa, NJ: Rowman & Littlefield.

Kelman, S. (1981). *Regulating American, regulating Sweden*. Cambridge: MIT Press.

Knudsen, D. D., & Miller. J. L. (Eds.). (1991). *Abused and battered: Social and legal responses to family violence*. New York: Aldine.

Krasner, S. D. (1988). Sovereignty: An institutional perspective. *Comparative Political Studies, 21*, 66-94.

McCarthy, J. D., Wolfson, M., Baker, D. P., & Mosakowski, E. (1988). The founding of social movement organizations: Local citizens' groups opposing drunken driving. In G. Carroll (Ed.), *Ecological models of organizations* (pp. 71-84). Cambridge, MA: Ballinger.

Manning, P. K. (1977). *Police work*. Cambridge: MIT Press.

Manning, P. K., & Van Maanen, J. (Eds.). (1978). *Policing: A view from the streets*. New York: Random House.

March, J. G., & Olsen, J. P. (1989). *Rediscovering institutions: The organizational basis of politics*. New York: Free Press.

Mendeloff, J. (1979). *Regulating safety: A political and economic analysis of the federal occupational health and safety program*. Cambridge: MIT Press.

Meyer, J. W. (1983). Centralization of funding and control in educational governance. In J. W. Meyer & W. R. Scott (Eds.), *Organizational environments: Ritual and rationality* (pp. 179-198). Beverly Hills, CA: Sage.

Meyer, J. W., Boli, J., & Thomas, G. M. (1987). Ontology and rationalization in the Western cultural account. In G. M. Thomas, J. W. Meyer, F. O. Ramirez, & J. Boli (Eds.), *Institutional structure: Constituting state, society, and the individual* (pp. 12-37). Newbury Park, CA: Sage.

Meyer, J. W., & Rowan, B. (1977)."Institutionalized organizations: Formal structure as myth and ceremony. *American Journal of Sociology, 83*, 340-363.

Mitroff, I. I. & Kilmann, R. H. (1984). *Corporate tragedies: Product tampering, sabotage, and other catastrophes*. New York: Praeger.

Near, J. P., & Miceli, M. P. (1987). Whistle-blowers in organizations: Dissidents or reformers? In B. M. Staw & L. L. Cummings (Eds.), *Research in organizational behavior* (Vol. 9, pp. 321-368). Greenwich, CT: JAI Press.

Nelson, R. (1988). *Partners with power: The social transformation of the large law firm.* Berkeley: University of California Press.

Noll, R. G. (Ed.). (1985). *Regulatory policy and the social sciences.* Berkeley: University of California Press.

Oliver, C. (1991). Strategic responses to institutional processes. *Academy of Management Review, 16,* 145-79.

Parsons, T. (1951). *The social system.* Glencoe, IL: Free Press.

Pizzo, S., Fricher, M., & Muolo, P. (1991). *Inside job: The looting of America's savings and loans.* New York: Harper Perennial.

Schmitter, P. C. (1990). Sectors in modern capitalism: Models of governance and variations in performance. In R. Brunetta & C. Dell'Aringa (Eds.), *Labour relations and economic performance* (pp. 3-39). Houndmills, UK: Macmillan.

Scott, W. R., & Meyer, J. W. (1983). The organization of societal sectors. In J. W. Meyer & W. R. Scott (Eds.), *Organizational environments: Ritual and rationality* (pp. 129-153). Beverly Hills, CA: Sage.

Scott, W. R. (1987). The adolescence of institutional theory. *Administrative Science Quarterly, 32,* 493-511.

Scott, W. R., & Meyer, J. W. (1991). The organization of societal sectors: Propositions and early evidence. In W. W. Powell & P. J. DiMaggio (Eds.), *The new institutionalism in organizational analysis* (pp. 108-140). Chicago: University of Chicago Press.

Scott, W. R. (1992). *Organizations: Rational, natural and open systems* (3rd ed.). Englewood Cliffs, NJ: Prentice-Hall.

Scott, W. R. (forthcoming). Conceptualizing organizational fields: Linking organizations and societal systems. In U. Gerhardt, H-U. Derlien, & F. W. Scharpf (Eds.), *Systems rationality and partial interests.* Baden-Baden, Germany: Nomos Verlag.

Seavoy, R. E. (1982). *The origins of the American business corporation, 1784-1855: Broadening the concept of public service during industrialization.* Westport, CT: Greenwood.

Selznick, P. (1957). *Leadership in administration.* New York: Harper & Row.

Selznick, P. (1969). *Law, society, and industrial justice.* New York: Russell Sage.

Sherman, L. W. (1982). *Scandal and reform.* Berkeley: University of California Press.

Skowronek, S. (1982). *Building a new American state: The expansion of national administrative capacities, 1877-1920.* New York: Cambridge University Press.

Smigel, E. O. (1964). *The Wall Street lawyer.* New York: Free Press.

Sproull, L. S. (1981). Response to regulation: An organizational process framework. *Administration and Society, 12,* 447-470.

Stewart, J. D. (1991). *Den of thieves.* New York: Simon & Schuster.

Stone, C. D. (1975). *Where the law ends: Social control of corporate behavior.* New York: Harper & Row.

Streeck, W., & Schmitter, P. C. (Eds.). (1985). *Private interest government: Beyond market and state.* Beverly Hills, CA: Sage.

Suchman, M. V. (1993, April). *Conceptualizing the legal environments of organizational activity.* Paper presented at the annual meetings of the Stanford Conference on Organizations at Asilomar, Pacific Grove, CA.

Sutherland, E. (1949). *White collar crime.* New York: Dryden.

Sykes, G. M. (1958). *The society of captives: A study of a maximum security prison.* Princeton, NJ: Princeton University Press.

Tamuz, M., & Sitkin, S. B. (1991, August). *The invisible muzzle: Organizational and legal constraints on the disclosure of information about health and safety hazards.* Paper presented at the national meeting of the Academy of Management, San Francisco, CA.

Vaughan, D. (1983). *Controlling unlawful organizational behavior: Social structure and corporate misconduct*. Chicago: University of Chicago Press.

Weaver, P. H. (1978). Regulation, social policy and class conflict. *The Public Interest, 50*, 45-63.

Weaver, S. (1977). *Decision to prosecute: Organization and public policy in the anti-trust division*. Cambridge: MIT Press.

Weber, M. (1946). The meaning of discipline. In H. Gerth & C. W. Mills (Trans. and Eds.), *From Max Weber: Essays in sociology* (pp. 253-264). New York: Oxford University Press.

Weisburd, D., Wheeler, S., Waring, E., & Bode, N. (1991). *Crimes of the middle classes*. New Haven, CT: Yale University Press.

Wilson, J. Q. (Ed.). (1980). *The politics of regulation*. New York: Basic Books.

Wilson, J. Q. (1968). *Varieties of police behavior*. Cambridge, MA: Harvard University Press.

2

The Legalization of Organizations:
A Multi-Theoretical Perspective

Sim B Sitkin

Robert J. Bies

> *Almost everything is litigation these days—and not just in baseball. It is a function of our time and our society.*
>
> Fay Vincent, Former Major League
> Baseball Commissioner (1992)

Managers in organizations are confronting what many perceive as a "litigation mentality" in today's workplace (Bies & Tyler, 1993). For example, the termination of an employee used to be a managerial action that left the employee with no recourse; today, however, such an action may result in an unjust dismissal lawsuit, in which the courts decide on the merits of the decision (Youngblood & Bierman, 1985). Such lawsuits provide evidence that managers and organizations are becoming the more frequent targets of lawsuits intending to modify or overturn many of their decisions ("A Plague," 1986; Lieberman, 1983; Olsen, 1991). In contrast, others have argued (Friedman, 1989) that the evidence is far from clear about whether litigation is actually on the rise.

AUTHORS' NOTE: Portions of this paper were originally presented at the 1986 National Academy of Management Meetings as part of a symposium titled *The Law Versus the Manager: The Encroachment of a Litigation Mentality into the Organization*. We wish to thank Thomas D'Aunno, Martha Feldman, and Elaine Romanelli for their helpful comments on earlier versions of this paper.

19

Regardless of whether the litigation rate is increasing, there is little controversy about whether legal considerations are receiving more attention and more weight in organizational decision making. More specifically, there is a "legalistic mentality" clearly gaining in prominence within American organizations (Sitkin & Bies, 1993). This legalistic influence has affected the actions taken by organizations and their members (Jasanoff, 1985; Meyer, 1983), as well as affecting how those actions can be legitimately justified (Kadish & Kadish, 1973). The impact of legalistic influences on organizational processes and structures is referred to as *legalization* (Meyer, 1983; Yudof, 1981a).

The legalization of organizations is a long-term social trend of substantial importance (Lieberman, 1983; Stone, 1975). Attention to legalization is stimulated by the observation that organizational decision making and procedures have become increasingly concerned with assuring legal acceptability for the organization at the expense of other important criteria (economic, humanistic, and the like). The impact of legalization has been observed across functional areas in diverse organizational settings, ranging from governmental agencies (Browning & Folger, this volume; Jasanoff, 1985) and public schools (Meyer, 1983; Tyack, James, & Benavot, 1987; Yudof, 1981a) to manufacturing firms (Barney, Edwards, & Ringleb, 1992; Bies, 1987; Randall & Baker, this volume), retail organizations (Sitkin, Sutcliffe, & Reed, 1993), and independent professionals (Turkington, 1986).

The implication of this trend is potentially significant. As decisions are increasingly dominated by a concern for what is legally defensible (versus that which is organizationally or interpersonally sensible), there is the potential for legalization to dominate attention, decision making, and structure at the expense of the organization's social and economic performance (Sitkin & Bies, 1993). Balancing the multiple criteria can create paradoxical outcomes when managers attempt to pursue legitimacy criteria and performance criteria—each at the expense of the other. As a result, legalization paradoxically poses serious threats to both an organization's legitimacy and its effectiveness.

Despite its pervasiveness, the growth of legalization and its paradoxes is not well understood (Friedman, 1989). While drawing on a number of disciplines (e.g., law, sociology, psychology, political science, communication), research on the phenomenon has rarely taken an explicitly organizational perspective, but instead has focused on individual or societal shifts in litigiousness. Yet, as only a few scholars have highlighted (Meyer, 1983; Selznick, 1969; Weber, 1947; Yudof, 1981a), the process of legalization is perhaps most significantly a problem of organizational adaptation, in that legalization is most often used to legitimate proposed organizational changes (e.g., by suggesting that the changes are legally required) or to avoid undesired change (e.g., by arguing that such changes are prohibited).

In this chapter, we focus on prior work that provides insights into how organizations come to exhibit legalistic features, and argue for the use of organizational theory as a potentially important—and previously neglected—source of insight concerning legalization processes and why the resultant paradoxes occur. The chapter is divided into four sections. First, we present basic definitions and summarize several salient aspects of legalistic organizations and the paradoxes they present. Second, we review the earlier work of Meyer (1983), Selznick (1969), Shklar (1964), Yudof (1981a, 1981b, 1988), and Weber (1946, 1947) as providing the cornerstones of current work on legalization processes. Third, we review the implications of four prominent organizational theories that offer distinct ways of predicting the forms that legalistic organizations and legalization processes can take. Finally, we outline several promising future directions that research on legalization can pursue.

■ Characteristics of Legalistic Organizations and the Legalization Process

Definition

We define legalization as a process that encompasses the diffusion of legalistic reasoning, procedures, and structures as a means of sustaining or enhancing the legitimacy of the organization (or an organizational subunit) with critical internal or external constituencies (Meyer, 1983; Sitkin & Bies, 1993b). Legalistic organizational responses to institutional pressures are not merely reactions to shifts in the expected values of options associated with legal/regulatory control. Instead, when organizations go beyond rational expectations associated with changes in the legal environment, they are driven by the symbolic value inherent in adopting easily recognized and readily acceptable legal forms (e.g., see Meyer, 1983). Thus our definition of legalization conceptualizes it as a particular type of institutionalization that is likely to be found in societies (e.g., the United States) in which the law and law-like forms offer a "normative . . . source of organizational legitimacy independent of [their] immediate organizational functionality, or any other criteria of internal rationality" (Friedland & Alford, 1991, p. 243). Such an institutional perspective on legalization is distinct from the legal-rational view of bureaucratization in that the bureaucratic perspective stresses the competitive, efficiency-enhancing, technology-driven effects of bureaucratic procedure; whereas the legalistic perspective stresses the circumstances under which mimetic institutional processes lead to the symbolically useful, but instrumentally dysfunctional, adoption of bureaucratic or legal procedures.

As Roth, Sitkin, and House (this volume) point out, a strictly legalistic view can also be distinguished from a more general institutional perspective. Specifically, legalization implies that organizations will respond to threats to legitimacy with increased use of legalistic features (e.g., formal decision criteria or due process procedures) and the decreased use of nonlegalistic sources of institutional legitimacy (e.g., cultural traditions or norms). In contrast, a purely institutional view would predict that both potential sources of legitimacy would increase as threat rises.[1] In support of the legalization view, Roth, Sitkin, and House found that decisions concerning employees with more stigmatized illnesses were based to a greater extent on formal, legalistic criteria and less on informal, cultural criteria.

As Selznick (1969, p. 8) noted, "to 'legalize' an institution . . . is to infuse its mode of governance with the aspirations and constraints of the legal order." Sometimes this process of infusion involves the adoption of an effective administrative technique, while other times it involves the adoption of the trappings of law in a context for which those trappings are largely inappropriate. Thus, the adoption of legalistic procedures can simultaneously serve two purposes— enhancing administrative coordination (Black, 1976; Lieberman, 1983; Stone, 1975; Weber, 1947), and enhancing institutional legitimacy by mimicking the readily acceptable formality of legal reasonings, procedures, and structure (DiMaggio & Powell, 1983).

Dimensions of Legalization

Drawing on the work of Meyer (1983), Selznick (1969), Shklar (1964), Weber (1947), and Yudof (1981a), we have identified five dimensions of legalization, as shown in Figure 2.1 (Sitkin & Bies, 1993b).

Formalization/Standardization. First, there is an increased use of formal, standardized policies and procedures that reflects the legal emphasis

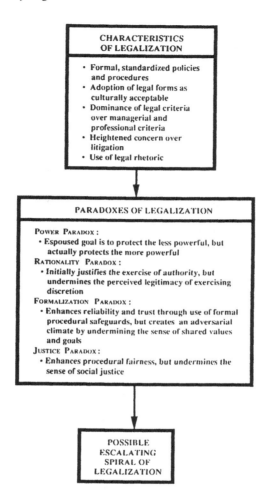

CHARACTERISTICS OF LEGALIZATION

- Formal, standardized policies and procedures
- Adoption of legal forms as culturally acceptable
- Dominance of legal criteria over managerial and professional criteria
- Heightened concern over litigation
- Use of legal rhetoric

PARADOXES OF LEGALIZATION

POWER PARADOX:
- Espoused goal is to protect the less powerful, but actually protects the more powerful

RATIONALITY PARADOX:
- Initially justifies the exercise of authority, but undermines the perceived legitimacy of exercising discretion

FORMALIZATION PARADOX:
- Enhances reliability and trust through use of formal procedural safeguards, but creates an adversarial climate by undermining the sense of shared values and goals

JUSTICE PARADOX:
- Enhances procedural fairness, but undermines the sense of social justice

POSSIBLE ESCALATING SPIRAL OF LEGALIZATION

Figure 2.1. The Legalization Process
SOURCE: Reprinted by permission, "The Legalistic Organization: Definitions, Dimensions, and Dilemmas," S. Sitkin and R. J. Bies, *Organization Science, 4* (3), August 1993. Copyright 1993, The Institute of Management Sciences, 290 Westminster Street, Providence, RI 02903.

on due process, formalization, and official written findings (Dobbin, Edelman, Meyer, Scott, & Swidler, 1988; Edelman, 1990; Scheppele, 1988; Tamuz & Sitkin, 1992; Yudof, 1981a). It is in this sense that Yudof (1981a) and Meyer (1983) use the term *legalization* to depict situations in which organizations go beyond the instrumental need for administrative bureaucratization as the organizations grow in size and complexity. Specifically, legalization refers to bureaucratic goal displacement, which is characterized by the increased utilization of excessively cumbersome or inappropriate administrative processes (Jasanoff, 1985; Meyer, 1983). Thus, legalization builds upon the Weberian legal-rational bureaucratic form by reflecting that in practice organizations depart from Weber's *ideal-type* in part because they are responding to institutional pressures to adopt the appearance of the legal-rational bureaucratic form (i.e., *legalistic* rather than *legal-rational*) in circumstances where the particular forms adopted may be instrumentally inappropriate, but nonetheless may be effective institutional responses.

Hallmarks of a legalistic approach (see Sitkin & Bies, 1993a) include: (a) high levels of formalization in operating rules and procedures (operating formalization); (b) reliance on standardization and uniformity in rule implementation and enforcement (standardization); and (c) the use of elaborate standards for the formal presentation of evidence in making decisions and resolving disputes (decision making formalization). These features have come to characterize a variety of organizational relations (Foote, 1984; Lieberman, 1983; Luhmann, 1981)—including those between managers and workers (Abzug & Mezias, 1993; Bies, 1992; Bies & Tripp, 1993; Near, Dworkin, & Miceli, 1993), between the public and the organization (Tamuz & Sitkin, 1992), between boards of directors and the organizations they govern (Kaplan & Harrison, 1993; Kesner & Kaufmann, this volume), and among cooperating organizations (Smitka, this volume; Stinchcombe & Heimer, 1985).

Internalization of Litigious Model of Conflict Resolution. Second, litigation has become a routine mechanism for resolving conflict in and between organizations (Lieberman, 1983). In addition to the traditional bureaucratic cornerstones of a legalistic approach cited above, two additional features are: (a) adversarial, winner-take-all procedures (adversarial conflict) and (b) ultimate reliance on judicial review (reconciliation through litigation) or quasi-judicial review (reconciliation through internal dispute resolution procedures). These features draw upon the legal system's emphasis on due process, the advocacy model of conflict, and the use of third-party arbiters of justice. The use of these legalistic procedures has tended to result in the diminished reliance on "control through consensus" (Bies & Tyler, 1993; Jasanoff,

1985, p. 157; Near et al., 1993; Sitkin & Roth, 1993). Thus, while these aspects of legalization for organizations can also be traced to Weber's legal-rational form of authority, they can be dysfunctional for the organization—as Weber (1947) himself noted in his explorations of a theory of bureaucracy. Weber's concerns were echoed more recently by Jasanoff (1985, pp. 155-156), who observed:

> Conceived and implemented by lawyers, administrative decision making in the United States is stamped with the procedural hallmarks of litigation: open and adversarial arguments, preparation of elaborate technical "cases," and a delegation of ultimate responsibility for resolving conflicts to the courts.

Whereas these features are appropriate for litigation between independent disputing parties and the protection of their legal rights, they may not be appropriate for cooperation and problem solving when taken inside the boundaries of the organization (Shapiro & Kolb, this volume; Sitkin & Roth, 1993).

Adoption of Legitimacy-Enhancing Legal Forms. Third, increased attention to institutional acceptability can foster the adoption of legal forms because they are readily recognized as culturally acceptable, which is particularly helpful in handling controversial or conflict-laden issues (Kirp, Yudof, & Franks, 1986; Sitkin & Bies, 1993a; Sitkin & Roth, 1993). For example, as Tamuz & Sitkin (1992) note, to sidestep controversial issues organizations may tap widely accepted legal precedents that allow for the routine destruction of potentially incriminating information. Conversely, organizations may bury stakeholders in a flood of data or procedural detail that simultaneously meets legalistic expectations for openness and formal procedure while effectively obscuring key information from detection (Clarke, 1989). These techniques represent the well-known use of elaborate information-processing routines as an important vehicle for managing perceptions of competence and responsibility, in that the mere adoption of formal or elaborate systems taps the symbolic acceptability of the careful collection, analysis, documentation, and availability of evidence used in decision making (Edelman, 1977; Feldman & March, 1981; Tamuz & Sitkin, 1992).

The institutionalization of civil rights reform provides another illustration (Edelman, 1990), in that one effect of the Civil Rights Act of 1964 on many organizations was to increase formal due process procedures beyond what was legally required. These procedures were adopted because they symbolically represented institutional legitimacy and responsiveness, even though Edelman concludes that they provided "no real benefits to employees" (p. 1436). That is, discrimination in hiring, promotion, and other personnel actions was not impeded by the imposition of a procedural routine since the routine could be used so easily as a legitimating cover for those who continued to discriminate.

Meyer (1983) and Yudof (1981a, 1981b, 1988) document similar uses of procedure in school settings. Because the use of readily recognizable and legitimate forms can reduce the perceived uncertainty and processing effort required by those who may judge the organization, legalistic responses may be used strategically to avoid the likelihood that questionable or clearly illegitimate actions will be recognized as such (Browning & Folger, this volume; Elsbach & Sutton, 1992; Tamuz & Sitkin, 1992; Van Maanen & Pentland, this volume).

Legalistic Decision Criteria. Fourth, law-like criteria can dominate other decision criteria and come to serve as critical guidelines and justifications for choices. It would be imprudent to ignore the legal ramifications of managerial decisions. However, when legal requirements (or the threat of litigation) are so heavily stressed that other factors relevant to organizational decision making are essentially ignored, such a bias can seriously distort the decision-making process in favor of the status quo and can limit the opportunity for a number of organizational constituencies to participate in and benefit from organizational decisions. This situation has led Wildavsky (1988, p. 170) to ask: "Why is everyone acting as if they are being regulated?" For example, to avoid employee lawsuits resulting from problems in pregnancy, some organizations have required female workers to undergo sterilization to get and/or keep jobs that involved handling hazardous materials in a plant that was closed just a few years later (Randall, 1985; Randall & Baker, this volume).

Heightened concern about the threat of litigation can significantly alter the risks associated with different choice options (Randall & Baker, this volume; Tamuz & Sitkin, 1992; Van Maanen & Pentland, this volume). As the number of competitors for corporate control and influence has grown (Abzug & Mezias, 1993; Kaplan & Harrison, 1993; Tamuz & Sitkin, 1992), organizational members are confronting what many perceive to be a "litigation mentality" in today's workplace (Bies & Tyler, 1993). Concern over potential litigation has even received a label—"litigiphobia" (Turkington, 1986)—and can be seen in the concerns expressed by corporate executives (Browning & Folger, this volume; Randall, 1985), human resource managers (Bies, 1992; Bies & Tripp, 1993; Cascio & Bernardin, 1981; Wooten & Godkin, 1983), board members (Kaplan & Harrison, 1993; Kesner & Kaufmann, this volume; Moskowitz 1987; Stone, 1975), and professionals (Makofsky, 1979; Sitkin & Sutcliffe, 1991). Under such conditions, decisions based on a single criterion (e.g., impact on firm profits) can obscure consideration of other equally important factors (e.g., employee or community safety). For example, Barney, Edwards, and Ringleb (1992) describe how organizations avoided the liability associated with employee exposure to hazardous materials by spinning off legally independent subsidiaries in a way that retained assets in the parent firm and divested liabilities to the subsidiary. Tamuz and Sitkin (1992) and Van Maanen and Pentland (this volume) examine how organizations keep (or destroy) records to enhance their chances of winning if taken to court—while largely ignoring the potentially devastating effect of such record-keeping practices on their own planning, operations, or their stakeholders. Citing legal liability and regulatory control as the two most influential changes in the legal environment of corporations, Foote (1984, p. 220) has noted that "the expansion of legal institutions has greatly altered the process of decision making . . . formerly private decisions are open for public scrutiny . . . [such that the] corporation loses control over the outcome."

Legalistic Rhetoric. Fifth, increased use of legal rhetoric both manifests and exacerbates the other aspects of organizational legalization. For example, Bies (1992) finds that in dealing with bad news, managers talk more about "getting their briefs ready" and "preparing their case" than they do about getting facts or persuading and motivating employees; similarly they talk more about giving employees "their day in court," rather than listening to the concerns of their employees. The use of legal rhetoric is on the rise, not just because of the increased influence of legal staff among top management, but also because in an environment that is dominated by legalistic decision criteria, the use of quasi-legal language can provide a legitimating edge in attempts at organizational influence. The use of legalistic rhetoric, in the sense described here, has received limited scholarly attention (exceptions include Bies & Tyler, 1993; Stutman & Putnam, this volume; Shapiro & Kolb, this volume; Sitkin, Sutcliffe, & Reed, 1993). However, studies of legalistic rhetoric are of great potential import because of the role that legal language can play in shaping the perceptions of and the interactions among organizational actors (cf., Pfeffer, 1981).

Paradoxes of Legalization

Legalization presents a complex set of organizational implications and tradeoffs for managers that merit careful review and consideration (see Sitkin & Bies, 1993b). On the positive side, legalization can lead to loose coupling among organizational units and can be particularly adaptive when institutional demands (e.g., legal requirements) diverge from economic-competitive requirements (Kaplan & Harrison, 1993; Meyer & Rowan, 1977; Pfeffer & Salancik, 1978; Weick, 1976). Moreover, in terms of broader social implications, Friedman (1989) notes that legalization frequently results in less discrimination against and disempowerment of various classes of workers (or other constituent groups), a positive social goal that is often overlooked in the rush to criticize legal constraints. In addition, legal remedies provide a source of influence for otherwise disempowered constituent groups. In addition, law can serve as a source of social protection and ·legitimacy of "greater significance to organizational survival than economic viability" (Pfeffer & Salancik, 1978, p. 194).

On the negative side, as managerial decisions are increasingly dominated by a concern for what is legally defensible, they necessarily shift concern away from that which makes organizational sense. Perhaps best reflected in the Peters and Waterman (1982) critique of American business, the essence of this argument is that businesses begin to fail when they lose sight of their core activities: providing useful products or services for customers. While the adoption of legalistic procedures may be motivated by the desire to enhance the efficiency, fairness, or effectiveness of existing practices, in practice such procedures frequently obstruct the achievement of these goals. Sometimes this is due to drawing managerial attention to real or imagined legal requirements or threats at the expense of attention to customer or task requirements (e.g., Edelman, 1990; Randall & Baker, this volume; Van Maanen & Pentland, this volume). Other times, organizations may become bureaucratically paralyzed in response to legal threats (Staw, Sandelands, & Dutton, 1981). In addition, contradictory demands are handled by "decoupling internal work activities from formal structures and external assessment as a means of maintaining faith [in] and legitimacy of the organization" (Oliver, 1991, p. 155; see also Meyer, 1983; Meyer & Rowan, 1977). While such actions can prop up otherwise "failing organizations" (Meyer & Zucker, 1989) in the short term, from this perspective legalization dominates managerial attention at the expense of long-term organizational health. Further, while legalization may arise to protect the less powerful, its actual effect can be the opposite: Those in power are protected as long as they adhere to the letter rather than the spirit of the law (Barney et al., 1992). Thus, while legalization is frequently an intendedly positive force, it can paradoxically undermine the very social goals it was designed to further (e.g., see Kirp et al., 1986; Sitkin & Roth, 1993; Yudof, 1981a).

Our analysis of the implications of legalization processes suggests the following four paradoxes created by the duality inherent in the process of legalization (see Figure 2.1).

Power Paradox. One of the primary motivations for utilizing legalistic approaches is to place constraints on the arbitrary use of power by those in positions of formal authority (Weber, 1947). Notwithstanding the pursuit of such a positive social goal, the actual effect often can be the opposite of that intended. This effect can occur either prospectively or retrospectively. For example, Browning and Folger's (this volume) study of the strategic use of "plausible deniability" shows how adherence to proper procedure can serve as an effective protection for almost any action taken by those in power. Van Maanen and Pentland (this volume) show how police officers and auditors use "generally accepted" forms, terms, and procedures to retrospectively cleanse their questionable actions and ward off the threat of perceived illegitimacy. These examples are consistent with Mosca's (1939, p. 70) observation that those in power "do not justify their power exclusively by *de facto* possession of it, but try to find a moral or legal basis for it, representing it as the logical and necessary consequence of doctrines and beliefs that are generally recognized and accepted." In other words, as a result of the skillful use of legalistic covers, a common outcome of legalization is that questionable actions taken by those in power are protected by the veneer of legal respectability.

One reason for this is that the fragmented state of the institutional environment provides a great deal of organizational discretion. As Abzug and Mezias (1993) point out, organizational actors not only can frequently "interpret" legal/regulatory constraints, but they can also often select among those constraints (e.g., local, state, or federal regulations) in choosing and justifying their actions. A number of studies have similarly described how organizations cope with competing or even incompatible requirements through selective compliance, coupled with the use of rhetoric or hollow formal reforms that offer the illusion of responsiveness (Edelman, 1977; Tamuz & Sitkin, 1992). In other words, those in power are not limited to power over instrumental resources, but frequently possess power over symbolic resources as well and, thus, the ostensible use of legalistic remedies for redressing power inequities can actually serve to preserve the status quo, rather than overturning it.

Rationality Paradox. Legal reasoning is held up as the epitome of rationality, and it is for this reason that many managers are drawn to the use of legalistic procedures and criteria in making decisions. For example, the use of legitimate law-like procedures in decision making provides an apparently authoritative basis for justifying managerial choices (Sitkin & Sutcliffe, 1991). This occurs in delivering bad news since managers often explain the procedures they followed to arrive at a decision by highlighting the detailed use of formal data collection and analyses (Feldman & March, 1981) or pointing to official "evidence" and the consistency in how that evidence was evaluated (Bies, 1992).

Paradoxically, however, the very reliance on that which is legalistic (e.g., an emphasis on strict rule adherence) may undermine the rationality of organizational actions. For example, strict rule adherence places authority for decisions in the previously specified rule or procedure, thus obviating the flexibility of positional authority. Further, strict rule adherence limits managerial discretion to make appropriate adjustments in response to changes in the organization's environment, or to create new rules in the face of new facts—both hallmarks of rationality in organizational decision making. In other words, an inflexible, procedural authority rooted in formal rules, and an obsessive consistency in applying those rules, can supersede the adaptive, flexible positional authority of managers (see also Cartwright & Schwartz, 1973, for a comparison of Durkheim's and Weber's views on this issue).

Formalization Paradox. Legalistic approaches are frequently adopted as a means for institutionalizing informal practices that have been particularly successful. Unfortunately, the very act of formalizing a successful practice may remove the sense of intimacy or interpersonal responsibility that was the cornerstone of its success (Macaulay 1963; Smitka, this volume). For example, the increasing emphasis on formal standards and documentation (e.g., in recruiting new or firing old employees, in describing product hazards, or in providing employee benefits) may undermine the informal and valued trust that managers share with their subordinates or customers (Shapiro, 1987; Sitkin & Roth, 1993). This idea implies that some attempts to minimize conflict (Bies & Tyler, 1993) or to reduce legal liability to "protect" the organization (Barney et al., 1992; Randall & Baker, this volume) may actually contribute to a growing adversarial climate in which fragile organizational relations are undermined anyway (Sitkin & Roth, 1993).

Justice Paradox. "Law without justice." For most of us, such a phrase is an intellectual, if not moral, contradiction. Yet in today's workplace, there is growing evidence that "law without justice" is becoming commonplace, as managerial decisions are dominated increasingly by a concern for what is "legal" at the expense of humanistic and social considerations, such as justice and fairness (Barney et al., 1992; Ewing, 1989; Randall & Baker, this volume). While highly formalized, legalistic procedures may "protect" managers and organizations legally (Bies & Tripp, 1993; Lieberman, 1983; Skupsky, 1989; Van Maanen & Pentland, this volume), they can also undermine social goals of justice and fairness by fostering a superficial reliance on that which has an acceptable *rationale* (i.e., meets the letter of the law) over that which is socially *rational* (i.e., meets the spirit of the law) (Bies & Sitkin, 1993a).

■ Alternative Theoretical Perspectives on Legalistic Organizations

Despite its pervasiveness, legalization is not well understood as an organizational phenomenon. Even when scholars have attempted to place legalization in a broader social context, the research has focused on the legal aspects of the phenomenon and has been grounded in legal theory (Jasanoff, 1985; Kadish & Kadish, 1973; Lieberman, 1983; Metzger, 1984).

Although research on organizational legalization has been sparse, legalization is essentially a problem of organizational design, decision making, and adaptation (Sitkin & Bies, 1993b). As a type of formalization (e.g., due to the legal emphasis on standardized, formal procedures), legalization is theoretically relevant to issues of organizational design from both a Weberian (1946, 1947) and an institutional perspective (Meyer, 1983; Selznick, 1969). In addition, by providing a ready-made set of accounts for questionable behavior, legalization provides a powerful (but usually hidden) heuristic for determining the acceptability of alternative decision-making criteria and choices (Sitkin, Sutcliffe, & Reed, 1993). Thus, in our attempt to understand legalization, organizational theory represents a potentially important—and previously neglected—source of insight.

Since past work has primarily emphasized a legal approach to the study of legalization, one intent of this research is to examine competing theoretical perspectives in developing empirically testable hypotheses about the legalization process. The sections that follow provide an overview of several theories and their implications for the study of legalization. These theories were selected because they differ in terms of their conceptualization of the determinants of organizational change, the role of managerial choice, and the characteristics associated with legalization.

There exists a variety of theoretical perspectives on determinants of the formal structure and decision-making processes of organizations (Scott, 1981). In this section, four major perspectives—drawn from organizational theory—are described in terms of their relevance for understanding the conceptual underpinnings of legalization and examining the structure and processes associated with the emergence of legalization in organizations (see Table 2.1 for a summary of the characteristics of each theoretical perspective). These perspectives are complementary in that, taken together, they take into account how legalization can be influenced by an organization's managers, the environment, or the stage of an organization's development.

Rational Perspectives

Rational organizational theories view the organization as a tool for efficient production, and focus on managerial decisions as the mechanism by which the tool can be adjusted to changing economic and technological conditions (Scott, 1981). Legalistic approaches—because they emphasize careful weighing of evidence, rule-governed behavior, and the standardized and efficient handling of decisions—can be viewed as exemplars of the rational perspective.

Weber's (1947) notion of bureaucracy captures some aspects of the "legalistic organization" concept quite well in that legalization involves the increased use of formal rules and procedures to clearly

Table 2.1 Comparison of Theoretical Perspectives on Legalization

Theoretical Perspective	Source of Legalization	Function of Legalization	Focus of Change Efforts	Assumptions	Examples
Rational	Management Economics of the Situation	Enhance Performance	Promote efficiency	1. Performance drives decision making. 2. Formal procedures are enacted as designed.	Organizational decisions based on computation of expected cost/benefit ratio for actions in terms of the potential for subsequent litigation (e.g., environmental pollution or collusive activities).
Institutional	Symbolic Environment	Survival Through Adaptation	Insure legitimacy through acceptable procedures	1. Organizations are composed of loosely coupled components. 2. Components are influenced more by environmental factors than by intraorganizational factors.	Requirement that newly hired employees sign a statement indicating that they are not bringing any proprietary information from their former employer.
Resource Dependence	Instrumental Environment	Survival Through Adaptation	Insure competitiveness through control of critical resources	1. Organizations are composed of loosely coupled components. 2. Components are influenced more by environmental factors than by intraorganizational factors.	Firm files for Chapter 11 bankruptcy to force labor union to renegotiate terms of union contract. A firm pursues patent registration unnecessarily because its venture capitalists prefer the use of patents, even in fast-moving, short product lifespan technological markets.
Life Cycle	Developmental Changes	N/A	Foster recognition of stages to avoid misinterpretation.	1. Legalization is not a strategic choice, but is simply a predictable developmental characteristic of organizational populations.	Degree to which organizations develop an internal legal staff and institute certain legalistic procedures increases as the organization prepares to "go public" or enters certain other specific stages of development.

define the rights and obligations of those in authority and their subordinates. Two motivating goals underlying the adoption of legalistic practices mirror the concerns that motivated the development of Weberian bureaucracy: (a) assuring that the exercise of authority is not arbitrary and capricious and (b) ensuring that consistent, replicable decision criteria are applied to the management of the organization. A Weberian conception of legalization involves the beneficial aspects of legalistic procedure: It is objective, it is a predictable and stabilizing force, it facilitates coordination and planning, and it enhances the fairness of organizational decision making by depersonalizing decision making.

A second rational conception of legalization can be captured in the transaction cost approach of Williamson (1975, 1981). At its core, the transaction cost approach suggests that organizations will internalize aspects of the marketplace that can be more efficiently handled through internal management control than through market forces. Williamson suggests that markets fail to remain sufficiently efficient when transactions become too uncertain to adequately estimate in advance, and, under these circumstances, firms respond by developing intraorganizational substitutes for external contractual or spot market relationships.

There are two distinct paths by which a Williamsonian view could predict increased legalization. First, the fundamental argument in the transaction cost approach is that some transactions are more efficiently handled via intraorganizational controls (i.e., bureaucracy) than via interorganizational controls (i.e., market relations). That is, this theoretical approach suggests that organizations internalize certain transactions because those transactions can be more efficiently managed through the use of internal mechanisms, including more actively "managed" formal procedures, standards, and hierarchical controls. Chandler (1977) explained the rise of American middle management in terms of the efficiencies associated with internalizing control over and facilitation of transactions that had traditionally been handled in the marketplace. Attention to the development of internal labor markets and the legalization of the employment relation can also be recast in a Williamsonian light: for example, research that has focused on the increased efficiency and formal control associated with the development of even elaborate internal labor markets (Doeringer & Piore, 1971; Wholey, 1985).

Second, as organizations internalize transactions, it is possible that the legal mechanisms used to control such relationships in the marketplace are simply carried along with the transaction itself as it moves inside the organization's boundary. It should be noted that this view is not consistent with the extant predictions of transaction cost theorists, although there is nothing in the "market failure" circumstance described by Williamson that would preclude such a process from occurring. That is, the proposed approach would suggest that not only could market failure be associated with the internalization of aspects transactions that can be more efficiently handled internally, but also that inappropriate (i.e., less efficient) aspects of the relations could be inadvertently internalized as well.

In addition to gauging the effect of legalization on decision making, a rational perspective would take note of the sanctioning power of threatened litigation and legal liability, and view these as influential factors in computing the expected value of alternative organizational options (Barney et al., 1992; Metzger, 1984). These factors need not include only direct monetary sanctions (such as liability suits or regulatory penalties). For example, in industries where customer or regulator trust is important (e.g., see Foote, 1984; Scott & Meyer, 1983), organizational legalization can serve as a cost-effective signal of trustworthiness (Zucker, 1986). Thus, rational approaches to understanding legalization focus attention on the benefits of adopting legalistic mechanisms for handling problems that are less effectively handled by market forces due to economic (e.g., Williamson, 1975), administrative (e.g., March & Simon, 1958), or ethical (Ewing, 1989; Matthews, 1988) considerations.[2]

Resource Dependence Perspective

Whereas the rational perspective focuses on intraorganizational influences on legalization, open systems approaches emphasize environmental influences. From an open systems perspective (Katz & Kahn, 1966), the primary impetus for legalization is to adapt to changing environmental requirements. Changes in the legal environment of organizations often affect large groups of organizations, and thus may be observed in the form of widespread adoption of similar responses. For example, recent publications have described the effect of legal/regulatory changes on the structure of corporate boards of directors (Kaplan & Harrison, 1993; Kesner & Johnson, 1990; Kesner & Kaufmann, this volume).

Stressing that organizations must acquire adequate resources to assure continued survival, open systems approaches note the importance of competitive control in assuring continued access to critical resources. The resource dependence form of the open systems approach (e.g., Pfeffer & Salancik, 1978) stresses how legalization can help the organization maintain control over critical instrumental resources (e.g., capital, raw materials, buyers). Thus, from a resource dependence perspective, increased threats to the organization—real or perceived—from the legal environment would be expected to lead to increased influence on the part of those organizational members who are able to manage legal issues (see Table 2.1). For example, Salancik and Pfeffer (1977) suggest that the legal department will gain in power when a firm is faced with increased lawsuits and that chief counsels will begin to become CEOs in industries in which legal factors overshadow production, marketing, or other considerations in determining the viability of the firm.

The resource dependence approach, and its grounding in open systems theory, highlights one way that legalistic responses may be quite functional for many organizations. Specifically, many organizations are confronting much more legally complex environments for a variety of reasons: government regulation, the use of technologies with less predictable effects, greater information availability, increased litigation, and international operations. To the extent that the critical environmental contingencies that organizations face have in fact become more legalistic, to remain isomorphic with their changing environment, organizations must become concommitantly legalistic. Thus, one implication of a resource dependence perspective is that legalization is a positive indicator of organizational adaptation and responsiveness—and thus may be positively associated with organizational competitiveness and survival. By extension, one would predict more legalistic features in industries in which lawsuits, regulatory influence, or patent protection issues were greater, and fewer legalistic features in industries in which customer service was paramount.

Furthermore, a resource dependence approach can be used to analyze the distinct requirements imposed on different subunits within the organization. When sub-units of the organization are decoupled to respond to conflicting environmental demands, these subunits may exhibit different legalization features, depending upon the unique environmental demands the subunits face. For example, a federal agency that distributes grant funds may create a highly legalistic "contracts office" to assure that all official contacts with prospective bidders are handled in a legally defensible manner. In contrast, a "program office" may actively solicit proposals and interact with prospective bidders more informally, so as to generate a greater number and higher quality of proposals.

The resource dependence approach can also accommodate a less rosy portrayal of the impetus and effects of legalization, as it is not a prescriptive theory but a description of how organizations tend to adjust to external control over critical resources when there is some conflict over means or ends (see Oliver, 1991). While Salancik and Pfeffer (1977, p. 5) note the benefits of allowing the influence of legal experts to "extend beyond handling legal matters and into product design, advertising, production, and so on . . . accompanied by appropriate, or acceptable, verbal justifications," it is clear that the administrative reach of legal experts may exceed their disciplinary grasp (Yudof, 1981b, 1988). It is for this reason, in part, that the escalating diffusion of legal interdependencies and its effect on organizational response patterns is of substantial practical and theoretical concern.

In addition, resource dependence theory can shed light on the paradoxical nature of adopting legalistic features. Specifically, legalization involves two features that work against the beneficial features of resource dependence. First, legalistic organizations involve more red tape—that is, more documents, more standard procedures, more administrators, and frequently more external regulators and other stakeholders. The increased involvement of outsiders in formal decision-making roles and the increased use of formal documentary procedures (e.g., to permit the review of what decisions have been made and how) serve to interject third parties into intraorganizational decision making and work relationships. The introduction of additional exchange partners incurs decreased control for the original partners, as they must meet additional demands from new participants (see Pfeffer & Salancik, 1978, for a similar argument). For example, employees, who invoked legalistic procedures to enhance their negotiating status and rights, may find that the third-party lawyers or regulatory agencies may have little interest in the employees' concerns, which have become dissipated in strength with the addition of two more decision participants. In addition, both managers and employees may find that the introduction of third parties tends to increase the degree of formalization and adversarial tone in the process. Finally, as the number of parties involved grows, the possibility of developing integrative solutions becomes increasingly remote (for examples, see Randall & Baker, this volume; Shapiro & Kolb, this volume).

Institutional Perspective

The institutional approach emphasizes the need to maintain legitimacy through the use of acceptable legalistic procedures or the adoption of other symbols of adhering to legally acceptable criteria (Selznick, 1969) (see Table 2.1). For example, recent publications have described the effect of legal/regulatory changes on the diffusion of due process procedures (Abzug & Mezias, 1993; Dobbin et al., 1988; Edelman, 1990) and accounting practices (Mezias, 1990).

Organizations have frequently been observed to engage in highly formalized, legalistic procedures that seem unnecessary (Meyer & Rowan, 1977) or even harmful from a purely instrumental point of view (Scott, 1987; Zucker, 1988). But, as institutionalists point out, the use of institutionalized forms can convey important symbolic messages that can affect the legitimacy of the organization with key constituencies (DiMaggio & Powell, 1991; Feldman & March, 1981). Thus, the use of seemingly superfluous routines is quite sensible for organizations for which sustained legitimacy is more important to survival than operating efficiency (Meyer & Scott, 1983; Meyer & Zucker, 1989). Institutional theorists point to the importance of sustained social legitimacy as both a resource and the basis for control over other resources essential for organizational survival (e.g., see Scott, 1987).[3]

The adoption of legally mandated formal policies and procedures, and the designation of parties who are officially "responsible" for handling the problem, reflect the notion that by categorizing a problem and establishing standardized ways of dealing with it, organizations can protect their institutional legitimacy (e.g., Meyer & Rowan, 1977; Meyer & Scott, 1983). By adopting a formally defined set of institutionally acceptable responses, the organization can cope with controversy while avoiding the difficulties associated with "taking sides" and alienating critical constituencies (Greenberg, 1990; Selznick, 1949; Sitkin & Bies, 1993a). Legalistic forms provide an effective and efficient "signal and symbol" (Feldman & March, 1981) of acceptability due to the salience and legitimacy of the law (Meyer, 1983; Nonet & Selznick, 1978; Selznick, 1969). This implies that legalization should be most prevalent in societies—or in industrial sec- tors (Meyer & Scott, 1983)—in which the law is most institutionalized.

Consider the case of trust in organizations. Because issues of trust and distrust are potentially volatile, simply having them arise can threaten the legitimacy of the firm or its leadership. In cases where trust is threatened, the use of personal, subjective judgment is likely to be suspect—after all, it is almost definitionally a part of any problem of distrust. As a result, organizations appear to respond by using formal, legalistic remedies (i.e., institutional forms of trust) that convey the use of impersonal, objective criteria to obtain the legitimacy that is often associated with institutionalized responses (Shapiro, 1987; Sitkin & Roth, 1993; Zucker, 1986). In addition, the mere use of formal, legalistic remedies can convey a sense that trust problems are minor, routine, and "under control." As Nonet and Selznick note (1978, pp. 66-67), "received authority, fact and logic . . . [are] weaker source[s] of legitimacy than appeal to procedure."

Institutional theory also provides a possible explanation for the problematic effects of the use of institutional substitutes for trust. Institutional theorists have noted that institutionalization, at its heart, involves making assumptions and routines tacit (see DiMaggio & Powell, 1991). For example, Zucker (1977) has argued that the more institutionalized something is, the more it would be literally unimaginable to question it or to consider alternatives. That is, institutionalized assumptions or routines are treated as objective facts or conditions that were determined externally and, therefore, are treated as given. A corollary of this idea is that when that which has been assumed (i.e., has been successfully institutionalized) is suddenly made explicit (e.g., through a written contract), this act inadvertently makes alternative assumptions or routines to those specified in the written document "imaginable." Thus, the mere act of making something explicit that was previously tacit (i.e., was institutionalized) can paradoxically serve to deinstitutionalize it.

In terms of trust, this helps to clarify one effect of increased use of formal, legalistic remedies: They make previously tacit interpersonal bonds of trust explicit, objective, and external. While these are the qualities that Zucker (1986) suggests permitted *impersonal forms of trust* to become an institutional "commodity," they simultaneously deinstitutionalize *interpersonal forms of trust* by transforming what was personal and tacit into something that is suddenly external and open for question and debate. Thus, the legalization of trust analyzed by Zucker (1986), Shapiro (1987), and Sitkin and Roth (1993) can be more clearly assessed as two simultaneous processes—one of institutionalization (of impersonal trust) and the other of deinstitutionalization (of interpersonal trust).

Life Cycle Perspective

Noting that organizations pass through a standard sequence of developmental stages, independent of human or environmental influence, life cycle approaches differ from the approaches just described by shedding light on how legalization may evolve as organizations move from one stage to the next. For example, the form that legalization takes may follow a standardized progression (e.g., increasingly formal—at least up to a point) as the organization passes through a set of developmental stages and grows in size.

The general insights provided by this theoretical approach can be readily applied to understanding the process of legalization, as many of the life cycle theories differentiate stages of develop in terms of legalistic features (e.g., Adizes, 1979; Greiner, 1972). In the early life of an organization, entrepreneurial leadership and operating styles become problematic as the organization grows and its coordination and administrative needs become more complex. Not only are more experienced leaders hired at this stage, but the trappings of bureaucracy begin to be adopted. From the perspective of standard treatments of life cycle stages, organizations not only pass through standard stages, but also experience predictable sequences of "crises" that stimulate the progression as the resolution of one set of crises requires that the organization adopt the features of the subsequent stage of development.

During its entrepreneurial years, an organization may be relatively free of legalistic features as its founders and staff focus on solving technical, product-related problems that will allow it to survive. But as life cycle theorists note, in response to the predictable crisis of leadership that ensues, chaos is reigned in through the use of simple bureaucratic procedures and increased reliance on mid-level managers to facilitate coordination in a growing organization. While the use of legalistic coordination devices is helpful for a time, organizations typically experience a revolt of sorts when midlevel managers feel that they have not been given sufficient autonomy to function effectively. The typical response to this second-level crisis is to adopt procedures for delegating authority, both in terms of formal guidelines for midmanagement and in terms of constraints on top management. The imposition of formal limitations on central control creates the next crisis: the need for coordination across autonomous midlevel managers. This results in the increased use of structural integration, planning and scheduling, and other forms of cross-functional systems. As the organization continues to grow in size and complexity, the need to simultaneously adapt to the needs of specialized employees and to specific customer groups may require the use of matrix forms, flexible teams, or network organizations.

Organizational characteristics described in life cycle theories are consistent with the proposition that organizations will become more legalistic as they mature and grow in size and diversity. Although both early (e.g., initial public offerings) and late (e.g., filing for bankruptcy) crisis-related transitions involve some degree of legalization, it is consistent with the general thrust of life cycle approaches that it is the developmental process itself that leads organizations to increasingly exhibit legalistic features over time, and for its members to become increasingly sensitive to legal issues.

Life cycle approaches emphasize that the level of legalization may not be a simple monotonically increasing function. Specifically, organizations that are able to move successfully into the more flexible last stage, described in recent life cycle approaches, appear to involve the reduction of legalization within the most mature and largest organizations. Sometimes this is associated with reduced size. For example, this type of institutional deconstruction can be seen in a number of recent analyses of network organizations (Pfeffer & Baron, 1988; Powell, 1990), in which formerly internalized market relations are exported to decrease the degree of formality, complexity, and inflexibility retained within the organization. In addition, this process can take place in large organizations, even if their size does not shrink, as long as their internal level of legalization is reduced. For example, it has recently been suggested that larger organizations may be better suited to the pursuit of institutional flexibility and learning (Brown & Duguid, 1990), in part because they are better able to build on the experience accumulated during earlier, more legalistic phases of development (Sitkin, 1992).

Life cycle theories provide a unique developmental perspective on legalization as a cascading set of standard solutions to presumably standard (but evolving) technical or institutional problems. Legalistic remedies are often adopted to reconcile problems associated with leadership (e.g., creation of formal checks and balances on administrator discretion), product quality (e.g., formal product standards), personnel relations (e.g., union contracts), public relations (e.g., airline policies on public discussions after accidents). Life cycle theories can help in analyzing the adoption of legalistic remedies for such problems by highlighting the degree to which the problems emerge in a predictable sequence of steps and the types of legalistic remedies adopted also conform to a predictable sequence.

Summary

While recent theoretical advances in organizational research have incorporated elements of the legal environment, the insights of Weber (1947), Selznick (1969), and legal scholarship more generally (e.g., Yudof, 1981a, 1981b, 1988) have remained largely neglected. In this chapter, we have demonstrated that such neglect is unwarranted. In addition, several dominant organizational theories have been shown to be directly relevant for understanding and analyzing the legalization process and identify the different variables that may explain the emergence of paradoxical outcomes. Even for institutional theorists, for whom formalization and legitimacy enhancement are central causal mechanisms, legalization has rarely been recognized as a distinct and growing organizational response pattern (Roth, Sitkin, & House, this volume). Researchers have treated individual elements of what we have referred to as a legalistic response, but have not identified the individual elements as part of a broader pattern or configuration of legalization. Thus, the importance of legalization to research using those theories has remained somewhat hidden.

Focusing on legalization and legalistic organizations represents an important new direction for organizational researchers for several reasons. First, the environment has been steadily shifting toward exhibiting legalistic attributes since before Weber's (1947) discussion of the issue, but the pace of the change appears to be quickening (see Bies & Sitkin, 1993a; Sitkin & Bies, 1993b).

Second, by identifying the organizational characteristics associated with legalization, and rooting these features in major organizational theories, we can begin to suggest fruitful new lines of research that can help predict the facilitating conditions, trajectory, and speed of the legalization process. For example, the study of legalization provides a unique opportunity to address a number of basic theoretical questions such as: (a) How do environmental characteristics enter the organization? (b) How do general societal culture features interact with organization-specific cultural features in influencing organizational adaptation? (c) When new institutional practices are adopted by an organization, to what extent is the process influenced by the symbolic versus the instrumental benefits offered by the new practice? (d) Does the form that legalization takes differ from society to society? For example, it may be that Japanese organizations have also become more legalistic over time, but that the term means something quite different within the Japanese cultural context than it does in an American one (see Smitka's discussion of contract versus contracting in the United States and Japan, this volume). Answering such questions can materially aid our ability to both understand and manage the process.

Third, even though Weber acknowledged that the bureaucratization process contained paradoxical elements, organizational theorists have not reflected the notion that organizational in a legalistic world is inherently paradoxical. By conceptualizing and exploring several fundamental paradoxes posed by legalization, we have tried to provide a springboard for future work on the distinct causes, effects, and processes underlying the paradoxical nature of legalization.

Finally, the practical implications of the proposed research are numerous. Increased understanding of the conditions that give rise to legalization may be helpful in identifying mechanisms for managing or regulating legalization. One practical goal of this research is to identify less useful forms of legalization, while retaining the beneficial effects that first drew attention to legalization as an important mode of organizational (i.e., efficiency-related) and social (i.e., fairness-oriented) reform. Although legalization has been heralded by regulators and worker advocates as a primary mechanism for fostering rational choice and constraining managerial abuse of discretion, evidence suggests that these laudable goals may in fact be undermined in some cases by the use of legalistic procedures (Bies & Tripp, 1993; Browning & Folger, this volume; Randall & Baker, this volume; Tamuz & Sitkin, 1992; Van Maanen & Pentland, this volume). In addition to cases in which the net effect of legalization is to exacerbate power disparities or to reduce the fairness of resource allocations, legalization can have a deleterious impact merely by slowing down or biasing the decision making or implementation processes of the organization. In fact, this is one of the primary arguments used by opponents of legalization: that legalization promotes inefficient and biased decisions through its emphasis on highly formalized and argumentative procedures. Thus, it is of substantial practical significance to explore the organizational contingencies that might mitigate the unintended and undesirable effects of legalization.

In conclusion, we would hope that scholars working from quite diverse perspectives will see the link of this theme to their work. To illustrate the broad applicability of legalization as an organizational phenomenon, we would like to conclude by making three links explicit. First, the rise in legalistic processes could be viewed as an example of formalization, structuration, or the diffusion of legitimized institutional forms, thus linking to research on structure, bureaucracy, structuration, and institutionalization. Second, communication about and interpretation of legalistic processes and language could also be conceptualized as related to organizational culture and communication. Finally, the notion of the law as a protector of fairness in employee relations and corporate responsibility is directly linked to conceptions of justice, ethics, and human resource management.

■ Notes

1. This is a slight oversimplification, but is used to emphasize the distinct issues highlighted by a focus on legalization. See Oliver (1991) and DiMaggio and Powell (1991) for a more fine-grained discussion of institutional predictions.

2. Despite their similarities, legal and rational approaches do have fundamental differences. In contrast to the legal veneration of precedent and tradition as a crucial basis for current decision making, the rational perspective eschews reliance on prior decisions as representing sunk costs (which are viewed as irrelevant to decisions that should be based on future-oriented expected values). Despite the logical link between rational approaches and the development of a Weberian "ideal type" bureaucracy, the natural tendency toward subideal bureaucratic red tape does not fit the efficiency-orientation of the rational model. Thus, to the extent that legalization gets bogged down in formal procedures at the expense of efficiently weighing evidence, it would be viewed as less "rational."

3. Although resource dependence theory is quite consistent in this view (e.g., Pfeffer & Salancik [1978, p. 196] refer to "social legitimacy" as a resource—see also Kaplan & Harrison, 1993), resource dependence theorists have actually limited their attention to the control of critical "hard" resources (e.g., capital, personnel) and its impact on decision-making influence. See Oliver (1991) and DiMaggio and Powell (1991) for more integrated discussions of these two theoretical approaches.

■ References

Abzug, R., & Mezias, S. J. (1993). The fragmented state and due process protections in organizations: The case of comparable worth. *Organization Science, 4*(3).

Adizes, I. (1979, Summer). Organizational passages. *Organizational Dynamics*, 3-25.

A plague of lawyers. (1986, November 17). *Barron's*, pp. 38-39.

Barney, J. B., Edwards, F. L., & Ringleb, A. H. (1992). Organizational responses to legal liability: Employee exposure to hazardous materials, vertical integration, and small firm production. *Academy of Management Journal, 35*(2), 328-349.

Bies, R. J. (1987). Bad news and the litigation mentality: Managerial strategies for liability reduction. In R. Bies & S. Sitkin (Co-chairs), *The law versus the manager: The encroachment of a litigation mentality into the organization*. National Academy of Management meetings, New Orleans, LA.

Bies, R. J. (1992). *The manager as intuitive politician: Blame management in the delivery of bad news in organizations*. Manuscript under review.

Bies, R. J., & Sitkin, S. B. (1993). Law without justice: The dilemmas of formalization and fairness in the legalistic organization. *Employee Responsibilities and Rights Journal*, 271-275.

Bies, R. J., & Tripp, T. M. (1993). Employee-initiated defamation lawsuits: Organizational responses and dilemmas. *Employee Responsibilities and Rights Journal*.

Bies, R. J., & Tyler, T. R. (1993). The "litigation mentality" in organizations: A test of alternative psychological explanations. *Organization Science, 4*(3), 352-366.

Black, D. (1976). *The behavior of law*. New York: Academic Press.

Brown, J. S., & Duguid, P. (1990). Organizational learning and communities-of-practice: Toward a unified view of working, learning and innovation. *Organization Science, 2*(1), 40-57.

Cartwright, B. C., & Schwartz, R. D. (1973). The invocation of legal norms: An empirical investigation of Durkheim and Weber. *American Sociological Review, 38*, 340-354.

Cascio, W. F., & Bernardin, H. J. (1981). Implications of performance appraisal litigation for personnel decisions. *Personnel Psychology, 34*, 211-226.

Chandler, A. D. (1977). *The visible hand: The managerial revolution in American business*. Cambridge, MA: Harvard University Press.

Clarke, L. (1989). *Acceptable risk? Making decisions in a toxic environment*. Berkeley: University of California Press.

DiMaggio, P. J., & Powell, W. W. (1983). The iron cage revisited: Institutional isomorphism and collective rationality in organizational fields. *American Sociological Review, 48*, 147-160.

DiMaggio, P. J., & Powell, W. W. (1991). Introduction. In W. W. Powell & P. J. DiMaggio (Eds.), *The new institutionalism in organizational analysis* (pp. 1-38). Chicago: University of Chicago Press.

Dobbin, F. R., Edelman, L., Meyer, J. W., Scott, W. R., & Swidler, A. (1988). The expansion of due process in organizations. In L. G. Zucker (Ed.), *Institutional patterns and organizations* (pp. 71-98). Cambridge, MA: Ballinger.

Doeringer, P. B., & Piore, M. J. (1971). *Internal labor markets and manpower analysis*. Lexington, MA: D. C. Heath.

Edelman, L. (1990). Legal environments and organizational governance: The expansion of due process in the American workplace. *American Journal of Sociology, 95*, 1401-1440.

Edelman, M. (1977). *Political language: Words that succeed and policies that fail*. New York: Academic Press.

Elsbach, K. D., & Sutton, R. I. (1992). Acquiring organizational legitimacy through illegitimate actions: A marriage of institutional and impression management theories. *Academy of Management Journal, 35*(4), 699-738.

Ewing, D. W. (1989). *Justice on the job*. Boston: Harvard Business School Press.

Feldman, M. S., & March, J. G. (1981). Information in organizations as signal and symbol. *Administrative Science Quarterly, 21*, 171-186.

Foote, S. B. (1984). Corporate responsibility in a changing legal environment. *California Management Review, 26*(3), 217-228.

Friedland, R., & Alford, R. R. (1991). Bringing society back in: Symbols, practices, and institutional contradictions. In W. W. Powell & P. J. DiMaggio (Eds.), *The new institutionalism in organizational analysis* (pp. 232-263). Chicago: University of Chicago Press.

Friedman, L. M. (1989). Litigation and society. In W. R. Scott & J. Blake (Eds.), *Annual Review of Sociology* (Vol. 15, pp. 17-29). Palo Alto, CA: Annual Reviews.

Greenberg, J. (1990). Looking fair vs. being fair: Managing impressions of organizational justice. In B. M. Staw & L. L. Cummings (Eds.), *Research in organizational behavior* (Vol. 12, pp. 111-157). Greenwich, CT: JAI Press.

Greiner, L. (1972, July/August). Evolution and revolution as organizations grow. *Harvard Business Review*, 37-46.

Jasanoff, S. (1985). The misrule of law at OSHA. In D. Nelkin (Ed.), *The language of risk: Conflicting perspectives on occupational health* (pp. 155-177). Beverly Hills, CA: Sage.

Kadish, M. R., & Kadish, S. H. (1973). *Discretion to disobey: A study of lawful departures from legal rules.* Stanford, CA: Stanford University Press.

Kaplan, M. R., & Harrison, J. R. (1993). Defusing the director liability crisis: The strategic management of legal threats. *Organization Science, 4*(3), 412-432.

Katz, D., & Kahn, R. (1966). *The social psychology of organizations.* New York: John Wiley.

Kesner, I. F., & Johnson, R. B.. (1990). Boardroom crisis: Fiction or fact. *Academy of Management Executive, 4*(1), 23-35.

Kirp, D. L., Yudof, M. G., & Franks, M. S. (1986). *Gender justice.* Chicago: University of Chicago Press.

Lieberman, J. K. (1983). *The litigious society.* New York: Basic Books.

Luhmann, N. (1981). Communication about law in interaction systems. In K. Knoor-Cetina & A. V. Cicourel (Eds.), *Advances in social theory and methodology: Toward an integration of micro- and macro-sociologies* (pp. 234-256). Boston: Routledge & Kegan Paul.

Macaulay, S. (1963). Non-contractual relations in business: A preliminary study. *American Sociological Review, 28*(1), 55-67.

Makofsky, D. (1979). Malpractice and medicine. In A. L. Strauss (Ed.), *Where medicine fails* (pp. 261-273). New Brunswick, NJ: Transaction Books.

March, J. G., & Simon, H. A. (1958). *Organizations.* New York: John Wiley.

Matthews, M. C. (1988). *Strategic intervention in organizations: Resolving ethical dilemmas.* Newbury Park, CA: Sage.

Metzger, M. B. (1984). Corporate criminal liability for defective products: Policies, problems, and prospects. *Georgetown Law Journal, 73*(1), 1-88.

Meyer J. W. (1983). Organizational factors affecting legalization in education. In J. Meyer & W. R. Scott (Eds.), *Organizational environments: Ritual and rationality* (pp. 217-232). San Francisco: Jossey-Bass.

Meyer, J. W., & Rowan, B. (1977). Institutionalized organizations: Formal structure as myth and ceremony. *American Journal of Sociology, 83*, 340-363.

Meyer, J. W., & Scott, W. R. (Eds.) (1983). *Organizational environments: Ritual and rationality.* Beverly Hills, CA: Sage.

Meyer, J. W., & Zucker, L. G. (1989). *Permanently failing organizations.* Newbury Park, CA: Sage.

Mezias, S. (1990). An institutional model of organizational practice: Financial reporting at the Fortune 200. *Administrative Science Quarterly, 35,* 431-457.

Mosca, G. (1939). *The ruling class.* New York: McGraw-Hill.

Moskowitz, D. (1987, July 13). Serving on a charity: It's getting safer. *Business Week,* p. 120.

Near, J. P., Dworkin, T. M., & Miceli, M. P. (1993). Explaining the whistle-blowing process: Suggestions for power theory and justice theory. *Organization Science, 4*(3), 393-411.

Nonet, P., & Selznick, P. (1978). *Law and society in transition: Toward responsive law.* New York: Harper & Row.

Oliver, C. (1991). Strategic responses to institutional processes. *Academy of Management Review, 16*(1), 145-179.

Olsen, W. K. (1991). *The litigation explosion.* New York: E. P. Dutton.

Peters, T. J., & Waterman, R. H. (1982). *In search of excellence.* New York: Harper & Row.

Pfeffer, J. (1981). Management as symbolic action. In L. L. Cummings & B. M. Staw (Eds.), *Research in organizational behavior* (Vol. 3, pp. 1-52). Greenwich, CT: JAI Press.

Pfeffer, J., & Baron, J. N. (1988). Taking the workers back out: Recent trends in the structuring of employment. In B. M. Staw & L. L. Cummings (Eds.). *Research in organizational behavior* (Vol. 10, pp. 257-303). Greenwich, CT: JAI Press.

Pfeffer, J., & Salancik, G. R. (1978). *The external control of organizations: A resource dependence perspective.* New York: Harper & Row.

Powell, W. W. (1990). Neither market nor hierarchy: Network forms of organization. In B. M. Staw & L. L. Cummings (Eds.), *Research in organizational behavior* (Vol. 12, pp. 295-336). Greenwich, CT: JAI Press.

Randall, D. M. (1985). Women in toxic work environments. In L. Larwood, A. H. Stromberg, & B. A. Gutek (Eds.), *Women and work: An annual review, 1,* 259-281. Beverly Hills, CA: Sage.

Salancik, G. R., & Pfeffer, J. (1977, Winter). Who gets power and how they hold onto it: A strategic-contingency model of power. *Organizational Dynamics,* 3-21.

Scheppele, K. L. (1988). *Legal secrets.* Chicago: University of Chicago Press.

Scott, W. R. (1981). *Organizations: Rational, natural and open systems.* Englewood Cliffs, NJ: Prentice-Hall.

Scott, W. R. (1987). The adolescence of institutional theory. *Administrative Science Quarterly, 32*(4), 493-511.

Scott, W. R., & Meyer, J. W. (1983). The organization of societal sectors. In J. W. Meyer & W. R. Scott (Eds.), *Organizational environments: Ritual and rationality* (pp. 129-153). Beverly Hills, CA: Sage.

Selznick, P. (1949). *TVA and the grassroots.* New York: Harper.

Selznick, P. (1969). *Law, society, and industrial justice.* New York: Russell Sage.

Shapiro, S. P. (1987). The social control of impersonal trust. *American Journal of Sociology, 93*(3), 623-658.

Shklar, J. N. (1964). *Legalism.* Cambridge, MA: Harvard University Press.

Sitkin, S. B (1992). Learning through failure: The strategy of small losses. In B. M. Staw & L. L. Cummings (Eds.), *Research in organizational behavior* (Vol. 14, pp. 231-266). Greenwich, CT: JAI Press.

Sitkin, S. B, & Bies, R. J. (1993a). Social accounts in conflict situations: Using explanations to manage conflict. *Human Relations 46*(3), 349-370.

Sitkin, S. B, & Bies, R. J. (1993b). The legalistic organization: Definitions, dimensions, and dilemmas. *Organization Science, 4*(3), 345-351.

Sitkin, S. B, & Roth, N. R. (1993). Explaining the limited effectiveness of legalistic remedies for trust/distrust. *Organization Science, 4*(3), 367-392.

Sitkin, S. B, & Sutcliffe, K. M. (1991). Dispensing legitimacy: Professional, organizational, and legal influences on pharmacist behavior. In P. Tolbert & S. Barley (Eds.), *Research in the sociology of organizations* (Vol. 8, pp. 269-295). Greenwich, CT: JAI Press.

Sitkin, S. B, Sutcliffe, K. M., & Reed, L. (1993). Prescriptions for justice: Using social accounts to legitimate the exercise of professional control. *Social Justice Research 6*(1), 87-111.

Skupsky, D. S. (1989). *Recordkeeping requirements*. Denver: Information Requirements Clearinghouse.

Staw, B. M., Sandelands, L. E., & Dutton, J. E. (1981). Threat-rigidity effects in organizational behavior: A multilevel analysis. *Administrative Science Quarterly, 26*, 501-524.

Stinchcombe, A. L., & Heimer, C. A. (1985). *Organizational theory and project management: Administering uncertainty in Norwegian offshore oil*. Bergen, Norway: Norwegian University Press.

Stone, C. D. (1975). *Where the law ends: The social control of corporate behavior*. New York: Harper & Row.

Tamuz, M., & Sitkin, S. B. (1992). *The invisible muzzle: Organizational and legal constraints on the disclosure of information about health and safety hazards*. Manuscript under review.

Turkington, C. (1986). Litigaphobia. *The APA Monitor, 17*(1), 1ff.

Tyack, D., James, T., & Benavot, A. (1987). *Law and the shaping of public schools*. Madison: University of Wisconsin Press.

Weber, M. (1946). *From Max Weber: Essays on sociology*. New York: Oxford University Press.

Weber, M. (1947). *The theory of social and economic organization*. New York: Free Press.

Weick, K. E. (1976). Educational organizations as loosely coupled systems. *Administrative Science Quarterly, 21*, 1-19.

Wholey, D. R. (1985). Determinants of firm internal labor markets in large law firms. *Administrative Science Quarterly, 30*, 318-335.

Wildavsky, A. (1988). *Searching for safety*. New Brunswick, NJ: Transaction Books.

Williamson, O. E. (1975). *Markets and hierarchies*. New York: Free Press.

Williamson, O. E. (1981). The economics of organization: The transaction cost approach. *American Journal of Sociology, 87*, 548-577.

Wooten, B. E., & Godkin, L. (1983). The specter of malpractice: Are personnel managers liable for job-related actions? *Personnel, 60*(6), 53-58.

Youngblood, S. A., & Bierman, L. (1985). Due process and employment-at-will: A legal and behavioral analysis. In K. Rowland & G. R. Ferris (Eds.), *Research in personnel and human resource management* (Vol. 3, pp. 195-229). Greenwich, CT: JAI Press.

Yudof, M. G. (1981a). Legalization of dispute resolution, distrust of authority, and organizational theory: Implementing due process for students in the public schools. *Wisconsin Law Review, 1981*(5), 891-923.

Yudof, M. G. (1981b). Law, policy and the public schools. *Michigan Law Review, 79*(4), 774-791.

Yudof, M. G. (1988). "Tea at the Palaz of Hoon": The human voice in legal rules. *Texas Law Review, 66*(3), 589-622.

Zucker, L. G. (1977). The role of institutionalization in cultural persistence. *American Sociological Review, 42*, 726-743.

Zucker, L. G. (1986). Production of trust: Institutional sources of economic structure, 1840-1920. In B. M. Staw & L. L. Cummings (Eds.), *Research in organizational behavior* (Vol. 8, pp. 53-111). Greenwich, CT: JAI Press.

Zucker, L. G. (Ed.). (1988). *Institutional patterns and organizations: Culture and environment.* Cambridge, MA: Ballinger.

Part II

Legalistic Procedures

3

Cops and Auditors:
The Rhetoric of Records

John Van Maanen

Brian T. Pentland

Organizational records, like any product of a social process, are fundamentally self-conscious and self-interested. What is recorded is never simply "what happened" because, first, no event can be fully or exhaustively described and, second, all records, as institutionalized forms, represent the collective wisdom of those who are trained to keep them. Records are not neutral, factual, technical documents alone, although when serving legitimate ends they must appear this way, and when serving illegitimate ones even more so.[1] They are designed—implicitly or explicitly—to produce an effect in some kind of audience, which itself actively uses records to interpret events. This is not to suggest conscious deceit or cynicism on the part of either record keepers or users (although, as we shall see, this is certainly possible). Rather it is simply to acknowledge and open up for analysis the conditions under which organizational records are produced and used.

Records often are produced to document the performance of a given organizational task, rather than allowing an impression of this performance to form upon an audience as an incidental by-product of the task activity itself. In such cases, organizational members devote at least a part of their labor to the creation of a desired impression as expressed by means of documentation. Records thus have rhetorical uses as, for instance, when they are used to convince some audience that those in the organization are taking care of business in quite proper ways.[2] The rhetorical uses do not undermine the technical work of records. Nor is the distinction between the rhetorical and the technical absolute. Certainly they may have instrumental or technical value as indexed by their use in decision processes, scheduling activities, and planning; as memory aids and counting devices; or in the making of comparative assessments. Both uses coexist and play off one another.

Whether one is concerned with technical content or rhetorical force, all records presume an audience. The audience for organizational records may include coworkers, subordinates, superiors, managers, customers, friends, clients, investors, auditors, jurors, regulators, family members, journalists, academics, crooks, trash collectors, librarians and archivists, industrial spies, pranksters, consultants, judges for the Baldrige Award, prosecutors and defense attorneys. Conceivably, anyone can stumble across an organizational record and read it. Far fewer, however, will be able to make much sense of most reports, for they are created with particular readers in mind. This chapter concerns the effects of a presumed kind of audience(s) on the production of rather specialized records. In particular, we are concerned with the effects of possible litigation on the production of working papers produced by financial auditors, and various event records produced by police officers such as arrest reports, duty logs, use-of-force statements, and charge sheets. Litigation introduces the possibility of an adversarial audience, one that can be counted on to construe every detail of the record as supportive of their contentions. In these circumstances, the general problem of impression management becomes acute.[3]

To a large degree, the paperwork associated with the keeping of records mediates the front (public) regions of an organization and the back (private) regions. Thus a phenomenon such as the impact of the law on the actions of the police or auditors is not so much obscured by routine practices, such as secrecy, collusion, selective enforcement, or faulty record keeping, as it is constituted by them. To try to edit out or analyze out these practices to get to the impact of the law would be futile and foolish. It would be the equivalent to pulling away the walls of a building to see what is keeping up the roof.

■ The Active Quality of Organizational Records

A theory of organizational records needs to consider both the production and the consumption of records as specialized genres or styles of text (Yates, 1989; Yates & Orlikowski, 1992). In general, there are elaborate conventions about what constitutes a proper example of a given genre. Our approach in this analysis is to examine how the legal context is implicated in these conventions and the organizational arrangements that sustain them. Specifically, how does the threat of an adversarial audience shape the records that organizations routinely produce?

Organization structure plays a role in all this since, from a microviewpoint, structure can be coded as the repeated behavior of individuals in particular places, using particular physical objects and communicating by the same symbolic expressions repeatedly with certain other people (Collins, 1981; Powell & DiMaggio, 1991, pp. 19-24). Records embody virtually all these definitional features and thus stand as structural attributes alongside others, such as the formal division of labor that is said to exist in the organization, or the degree to which reporting relationships are considered to be centralized or decentralized. And, like other structural attributes, records have importance as legitimizing symbols to both insiders and outsiders (Meyer & Rowan, 1977; Meyer & Scott, 1983). This legitimizing function may, of course, be of more value than whatever instrumental role records play in directing activities within the organization. Good record keeping, for example, may enhance the reputation of the organization by suggesting that managers have at their fingertips information useful to guiding intelligent choice, and, by implication, are using it (Feldman & March, 1981).

Records may also be recommended on the grounds of the indirect—if not unintended—effects their keeping can be seen to have on those who keep them. Such things as spreadsheets and end-of-shift summaries are tools for improving the minds of members, exercising their wit and wisdom, exposing them to disciplined ways of thought and expression, impressing on them a devotion to duty, and so forth. Those who do not adhere to the keeping of careful (and conventional) records may find they arouse the suspicion of others in the organization who do, and therefore come to be seen by them as slothful, ignorant, and unworthy. These depressing effects may be enlarged considerably when the record-keeping practices of the organization at large are examined.

Actions taken in the name of the organization are generally reported and recorded after the fact. This is in line with the Weickian observation that action can also be scripted after the fact and then legitimized by reference to culturally available accounts. This potential is a matter of common knowledge; so common that its potential can also be used before the fact, thus allowing "facts" to be recorded prior to their occurrence, on the usually bankable grounds that such "facts" will soon come into being. As we shall see, auditors routinely write their conclusions in advance, safe in the knowledge that they will eventually arrive at them. Production of records can thus move forward and backward in time, while appearing fixed to inscribed temporal particulars.

All of this argues for a perspective on records that recognizes their multipurpose and flexible character. Experienced makers, fakers, and takers of records recognize this too, forcing them to be alert to the numerous demands, constraints, dangers, and designs that surround record production and consumption. On the production side of the house, there are, for example, what Garfinkel (1967, pp. 186-207) calls "good organizational reasons" for "bad" (clinical) records. But, "bad" is a shifty matter and, as Garfinkel would be the first to point out, it depends fully on who is doing the labeling.

Records in Context

The good reasons Garfinkel discusses for the bad records he finds in an outpatient psychiatric clinic are many. At the simplest level there are good reasons that flow from what might be termed economic considerations concerning what data should be collected and kept. Garfinkel points to a kind of cost-benefit logic that seems to operate here, noting that costs are perceived as fairly immediate (i.e., lengthening the patient's intake interview), while the benefits are somewhat vague and speculative. Even if one assumes that what is recorded is somehow meant to be objective, one must grant that it is always selective.

Cochran, Gordon, and Krause (1980) review a wide range of studies that demonstrate what they call the proactive nature of records. Using examples from the airline industry, social welfare programs, parole officers, and other bureaucratic settings, the authors demonstrate how the contents of records depend on the record keeper's interests. Citing Ridgway (1956), they point to several examples of the "unintended effects of performance records," whereby supposedly rational organizational decision making was subverted by the pressure to meet sub-organizational goals (e.g., in a social service agency, cases were selected according to the length of time necessary to process them, instead of their urgency or the sequence in which they were received). The theoretical point here is not so much that records are generated to "beat the system," but that the system imposes systematic pressures "to maintain interpersonal relationships, control the behavior of others, protect oneself, save time, eliminate busy work, avoid unwanted scrutiny, exercise discretion over one's work, document cases that have been successfully resolved, and document that work has, in fact, been done" (Cochran et al., 1980, p. 13).

While this list can be expected to vary by organizational and occupational setting, it illustrates well the variety of ways in which record production may be self-interested. Rest assured, however, that such self-interest will not surface easily. Most record producers must act as if there were but a single standard of conduct—that which the law prescribes. If members are to meet their own varied interests, while performing for a pluralistic and educated audience who will not accept just any version of their conduct, it is essential that they avoid intensive scrutiny, while suggesting at the same time that they are fully accountable to the law. Groups that are held to high standards of accountability, such as police and financial auditors, do their best to maintain the secrecy of their work. Records play a role on the secrecy side in terms of both their accessibility (or lack thereof) and their content (or lack thereof).

Garfinkel (1967, p. 197) also argues that there are at least two possible readings of clinical files. There is an *actuarial* reading, which one could think of as a kind of journalistic reading—asking the standard questions of who, what, when, where, why, and perhaps how much. An actuarial reading of a clinical file would seek out a history of all activities concerning a particular patient. In this regard, the case files examined by Garfinkel were terrible, with all kinds of glaring omissions. It was not possible to construct an account of each patient's treatment history that was adequate for the needs of Garfinkel's study, which asked simply: "By what criteria were applicants selected for treatment?"

But records can also be given what Garfinkel calls a *contractual* reading, which emphasizes the relationship between the patient and the provider. The contractual reading seeks to establish that services were rendered in a responsible manner; in accordance with the generally accepted, customary norms for such cases; reflective, more or less, of the legal environment to which the clinic must respond. From this perspective, the case files were much better. Clinic personnel apparently sought to construct case files that reflected their relationship with the patient. Although Garfinkel uses the term metaphorically, it is the contractual reading that is closest in spirit to the issues we wish to highlight. What plaintiffs seek in organizational records is some indication that the defendants have breached their legal responsibilities.

There is, no doubt, a good deal of game playing and cunning in the record production business. It is subtle. Producers of records strive to create impressive facades, while antagonistic consumers of records attempt to tear them down. Certainly, it is possible for clever organizational members to engineer reports designed to give savvy readers a set of incidental clues, which allow them to conclude that the organization behaves in a way that it, in fact, does not. Since the signs are taken as incidental, not intentional, they may seem more significant. Presumably, coffee stains provide the evidence of late-night labor, sloppy strike-outs the appearance of spontaneity, tidiness the mark of an orderly process, multiple signatures the assurance of labor intensity or oversight, polysyllabic words the sign of intelligence, numbers and charts the stamp of precision. Both readers and writers of records are concerned with the information both given in and given off by reports (Goffman, 1969, pp. 3-9).

Even if record keepers were in some way unconcerned with managing impressions, they would nonetheless still create them, for their records are subject to interpretation. Neutrality, objectivity, dispassion, expertise, and so on are, after all, claims seeking affirmation, and, like any other claim, they have rhetorical foundations as well as technical ones. In the sections to follow, we will see how members of two particular occupational groups—financial auditors and police officers—go about their work and, in the process, produce records that they know may draw the sharp eyes of the legal eagles perched outside their organizations.

■ Auditors and Cops

To compare cops and auditors may appear on the surface audacious and silly. Auditing is safe; policing, risky. Auditing is the archetypal boring occupation, and its practitioners are seen as methodical and dull. Cops, on the other hand, personify excitement and have gained a rather high symbolic place in the public imagination as those determined to prevent and detect acts subsumed under the generic (and quite simplistic) classification of crime. Both images are off the mark. Auditing is less repetitious and routine than it appears, and policing is less spontaneous and fierce. To be sure there are crucial differences between the two, and it is difficult to imagine auditors and cops trading places. But there are analogies, as well, and some of them are striking.

In a sense, auditors are the police of the accounting world. They perform an enforcement function in the world of finance. Since the turn of the century, they have been given increasing responsibility to protect the interest of investors and the public at large through their appraisal of the financial statements of the corporate entities they audit (Johnson & Kaplan, 1987, pp. 129-135). There is, as we shall see, a rather heated, ongoing debate on the extent to which auditors can actually fulfill this responsibility, given their close relationship to the firms they audit (see, for example, Sternberg, 1992). Nonetheless, independence and objectivity are fundamental parts of the professional code of ethics for auditors. Furthermore, this responsibility forms the basis on which auditors can be sued for malpractice in the event that financial statements prove willfully or carelessly inaccurate. This is termed *audit failure* and, as the term suggests, the implication is that the auditor has negligently failed to correctly assess the financial condition of the client.

The police carry a different enforcement burden in society. If auditors enforce the GAAP (Generally Accepted Accounting Principles), police enforce nearly everything else. Police are rather nontechnical specialists, whose workplace is more likely to be out in the street or in a car than in an office building. But, like auditors, their work is governed by an esoteric code (both formal and informal). And, again like auditors, their work can be challenged if not performed in accordance with parts of that code. Cases can be thrown out of court, based on errors in police procedure, and the officers themselves are subject to claims of negligence and brutality.

The documents produced by auditors and by cops have some important parallels as well. First, they purport to record what the enforcer did in the act of enforcement. Auditors' working papers show the steps of the audit: when they were conducted, how audit evidence was collected, what accounts were tested, what inventory was observed and, ultimately, what the results were. Similarly, police arrest records attest to the actions of the officer or officers who make the collar—the reasons for a street stop, its location, time and special circumstances, the observed or inferred grounds for the charges filed, and so forth. Second, these records are subject to litigation only on a contingent basis. That is, not every set of working papers is challenged in court. Neither is every arrest report. Realistically, cops can expect their handiwork to show up in court more often than that of auditors, but not for improper procedure or brutality charges. Finally, as we shall argue below, the specific form these records take, the language used in them, the process of their production, and, to some extent, their very existence are all determined in part by the record producers' shrewd sense of the requirements of prospective audiences to whom their records may be given.

On this last similarity, a larger matter rests. Cops and auditors deal with a reality that is in various ways imperceivable—at least in any direct, immediate way. Both have mandates to protect the public by exposing wrongdoing, but the level of wrongdoing in society is impossible to know in any unquestionable way. In general, there is great public concern over the affairs attended to by auditors and cops. But, in both cases, organizationally orchestrated appearances must ordinarily satisfy this broad public concern for wrongdoing, because there is no other information available. Thus, the more we are concerned with the reality of crime or the financial health of our institutions, the more we must rely on appearances created by organizations whose very success is judged by the appearances they create.

■ A Word on Method

The data reported here come from several sources. Pentland conducted fieldwork among auditors as part of a study on how auditors create and use working papers. Observations, interviews, and verbal protocols of working paper reviews represent the primary techniques followed in the field (see Pentland, in press, for details). Van Maanen conducted fieldwork among the police, and the work is described in detail elsewhere (Van Maanen, 1981, 1991). We also draw on materials reported in the press, in trade publications, by investigatory bodies, and, of course, by other researchers as noted in the text. Our intent is to fashion something of a "critical tale" (Van Maanen, 1988, pp. 127-130) that speaks to the broader meaning of certain documents regularly produced by cops and auditors, rather than resting on the meanings (and uses) indigenous to them alone.

The approach we take to fashioning our critical tale—two tales, really—is to locate our respective subjects within the larger social worlds in which they operate, by providing a few broad-brush vignettes of police and auditor operations drawn from distinctly nonethnographic materials. These vignettes provide something of a point of entry for the more detailed fieldwork-based cultural descriptions of organizational life that follow, the assumption being that the latter makes sense of the former. The theoretical hook on which we hang our understandings of auditor and police reporting practices is, as noted, the rhetoric associated with impression management. The reporting practices of both of these groups are permeated by the need to legitimate their work in the eyes of critical and often litigious audiences. Prescriptively, record keeping is a purely technical act, but descriptively, it is a symbolic use of legalistic rhetorical forms to create (sometimes false) impressions of legitimacy and rationality. This idea appears throughout our tale-telling and is again revisited in the commentary that concludes the chapter.

■ Audit Work and Hard Copy

Accounting professors occasionally tell jokes. Many involve auditors whose staid but feeble public image seems to invite a disproportionate share of the barbs slung in financial worlds and words. A well-known joke of this genre is one that has an auditor responding to a potential client's question, "How much is two plus two?" with the unblinking response, "How much do you want it to be?" One need not be a deconstructionist to see that the joke itself plays off a rather deep source of tension for members of this distinctly unglamorous occupation. Independence—or, at least, its appearance—is a vital matter that lies at the very core of the appeals auditors make for professional status.

Such claims are issued most forcefully by The American Institute of Certified Public Accountants (AICPA), an association with about 300,000 members. This powerful voluntary association owes much of its growth (and prestige) to the audit function required by state and federal laws designed to produce truthful financial recording by American corporations. These laws—and their interpretation—have emerged historically as legislative and judicial responses to periods of unbridled capitalism, to stock market crashes and scandals, and to investment scams in various industries that cost investors and taxpayers billions of dollars. By law, then, publicly held companies are required to have their financial statements audited by independent public accountants. There is a rub, however, for the law is relatively silent on how this audit function is to be carried out. The system operates on the basis of companies hiring their own auditors, which means that auditors can be (and are) fired by firms unhappy with their work. And, in some cases, an auditor's choice is to either see things the way management does, or walk off the job and leave it for another auditor to pick up the trade. Since management selects its own auditors, the situation is not unlike allowing students to pick those whom they will let grade their own exams.

There is, however, a good deal of variation in just how seriously companies—large and small—take their SEC-required audits. Some managers and corporate boards may regard it as a bothersome ritual, others as an important check on internal affairs. Yet few sophisticated investors are likely to take audited financial statements at face value, for several reasons. First, the audit function, while mandated, is one firms can meet by shopping around. Bargain basement audits are as possible as top-of-the-line work, but certified financial statements are produced in either case, and it is difficult for an outsider to know how carefully a given audit was conducted. Second, auditors define their task as "testing" to see whether the financial records offered for inspection follow "current and accepted" accounting principles. These are principles that shift over time and are marked (variously) by a good deal of ambiguity and debate as to what constitutes "good" accounting practices (Kaplan, 1987). Third, most observers know that, inside firms, there is a good deal of horse trading, negotiating, imperfect estimation, and conflict taking place with regard to the figures that are submitted to auditors. Cost measures, for instance, are highly contestable matters, and the numbers managers eventually report may have less to do with some actual situation than with the results of intrafirm politics (Covaleski & Dirsmith, 1988; Eccles, 1985; Thomas, 1992). Tracing back the source of certain numbers may be too costly, or even impossible. Auditors know this, too, and while they may raise questions about how costs are accounted for in a com- pany's books, given the constraints under which they work, they are often stuck with what they are given and must make the best of it.

Finally, a clean audit—*unqualified* in audit terms—means only that the audit firm judges the company's financial statements to be free of material and conscious deception (i.e., that shareholders are not being cheated). Such final opinions, as issued over the signature of the audit firm, carry the implication that the audited firm's records represent fairly its economic transactions. The so-called bottom line here is that the audit statements provide only a judgment about the record-keeping practices of the audited firm and are not intended, legally at least, to pass judgment on the economic health and viability of the firm—although auditors are supposed to note if they have doubts about a firm's short-run survival.

Auditors are of course altogether aware of their own practices and limitations. And they take great care to distance themselves from business failures of all types. They note that their job is merely to attest to the fair presentation of organizational data. From the inside, auditors define their work largely in terms of "getting comfortable with the numbers" (Pentland, in press). Auditors note, too, that even if a business failure occurs after an auditing firm has provided a clean audit, such failure may say nothing about the audit itself. Business conditions could suddenly deteriorate, or the market might shift in unanticipated ways. Or maybe the managers of the audited firm were altogether ingenious at covering up illicit activities. As most accountants are quick to point out, there is an "expectations gap" between what the public believes auditors do (or are supposed to do) and what auditors can, in fact, do (Kaplan, 1987).

Moreover, even if auditors do stumble on misconduct in the keeping of corporate books, the most they are required to do is report improprieties to the company's management and board. If the company refuses to take action, the auditing firm is to withdraw from the "engagement" and leave it to the company they worked for to inform the SEC as to why the relationship has been terminated. This is an odd system, to be sure. One business commentator notes that "it is hard to imagine a system more flawed than the one now in place, a system that has undermined the very confidence it is supposed to engender" (Sternberg, 1992). Apparently, the ability of some corporate managers and directors to play it fast and loose with the books is not often discovered by auditors, or, if discovered, is not often acted on by even the most prestigious of firms. Some examples follow.

Cooking the Books

Built into the culture and language of the auditing world is the idea that service and confidentiality characterize good practice. Certainly, the very term *client* suggests a particular—and perhaps problematic—relationship between accounting firms and those for whom they labor. Clients, most auditors say, are the managers of the companies that have hired their firm. Such a view, however, runs smack up against another impression auditing firms would also like to convey, which is about their loyalty to principles higher than those specified in a mere employment contract. In fact, a recent U.S. Supreme Court ruling (*U.S. v. Arthur Young*, 1984) held that auditors have a public responsibility that goes beyond their employee status and duties. From the Court's point of view, the job of an auditor is not to simply satisfy clients, but to perform a public service by acting as a watchdog over corporate dealings, while maintaining a strict independence from the firm whose books are being examined.

Easier said than done. The fall of Silverado Savings and Loan is instructive in this regard. It is also a useful illustration of the kinds of trouble auditing firms have experienced in the savings and loan (S&L) industry (and elsewhere), where a number of costly malpractice suits have been filed as a result of clean audits provided various S&L firms shortly before they defaulted on critical loans and went belly-up—28 of 30 California S&Ls received "unqualified" audits less than a year before they went bankrupt (Sternberg, 1992). Silverado offers a glimpse at what can only be called creative accounting on the part of the firm, and the willingness, if not eagerness, of an auditing firm to also play the game.

As sketched out by Wilmsen (1991), Silverado was audited in 1985 by Ernst & Whinney, a Big-Six firm, who forced the thrift to report to shareholders some $20 million in losses from bad loans the bank had issued. Silverado's management team—including bank directors and senior executives—was not pleased with the work of Ernst & Whinney and fired them. They hired another Big-Six firm, Coopers & Lybrand, whose audit team took a rather different view of Silverado's books. The following year, Silverado reported in excess of $15 million in profit, and the managers of the enterprise pocketed almost $3 million in bonuses. A little over a year later, the company folded. Coopers & Lybrand is still settling claims that have flowed in response to their Silverado work.

Despite what appears to be a rash of spectacular recent cases, litigation historically involving audits has not been frequent. Palmrose (1988) reports the results of a study of audit-related litigation against the (then) Big-Eight and non-Big-Eight firms between 1960 and 1985. During that period, 472 lawsuits were filed, out of some 19,702 audits in the sample. Palmrose estimates that the overall frequency of "metitorious cases" against the Big Eight was less than 2%, while against the smaller firms it averaged less than 4% for the same period.[4] Such a study does not, of course, say much about those cases where the threat of litigation was apparently sufficient to bring about an out-of-court or before-filing settlement. Nor does it say much about the symbolic power of dramatic cases, such as Silverado, for focusing public attention on the audit process. The Keating Five scandal, for example, revealed that the managing partner of Arthur Young's Phoenix office, who signed off on the "unqualified" audit of Charles Keating's troubled Lincoln Savings and Loan, left Arthur Young shortly after this audit to work for American Continental (Lincoln's parent company) at a modest salary of about $1 million per year (Sternberg, 1992). Whether subsequent litigation could be deemed "meritorious" is beside the point; the appearance of misconduct in this case was so strong that it cast considerable doubt on the myth of auditor independence.

Audit problems are not always necessarily, or perhaps even typically, associated with guile on the part of managers or auditors. A close look at the routine, everyday features of auditing itself suggests that audits may sometimes be more a matter of form than function (Pentland, in press). There is a good deal of impression management and ritual respect involved in audit work. Much of it escapes notice by outsiders. Insiders also may fail to appreciate just how central such practices are to the trade—although they will not fail to put such practices into play. Just how deep some of these matters go can be seen by a quick look at working papers, the secret and sacred texts of the auditing world.

■ Auditor Working Papers

Financial auditors create working papers to document the financial statements of the entities they audit. To an outsider, the term *working papers* conveys something incomplete or in process; but, to an auditor, working papers are something very different. As a genre of text, audit working papers are highly specialized and codified. The general idea is that working papers support the auditor's conclusions about the financial statements of the client firm.[5] Since financial statements have a conventionalized structure that includes entries like cash, accounts receivable, accounts payable, accruals, and so on, working papers have a parallel structure. The papers themselves are physically divided into *files*, each of which corresponds to a particular "component" or entry in the financial statement. Each file contains a collection of "schedules" (which are essentially spreadsheets that itemize entries in each account) and a variety of supporting documentation. All of these materials are corner-punched and bound together between color-coded cardboard covers. At one of the observed sites, working papers for the prior year were organized into more than 30 separate files, which ranged from about 1 inch to almost 4 inches thick. Although the degree of automation varies from job to job and firm to firm, the majority of these papers are still produced by hand, with a pencil and a calculator.

Unlike some kinds of official documents that are produced on forms or letterhead, there is a rather fine line that distinguishes a working paper from mere scrap paper. Auditors on the job can create a schedule using any random sheet of paper that is convenient. It is transformed into a working paper by the addition of a title, page number, date, the signature of the person preparing it, and ultimately, its inclusion in a corner-punched file. Perhaps the most important feature of working papers is the omnipresent "sign-off" by the individuals who prepare and review them. Every section, page, and conclusion must be signed off by the staff auditor and the senior. The managers sign off on every page and the conclusions of each section, and the partner signs off on the conclusions of each section and of the audit as a whole. When the sign-offs are complete, then the working papers are complete.

The main audience for working papers is the higher-level members of the audit team: the senior, the manager, and the partner. At each stage of preparation, working papers are viewed by the senior. When audit sections are well along (but not necessarily finalized), they are reviewed by the manager. When they are nearly complete, they are reviewed by the partner. At each level of review, the interests of the audience vary somewhat. The senior is interested in mechanics. Were the audit steps followed by the team performed and documented correctly? The manager is interested in questions of scope and coverage, as well as reasonableness and risk. The manager assumes that the mechanics are right (because the senior says so) and asks broader questions about whether the steps performed seem adequate to reach the conclusions, and do those conclusions seem reasonable. Finally, the partner reviews the working papers as a whole.

The possibility of litigation introduces the potential of an adversarial third party into the audience. Working papers are the confidential property of the audit firm, but they may become public in the event of litigation by shareholders. As one senior auditor explained:

> The work papers are our evidence of the work we perform and that we knew what we were doing. . . . If we had to go to court, the work papers would be the main evidence of what was going on and of the work we performed.

It's a hard copy. It would be hard to falsify that. If you were up on the stand and had to give a statement or something and said, "Oh, we knew what was going on then." Well, then why wasn't it in the work papers? If I was the judge I'd say you should have included it in the work papers if you knew what was going on.

The image of being "up there on the stand," explaining what went into the work papers, is a vivid one for auditors. As a result, work in process is treated as though it were also a finished public document, ready for scrutiny by opposing counsel. This point is explicitly addressed by the teaching materials of one such public accounting firm:

A well-documented set of audit working papers can be of enormous assistance when audit work is challenged. Conversely, our audit working paper files may provide support to an adversary if they show, for example, unresolved questions, facts not followed up, or inadequate treatment of important matters.

The possibility of litigation therefore insinuates itself in the detailed conduct of auditing work. For example, norms concerning the use of erasers, correction fluid, and other routine correctives are directed not only toward the completion of the audit, but also toward the possibility of how they might appear and be explained under cross-examination.

As mentioned earlier, auditors are responsible for verifying that the financial reports issued by their clients are "fairly stated." When an auditor issues this assurance (which can be found at the end of every annual report), he or she assumes a degree of liability, as do the firm and its partners. In the event that the financial statements turn out to be "materially incorrect," this is an "audit failure" and the auditor can be sued for negligence.[6]

The threat of litigation is a clear and present danger in the minds of auditors on the job. The detailed conduct of their work is oriented toward producing, inside the time and resource constraints placed on them, a set of working papers that will "stand up in court." This translates not only the content of the working papers, but also their form and details of presentation. For example, in the process of an audit, there are numerous pages of review notes produced. Review notes are essentially questions that seniors and managers have about the work of their subordinates, and typically contain "to dos," things that the subordinate needs to change before the working paper can be signed off. These reflect the evolution of the work in progress. However, they are systematically purged in the end from finalized working papers to avoid the appearance that such questions ever existed.

Teaching the Staff to Do it Right

The working paper review process is a critical vehicle for socialization of new staff. In particular, review notes tell staff what is acceptable and what is not. They are reminded to sign off if they forget, they are corrected if they make an error in interpretation or style. Consider these comments, which are taken from a verbal protocol of a senior reviewing a case file:

> The Staff used the same tick mark he used on [another account] but neglected to alter the tick mark in the sense that he's saying these costs relate to [that account], when in fact they relate to [this account]. I'm therefore going to write a review note for him to change it.
> The Staff put a note on the bottom of the page, so I'm reading it. The Staff did not sign off the note on the bottom of the page, so I will write a review note to do so.
> The last step is to conclude, so I read the Staff's conclusion. I agree with the Staff's conclusion, so I am writing "Agree" and I am dating it. I note that the Staff dated his conclusion 5/19/90. I know that the Staff could not possibly have performed the work prior to that time, so I'm going to write him a review note to change the date on the conclusion.

The manager on his job emphasized that review notes are the most important single means of educating and developing the staff. From this selection of the senior's review notes, it is easy to see what he meant. These "to do's" deal with what could be regarded as cosmetic aspects of working paper preparation: using unambiguous tick marks, signing off on work, and dating the work correctly. The actual analysis was complete; there were no questions raised about the content of the document or the conclusions reached. Rather, what mattered was the form. The senior agreed with the staff's conclusions, but the date was wrong.[7] Even though the senior knew the work was complete, the apparent errors in dating and signing off could raise doubts about the integrity of the work.

Specialized Language in Working Papers

The language that auditors use in their work carries a great deal of significance as a means of demonstrating due diligence on one hand and hedging their conclusions on the other. A constant concern in auditing is how accounts are sampled and tested for accuracy. This is referred to as the *basis of selection*. Imagine a company who claims to have $5,000,000 in accounts receivable, spread over thousands of customers. How can auditors tell if these creditors are genuine? Since they don't have time to contact all of them, they must select a sample. The problem is identical, in principle, to the scholarly problem of sample selection, but auditors can be sued for malpractice if they get it wrong. The wording used to justify the sample is the key: Auditors can select a "judgmental sample" or a "statistical sample." Since statistical sampling is expensive and time-consuming, the phrases "judgmentally selected" and "non-statistically selected" appear constantly in working papers.

The wording of conclusions is also important. Auditors will never conclude that the financial statements are literally correct. Even for "unqualified" or clean audits, auditors will only conclude that "taken as a whole," financial statements are "fairly stated." The difference between "correct" and "fairly stated" encompasses a large part of the audit expectations gap mentioned previously. Here we have another kind of audience effect in the use of auditor records, but this time the record is public. While lay people (non-accountants) may interpret a clean audit of company records as a kind of guarantee of that company's financial health, auditors see their results as, at best, a kind of filter; they may screen out some of the worst problems, but there is no guarantee that other problems do not get through.

Within the general semantics of auditing work, words and phrases are selected to create the impression of due diligence and certainty on the part of the audit firm. Such may not have been the impressions of the auditors while they conducted they work. At one engagement, a senior erased an inappropriate comment on a schedule and explained, " 'Bogus' is not a good word to use in work papers." Of course, it was commonplace to hear staff use terms like this, or worse, when talking among themselves about client accounts and personnel. The spoken language, which is filled with expressions of uncertainty and distrust, is systematically replaced with language that preserves a veneer of objectivity and confidence when committed to paper.

Cleaning up the Working Papers

The role of working papers in the production of financial statements can be illustrated with a story. On one observed engagement, work papers left over from a recently completed job were being reviewed by the audit team. The job had been completed under severe time pressure, so even though the financial statements had been approved and sent out, the work papers still needed to be "cleaned up" and "signed off." At first, this was puzzling: How could the opinion have been rendered if the work papers were not complete? The partner in charge of this job happened to be on site that day, and was sitting in the main workroom with the rest of the audit team. When asked why any further work was necessary on that job, he responded that work papers serve two functions. First, to get comfortable with the work, and second, to defend the work against an adversarial third party. To the extent that he had already rendered his opinion, and the financial statement was on the way to the printers (and ultimately to the shareholders), he must have been comfortable with the work. What remained was to defend that work against third parties by editing out anything that might raise questions about the objectivity or diligence of the audit.

There were several specific things that remained to be done. The draft financial statements were still in the audit summary file and needed to be replaced with the final copy. It is standard practice to remove the draft financial statements (even though these are the ones on which the audit conclusion is actually based) and substitute the final, printed version of the statement. Several of the files still had review notes attached to their covers, notes that also had to be removed. As he cleaned up the file, the manager removed miscellaneous Post-its™, paper clips, and fax cover sheets as well. In one case, a schedule had question marks where numbers should have been. Unruffled, the manager located the sources for these numbers, and the blanks were filled in. Anything that might detract from the internal consistency of the file was removed or repaired. This is a part of what might best be considered an institutionalized purification process.

Working papers are designed and produced to present an air of infallibility, to eliminate the possible inference on the part of potential readers that the conclusion could be materially different. The process of cleaning up or purifying working papers highlights the fact that this presentation is unnecessary for insiders. Insiders (particularly those who have worked on the audit and know the client) can get comfortable enough to sign an opinion, even if all the cross-references aren't checked yet, or all the numbers aren't in the proper places. Working papers, in the final analysis, are not only for the use and consumption of the audit team but are prepared "just in case" for those beyond the organization.

■ Policework and Paperwork

Unlike auditor working papers, police reports of most varieties have been subjected to considerable scrutiny, ethnographic and otherwise.[8] That they usually come up wanting in terms of actuarial accuracy is less the point here than the fact that a contractual reading in Garfinkel's sense would grant them considerable merit. The police know well that what they write down may be read carefully and in great detail by individuals and groups they regard as adversaries. In response, they are careful writers of reports, knowledgeable of the many ways their crafted prose can be used. The records they create are as much proactive as reactive in the sense of anticipating the uses to which their paper may be put.

Proactive uses of police records include such matters as cleaning up procedures followed in the field, so they appear later to be in line with departmental regulations and legal limits; selectively representing evidence—material discoveries, witness accounts, defendant statements, and so on—that may have bearing on future case disposition; recording crimes in such a fashion as to increase or decrease their net effect on crime and clearance rates;[9] and so forth. All these practices are well known to the police and attest to the creative uses to which police records can be put. Frequencies of use vary over time by departments, by units, by individual officers, and so on; but, to the police, the availability of such strategies is crucial for plying the police trade.

Street officers view a large part of their trade as controlling the behavior of those they regard as dangerous, deviant, and otherwise up to no good. To insiders, the department is most distinctly a police force, not a police service. Officers entertain few doubts as to whom the force should be directed. One attention-getting category is comprised of "assholes," who contrast to others with whom the police interact by their perceived refusal to accept the police definition of the situation at hand (Van Maanen, 1978). They mean trouble for the police and are dealt with in no uncertain terms.

Trouble to the police is also a source of excitement and job satisfaction. Assholes are to street cops what bad guys are to detectives.
They provide a constant source of bread-and-butter "stats" and "body
counts"—arrests for such misdemeanor and minor felony offenses as
drunk and disorderly, possession of drugs (or paraphernalia), loud
and abusive language, fighting, disturbing the peace, resisting arrest,
disorderly conduct, and so forth.[10] They are central to the occupation,
and, indeed, some officers define their role as "not letting the assholes
take over the city" (Van Maanen, 1981). The category is, however, an
ethno-technical one, not a legal one, and this can cause difficulties
for the police, because the technical recipes that hold within police
circles for just how assholes are to be identified and treated may not
necessarily be those thought by the courts to be consistent with
current legal restraints.

This is an inconvenience for the working police, for they are
convinced that they know their trade well and do not like to be tied up
—hamstrung—by tiresome legalities and red tape. Thus, a good deal
of lore, habits of the mind and body, routine practices and cautionary
wisdom, exists as to how one is to survive and maintain respect in
the police world by circumventing the spirit, if not the letter, of
the law. Such guidelines are cultural ones, occupational rather than
organizational. But they are of a most practical sort, and legal matters
are mostly of background relevance. Moreover, since so much of what
the police do is out of public sight, the law is felt most keenly when
episodes are described after the fact than during the fact-producing
moments themselves. Consider a recent and rather chilling example.

■ L.A. Law [11]

Rodney King and two friends were cruising north on the Foothill
Freeway on the night of March 3, 1991. They were pleasantly high on
booze and marijuana and apparently moving along at a good clip, with
no particular place to go. Around midnight, a husband-and-wife team
of CHP (California Highway Patrol) officers spotted King's white
Hyundai running at a speed of what they estimated to be more than
100 mph. Hitting their emergency blue lights and siren, the officers
began a high-speed chase that was to end miles away at a red light
on a surface street in front of the Mountain View Apartments in Lake
View Terrace. It was a chase joined in by at least two squad cars from
the Foothill Division of the Los Angeles Police Department (LAPD).

The run was, by police standards, a good one. It was a pursuit that brought out the troops, enlivened an otherwise quiet Saturday night and gave a few officers the chance, in the police vernacular, to get in a little "stick time" and "deliver a service" (street justice). In the words of the LAPD dispatcher requesting aid for the pursuing officers that evening: "[King and his friends] should know better than to run, they are going to pay a price when they do that."

When the pursuit and its mop-up were over, one man, Rodney King, was in custody for "evading arrest" (a charge dropped by the department 4 days later). The end-of-shift report filed by Sergeant Stacey Koon —the supervising shift sergeant and a participant in the chase and arrest—noted that "felony stop procedures" were followed after King finally pulled his car over. The three passengers were ordered out of the Hyundai by loudspeaker. Two quickly complied and exited on the right-hand side of the car in cop-wise fashion, with their hands high and visible. They were put to the ground and handcuffed. The driver, King, balked at the command, according to Koon, refusing to immediately exit the car and "prone-out" (place himself face down on the pavement). When he did move from the car, he was said by Koon to have offered so much resistance that the officers had to subdue him by force—using several "power strokes" (baton blows) administered by LAPD officers Powell, Wind, and Briseno, and several electrical jolts from Koon's Taser stun gun. When King was finally "brought under control," an ambulance was summoned and he was taken to the emergency ward of a local hospital. On the department's standard form arrest report, Officer Powell presented the incident in the following way:

> Deft [defendant] recovered almost immediately [from the effects of the Taser] and resumed his hostile charge in our direction. Ofcr Wind and I drew our batons to defend against deft's attack and struck him several times in the arm and leg areas to incapacitate him. Deft continued resisting kicking and swinging his arms at us. We finally kicked deft down and he was subdued by several ofcrs using the swarm technique.

Such actions as inscribed on the documents completed by LAPD officers that night offer an account of the incident that is hardly unusual in police circles. So common are police encounters entailing the "use of force" that the LAPD—along with most other big-city agencies in the United States—has a special form devoted to its efficient description. Officers need only check boxes (ranging from "firm grip" to "deadly force") to indicate the extent of their street actions. Similar check-off forms are available to describe the actions of those receiving police attention. Thus, Powell and Wind put tick marks in the boxes labeled "attacked officer," "continued resistance," and "increased resistance." Their estimate of Rodney King's injuries was marked by a tick in the box "contusions and abrasions." The senior supervisor, Sergeant Koon, included a short narrative attached to the bottom of his end-of-shift report: "[King] was subdued by several baton strikes and his injuries were slight . . . several facial cuts due to contact with asphalt. Of a minor nature. A split inner lip. Subject appeared oblivious to pain." As to the apparent difficulties of the officers to put King down, and the cause of his stubborn tolerance of pain, Koon offered his experienced opinion, which later turned out to be wrong, that "[King] appeared to be under the influence of PCP."

For most police officers and their superiors, the King incident, as told in the official paper submitted to the department, follows a rather well-established and highly regarded formula. It highlights the celebrated pursuit-and-capture aspects of policing as accomplished through the thrilling high-speed chase. It demonstrates the recalcitrance of a bona fide asshole—a dusted ex-con, to boot—who did not accept the police definition of the situation and was brought up short for carrying an attitude into his encounter with the police. Insiders would naturally read a good deal more into the official paper than put there by the reporting officers. But, by the end of the shift, no further information was needed to complete the record. A righteous bust. Case closed. As codified in the reports, the LAPD had once again illustrated a textbook arrest in conjunction with the proper use of force. This was proactive policing at its best.

This is no doubt where the case would have ended—filed and forgotten—were it not for the new Sony Handicam, recently purchased by George Holliday and used to record the action on the street below his Mountain View apartment, as Rodney King earned his hard time and split lip. And action there was. Unlike the tamed and muted depiction of the scene put forth by the police reports of the incident, the scene that drew Holliday's attention was wild. The street was lit up by the searchlight from a booming police helicopter overhead. There were policemen and policewomen everywhere. Prowl cars squealed into and out of the frame. In all, there were at least 23 LAPD officers wandering about the scene, 2 more in the police chopper above, and 4 officers from other departments, including the CHP officers who had begun the chase.

What appears on Holliday's tape bears no relation whatsoever to the official records of the incident as filed by the police. The tape begins with King already "proned" and the wires from Koon's stun gun visibly stuck in his body. No resistance is offered by King—indeed, he appears half-dead on the tape—as four LAPD officers clobber him with their 2-foot-long, solid aluminum batons and kick him repeatedly with steel-toed shoes. What were described in the police reports as "light injuries," turned out to be a fractured cheekbone, facial nerve damage, a severe concussion, a broken ankle, and 11 broken bones at the base of the skull, as a result of the kicks and blows from the police. Fillings had been knocked from King's teeth as his face was smashed into the asphalt. Twenty stitches were required for the deep cuts and scrapes he received from being dragged across the pavement. When Holliday called the LAPD on Monday morning to inquire on the condition of his videotaped motorist, he said he was told by the desk officer, "We do not give out information like that." Yet, a good deal of information "like that" was soon to come out.

Holliday sold his tape of the incident to a local TV station for $500. Soon thereafter it was running on all channels across the country. A major investigation was undertaken in Los Angeles, by an independent commission appointed by the mayor, in which almost nothing the LAPD did that night in March could be construed in a favorable light. Probably the most damaging aspect of the entire incident was the indifference to the beating displayed by the other officers on the scene. Indeed, what was most revealing about the tape was what it did not show. No one moved to stop the beating.

Further damage to the reputation of the department and its official version of the King episode came from the release of MDT (Mobile Digital Terminals) transcripts for the night of March 3. MDTs, located on the dashboards of most of the LAPD squad cars, allow units to communicate with each other and headquarters without going on radio. The transcriptions, published in the *Los Angeles Times* on March 19 (and later in the *Report of the Independent Commission*, released in July 1991), provide a very different picture of the event than is to be found in any official reports. An excerpt reads:

> 12:56 AM: "U just had big time use of force . . . tased and beat the suspect of CHP pursuit, Big Time." (from Sgt. Stacey Koon to Watch Commander's Office)
> 12:57 AM: "Oh well . . . I'm sure the lizard didn't deserve it . . . ha, ha . . . " (from Watch Commander's Office to Koon)

The use of "big time force," "the lizard," and the appearance of "ha, ha" on the transcripts do not appear on any official paper. Nor do they reflect the language the public is accustomed to hearing from the police. What became visible in the King episode was a quick and unnerving glimpse of the everyday realities of police work—albeit in a condensed and highly dramatic form. As was patently obvious, the street officers swarming in on Lake View Terrace were enacting their own version of *L.A. Law*, a version that had little or nothing to do with policy, procedure, or practice as legally prescribed. Only the paper produced by the routine reporting carried on following the episode could conceivably be tied to such normative matters. These are the "working papers" of the police, and it is well worth looking at what they represent within the police culture, for they shed a good deal of light on how the police regard their legal mandate.

Taking the Power

The police themselves often put forth a view of their record-keeping duties as distasteful—an annoying documentary task that infringes on their "real work" and ever-increasing in terms of its demands on their time. Street officers in particular hold that paperwork is one of the most time-consuming and pointless of their duties. They go on often to invoke a sort of mythical Dreamtime when talking about what they see as escalating paperwork:

> In the days when I first came on the force, we had a couple of forms and that was it. . . . I'd throw a bunch in the car and head out for my district. But, nowadays, I must have fifty different forms, one for every imaginable offense and contingency. It's more important these days to be a good writer than a good shot. . . . (excerpted from fieldnotes)

The issue is not whether the paperwork demands associated with routine patrol work have increased in recent times. The issue is that officers everywhere consider paperwork to be a nagging but unavoidable aspect of their work—and, as the quoted officer begrudgingly suggests, its importance to the trade cannot be overlooked. So important is writing to cops (and their supervisors) that individual officers establish reputations among their peers as to their writerly skills. Nicknames such as "Word Perfect," "Hemmingway," "Squint," "The Little Professor," "Sergeant Bic," and "The Man with the Golden

Arm" are attached to some of the more appreciated—if not always respected—masters of departmental paperwork.

The skills that stand behind such labels are varied. Speed, comfort, and technical abilities, such as knowledge of proper spelling, rules of punctuation, and grammar, are obviously of importance. But, more critically, subtle contextual use of pat phrasing, wise precedent (legal and departmental), and person-specific cultural rules surrounding what will be regarded by certain senior officers as a proper account (given a particular report or incident genre) are crucial in construct-ing good paper. Developing skill is a matter of training, experience, and aid. Consider, for example, a brief learning episode in this regard:

> Returning to the station house, Barnes filled out the many reports associated with the incident and passed each of them to his sergeant for approval. The sergeant carefully read each report and then returned the paper to Barnes saying that he better claim he was kicked in the face BEFORE he entered the patrol wagon or Barnes would get a heavy brutality complaint for sure . . . after some discussion and two rewrites, Barnes finished a report that the Sergeant said "covered their asses." (Van Maanen, 1983, p. 273)

What begins in the street with the arrest of a "stand-up drunk" ends for the officer(s) involved in the station house with the filing of a "public intoxication" charge. The conversion involves the production of a "file" (a report or set of reports) that contains enough evidence (broadly defined) to make the charge fit and assure the officer(s) a better than 50% chance of winning the case, should the charge be contested in court. The police know well that most of those they charge with minor infractions (the bulk of the street cop's "stats") will not contest the issue, and the files are completed in an altogether routine fashion. When troublesome cases arise, there is usually a battery of checkers and administrators in the station house whose job it is to discover potential flaws in the files (and make sure they are corrected), for they must sign off on the work that passes before them. Thus the complexities of social behavior are reduced to paper with a little help from one's friends within the department.

Such retrospective work of cleaning up past events is also a pro-spective matter because the police, like auditors, assemble and write their records with particular goals and audiences in mind. Again this is a critical point, for if we see records only as reactive, then merely the form and formula for completing the record draws causal attention.

But, if the record itself is seen to have purpose—where records are actually or potentially used to legitimize, hide, cover, bend, or otherwise account for action—then the people who produce records, and the context in which such records are produced, become the principle focus of attention. Record keeping and use among both the police and auditors cannot be understood without an appreciation of the intentionality and opportunism exercised by those who create records.

The Department Speaks [12]

Law enforcement agencies in the United States seek to appear—like all organizations—responsible, moral, efficient, effective, and law-abiding. But the creation and maintenance of such an image is both historically situated and highly problematic. One claim police officials emphasize in public appeals for legitimacy is their thoroughly constrained and closely monitored custodianship of their state-granted monopoly on violence. Such custodianship is seen particularly clearly when the police are involved in the direct use of force, and their actions become subject to outside scrutiny.

Ideally, what administrators wish to demonstrate when publicly presenting an official version of a problematic police episode involving force, is (a) that the events leading up to the incident were matters of appropriate police concern and response, and (b) that those members of the organization involved in the episode were behaving within well-known and well-prescribed limits of individual discretion. The first purpose then is to place the action squarely in the domain of public life by showing that the police presence on the scene was warranted. The second purpose is to fit selected facts of the case to the legal justifications for the use of force by law officers. These purposes are not unrelated, of course, and a failure to adequately fulfill one may lead to the collapse of the other. Taken together, however, their accomplishment converts a reaction into a guided action and thus may help maintain (or build) public support for the necessity of police use of force.

As suggested by the Rodney King story, this legitimating activity has become rather institutionalized within police organizations. There are pre-coded reports to fill out and standard kinds of questions to answer. Even in controversial cases, where the police version of events is widely and publicly questioned, there are particular reviews to undertake, hearings to hold, audiences to assemble, statements to be written, spokespersons to be briefed, and so forth. There are, in effect, standard operating procedures to be followed in such cases, so that at a minimum the organization itself will be viewed by the public—or particular segments of the public—as acting responsibly, properly, and well within the letter and spirit of the law (even if individual police officers are not seen in the same light). Such damage control or crisis management routines are formalized and are regarded by administrators as absolutely necessary.[13]

In light of such procedures and the experience on which they have been built, a language is chosen as a way of framing a particular incident. In short, a reality is created (that may or may not be accepted outside the agency), which attests to the fact that all is functioning well within the department. It is, however, a weak paper reality to the officers involved, for the official words will always prove inadequate descriptions of what happens on the ground.

> [After a shooting] . . . I had to write that major (i.e., arrest report) about six times. Each time some different asshole in the department wanted it redone. Where was I standing? Where was Louie my partner? What exactly did I say before I squeezed off the round? When did I unsnap my gun, release the safety? Did I see him before or after his scrod buddies pulled off the road? I figure the people upstairs know what's important (administrative staff) but there's no way I could answer those questions. It happened. It happened fast. It happened faster than I could think about it. . . . When I read these reports it doesn't mean like the same thing . . . (Van Maanen, 1980, pp. 150-151)

What is constructed from such procedures is a version of an incident such that the reputation and stature of the organization itself (and its members, particularly the leadership) are not harmed and, if possible, are even enhanced. The "facts" relevant here are the facts relevant for organizational purposes and not circumstantially fleeting facts that those involved might regard as critical. The fact that the recipient of a police bullet was not a felon until he was seen as fleeing, or that a given officer was unsure that the "glaring metal object" held by a citizen was a knife, a flashlight, or a cigarette lighter, are of importance only when the many possible facts are sifted, selected from, and ordered according to a logic rather different from what is on an officer's mind while engaged in the particular white-heat responses of the moment.

At a somewhat more mundane and altogether routine level, individual officers speak for the department (as do their records) when making a court appearance. The court appearance, coming long after the real work and control of an incident has taken place at the street level, is invariably seen by the police as an adversarial legal game, involving two sides, in which a peculiar institutional truth is sought. The game is played with a concern for evidentiary and conduct rules quite at odds with the rules of a practical sort that guide an officer's everyday actions. Since it is a game to the police, their control moves (testimony and reporting) are designed to increase the likelihood that the results of court proceedings are ones they find least objectionable. Words and records are produced with these ends in mind.

This is to say that nothing counts as the "action that was taken" independent of the background understandings of those in the department. Among other things, these background understandings link the legitimacy of police practices to just certain kinds of accounts. A given street stop, for example, may be justified on the grounds of a "furtive gesture," "suspicious behavior," a minor traffic violation or a vehicular one, such as the police classic "no rear plate illumination." Those in the know are quite aware that behind this stop stands a common but hidden criterion, such as the unexpected appearance of a black face in a white neighborhood. The latter cannot be used on an official report, so a cover story is created for the record. These are the background understandings of the police, and most emerge from the intimate practical world of street work.

■ Comment

By way of summary, several points stand out. First, both cops and auditors have enforcement functions that are mandated and, to a degree, governed by law. As such, their records are historically, situationally, and organizationally determined tactics of demonstrating to outsider groups that the enforcement tasks they perform are being conducted according to legitimate and approved procedures—means that are both codified and explicit. Second, in both cases, there are systematic ways that the respective organizations try to produce records that are "done right," and these procedures are backed up by those in the organization who read and sign off various reports— usually direct supervisors (seniors and managers in audit work and sergeants and watch commanders in police work). In both contexts, there are elaborate socialization processes that involve training recruits how to write a proper report. Included in such processes are practices like "kicking back" a report so that the person will "do it right." It is also apparent that in both auditing and policing, "doing it right" involves, among other things, a highly specific and specialized use of language, order, and form. Insiders believe their records may be challenged unless, for example, certain key words and phrases appear in a particular place and sequence. Third, these examples show how the legal environment can influence the information-processing routines of an organization in rather subtle and pervasive ways. Unlike formal reporting requirements for toxic materials and workplace safety, which attempt to directly regulate disclosure (Tamuz & Sitkin, 1992), the potential for litigation operates indirectly. But the effect on organizational practices is just as pronounced. Finally, it seems that procedural records documenting the work that was done have the potential to be either the best defense or the worst liability if a cop's or auditor's judgments are challenged.

Records that claim work was done in a certain way serve, of course, as accounts for the results of that work—be the results an unqualified audit or the arrest of a drunk and disorderly person. Typically, records suggest that actions taken were the only ones possible, given the circumstances as rendered in the report. To provide an account in both the auditing world and the police world means adhering to descriptive devices (numerical and narrative) that are by and large conventional and arbitrary.[14] They are neither right nor wrong but stand as coding or reporting standards that are "generally accepted" as adequate for the task. They can be regarded as strategic representations, collectively validated by members, designed to put the organization's best foot forward. This is to say that what goes into working papers or arrest reports are numbers, words, phrases, opinions, and logic that have precedent and warrant, not only among organizational colleagues but among outsiders as well.

In this sense, organization documents serve as cognitive devices that order and frame, sort and name. Documents turn a "this" into a "that." It is not a matter of making excuses, because the production of records precedes any public suspicion that anything needs excusing. As institutionalized classification schemes, reports depersonalize actions by substituting an organizational voice—in terms of the learned categories of description—for an individual one. And, by virtue of the accumulation of records that select and squeeze information about the world in more or less identical ways, a belief is fostered among members that an "objective" social (or economic) reality exists "out there" that is subject—with some reservations, of course—

to representation and measurement. But, each item or category reported has a definite place and relation to all other items or categories. Because categories are relatively permanent, comparisons of both a temporal and a spatial sort can be made. The effect on organizational members of following such reporting conventions time after time, year after year, may be quite powerful. A famous suggestion for just how powerful is provided by March and Simon (1958, p. 165):

> The world tends to be perceived by organizational members in terms of particular concepts that are reflected in the organization's vocabulary. The particular categories and schemes of classification it employs are reified and become for members of the organization attributes of the world rather than mere conventions.

Instances of this kind of reality structuring are not difficult to locate in the worlds of either cops or auditors. Street officers, for whom "breaches of the peace" are continually being performed, owe at least a part of this peculiar social disorder to their trained capacity to recognize them and write them up. Auditors, likewise, learn to see corporate assets at General Motors "attached" to rolling stocks of automobile inventory, rather than seeing, as others might, clunkers and costs. In both cases, the classification scheme, provided by the respective organizational/occupational worlds and enshrined by the received categories that appear on routinely used reporting forms, becomes the reality to which individuals respond and hence record or, at other times, record and hence respond.[15]

What we have set forth, in our brief descriptions of police reports and working papers, is not simply a story of how a few rough cops or hard-pressed auditors utilize certain impression management tactics to cover up activities that might prove embarrassing to themselves or the organization were they to come to light. Rather what we have tried to suggest is that impression management is literally built into the very reporting practices of the two trades. In addition to whatever else auditors or police officers may do, they must demonstrate a willingness to cooperate with colleagues by helping present and project a serviceable public image of the organization. Those who, for various reasons, cannot or will not meet this requirement, will soon find themselves unemployed.

To a large extent, the ability to create favorable impressions of the organization depends on the degree to which members can conduct their business in private and account for their conduct by standards of their own making that are taken as legitimate by the public(s) for whom they perform. Accounting for conduct is precisely what the construction of working papers and police reports is about. Both carry heavy symbolic loads for they both allow readers to assess the claims of practitioners and provide readers with a glimpse of what those behind the occupational masks might be up to. As symbols, working papers and police reports are rhetorical forms designed to convince an audience of the legitimacy of some organization action or result (and, more generally perhaps, the organization as a whole). These rhetorical ends, as we suggested much earlier, do not, of course, preclude whatever technical or utilitarian uses such documents may also provide. But, viewed alongside one another, it seems to us that the symbolic or rhetorical value of the information put forth in working papers and police reports is of greater importance generally to organizational members than whatever technical value such records convey. The elaborate care associated with the production of these documents suggests that members are as concerned with the appearance of a record as they are with whatever substance is to be stuffed in them. Concerns for sign-offs, phrasing, timing, missing data, tidiness of the report, filling in the blanks, misspellings, proper order, and so on all highlight form over function. Crucially, these documents are essentially prepared for outsiders. They are written with the explicit contingency in mind that others beyond the organizational boundaries will read what they contain. And, unlike insiders who have little need to be reassured or convinced of the legitimacy of their own actions, outsiders may need a good deal of such reassurance and convincing.

What might account for the prominence of the rhetorical uses served by working papers or reports? Obviously, some of their symbolic importance flows from the fact that both deal with rather emotional and evocative public issues. Financial states and crime rates are troublesome and highly charged matters in American society. Both kinds of documentation produce information about activities that are illegitimate and stigmatized. This would seem to increase the symbolic importance of records that offer information about the presence or absence of what is widely regarded as evil. Further rhetorical punch comes from the lack of any hard-and-fast performance standards in either domain. What constitutes public order or disorder? Is an organization financially sound or not? These are matters for which conventions only can be applied, and while working papers and police reports apply them surely, they cannot defend them in any technical—

scientific or statistical—fashion. What is sought in both domains by the public at large is valued but vague, for there exist no reliable alternative means, beyond those the respective organizations choose to report about their activities, to judge the knowledge and truth contained in their records.

It would seem, therefore, that we have a good empirical match for the provocative but largely conceptual work of Feldman and March (1981) on the conditions under which information gathered by organizations is used primarily for rhetorical or symbolic purposes. We must note, however, that gathered information must also be organized or textualized and put forth somehow if it is to have any impact or value. Records, reports, and organizational documents of all sorts are employed to this end. Information is text. The display may be dramatic or subtle, but for information to work as Feldman and March suggest, not only must it be collected, but others must also be made aware of the collection. What Feldman and March tag "ritual assurance" seems best to fit the observations we have presented on police reports and working papers.

Ritual assurance represents a desire on the part of organizational members—sometimes all, sometimes a few—to convince those interested in the affairs of the organization that the choices made within it are guided by proper social values; including, most critically in this society, an appreciation for keeping careful track of the actions of the membership so that they can be held responsible for what they do or don't do on behalf of the organization. Whether records are used in such a fashion is entirely another matter, but the presence of files and piles of records offers an appearance of concern for responsibility that is important in and of itself. Ritual assurance comes also by the way records can demonstrate a degree of organizational competence and authority simply through the completion and accumulation of records in a reasonably timely and consistent manner. This may inspire confidence in the organization from the outside and help legitimate decisions reached inside by organizational members. All this is to again argue that the busy round of activities set off by organizationally initiated record keeping may persist, not because there are any technical advantages associated with such paperwork, but because such paperwork carries symbolic advantages of critical importance to the persistence of the organization itself.

■ Notes

1. We are suggesting here that many organizationally produced documents conceal, misrepresent, or unwittingly mislead in a variety of ways. Concealment or cover is perhaps the most common aim in the kind of information games we consider in this paper. The point raised in the text notes merely that records designed to create false impressions must be constructed along the same basic lines as those designed to create accurate ones. The student of records is then well advised to examine faked records for guides to the production of truthful ones, since what is picked up as conjured by readers of the former may be precisely what is critical to readers of the latter. Thus, records fitted up to convey a fiction must look as forthright, sturdy, objective, direct, and perhaps neutral as those fitted up to convey the facts. Consequently, there are times when the best record may be the worst. The master cryptographer is, of course, Erving Goffman, and we follow his lead throughout this paper. Two essays serve as guides to our writing here: Goffman (1959, pp. 208-239) and Goffman (1969, pp. 3-81), which emphasize that impression and expression are two sides of the same coin.

2. By rhetoric, we mean simply the methods used to put forth a persuasive argument. Burke (1969, p. 42) notes that rhetoric serves to "induce action or the attitude that precedes it." The function of rhetoric is to convince, and the analysis of what precisely is convincing depends on just who is trying to convince whom of what and where, when, and why they are doing so (Scott & Lyman, 1968).

3. The general problem of impression management is moral. Individuals (and the organizations they represent) are concerned with appearances that sustain the view that they (and their organizations) are fully deserving of respect. Such respect flows from living up to standards that they themselves have put forth, or otherwise defer to, as to just how their work is to be judged. Yet these standards are many and create what Goffman (1959, p. 251) suggests is a fundamental irony: "Individuals are concerned not with the moral issues of relaxing these standards but with the amoral issue of engineering a convincing appearance that these standards are being realized." It is this dramaturgic sense of record keeping that informs our work here.

4. Palmrose (1988) also reports on the cases for which resolution data were available and notes that some 30% resulted in settlements of more than $1 million, 31% resulted in settlements of less than this, and some 39% were dismissed (or resulted in no payments by the audit firm). The term *meritorious* is defined by Palmrose as those cases where there was "actually some evidence of audit failure." We must note, however, that Palmrose's figures do not reflect recent events. Sternberg (1992) reports what he calls a "tidal wave of litigation" swamping big accounting firms as a result of the downfall and bankruptcy of many enterprises (notably in the savings and loan industry): "As of last May (1991), federal banking regulators alone had thirty-two lawsuits pending against accounting firms, seeking 2.5 billion dollars for damages to government insurance funds from accounting malpractice." This litigation could easily be followed by billions more as a result of piggybacking plaintiffs. The Big Six might well be the Big Five (or Four) in a few years if major litigation goes against one or two of the large firms.

5. The basic content of working papers is spelled out by the GAAS (Generally Accepted Auditing Standards); however, the details and the form are left largely open to local norms and practices. The final form working papers take may or may not be "rational" in terms of the firm that makes use of them. But, given the need for auditing

firms to maintain their reputations, the use of the general GAAS categories and standards is certainly understandable. What eventually fills up these categories and meets these standards is a local matter that often appears to be a result of what Heimer (1985) calls "a negotiated information order."

6. A discussion of the scope of auditor liability goes far beyond the interests of this chapter. Interested readers may wish to consult Gormley and Stanger (1988) or Wilson (1990) for additional details (and arguments).

7. The error in the date is quite likely to have been caused by the general practice of writing the conclusions first. The senior auditor on this engagement explained the situation in the following way: "[A] lot of times staff write the conclusions the first thing (for an audit section). The first couple of days of the audit you don't have enough information to really crank, so you start doing all the little things that will save you time in the end" (Pentland, fieldnotes).

8. The police and their records have been closely attended to by a number of interested groups, from crusading journalists attempting to open up police reporting practices to management consultants attempting to tighten them down. Sociologists are in the middle, but have created something of a cottage industry in at-home ethnography with their close, detailed studies of police agencies. Some of the best works issuing from the sociologically informed studies of the police include Bittner (1970), Rubenstein (1973), Manning (1977, 1983, 1988) and Brown (1981). None of these works is silent on the role of records, and all take care in showing just how particular records—usually arrest reports—are fashioned and shaped by the cultural rules that operate in the examined police worlds. More focused studies on other kinds of records, such as reported crime rates, use-of-deadly-force reports, police recorded citizen complaints, and so forth, are found in Kobler (1975), Sherman (1978), Fyfe (1981) and Ericson, Baranek, & Chan (1987, 1988).

9. In this regard, there is a joke told by the police that parallels the joke told by accountants and mentioned earlier in the text. In the police version, a naive character, the fool, often a sociologist or a journalist, poses the question to a street-wise cop: "How many crimes were committed today (this week, this year)?" The wise veteran then pauses, scratches his chin, and replies: "How many do you want?" Behind the joke stands a good deal of truth. Young (1991, pp. 369-396) provides a superb account of the "counting rules" followed by detectives in a British policy agency. These rules are quite explicitly impression management rules. It is well worth noting also that up until about the mid-sixties, police agencies in the United States seemed more concerned with deflating the appearance of crime by following "under-reporting" rules, thus impressing upon us just how well they were managing the problem of order in society. Since that time, the police seem to have switched tactics and now appear concerned with inflating the appearance of crime by following "over-reporting" rules, thus impressing upon us just how much we need them to stem the rising tide of disorder in society. On the dramaturgic properties of police work, see Manning's (1974) much and justly cited article.

10. These bread-and-butter charges are the tools street cops have at their disposal to maintain order and preserve the peace. Critically, the police themselves decide when the line between order and disorder has been breached. Thus the use of these charges is such that virtually everything depends on the judgments of the police at the moment: on context, on mood, on stereotype, on gut reaction. These are matters that simply cannot be recorded in the log book, the arrest form, or the use-of-force report. See Van Maanen (1974).

11. This account of street justice in La-La Land is drawn from public materials. Most important is the report issued by the Independent Commission on the Los Angeles Police Department, released to the public on July 9, 1991. So public is this document that we had to smuggle it out of Los Angeles County, where it is supposed to remain in law libraries under lock and key. Other sources include John Gregory Dunne's deep reporting of the incident in his two-part article, "Law and Disorder in LA," which appeared in the *New York Review of Books* (Dunne, 1991). Various newspaper clippings were also used, as mentioned in the text.

12. Much of the material appearing in this section (and the next) represents a modest updating and reworking of Van Maanen's (1980) account of the events that typically occur in the aftermath of a police shooting.

13. There is good cause for these procedures. From 1986 to 1990, 2,151 allegations of police misconduct (excess force) were filed against the LAPD, but only 42 were sustained by the department. To expect the police to look very closely and critically at their own affairs is to expect them to have an interest in doing themselves in—an unlikely situation (see, for example, Skolnick, 1966; Manning, 1977; Fyfe, 1982; Wilson, 1983). During this same period, however, more than 300 successful lawsuits were filed against the department, on the grounds of excess force, that resulted in judgments costing the City more than $20 million (*Independent Commission Report*, 1991, pp. 36-39, 55-61, 153-158).

14. It is (alas) usually the case that information put into numerical form is more convincing to most readers of record than information cast in narrative form—the graphic literary phrase being seen perhaps as too open to interpretation, and thus unpredictable and unsafe in terms of its reception. Witness, for example, the reputation of qualitative fieldwork in the social sciences as "anecdotal." Certainly participant-observation research, with its characteristic narrative representation, is regarded by many potential subjects of such research—including cops and auditors—as some distance away from the "safe" and "clean" research of a quantitative sort. Today the legitimacy of numerical evidence is taken for granted as "objective" (or at least more "objective") than narrative evidence. It was not always so, as Goody (1986) usefully reminds us. In the police world, numerical accounts have reached new levels as most departments now have their own statisticians, demographers, quantitative modelers, and other number-crunching advocates on the payroll. An illustration of just how far these quantitative trends have moved in police agencies is found in the scale LAPD developed to "measure" the use of force, and mentioned in passing during our discussion of the Rodney King episode. In full form, the use-of-force scale provides a 0 for "verbalization," a 1 for "firm grip," a 2 for "compliance hold," a 3 for "intermediate force" (defined as "baton blows, kicks, use of gas, sap or Taser") and a 4 for "deadly force" (consisting of, on the form, "upper body holds, carotid chokes and firearms"). The implications, rhetorical and otherwise, of the replacement of narrative by number is a topic sorely in need of study.

15. Johnson and Kaplan (1987) make the argument that current forms of accounting carried on in large U.S. corporations reflect what auditors, not managers, regard as important. In their view, cost accounting has lost touch with the sort of things managers should be paying attention to, such as the manufacturing and delivery of real goods and services. If, in fact, this argument is sound, and auditing as currently practiced is becoming less and less valuable to managers, it would seem then that the rhetorical properties of an audit become more important, as a consequence of its declining technical use in organizational decision making.

■ References

Bittner, E. (1970). *The functions of police in urban society.* Bethesda, MD: National Institute of Mental Health.

Brown, M. K. (1981). *Working the street.* New York: Russell Sage.

Burke, K. (1969). *A grammar of motives.* Berkeley: University of California Press.

Cochran, N., Gordon, A. C., & Krause, M. S. (1980). Proactive records: Reflections on the village watchman. *Knowledge: Creation, Diffusion, and Utilization, 2*(1), 5-18.

Collins, R. (1981). On the microfoundations of macrosociology. *American Journal of Sociology, 86*(5), 984-1014.

Covaleski, M. A., & Dirsmith, M. W. (1988). The use of budgeting symbols in the political arena: An historically informed field study. *Accounting, Organizations and Society, 13,* 1-24.

Dunne, J. G. (1991, October 10, 24). Law and disorder in LA. *New York Review of Books.*

Eccles, R. G. (1985). *The transfer pricing problem.* Lexington, MA: Lexington Books.

Ericson, R. V., Baranek, P., & Chan, J. (1988). *Negotiating control.* Toronto: University of Toronto Press.

Ericson, R. V., Baranek, P., & Chan, J. (1987). *Visualizing deviance.* Toronto: University of Toronto Press.

Feldman, M. S., & March, J. G. (1981). Information in organizations as signal and symbol. *Administrative Science Quarterly, 26*(2), 171-186.

Fyfe, J. J. (1981). *Police use of deadly force.* Washington, DC: Police Foundation.

Fyfe, J. J. (1982). Blind justice: Police shootings in Memphis. *Journal of Criminal Law and Criminology, 73,* 702-722.

Garfinkel, H. (1967). Good organizational reasons for bad clinic records. In *Studies in ethnomethodology* (pp. 186-204). Englewood Cliffs, NJ: Prentice-Hall.

Goffman, E. (1959). *The presentation of self in everyday life.* Garden City, NY: Doubleday.

Goffman, E. (1969). *Strategic interaction.* Philadelphia: University of Pennsylvania Press.

Goody, J. (1986). *The logic of writing and the organization of society.* Cambridge, UK: Cambridge University Press.

Gormley, J. R., & Stanger, A. M. (1988). Developments in accountants' liability to nonclients for negligence. *Journal of Accounting, Auditing, and Finance 3*(3), 185-216.

Heimer, C. (1985). Allocating information costs in a negotiated information order. *Administrative Science Quarterly, 39,* 395-417.

Independent Commission on the Los Angeles Police Department (W. Christopher, Chair). (1991, July 9). *Report of the independent commission on the Los Angeles police department.*

Johnson, H. T., & Kaplan, R. S. (1987). *Relevance lost: The rise of managerial accounting.* Boston: Harvard Business School Press.

Kaplan, R. L. (1987). Accountant's Liability and Audit Failures: When the Umpire Strikes Out. *Journal of Accounting and Public Policy, 6,* 1-8.

Kobler, A. L. (1975). Police homicide in a democracy. *Social Issues, 31,* 1963-1984.

Manning, P. K. (1974). Dramatic aspects of policing. *Social and Social Research, 59,* 21-29.

Manning, P. K. (1977). *Police work.* Cambridge: MIT Press.

Manning, P. K. (1983). *The narc's game.* Cambridge: MIT Press.

Manning, P. K. (1988). *Symbolic communication*. Cambridge: MIT Press.

March, J. G., & Simon, H. A. (1958). *Organizations*. New York: John Wiley.

Meyer, J., & Rowan, B. (1977, September). Institutionalized organizations: Formal structure as myth and ceremony. *American Journal of Sociology, 83*, 340-363.

Meyer, J. W., & Scott, W. R. (1983). *Organizational environments: Ritual and rationality*. Beverly Hills, CA: Sage.

Palmrose, Z. (1988). An analysis of auditor litigation and audit service quality. *The Accounting Review, 63*(1), 55-73.

Pentland, B. T. (in press). Getting comfortable with the numbers: Auditing and the micro-production of macro-order. *Accounting, Organizations and Society*.

Powell, W. W., & DiMaggio, P. J. (1991). Introduction. In W. W. Powell & P. J. DiMaggio (Eds.), *The new institutionalism in organizational analysis* (pp. 1-38). Chicago: University of Chicago Press.

Ridgway, V. F. (1956). Dysfunctional consequences of performance measures. *Administrative Science Quarterly, 1*, 240-247.

Rubenstein, J. (1973). *City police*. New York: Farrar, Strauss, & Giroux.

Scott, M., & Lyman, S. (1968). Accounts. *American Sociological Review, 33*(2), 309-318.

Sherman, L. W. (1978). *Scandal and reform: Controlling police corruption*. Berkeley: University of California Press.

Skolnick, J. (1966). *Justice without trial*. New York: John Wiley.

Sternberg, W. (1992). Cooked books: Practices of large accounting firms contributed to financial scandals. *The Atlantic (269)*1, pp. 20-27.

Tamuz, M., & Sitkin, S. B (1992). *The invisible muzzle: Organizational and legal constraints on the disclosure of information about health and safety hazards*. Manuscript under review.

Thomas, R. J. (1992). Organizational politics and technological change. *Journal of Contemporary Ethnography, 20*(4), 442-477.

U.S. v. Arthur Young Co. 104 S.Ct. 1495 (1984).

Van Maanen, J. (1974). Working the street. In H. Jacob (Ed.), *The potential for reform of criminal justice* (pp. 83-130). Beverly Hills, CA: Sage.

Van Maanen, J. (1978). The asshole. In P. K. Manning & J. Van Maanen (Eds.), *Policing: A view from the streets* (pp. 115-128). New York: Random House.

Van Maanen, J. (1980). Beyond account: The personal impact of police shootings. *The Annals of the American Academy of Political and Social Science, 451*, 145-156.

Van Maanen, J. (1981). Notes on the production of ethnographic data in an American police agency. In R. Luckham (Ed.), *Law and social enquiry* (pp. 189-230). Uppsala: Scandinavian Institute of African Studies.

Van Maanen, J. (1983). The moral fix. In R. Emerson (Ed.), *Contemporary field research* (pp. 269-287). Boston: Little, Brown.

Van Maanen, J. (1988). *Tales of the field: On writing ethnography*. Chicago: University of Chicago Press.

Van Maanen, J. (1991). Playing back the tape. In W. B. Shaffir & R. A. Sebbins (Eds.), *Experiencing fieldwork* (pp. 31-42). Newbury Park, CA: Sage.

Wilmsen, S. K. (1991). *Silverado: Neil Bush and the savings and loan scandal*. Washington, DC: National Press Books.

Wilson, D. (1990). Opening the door to third party liability: Are CPAs Accountable? *Commercial Law Bulletin, 5*(3), 10-13.

Wilson, J. Q. (1983). *Crime and public policy*. San Francisco: ICS Press.

Yates, J. (1989). *Control through communication: The rise of system in American management.* Baltimore, MD: Johns Hopkins University Press.

Yates J., & Orlikowski, W. J. (1992). Genres of organizational communication—A structurational approach to studying communication and media. *Academy of Management Review, (17)*2, 299-326.

Young, M. (1991). *An inside job.* New York: Oxford University Press.

4

Contracting Without Contracts:
How the Japanese Manage
Organizational Transactions

Michael J. Smitka

[A]ll legal systems must have a set of rules to govern the making and enforcement of agreements, and we hope that much of what we say about the English law of contract will have parallels in the law of contract in other legal systems.

(Harris & Veljanovski, 1986, p. 109)

[I]n negotiating the settlement . . . it is a waste of time and expense to investigate the precise legal position. . . . It would clearly not make economic sense to settle all contractual disputes out-of-court . . . [but] An appreciation of this situation should lead contract lawyers to the conclusion that legal rules on remedies for breach of contract should be designed to take into account the fact that in the vast majority of cases the rules will be used to guide out-of-court settlements and to induce compromises.

(Harris & Veljanovski, 1986, pp. 116-117)

■ Introduction

This book seeks to pull together two approaches to institutions, those of law and organizational theory. As an economist, I stand somewhat apart from both of those approaches. Within economics, law on the one hand is presumed to provide an essential support for

AUTHOR'S NOTE: The initial version of this paper was written under a Japan Foundation Research Fellowship while a visiting professor at the Faculty of Law, Rikkyo University, Tokyo. I gratefully acknowledge the efforts of that Faculty to teach an economist law. I also benefited from the editors' extensive comments.

market transactions, but the nature of that support is seldom specified. On the other hand, organizational studies focus upon hierarchy, the locus of most day-to-day economic activity in the United States. Economics, however, typically treats the subject of organizations as a black box that is best left unopened. Here my focus is on the presumed centrality of contract law, drawing upon empirical work on the Japanese auto industry (Smitka, 1991).

My analysis draws upon the transactions cost approach of Coase (1992) and Williamson (1985), and recent work in game theory (various chapters in Gambetta, 1988). Ironically, in their work, Coase and Williamson retreat to an analysis based on the formal structure of law and of the organization of the firm. While these provide a convenient starting point, one motivation for this book is the need to understand a world in which these pure structures cannot be empirically isolated. Indeed, neither law nor organization by themselves provide an adequate theoretical framework for understanding the base on which transactions are grounded. Thus economics as a field can benefit from —and by providing another perspective, contribute to—a richer research paradigm.

In the following I argue from my own empirical work, which highlights the pervasiveness of complex, deep-reaching interactions among firms that maintain many of the features of intraorganizational transactions. As such, they fall outside the realm of hierarchy but are also outside the scope of the market of neoclassical economics and the classical contract theory in law. However, I believe that the relational contracting and network organizational forms that are central to the Japanese auto industry are typical of economic transactions in general.

The central feature I see in such transactions is both the necessity for and the possibility of relying upon trust among parties, where legal remedies are too awkward and ineffective to be central. (See, likewise, Black, 1976, p. 40, who as a sociologist argues that law will be comparatively dormant when interdependence is central.) But if trust is effective—and by "trust" I mean a willingness to act in reliance on the other party, where circumstances do not compel them to be trustworthy—then what constructive role can contract law play? (Similarly, then in what way is formal organization—the firm—important?) These are clearly extreme positions, but taking them as a starting point will, I believe, lead both to better empirical work and to more precise theory. In the conclusion I briefly look at issues that my own and other recent studies of contracting raise for organizational studies. The bulk of this chapter, however, will focus upon the role of law.

Briefly, I posit that law—or more precisely, contract law—is unnecessary. In other words, *contracting*—the framing of the environment for transactions—is quite possible without *contracts*, the potential for legal enforcement of the agreements that accompany transactions. Indeed, I argue that the Japanese economy is best characterized as functioning without contract. (See Haley, 1991, for parallel arguments about the overall role of law in the Japanese polity.) At least when Japan's performance is viewed from afar, it is easy to presume that economic efficiency suffers little or may even be enhanced in such a "lawless" society. Let it suffice that Japan demonstrates that it is possible to have a complex, vigorous economy without contract law and associated legal institutions playing a central role.

As noted, the null hypothesis that law is irrelevant runs against the grain of legal scholarship. It does, however, serve a useful purpose by forcing careful arguments for how law actually matters. One role that I believe law should play is to suggest how transactions ought to be framed to encourage trust and avoid dispute-prone situations. In this normative and pedagogic role, drawing up a contract serves primarily as a check that each side has thought through the core business elements, to try to assure that both parties have an ex ante interest in carrying through their end of the deal. The training of lawyers in the United States, however, stresses the importance of contracts over contracting; that is, the need for protection, should things go wrong, over the prevention of things going wrong. The emphasis on carefully drafting a document all too often diverts the parties' attention from the business at hand. Indeed, lawyers, in a careful professional stance, will claim that their purview should be limited to narrow legal advice. I believe this combination produces unnecessary (if for lawyers, fruitful) levels of dispute.

Second, the prevalence of complex transactions, and the often tenuous connection that contracts bear to the real world of business contracting (a point long ago made by Macaulay, 1963), should serve as a cautionary tale for the ability of courts to resolve disputes. In one sense, this is what lies behind the death of classical contract law that Gilmore (1974) portrays as occurring through the accretion of exceptions to the classical doctrine, stemming from the willingness of courts to try to handle increasingly complex cases. Ironically, this may have made matters worse, because it creates pressures for more specialized and complex documents and hence a greater role for lawyers. Instead, a greater reticence by courts to attempt to resolve disputes would encourage parties to exercise more care up front.

However, restricting the role of the legal system makes sense only if it is indeed practical in most situations to rely upon trust and relational mechanisms to support contracting. There are situations—fraud, incompetence—that are appropriately recognized under current contract law (or shifted over to torts). We may as a society wish to provide protection to "small" parties who find it hard to self-insure through numerous independent transactions and who have neither the resources nor the experience to carefully craft transactions. (In fact, reforms to make available "small claims" procedures are now being discussed in Japan.) But I think that such situations should be viewed as exceptions to the general rule and that the granting of these exceptions should be grounded in careful theoretical and empirical work.

This argument is in accord in many ways with the findings of the Wisconsin school. Macaulay (1963) stresses the divergence between what contract law says and what businessmen do; Macneil (1985) argues that the contract law conception of a world of spot transactions is at variance with the pervasiveness of relational contracting. Both, however, start from the presumption that law matters or ought to matter, that the real world operates under the shadow of the law. Closer in spirit is the recent study of Ellickson (1991), who highlights how (in his case) neighbors settle disputes outside the shadow of the law, and why non-neighbors in similar situations may have recourse to law.

With these themes in mind, let me now leave contracts behind and turn my attention to the world of contracting. In the conclusion I will briefly turn my skeptical eye to studies of the firm.

■ Transactions and Trust

The Larger Literature

Many fine studies of contracting and interfirm organization have appeared in the past 5 years; most of these are of manufacturing, and many were stimulated by an interest in reputedly distinctive Japanese practices. (Much of this work is also informed by, if not inspired by Williamson, 1975, 1985.) Along with my study of the Japanese automotive industry, there is Helper's (1986, 1991) work on the U.S. auto industry, Sako's (1993) book on British printed circuit board makers, Nishiguchi's (1993) book on autos and consumer electronics, Lorenz's paper (1988) on French machine builders, Dore's (1986) book on the

Japanese textile industry, and Joskow's (1985) analysis of coal markets. In addition to these studies by economists and sociologists are a series of anthropological studies of wholesale food markets—Acheson (1991) on Maine lobsters, Bestor (1993) on Tokyo's seafood market, and Silin (1972) on Hong Kong produce markets.[1]

Two common themes are found in these studies. One is an emphasis on the wider context of the relationship; the atomistic spot transactions envisioned in classical contract theory (and the atomistic, anonymous markets of introductory microeconomics) are not what one finds in the real world. (Again, note Macneil, 1985.) Another implicit and often explicit theme of these recent studies is the role of trust in contracting. Virtually any economic transaction requires that parties rely upon each other, that one or both sides place themselves at risk. Formal contracts can highlight where risks lie, and provide penalties for reneging. But contracts in themselves are inadequate to produce active compliance and provide little guidance on how to adjust terms when problems arise but, as typically is the case, both sides still wish to carry through. Trust can help parties muddle through; contracts invite conflict. But these are only a few of the facets of trust; for other examples, see Gambetta (1988), my own study (Smitka, 1991, chapter 6), Sako (1991), and Sitkin & Roth (1993).

To reiterate, the thrust of these studies is that contracts are neither sufficient nor even necessary to provide assurance of performance. Indeed, below I make two simple, primarily empirical claims. The first is that trust is not primarily a cultural phenomenon. It is certainly true that goodwill is widespread in Japanese and American society— as stressed by, respectively, Dore (1983, 1986) and Macaulay (1963)— while a cultural legacy of distrust of others is similarly a barrier to development in many ethnically diverse societies. Clearly, without trust there is no civilization. But in business mere goodwill is insufficient; for example, the village and ethnic ties in Silin's (1972) Hong Kong wholesale market and the familial ties in Bestor's (1993) Tokyo fish market provided at most a common starting point. Whatever the social or cultural foundation, parties invest much time and energy to develop trust as a conscious part of their business strategy.

Indeed, the ability to deliberately foster trust leads to my second point, that trust offers an effective substitute to law as a basis of contracting. Parties require a concrete reason to trust each other, to risk nonperformance by the other party. Such trust can be, and in Japan is, deliberately fostered through appropriate contracting strategies, which I sketch below. I believe, furthermore, that similar strategies can be employed in the United States. Trust then in general offers a viable alternative to contracts—indeed, trust is necessary even with contracts. But in that event the Hobbesian specter of chaos in the absence of law reduces to a ghostly mist. The opposite problem may be more important: Law imposes an artificial structure upon contracting that all too often blinds parties to the need and the potential for crafting transactions in a manner that facilitates trust, as Sitkin and Roth (1993) also argue.

Contracting in Japan

As is reasonably well known, lawyers play a small role in Japanese society. The Bar is kept small; only about 600 individuals a year pass the written exam and go on to the mandatory legal apprenticeship. As a result, Japan, with a population of 125 million, has approximately 14,000 lawyers, or fewer than Manhattan. Furthermore, from this group are drawn not only the nation's 3,500 judges—again a small number relative to the population—but also public prosecutors, private practitioners, and the elite of the law school faculties.[2] The result is long dockets—an average of a year even for simple civil cases—and, relative to the United States, a small body of case law.[3] In short, whatever the theoretical possibilities are for using courts and other quasi-legal fora to resolve contract disputes, the remedies they provide in Japan are almost always too little and too late. (Indeed, I am aware of only one instance in the auto industry in which a dispute was taken to court.[4]) The legal system well-nigh forces parties to rely upon their own devices. Upham (1987) eloquently argues that this reflects a deliberate choice by the government during the post-World War II era, and he and Haley (1991) provide other examples besides contracts where formal law plays a minor role relative to the United States.[5] In any event, formal contracts tend to be brief—one typewritten page—and leave many details to be specified elsewhere.[6] As a result, except for international transactions and the occasional real estate case, lawyers are not involved in drafting contracts.[7]

Of course, a sophisticated commercial economy is symptomatic of an environment of interfirm specialization and the routine reliance upon transactions with other legal entities. There is clearly a need for some sort of framework for governing these everyday transactions. The standard assumption has been that, absent a Hobbesian legal order, anarchy reigns. But the Japanese example makes this claim suspect, though even in the best of circumstances, there is seldom time to wait for a court to act in the real world. Still, whatever the framework, these independent parties must reach an accord on price and other transaction terms, and so contracting (though not contracts) remains important. For less complex transactions, parties may insure themselves against problems by dividing business up into small units with different parties.[8] But another alternative is to try to do all business on the basis of relational contracts. What I outline here is the manner in which the auto industry structures transactions, contracting on the basis of trust rather than on the basis of contracts.

The Auto Industry

Whatever the legal and institutional environment, auto makers face a complex problem in contracting for production parts. First, they require up to 20,000 different parts for a single vehicle—and more when engine, trim, and color variations are included. These parts, furthermore, must be produced for the 4 or more years that a car remains in production. Second, many of these parts are unique to a given model: A windshield wiper motor will be specific to a single car of one manufacturer. But because the manufacture of a part often requires costly tools and dies, the assemblers face strong pressures to purchase from a single supplier. Similarly, from the supplier's standpoint, such assets can only be used to service one customer. There is thus a strong degree of interdependence among parts firms and their automotive customers, as transactions are neither spot nor short in duration. This is, of course, true whether the supplier is an internal division of the company, the pattern at the U.S. Big 3 and particularly at GM and Ford, or an independent firm, the prevalent pattern in Japan, where firms are not as vertically integrated. Because of such complexity and interdependence, automotive parts purchasing is thus not a typical business transaction, though I believe that the use of this nonrepresentative example is not fatal to my larger argument.

In any event, a little thought experiment provides the clearest way to understand the methods that are actually used in the Japanese auto industry. Let us assume that contracts have absolutely no legal standing, so that the parties to a transaction cannot rely on courts or other outsiders to enforce a bargain. How, then, can one go about initiating a transaction, and then maintaining and reinforcing it over time?

Commencing Transactions: Conceptual Aspects[9]

Choose Partners Carefully. As a first step, firms must obviously be very careful in choosing their partners. Even though in certain aspects Japanese businessmen are unusually honest, there are plenty ready to fleece the presumptuous newcomer. Thus firms ought to and do expend energy up front, searching among possible suppliers or customers before commencing a business relationship. Even in the United States it is common sense to run a credit check and, for a smaller firm, to check with the Better Business Bureau and similar sources. More generally, if a contract is worth only the paper it is written upon, firms ask questions such as: Is senior management committed? Will they be interested in doing business next year, too? Do both sides get along together personally? Do both sides have a good reputation? And so on. This courtship is time-consuming and expensive, and helps explain why business entertainment accounts for 1% of Japanese GNP. It is the antithesis of the quick handshake of a go-go American businessman.

Begin Gradually. However careful the initial search, the telling is in the making, to twist an aphorism. Both parties reduce their risks when the first transactions are small in scale and are restricted to unimportant items. This serves other functions as well in the automotive industry, because the contracting environment is complex and each firm has its idiosyncracies. Competence is hard to measure in advance, while terms are complex and most readily learned through experience. Can the firm actually deliver quality parts on time, as promised? (And how does the customer measure quality?) Does delivery in the morning mean by 7 a.m. or by noon? With whom does one communicate regarding a minor hitch?—remembering that a minor problem, if not resolved quickly, can stop the assembly line and turn into a major disaster. In short, actual transactions are needed to provide a meaningful test of good faith and competence. And since minor mistakes are inevitable in the process of learning the ropes, it is best to start small. When successful, this process locks parties into closer ties, since the costs of first finding new partners and then teaching them the ropes make it desirable to continue doing business. When unsuccessful, a small and gradual start facilitates damage control.

Commencing Transactions: Empirical Aspects

The above advice fits what is observed in the Japanese auto industry. The major automotive suppliers have been dealing with their major customers continuously from day one, sometimes for more than 50 years. For most auto companies, turnover of suppliers is less than 5% per year. Of course, new entry is similarly rare, to the discomfiture of outsiders, both Japanese and foreign.[10] Even when a new supplier can gain a foothold, the buildup in volume is slow. The resulting frustration for firms unused to that environment has helped turn auto parts into an ongoing source of U.S.-Japan bilateral tension.

Popular culture reinforces that success is gradual. From early in life the Japanese are taught that it is necessary to persevere in the face of challenges, whether it be at school, work, family, or riding the subways. One is taught that hierarchy cannot be defeated, and indeed must be respected. At the same time no one need, or in fact will, stay forever on the bottom rung. Even sports reflect this: While victory in an individual sumo match is decided in a momentary struggle, the result is interpreted as reflecting the outcome of years of practice that add strength, weight, and mental stamina. Furthermore, even the successful wrestler can advance but one or two rungs at a time, so reaching the top takes years of effort and, at the last rung, repeated triumphs.

Because of the recent success of Hawaiian wrestlers, this sports image is now familiar to non-Japanese readers. But the same images pervade descriptions of business life. The young salesman will carefully cultivate potential clients, perhaps for years, until he (seldom she) is a well known and even trusted figure. Then, one day, a new need arises, and by dint of constant effort he is on hand to serve—while, implicitly, the invisible rival, who thus far had dominated the business, has grown complacent. The result: a token order, but with the obvious message that further inroads will follow with continued effort.[11]

Never in these stories do we see the jubilant man in the concluding moments waving a piece of paper in front of his boss (much less springing the news to his wife) that "I got the contract." First, the news wouldn't be broken to her because, by the time our Dagwood Tanaka got home from socializing with customers new and old, his wife would have long since been asleep in her room, next to the kids. Second, we do not see the scene in the boss's office, either—and when we do, there is no piece of paper. Third, what he would have is not *the* business, but one portion of the business. Indeed, these three scenes are a piece of the same cloth, of contracting without contracts.

Supporting Ongoing Transactions

In the Japanese auto industry, firms find it important to maintain ongoing ties. As noted, even when the initial courting of two firms goes smoothly, it consumes significant managerial resources. For administrative efficiency, it is thus important that relationships be kept on a steady and smooth course. Yet as time passes, the complexity of the auto industry makes disputes inevitable, in part because initial conditions will not remain in effect as the years pass. Furthermore, firms are interdependent across many facets. For example, independent parts suppliers account for up to half the engineering hours required to develop a new car, including testing designs and drafting final blueprints. Quite literally, a car cannot be designed without supplier assistance. (In the United States, the Big 3 historically undertook this work themselves.) Overall, then, it is important to maintain more than a mere facade of cooperation. Strategies to maintain and strengthen trust are thus at least as important over the long run as exerting care at the start.

Making Credible Commitments. Firms strive to make their mutual commitment to the transaction tangible, to provide assurance to each other that they have a vested interest in continuing the relationship. In Japan, the auto assemblers have avoided vertical integration into parts manufacture, and do not maintain production facilities for items such as small metal stampings. Unlike GM in the United States, which often invested in parts production in competition with outside suppliers, Japanese firms made a clear commitment to purchase from someone. This lack of internal capacity in Japan even extends into engineering, as noted above. In turn, suppliers have often specialized in the automotive market and in many cases built dedicated production facilities near their prime customers' plants. Both sides are thus visibly interdependent, with a clear separation of roles. Furthermore, a supplier typically has overlapping contracts for different types of parts with different time horizons. This makes it virtually certain that both sides will be interacting into the foreseeable future. In the short term it is simply impossible for either side to walk away from the other. Indeed, the auto companies have repeatedly bailed out suppliers who suffered large losses due to financial speculation because of the difficulty of finding alternative capacity at other firms. An additional reason, of course, is what potential supplier would want to make a substantial commitment of resources to a firm that has just let its previous supplier go bankrupt? Indeed, it is partly the fact that purchasers entail such costs that makes their commitment credible.

Establishing Rules and Norms. Written contracts are exceedingly simple, but the overall transaction is not. The timing of delivery, containers, lot sizes, and payment methods obviously must be fixed, along with myriad other details. But in practice the only enforceable contract for parts is normally the monthly purchase order, where a concrete order for a specified quantity at a stated price is made for the first time. However, even that contracted quantity seldom matches actual deliveries since, under just-in-time production controls, the actual production schedule is set on the factory floor in response to sales to dealerships, while the purchase order reflects planned production based on projected sales. Actual production thus will vary from the forecast reflected in the purchase order, with discrepancies reconciled after the fact. In any event, both parties over time learn what each expects from the other for these and countless other details. The ongoing nature of the relationship permits this to be done, and in a more informal and flexible manner than provided by formal contracts, since the pretense of keeping to the letter of the agreement need not be maintained, nor need energy be spent constantly rewriting contracts.

More importantly for trust, elaborate norms have been worked out to cover such potentially fractious issues as initial pricing, compensation for deviations from projected volume, defective parts, and engineering changes. In the case of pricing, firms seldom employ American-style competitive bidding. Instead, prices are set by adding a prespecified margin to costs, where costs are broken down to separate out such objective items as material costs. (The supplier must use this fixed margin to cover overhead and provide a profit.) In addition, the continuity of transactions in most cases permits the use of previous costs as a starting point, with corrections made for the targeted productivity increase for the period, which is announced publicly by the automaker. As many elements of price as possible are therefore removed from the bargaining table, either by basing them on historic data or currently observable market prices, or by making them a common element to all suppliers. And, when a contract is lost against a rival, the auto company can provide a concrete reason, such as that costs for process X were out of line with those at rival firms. Norms for pricing thus provide a wealth of information that both parties can use for future transactions, and more importantly, limit the ability of one or the other side to employ hardball tactics that impinge upon trust.

The gradual buildup of a contracting relationship provides an opportunity for new suppliers to learn the ropes. But the auto companies have also instituted formal means of communicating with suppliers as a whole. Each firm has a formal supplier association with newsletters, working committees for technical issues, and regular meetings with senior management. In addition, purchasing departments are responsible for monitoring the overall flow of information, including that from engineering, marketing, and other functions, to try to see that wires do not get crossed or issues fall through the cracks. The purchasing department thus fulfills a strategic management role, in sharp contrast to the clerical roles that purchasing staff played until recently in Detroit. In turn, suppliers maintain a gatekeeper, who plays a similar coordinating function.

Investing in Information and Reputation. Even with shared norms and expectations, how can one feel confident that they will be honored? The presence of the credible commitments outlined above is clearly important. In addition, both suppliers and particularly the auto firms invest heavily in reputation. Even if they cannot provide ironclad assurances of future performance, they can at least make clear past behavior. Part of this information is obtained automatically, in the course of the extensive interactions that take place at the individual level between supplier and assembler. But the range of experience of any given firm with the treatment of exceptional circumstances will, by definition, be limited. What will happen if the advent of plastics or other new materials makes current production capabilities obsolete? Who will bear the costs of an after-the-fact discovery of a major design error? If a customer encourages a firm to expand its capacity to produce parts for a new model but the car flops when it hits the market, are suppliers then left holding the bag? While an individual firm may not have faced such issues, at least a few firms in the supplier universe will have done so. In addition, a single firm cannot be sure it is being treated fairly when its customer demands a price decrease during hard times. Suppliers will want reassurance on these and other such what-if scenarios.

In fact, the automakers are acutely aware of the need for suppliers to trust them on such issues, since the sheer number of parts transactions makes it a practical necessity that, as the general rule, each side accept the other's word without challenge. But most possible contingencies will in fact have been faced by at least a few of an auto company's suppliers. Here the supplier associations are again important for creating and maintaining trust. The occasional meetings of the association as a whole provide a forum for top management at the auto companies to present market projections and policy changes to all suppliers equally and consistently. The associations are also the organizational nexus through which joint technical issues are addressed and new management methods are taught (including in the past cost accounting, engineering management, quality control, and management information systems). Suppliers also interact with each other through these associations on many different levels, and not just with their customer. They know a lot about each other, and can readily learn how exceptional circumstances were handled, and whether they are receiving equal treatment. In addition, the associations provide a route for suppliers to voice their concerns, as the directors, typically the CEOs of a cross-section of suppliers, meet regularly with the executives of their "parent" company. [12]

Avoid Threats, Provide Positive Incentives. If the legal system (or a hierarchical analog) does not provide glue to hold parties together, then threats are highly dangerous: Unless both sides want to continue to do business, there is ultimately nothing to bind them. Threats are antithetical to the credibility of commitments, and can rapidly extinguish any trust that has been built up over time. Furthermore, as repeatedly stressed above, complexity and interdependence make willing cooperation crucial; both sides in general must be willing to go the extra kilometer.

The psychology literature supports the importance of socialization and of a gradual buildup to a relationship, and the strength of positive incentives over threats. [13] Of course, when outside sanctions are unavailable, a threat to terminate a contract (or a promise not to) holds no force in and of itself. But the entire contracting environment seeks to minimize the role of threats, from the use of rules that keep gross margins sacrosanct in the price-setting process, to the explicit policy of not dropping a supplier without strong cause, and even then not doing so suddenly. A troubled firm in fact often turns to its customer and/or suppliers for assistance to overcome difficulties in remaining competitive, or for help in recovering from gross management mistakes. At the same time, the automakers seek to steer new business to existing suppliers when possible, and strive to keep profits high enough for their suppliers to be willing and able to keep investing in new production equipment. Another aid to limiting conflict is that suppliers simultaneously are making several hundred or even thousand different parts. The multiplicity of contracts of different value, complexity, and duration allows both sides to balance a loss in one potential dispute with a profit on another transaction. As Ellickson (1991) noted, and the mathematical theory of repeated games shows, it is far easier to bury the hatchet and maintain cooperation when the books do not have to be closed at the end of each transaction.

Summary

Automotive contracting in Japan relies upon trust; both parties put themselves at the risk of loss, without assurance of long-term gain, out of the belief that the other party would not take unfair advantage of them. But in a business environment, blind trust is foolish, and reliance upon personal trust among individual members of larger organizations is equally untenable. Nor can either side systematically structure the relationship so that the other party is effectively compelled by commercial considerations or legal threat to always carry through, even to the bitter end.

Ultimately, then, contracting in Japan is governed neither by recourse to legal authority nor by reliance upon command within an organizational hierarchy.[14] Instead, both sides invest substantial resources to obtain information and generate reputation about past behavior and future expectations. This is buttressed by the establishment of norms, the fostering of communication channels, and the adoption of measures to reduce risk by a search process and the structuring of initial transactions. There is nothing in these methods, of course, that limits their applicability to the auto industry or to Japan. Indeed, I am convinced that even cursory empirical research will show that such techniques are widely employed (if poorly conceptualized) in the United States.

■ Concluding Thoughts

In the introduction I argued that contract law is not a prerequisite of a commercial economy; the above description of contracting parties in the Japanese auto industry has given a sense of how contracting without contracts can operate. Few transactions in Japan lead to disputes, and most disputes are resolved amicably outside the shadow of the law—as in the United States. While readers ought to be skeptical of my academic revisionism, it is surely both disingenuous and a disservice for lawyers to claim that documenting contracts is their job, and contracting is solely that of their customers. Surely the specialization and breadth of exposure of lawyers ought to leave them ideally equipped to provide the latter invaluable service. It is ultimately a legal fiction that contract law governs business transactions. The profession should not permit an unwarranted faith in both the importance and necessity of law to turn lawyers into mere clerks. As Macaulay (1985, p. 480) phrased it, "Students must understand a game to learn to play it well."

At the same time, organizational theorists need to avoid making the similar error of focusing on the form of an organization and ignoring the actual workings of individuals and the means through which transactions are carried out. In the Japanese auto industry, many highly complex interactions occur on an ongoing basis across organizational boundaries. The day-to-day partner of an automotive engineer may be a supplier engineer seconded to the next desk or attached to the same computer network. Pfeffer and Baron (1988) argue that such blurring of organizational membership is widespread in the United States as well. More generally, as Powell (1990) argues, it strains both received concepts and commonsense language to classify such interactions as an admixture of market and hierarchy, rather than as something qualitatively distinct. But while organizational theory may be better aware of the gap between form and function, caution remains in order. To me it is ironic that Coase (1992) is currently involved in an effort to assemble a large collection of formal contracts of large corporations. While assuredly an astute student of transactions, even he finds it difficult to move away from the assumption of the centrality of formal institutions.

In closing, however, let me pose a parallel conjecture about organizations: that trust will prove equally central to the smooth handling of transactions among members of the same firm, and not merely to those between firms. Trust, I posit, is not only the substance of contracting, but the substance of bureaucracy. I have for now few insights as to how formal rules and structures within organizations support trust, and the extent to which they are essential. (But see, for example, Sitkin & Roth, 1993.) However, I believe the same null hypothesis—that formal structures are unnecessary—will provide a fruitful starting point for clarifying the essential elements of formal organization, just as I believe it will clarify the role of contract law.

■ Notes

1. Other studies use organizational theory as a framework. See Moorman, Zaltman, and Deshpande (1992).

2. Tamiya (1992, pp. 19, 56-57). There are, however, several types of paralegals specializing in tax, patent, and administrative filings, tasks that are largely clerical in nature. There is also a mediation (*chotei*) system that mobilizes community leaders and other lay individuals to attempt to resolve disputes brought into courts. Bureaucrats and police also play such roles. In addition, Japanese law schools admit about 30,000 undergraduates a year. Business newspapers carry regular "how-to" columns, and bookstores all contain sections on law for businessmen. Even if the knowledge of law school graduates is modest, it is thus wrong to automatically conclude that businessmen are totally ignorant of the law. Whether they make use of this knowledge is, of course, a separate issue.

3. Uchida (1990). Japan is a civil law jurisdiction, so that in principle the discretion of judges is more narrowly restricted to applying statutes. These, however, are phrased in general terms, and courts do not have a high reputation for consistency. Furthermore, judges try to force disputants to privately mediate their differences, and final judgments exhibit a strong tendency to split down the middle rather than to find fully for one or the other party. For a brief overview of current issues, see Choy (1992).

4. Ueda (1987). This case was filed by the union of a company that went bankrupt after an automotive customer abruptly canceled its contracts. I am told that ultimately a modest settlement was reached out of court.

5. I did not come across Haley's work until after this article was in process, and so do not fully integrate his study here.

6. Even then, many agreements are oral and may not specify price or other variables that would be needed for a proper contract. Written documentation is most prevalent in response to specific government guidance, as with the Subcontractor Law that seeks to regularize the terms of subcontracting arrangements (my own research) or to satisfy regulators in the Tokyo fish market (discussion with Theodore Bestor).

7. Many Japanese businessmen are graduates of law faculties, as noted. Furthermore, large firms often maintain legal departments. However, virtually no firms in Japan employ a full-time lawyer. In addition, I am told that legal department staff are not always graduates of law faculties, and are in any case rotated to other functional positions in 2 to 3 years, so that the depth of expertise is not great.

8. As an example of self-insurance, most stores in the small town in which I reside readily accept personal checks for small amounts. Indeed, one store no longer accepts credit cards, having found that losses from the occasional bad check were in the aggregate less that the 3% to 5% fee that card companies levy on small stores.

9. The following discussion draws heavily on Smitka (1991, chapter 6).

10. Structural shift in the Japanese auto industry is now producing greater opportunities for new entry. Technologies are evolving rapidly, permitting new firms to break in, while the rapid rise in labor costs has hurt the competitiveness of many domestic auto parts firms. This is providing a window of opportunity for exports from the United States and elsewhere. See Smitka (1992).

11. Iwata (1982) offers such anecdotes in English; see, too, the several "business novels" now available in translation, for example, Arai (1991).

12. See Helper (1990) on "voice" versus "exit" in auto parts contracting in the United States.

13. See the essays in Gambetta (1988), and Sitkin and Roth (1993).

14. Despite much discussion of *keiretsu*, in the automotive industry the assemblers in general do not have equity ties or other means of potential control over their suppliers. The *keiretsu* are thus a reflection of the desired continuity of transactions, and are not a hierarchy to which the auto companies can issue commands.

■ References

Acheson, J. M. (1991). *The lobster gangs of Maine*. Hanover, NH: University Press of New England.

Arai, S. (1991). *Shoshaman*. Berkeley: University of California Press.

Bestor, T. (1993). *Tokyo's marketplace: Culture and trade in the Tsukiji wholesale fish market*. Stanford, CA: Stanford University Press.

Black, D. (1976). *The behavior of law*. New York: Academic Press.

Choy, J. (1992, November 13). Japan's legal system: Agent or barrier to change? *JEI Report, No. 43A*.

Coase, R. H. (1992). The institutional structure of production (Nobel Prize lecture of December 9, 1991). *American Economic Review, 82*(4), 713-719.

Dore, R. (1983). Goodwill and the spirit of market capitalism. *British Journal of Sociology, 34*(4), 459-482.

Dore, R. (1986). *Flexible rigidities*. Stanford, CA: Stanford University Press.

Ellickson, R. C. (1991). *Order without law: How neighbors settle disputes*. Cambridge, MA: Harvard University Press.

Gambetta, D. (Ed.). (1988). *Trust: Making and breaking cooperative relations*. London: Basil Blackwell.

Gilmore, G. (1974). *The death of contract*. Columbus: Ohio State University Press.

Haley, J. O. (1991). *Authority without power: Law and the Japanese paradox*. New York/London: Oxford University Press.

Harris, D., & Veljanovski, C. (1986). The use of economics to elucidate legal concepts: The law of contract. In T. Daintith & G. Teubner (Eds.), *Contract and organization: Legal analysis in the light of economic and social theory* (pp. 109-120). New York/Berlin: Walter de Gruyter.

Helper, S. (1986). *Supplier relations and technical change: Theory and application to the U.S. automobile industry*. Doctoral dissertation, Department of Economics, Harvard University.

Helper, S. (1990). Comparative supplier relations in the U.S. and Japanese auto industries: An exit/voice approach. *Economic and Business History, 2nd series, 19*, 152-161.

Helper, S. (1991, Summer). How much has really changed between U.S. automakers and their suppliers? *Sloan Management Review*, 15-28.

Iwata, R. (1982). *Japanese-style management: Its foundation and prospects*. Tokyo: Asian Productivity Organization.

Joskow, P. L. (1985). Vertical integration and long-term contracts: The case of coal-burning electric generating plants. *Journal of Law, Economics and Organization, 1*(1), 33-80.

Lorenz, E. H. (1988). Neither friends nor strangers: Informal networks of sub-contracting in French industry. In D. Gambetta (Ed.), *Trust: Making and breaking cooperative relations*. London: Basil Blackwell.

Macaulay, S. (1963). Non-contractual relations in business: A preliminary study. *American Sociological Review, 28,* 55-67.

Macaulay, S. (1985). An empirical view of contract. *Wisconsin Law Review, 47*(3), 465-482.

Macneil, I. (1985). Relational contract: What we do and do not know. *Wisconsin Law Review, 47*(3), 483-525.

Moorman, C., Zaltman, G., & Deshpande, R. (1992). Relationships between providers and users of market research: The dynamics of trust within and between organizations. *Journal of Marketing Research, 29,* 314-328.

Nishiguchi, T. (1993). *Strategic industrial sourcing: The Japanese advantage.* New York: Oxford University Press.

Pfeffer, J., & Baron, J. N. (1988). Taking the workers back out: Recent trends in the structuring of employment. In B. M. Staw & L. L. Cummings (Eds.), *Research in organizational behavior* (Vol. 10). Greenwich, CT: JAI Press.

Powell, W. W. (1990). Neither market nor hierarchy: Network forms of organization. In B. M. Staw & L. L. Cummings (Eds.), *Research in organizational behavior* (Vol. 12). Greenwich, CT: JAI Press.

Sako, M. (1991). The role of "trust" in Japanese buyer-seller relationships. *Ricerche Economiche, 45*(2-3), 449-474.

Sako, M. (1993). *Prices, quality and trust: Japanese and British management of buyer-supplier relations.* Oxford, UK: Oxford University Press.

Silin, R. H. (1972). Marketing and credit in a Hong Kong wholesale market. In W. E. Willmott (Ed.), *Economic organization in China*. Stanford, CA: Stanford University Press.

Sitkin, S. B, & Roth, N. R. (1993). Explaining the limited effectiveness of legalistic "remedies" for trust/distrust. *Organizational Science, 4*(3), 367-392.

Smitka, M. (1991). *Competitive ties: Subcontracting in the Japanese automotive industry.* New York: Columbia University Press.

Smitka, M. (1992). *The decline of the Japanese auto industry: Domestic and international implications.* Working Paper, Center on Japanese Economy and Business, Graduate School of Business, Columbia University.

Tamiya, H. (1992). *Nihon no saiban* [The Japanese court system]. Tokyo: Kobundo.

Uchida, T. (1990). *Keiyaku no saisei* [Resurrection of contract]. Tokyo: Kobundo.

Ueda, K. (1987). Jidosha ni okeru shitauke kanri [The management of subcontracting]. *Shoko Kinyu, 62*(9) 12.

Upham, F. (1987). *Law and social change in Japan*. Cambridge, MA: Harvard University Press.

Williamson, O. E. (1975). *Markets and hierarchies: Analysis and antitrust implications.* New York: Free Press.

Williamson, O. E. (1985). *The economic institutions of capitalism.* New York: Free Press.

5

Effects of Legal Context on Decision Making Under Ambiguity

Martha S. Feldman

Alan J. Levy

■ Introduction

The questions that motivate this volume are why organizations have become increasingly legalistic and how this increased legal context influences what organizations do. In this chapter we discuss a phenomenon that affects both of these questions. We observe that organizations often turn to the legal context for help in making decisions or resolving problems when there are competing claims on a decision or solution. We suggest this happens because the lack of agreement about what would be an acceptable decision or solution deprives all proposed solutions or decisions of legitimacy. The legal system provides an alternate basis for legitimacy. The basis of this legitimacy is agreement on the process, rather than agreement on the substance of the decision. This line of reasoning suggests that one of the sources of the increasingly legalistic nature of organizations may be the decreasing existence of agreement on substance.

We begin the exploration of these ideas with some general comments about decision making and problem solving. We discuss particularly the general problem of making decisions under conditions of multiple

AUTHORS' NOTE: Both authors are equal contributors; names are listed in alphabetical order. We are grateful to Lynn Eden, Elisabeth Hansot, Jonathon Simon, and Sim Sitkin for helpful comments and conversations.

claims. We then discuss three cases in which there are multiple claims and the law substantially influences the outcome. Next, we discuss some of the ways that legal considerations facilitated decision processes and affected decision outcome in these cases. Finally, we briefly discuss two issues raised by the argument we make and the cases we examine. One is the possible appearance of perversity in the outcome of decisions affected by legal considerations. The other is why we may be experiencing an increase in multiple claims in organizations.

Decision Making

Discussions of decision making have been dominated for decades by a particular model of decision making called the rational model. The model is defined by a process that is heavily dependent on information. In the most common formulation of this process, problems are recognized, goals are established, alternative solutions are formulated, and information is gathered and analyzed to assess the consequences of the alternative solutions, and on the basis of this assessment, one of the solutions is chosen (Feldman, 1989; Stone, 1988). The importance of information cannot be underrated in this process. Good decisions are based on relevant information.

This process is not always followed. There is a tendency to attribute the deviation to a deficiency of some sort in the people or organizations making the decisions. Years of research have identified specific problems in cognitive abilities and organizational structures. People have limited attention and memory (March & Simon, 1958). People have limited capacities to calculate (Simon, 1956; Tversky & Kahneman, 1974). Organizations have structures that impede the flow of information (Galbraith, 1973; Wilensky, 1967) and systems of power that subvert the rational use of information (Benveniste, 1972; Pfeffer, 1981).

An alternative to this tradition claims that what appears to be a failure may, in fact, be very sensible. Contributions to this literature have suggested that information used in unusual ways may make unusual sense. Thus, it is proposed that gossip may maintain channels of communication (March & Sevon, 1984); that apparent foolishness in the form of forgetting, being hypocritical, and trusting intuition may promote useful changes (March, 1972); that information not used for decisions may be useful for legitimating them (Feldman & March, 1981); and that commitment to action may be in conflict with and preferable to commitment to rationality (Brunsson, 1985).

One of the bases for these latter arguments is that much of the be-havior that seems strange from a rational standpoint makes sense when you appreciate the ambiguity or equivocality of the decision making context (March & Olsen, 1976; Weick, 1979). Ambiguity and equivo-cality are terms that refer to the fact that some situations have many meanings.[1] These meanings arise from many sources (March & Olsen, 1976). For instance, sometimes people differ about the way they define a problem, or the preferences they have for the solution, or the means of achieving a goal. People may even disagree about whether a problem has been solved. Each of these sources of disagreement is discussed below. Though these are surely not the only sources of disagreement, they do help to make the point that differing perspectives are common phenomena in decision making. In the following we use examples drawn from commonly known issues to illustrate these sources of disagreement.

A classic approach to decision making requires first that there be a well-defined problem that is being solved (Allison, 1971; Downs, 1957). Policy decisions, however, are often made in circumstances of either ill-defined problems or multiple problems (Cyert & March, 1963). For instance, was the Iraqi occupation of Kuwait a national security problem or an energy and trade problem for the United States? Is the savings and loan crisis in the United States a regulatory problem or a problem related to the role money plays in the electoral process? When we say that students in the United States are falling behind students in other parts of the postindustrial world, are we talking about a problem in the school system, in the family structure, or in the social structure and the incentive system to which students respond? In many cases it is very difficult, if not impossible, to discern what is the most relevant problem.[2]

Even once there is agreement about what the problem is, there may be considerable disagreement with regard to the preferences people hold about solutions. Even individuals may have trouble knowing always what they want. The problem increases with more people. There are at least three levels at which preferences may pose problems. One is that we may truly not know what we want. Do we want to bring an end to the rule of Saddam Hussein? The answer is not entirely clear. The second level is that we may know what we want, but not know what it means. Though we may all agree that we want "national security," we may not all agree on what that means or on what actions are likely to help us secure it. Third, we may not know what we want because we don't know what we are willing to give up to have it. For instance, if we agree that the Iraqi occupation of Kuwait was a serious threat to our economy or to the security of international boundaries, do we also agree that we were willing to send troops to fight to reverse the occupation? Even an individual may have ambivalent feelings about using offensive measures to ensure the availability of oil; a mixture of feelings are sure to arise within the collective. Since solutions virtually always entail tradeoffs, preferences can be very stressful. The problem is reminiscent of the numerous folk tales from all parts of the world of people who become unhappy because of the unanticipated consequences of having their wishes granted.[3] The story of King Midas and his wish to turn everything he touches into gold is perhaps the best known of these stories.

This latter problem of preferences is closely linked to the problem of technologies. Even when we know what we want, we may not know how to get it. For example, we may all be able to agree that we want less crime and fewer traffic accidents, but we do not necessarily know how to achieve these ends. Many options have been proposed for reducing crime rates. Some favor the death penalty, fixed sentencing, and other forms of sanction aimed at deterring people from committing crimes. Another approach suggests the restriction of the means to commit violent crime. Gun control is one form of this approach. There is considerable disagreement about whether either of these general approaches has much effect on crime rates.

Another source of disagreement is that it is often very hard to tell whether you have achieved what you wanted. Crime rates, for instance, are affected not only by how much crime is committed but also by how much crime is reported. Efforts to reduce certain types of crime may simultaneously legitimize the reporting of these crimes. The result may be that the reported rate of the crime stays the same or even increases. In addition, attempts to measure the effects of policies may not only be inaccurate but may also actually subvert the policies. For instance, policies aimed at increasing student test scores may encourage teachers to focus on the students who are most likely to improve, rather than on the students who need the most help. Measurements may even be simply changed to have the appearance of bringing about the desired effect. An example of this sort of dynamic occurred in the 1920s when several schools instituted policies aimed at combatting the problem of the low grade point averages of boy students. With sufficient encouragement from their principals, teachers apparently simply gave higher grades to the boys (Tyack & Hansot, 1990).

Measurement problems are not the only reason that there is considerable disagreement about the effects of policies. There are also problems of time frame. Policies that look good at one point in time later turn out to have problems that were not anticipated (Feldman, 1990). The decision to support nuclear energy as an alternative to fossil fuels at one point looked very promising. It was only several years later that the problems of nuclear waste and leakage made the nuclear option seem less acceptable. This situation continues to unfold, and the nuclear option may become more or less acceptable in the future.

These many sources of disagreement complicate decision making considerably. Legitimacy is a major problem. Where there are many competing claims, it may be very difficult to produce decisions that are generally seen as justifiable and capable of enforcement. Traditional rational theories of decision making suggest the decision produced will be legitimate because of the prior agreement on goals, alternatives, relevant information, and the basis for choice (e.g., utility maximization). Agreement on these elements assures that choice will be pro forma once the information gathering and analyses are complete, and that any reasonable person will agree on the choice. Ambiguity or equivocality in the areas previously discussed, however, disrupts this progression from stated goals and alternatives through information gathering and analysis to choice. Goals and alternatives, and what constitutes relevant information or appropriate analyses, are unlikely to be agreed upon. Not only are final choices likely to be the subject of dispute, but the entire process of making the decision lacks consensus. Any resulting choice is deprived of legitimacy.

Students of decision making have noted that there are ways that legitimate decisions can be made in such situations. One theory about how such decision making occurs is called the garbage-can theory (Cohen, March, & Olsen, 1972). Other theories can be grouped together under the rubric of incrementalism. These include Lindblom's branch theory (1958), Steinbruner's cybernetic theory (1974), and Allison's organizational process theory (1971). From the perspective of these theories, the emphasis is on how an organization can take action despite unresolvable differences in interpretation. All of these theories suggest that action takes place, but not because the grand differences in ways of perceiving a problem are resolved. Rather, it is the existence of procedures that allows action. Action takes place because organizations have procedures that organizational members follow. These procedures are followed both when there are and when there are not competing claims, but they are most evident when there are competing claims. When a logic of consequentiality or rationality is not available, a logic of appropriateness is an alternative (March & Olsen, 1989). The resulting decisions are legitimate because of the agreement on the procedures, rather than the agreement on the substance of the decision.

We might call this procedural legitimacy since it is the way the decision is made, rather than the substance of the decision, that forms the basis of the legitimacy. There are many examples of procedural legitimacy in everyday life. We may not always agree with the choice of elected officials, for instance, but we (generally) acknowledge the legitimacy of the process of voting, through which the choice was made. Similarly, we may not always agree with the choices the boss makes, but in domains where it is appropriate for him or her to make decisions, we acknowledge the legitimacy of the decision. Of course, in neither case does acknowledging the legitimacy preclude attempts to change the outcome at the next possible chance.

Our cases suggest that procedural legitimacy may not just rely on procedures that are internal to the organization. In these cases procedures external to the organization, in the form of laws and judicial procedures, are instrumental in creating legitimate courses of action. As in the previous discussion, the competing claims are not resolved. In no sense do the actors find the right answer. Instead, they find a reason to take one action rather than another. The action becomes legitimate because it is sanctioned by legitimate authorities acting in legitimate ways. In the following cases, we suggest that these authorities provide solutions for organizations, regardless of whether they want them, in situations where the relevant players cannot agree on substantive solutions. The three cases we explore are all taken from a university context and all pertain to issues of student life. Among issues at the university, those pertaining to student life are particularly likely to display ambiguity or equivocality, because the range of relevant actors is so broad. Though the specifics of these cases are perhaps unique to the University of Michigan, the issues are of general concern on many campuses (Barr, 1988; Gehring, 1992).

■ Case 1: Asbestos

Asbestos is the common name for a group of naturally occurring minerals that are heat- and fire-resistant, durable, strong, and flexible.

From the 1940s up until the early 1970s, when the link between asbestos fibers and lung cancer and other pulmonary diseases was confirmed, it was a very common material employed in building construction in as many as 3,000 products, especially in pipe insulation, ceiling tiles, and roof shingles.

Beginning in the 1970s there was increasing evidence connecting the inhalation of airborne asbestos dust particles with lung lesions (asbestosis), cancer (lung or mesothelioma), and related respiratory conditions. The U.S. Environmental Protection Agency (EPA), acting on this growing body of scientific study, initiated action to protect certain categories of workers from exposure to asbestos. The most stringent requirements were put into place in 1987, when Congress passed the Asbestos Hazard Emergency Response Act, which required school systems in the United States to institute comprehensive asbestos removal and abatement programs with estimated costs in the billions of dollars.[4] In 1989 the EPA banned the manufacture, use, and export of asbestos; the ban is to be fully in place by 1996.

During the 1980s there was a great deal of publicity engendered by asbestos lawsuits. It is estimated that there are more than 33,000 asbestos cases in federal courts and another 70,000 in state courts, making asbestos by far the most substantial personal injury issue ever to be adjudicated in the U.S. legal arena.

Recent scientific and public health studies, mostly published in the past 3 years, have put forth some strong cautionary recommendations regarding large-scale asbestos removal efforts. An international symposium at Harvard University concluded that nonoccupational exposure to undisturbed and undamaged asbestos is a risk considerably smaller than exposure to environmental cigarette smoke or radon (Energy and Environental Policy Center, 1989). The research claims that the amount of asbestos individuals are exposed to inside buildings is comparable to the level of asbestos in the outside air, both substantially below the threshold health safety level. Further, studies argue that removal of undamaged asbestos could lead to increasing rather than decreasing the risk of exposure, because the containment methods are not efficient enough to keep dust fibers from escaping into the air. Another group of scientists released a similar report, substantiating the Harvard symposium's conclusions (Mossman, Bignon, & Corn, 1990). All these studies acknowledge that the risk for construction, maintenance, custodial workers, as well as those directly involved in asbestos removal, is considerably higher than previously believed, and that for decades such workers were not adequately protected from the hazardous asbestos exposure.

The EPA has recently responded to the new research by issuing new guidelines that attempt to modify the agency's more hardline stance promulgated throughout the 1980s. These guidelines, "Managing Asbestos in Place" (Environmental Protection Agency, 1990), suggest that the emphasis should be placed on proper containment of asbestos, rather than removal, unless there is a clear and present danger from deteriorated, exposed asbestos. The EPA administrator, in justifying these new guidelines, said at the time that in-place asbestos management "can protect public health, reduce costs and guard against liability" and that "millions of dollars have been wasted on unnecessary asbestos removal operations" (Askari, 1990).

Throughout this period, officials in charge of university housing systems have had to make decisions about asbestos. While university housing is not the only affected system, it does account for a large proportion of the buildings on campus. At the University of Michigan, for instance, the Housing Division is responsible for maintaining approximately 25% of the total square footage of university buildings, consisting of 16 residence halls and a family housing apartment system of 1,700 units. Furthermore, the fact that people live in these buildings, and the sustained contact that implies, make the asbestos issue particularly pertinent to housing officials, who have received pressure from parents, the public, university administrators, students, and staff. There are people who want all asbestos removed, people who want as little money as possible spent, people who want the buildings to be used as much as possible, people who want exposure to asbestos minimized (which may or may not be the same as removing all asbestos). There is no convergence on these demands, and there is no emergence of a "right answer." How can officials make decisions in such a situation?

When one looks to the law for an answer, there are two relevant legal environments. One is the legislative/regulatory environment, represented by the EPA mandates and guidelines. The other is judicial. The regulatory environment has provided guidelines, but they have been both vague and rapidly shifting. The judicial message, in those cases not held up by interminable continuances, has been more straightforward, if simplistically, interpreted. Repeatedly, favorable verdicts, and in some cases large settlements, have been granted to claimants that have been able to show harm ("Appellate Court," 1992; Feder, 1990; Oppat, 1992). As a result, even though the settlements have revolved around occupational exposure, organizations and institutions where such exposure is unlikely to occur have still tended to focus on liability avoidance. Many school districts around the country have spent considerable sums to remove asbestos from all their buildings in order to avoid liability claims from either workers or students, even though the 1986 federal law on asbestos in schools stipulates that it is acceptable practice to leave undamaged asbestos in place (Stevens, 1989).

In general, colleges and universities have participated in legal actions as plaintiffs, pursuing cases against asbestos manufacturers such as the Manville Corporation, for decades a primary manufacturer of asbestos. In part because of stipulations in worker compensation statutes that prevent employees from suing their employers while being compensated under workers' compensation, colleges and universities have rarely had to deal with anything other than complaints filed about unsafe asbestos exposure. Recently, however, the Universities of Minnesota and Pennsylvania have been named as defendants in lawsuits that claim the institutions "knowingly allowed people to be exposed to harmful levels of asbestos on their campuses" (Magner, 1990). In the Minnesota case, a construction worker is filing suit, based on the university's failure to notify workers of the level of asbestos insulation present in a residence hall undergoing renovation. It should be noted that universities and residence hall systems have been held legally responsible for taking reasonable steps to inspect, maintain, and repair their facilities and grounds so that known and sometimes unknown physical hazards are dealt with on a timely basis (Magner, 1990). Although asbestos litigation has not yet been applied to colleges and universities, using this more general standard, it remains a possibility. From this perspective a central question for university officials is: Given the national and legal climate related to asbestos, will the university be sued if it does not take affirmative and very expensive steps to remove asbestos from its buildings and work areas?

Many institutions have acted as if such expensive steps were necessary (Main, 1991; Miller & Arnone, 1988). The Housing Division of the University of Michigan, for instance, has spent more than $1.2 million on asbestos abatement and removal since 1987. All residence hall and family housing units were surveyed by an independent asbestos specialist, who assisted in setting priorities for areas identified as needing repair, encapsulation, or removal of asbestos. Not all asbestos has been removed. In cases where the asbestos was determined to be secure and in good condition, it was not removed. If the asbestos was in a publicly visible area, a warning label was placed on the pipe, indicating that it contained asbestos and not to place any sharp objects on or near it. Housing facilities staff continue to monitor asbestos on an ongoing basis and have in place the ability to call in an asbestos speciality firm on an emergency basis. In addition, to help educate student residents, parents, or other concerned individuals, Housing publishes a brochure that describes what asbestos is, the current understanding of relative risk levels of environmental hazards, and what Housing is doing with respect to asbestos management.

■ Case 2: Commercial Solicitation

There are a number of important public policy issues for which colleges and universities claim that a campus environment is a special kind of community that sometimes necessitates variations in what would be tolerated or expected in nonuniversity settings. One such area revolves around what sort of commercial activities are permitted on campus, particularly those directed at student audiences. Universities tend to be very attractive locations for commercial vendors seeking to market and sell products of interest to a college-age population. Residence halls, in particular, have the advantage of offering a captive audience in very contained settings, so that a solicitor can reach many prospective customers in an extremely cost-effective manner.

There are several critical factors involved in determining how much and under what terms commercial solicitation can take place in university residence halls. First, one must deal with whether access of commercial solicitors can be restricted in residence halls, and if it can, what are the parameters of that access? In looking at this question, colleges and universities have attempted to determine whether residence halls are public buildings or more akin to a private residence and to identify the fundamental differences and similarities between residence halls and private residences (Gibbs, 1986; Luna, 1987). Second, universities operate in a position of trust and accordingly assume a fiduciary responsibility for the safety and security of student residents, which means that attention must be paid to how visitors of any kind are permitted entry into residence halls. Third, residence halls exist within a larger educational environment and are, at least philosophically, designed to facilitate students' ability to maximize their participation in campus life, both academic and non-academic. So, in summary, commercial solicitation policies are generally designed to take into consideration issues of privacy rights of individuals, security and safety of people and property and the overarching goal of a college or university to maintain an educational atmosphere in all its facilities on campus.

There are many competing preferences in this area. These preferences are held by faculty, administrators, students, parents, and the public. Sometimes the same group or even the same individual holds more than one of these preferences at the same time. One preference is for the maintenance of an orderly environment that is conducive to learning. Another preference is for protecting the privacy of people in residence halls. A preference that sometimes competes with the previous two is a desire to provide convenient services for students and other residents. And there is a desire to try to ensure that students are not commercially exploited.[5] Somewhat in conflict with this desire to protect students is a preference not to return to acting *in loco parentis*, a guiding framework that administrators could use to determine even very personal aspects of student behavior. This approach fell into considerable disfavor in the 1960s and has returned only in small degrees since then. What is the proper balance of these competing preferences?

There are several ways in which campuses can go about dealing with commercial solicitation. They can do what colleges do best and educate students about good business and personal finance practices. They can choose to offer or expose the campus community to a wide range of services, options, and conveniences, and let individuals select what they are interested in pursuing or learning more about, with the operative assumption of caveat emptor. Or, the argument can be made that because of the special nature of the community and the unique vulnerabilities of a captive student audience, no commercial solicitation will be permitted or commercial solicitation will be permitted only in specific settings under rigorously determined conditions.

Finally, there are many possible questions about outcome. What is a good outcome in this area? Is it a good outcome if students never encounter problems of commercial misrepresentation or never confront financial problems while they are at the university? If the university is a place to learn about life as well as a place to learn about academic subjects, then this hardly seems to be serving both goals. By contrast, is it a good outcome if students have lots of services, but are so distracted that they cannot study? Most people will readily agree that there must be some balance, but there may be considerable disagreement about what constitutes a balance that promotes the welfare of the students.

Most of the considerable case law on commercial solicitation in residence halls and college campuses is an effort to define whether dissemination of sales information qualifies as commercial speech under the Constitution and if so, what the legitimate reasons are that a university may restrict such speech (Fields, 1984). Commercial speech, which involves dissemination of information about a product or service, is distinguished from actual commercial transactions, and consequently most policies permit only the former in residence halls. Commercial speech has been consistently found to be protected under the First Amendment. Courts, up to the Supreme Court, have, however, supported the ability of colleges and universities to make restrictions on commercial speech if they result from stated educational and administrative goals.

Following from this general grant of permission, the courts have permitted schools to restrict commercial activity to specific times, places, and locations, and in some instances, to prohibit it entirely. In general, the courts expect colleges and universities to restrict commercial speech only as far as justified by their substantial interests. There are further expectations placed on institutions in carrying out these restrictions. First, a written policy, even one subject to interpretation, is better than unwritten policies. Second, once a policy is adopted, it must be adhered to consistently; any solicitor should receive the same treatment as any other. Practices that leave an institution subject to claims that it is behaving toward commercial solicitors in an arbitrary or capricious manner may subject it to lawsuits based on abrogation of constitutional rights to commercial speech.

Most campuses have adopted in writing, or by common practice, policies and procedures related to commercial solicitation by non-campus companies or commercial entities. These policies and procedures usually attempt to draw distinctions between the community living environments on campus and personal residences elsewhere.[6] At the University of Michigan, for instance, the Housing Division's written commercial solicitation policy begins by stating:

> Residence halls . . . serve a primary purpose of providing an atmosphere conducive to study and academic pursuit as well as a comfortable, supportive, and challenging living environment. Since they are restricted access

facilities, commercial solicitation can take place only under [certain] conditions . . .

In attempting to balance the rights of the community to be exposed to a wide variety of options and available services with the privacy rights of individuals to be left alone, the policy sets boundaries on how and where solicitation can take place in residence halls by treating resident rooms as private residences. No solicitors are permitted on residential corridors, except under very specific circumstances if sales demonstrations are taking place in a resident room at the specific invitation of a resident. All authorized commercial solicitation must take place in public areas of residence halls. This permits those who are interested in a particular display, service, or product to get additional information while not forcing the contact on everyone. Commercial solicitation must be registered in advance with the Housing Division, and all solicitors are provided with a set of guidelines clearly articulating permissible activity in residence halls.

There still remain considerable questions about the proper balance of services. Here is where the legal context has, perhaps, its largest effect. The course of action least likely to result in lawsuits by aggrieved vendors is to adopt a set of consistently applied and enforced policies and procedures for all commercial solicitation on campus. The courts have generally been willing to allow college campuses to place restrictions on when, where, and under what circumstances solicitation can take place, as long as the institution does not make invidious distinctions between otherwise similar vendors or solicitors. The legal context, therefore, tends to alter the focus of decision making on this issue. While the welfare of the students is still a consideration, there are no good or right answers to the questions of what serves the students best. The differences in preferences and questions about outcome, however, do not have to be resolved in order to have a legally acceptable policy. Thus, the legal issues tend to become the primary criterion of policy, the sine qua non. Decision making can proceed by focusing on the more straightforward question of vendors' rights, rather than on the more problematic questions about the students' welfare.

■ Case 3: Speech Codes on Campus

In a commencement address in May 1991 at the University of Michigan, President George Bush said:

Ironically, on the 200th anniversary of our Bill of Rights, we find free speech under assault throughout the United States, including on some college campuses. The notion of "political correctness" has ignited controversy across the land. And although the movement arises from the laudable desire to sweep away the debris of racism, and sexism, and hatred, it replaces old prejudices with new ones. It declares certain topics off-limits, certain expression off-limits, even certain gestures off-limits. (Bush, 1991)

President Bush was speaking at a campus that had enacted the most comprehensive policy on racial and sexual discriminatory harassment of any U.S. college or university. This policy, more commonly referred to as a speech code, resulted from a series of disturbing racially motivated incidents on the Michigan campus in 1987. More generally, campuses have experienced dramatic increases in such incidents, including verbal and physical abuse directed at members of minority groups, and gay men and lesbians in particular. The effort to create a more tolerant, civil, and multicultural campus has revolved around two primary paths: the development of policies designed to restrict in some manner offensive speech that creates a hostile and intimidating environment for specific populations on campus, and programmatic, curricular, and personnel initiatives to promote diversity in all facets of university life.

The development of speech codes, the focus of this section, has become an issue of extreme contention on and off college campuses. It has produced unusual alliances between liberal and conservative groups, who otherwise have little in common, either philosophically or in terms of public policy stances. Generally, campuses have adopted speech codes only under stressful and reactive circumstances, after serious incidents have demonstrated the need for significant institutional response. In the previous section on commercial speech, it was noted that the courts have generally upheld reasonable restrictions imposed by colleges and universities. However, in dealing with "pure" speech, the courts have applied a much more stringent standard in permitting restrictions on First Amendment rights, and finding the allowable level of restrictiveness in proscribing offensive speech has proven to be very difficult for campuses. An academic environment is fundamentally based on the need for free and open exchange of ideas, and this allowance for open inquiry in the context of academic freedom may be the overarching organizing principle of an institution of higher education. Consequently, institutions seeking to find some way to mitigate the impact of hurtful speech on specific populations are faced with fundamentally competing interests. The tension between the need to preserve free speech and academic freedom and the expectation, both legal and moral, that the institution provide an environment for students and staff that leaves them as free as possible from discriminatory harassment forms the battleground on which the validity of speech codes is fought.

The Michigan policy on discrimination and discriminatory harassment tried to deal with this tension by arguing that enforcement of antiharassment procedures could be variable, depending on the campus location at which the inappropriate speech or conduct occurred. It drew a distinction between public forums, classroom and academic settings, and residence halls. The most expansive definition of allowable speech was permitted in public forums, such as public gathering spots on campus and the student newspapers. A somewhat more restrictive definition was applied to academic settings, because of the university's substantial goal to ensure that the educational progress of students not be unduly influenced by harassment. Finally, the most restrictive definition was reserved for residence halls, on the assumption that no persons should be required to tolerate discriminatory behavior in their homes. The policy, following language employed in federal and state statutes and regulations on sexual harassment, proscribed any behavior, verbal or physical, that "stigmatizes or victimizes an individual on the basis of race, ethnicity, religion, sex, sexual orientation . . . [and that] creates an intimidating, hostile or demeaning environment for educational pursuits . . . " ("Discrimination and Discriminatory," 1988). Sanctions for students ranged from a reprimand to expulsion from the institution.

The residence hall incident at Michigan that helped precipitate the adoption of the discriminatory harassment policy is a good example of the complexity of this issue. A group of black women was meeting in a lounge. A flyer was slipped under their door, and upon picking it up to read it, the women saw that it was a photocopy that mimicked a State of Ohio governmental transmission regarding hunting regulations. In this instance, it was black people who were being hunted; the flyer was filled with racially derogatory epithets, slurs, and obscenities. After investigation by housing authorities, the individual who had slipped the flyer under the door was identified and his housing lease was terminated.

As a function of the intensity of residence hall environments and the fact that they purposefully bring together as roommates and housemates students from highly diverse origins and backgrounds, residence halls are often a social laboratory, reflecting both the strengths and weaknesses of the society at large, but in a concentrated form. Unquestionably, the strains in race relations that plague American society are evidenced in residence halls. Residence hall staff deal frequently with racist graffiti, racially directed speech and occasionally behavior, and with conflict, actual or perceived, with racial origins. The advent of the discriminatory harassment policy at Michigan was generally viewed positively by housing administrators, who had often felt at a loss in holding students truly accountable for significantly problematic behavior in this area, although it also represented a dilemma for them in restricting the free exchange of ideas. The Living at Michigan Credo, adopted by the Housing Division after the 1987 racial incidents as a statement of its core values with respect to intolerance and bigotry, reflects this tension by saying that "acts of racial hatred and other forms of bigotry . . . will not be condoned or tolerated," while simultaneously viewing the university as a "community designed to foster freedom of thought and unconventional, even uncomfortable opinions." To act on the aspirations of the Credo, Housing administrators developed policies and procedures that followed from the general university speech code.

The approach to this problem taken by the University of Michigan officials, as represented in this 1989 speech code, had two significant legal effects. It provided evidence that the university was concerned about protecting its students and employees from harassing speech. While this may not be sufficient in itself as a defense in possible future lawsuits, it is undoubtedly relevant evidence. The 1989 speech code also placed the thorny decision about how much free speech is appropriate squarely in the hands of the courts. The university had taken the first step. It was time now for a response from the courts.

The courts responded by overturning portions of the Michigan policy as overly broad in its restrictions on bias-related speech and, consequently, an unconstitutional infringement on First Amendment rights. Federal District Judge Avern Cohn, in 1989, said sections of the policy were so vague that persons of "common intelligence must guess at its meaning." (Reynolds, 1989). The decision (*Doe v. University of Michigan*, 1989) focused on three primary concerns. First, it stated that the terminology such as "stigmatize," "victimize," and "demean" was too vague and subject to overzealous and inappropriate enforcement. Second, Judge Cohn did not find the distinctions as to where the speech took place compelling. Finally, the decision did not support applying the hostile environment standard, used in sexual harrasssment cases in employment settings, to offensive speech directed at members of the university community by a student. Similarly, in 1991, another federal district judge overturned the University of Wisconsin policy on almost identical grounds to the Michigan case. The decisions of both courts seemed to indicate that restrictions on speech on campuses should flow much more clearly out of the "fighting words" doctrine with imminent danger of a violent reaction, and not out of the more abstract or nonspecific hurt or anguish felt by individuals offended by someone's use of language or speech (Stevens, 1991).

In deciding not to appeal Judge Cohn's decision, the University of Michigan modified the original harassment policy, and an interim version that was more specific and limited than the original version remained in place until June 1992. At that time, the U.S. Supreme Court, in *R.A.V. v. St. Paul*, rendered a decision that resulted in the constitutional end to campus speech codes in the Michigan and Wisconsin form. The two-pronged decision concluded that it was impermissible to silence speech based on its content, even if it could be interpreted as threatening, and second, that it was unconstitutional to specifically target offensive speech because it was racially or sexually directed (Greenhouse, 1992).

Support for all of these court decisions came from both the right and the left. The director of the Michigan branch of the American Civil Liberties Union stated that "You do not address the problem of racism by attacking the Constitution and the First Amendment. . . . If there is any institution in the country where controversial, in fact outrageous and even offensive, ideas ought to be aired . . . it ought to be a university" ("ACLU Says," 1989). A column by George Will noted that "in attempting to temper individualism with communitarian concerns, academic liberals are asserting a right they ferociously deny to every other community . . . the right to defend community values by circumscribing individual rights" (Will, 1989). While there is little dispute that actual conduct that is racially or sexually harassing should be subject to enforcement provisions and protections for the victims, the restriction of speech, however repugnant, in order better to regulate and achieve civility and tolerance toward difference on campus, remains very controversial.

■ Conclusion

Van Maanen and Pentland (this volume) make a compelling claim that the role of law in decision making is remote. In the cases they present—cops and auditors—legal constraints mostly affect the rhetoric surrounding the decisions. Both cops and auditors are careful to present their decisions in ways that suggest that the decisions and the decision processes are legally justifiable. The authors present evidence in both cases that actual decisions and decision processes are, at least some of the time, quite different from what is presented.

The cases we have presented suggest a very different story. In our cases, drawn from a university setting, the law seems to have very great influence on decision outcome. How can we account for this difference?

Of course, it is possible that one of us is wrong. It is also possible that university officials are more naive than cops or auditors. We suggest, however, that a more interesting and possibly more compelling reason for the difference lies in the context of decision making. In particular we think that cops and auditors tend to have a well-defined frame of reference for decision making. That is, they have fairly well-established notions of what information or action is relevant to the decision and what is irrelevant, and they have well-defined ideas about what is a good decision. The work of Manning and of Van Maanen has provided a great deal of insight into what constitutes a "good" decision for the police, and how new police learn what a "good" decision is and how to produce one (Manning, 1977, 1980; Van Maanen, 1973). The case material in the Van Maanen and Pentland chapter about auditors makes it clear that for an auditor a "good" decision is determined by the clients' interests.

In the cases we have presented, the appropriate frame of reference for the decision is not clearly defined. There are multiple clients and multiple claims. The decision makers do not have a clear bias in favor of one client or one claim. They do, we suggest, have a clear bias for making decisions that are justifiable and enforceable. In this they are not peculiar. What is peculiar, or at least problematic, is that the multiple claims make it so difficult to find a course of action that is readily understood as justifiable to the many different claimants. The law provides a basis for producing decisions that have this desirable quality.

The law is not the only basis for making "good" decisions in the face of multiple claims, and it is not a basis that is always available, or always used when available. As Weber pointed out, however, the legitimate form of authority in modern society is legal-rational (Weber, 1946). This form of legitimacy is based on belief in the "rightness of rules." Thus, rules and rule-following create legitimate action. Of course, rules themselves have to be formulated properly, that is, in accordance with the rules for rule making. As discussed earlier, rules are often internal to an organization, but they may emanate from a larger sphere, such as the judicial, legislative, and regulatory rules that apply to the organizations and individuals within a common political sphere. Rules are such an important source of legitimacy in our culture that we would expect to find their use fairly common.

Effects of Legal Context on Decision Making

Ambiguity and equivocality are impediments to action, in part, because it is not clear what information is relevant to making a decision. When we cannot specify what the problem is, we cannot know what information is relevant to resolving it. When we don't know what we want, we are at somewhat of a loss for figuring out how to get it. When the frame of reference is so broad, it is hard to determine what information is relevant.

While there are many means of resolving multiple claims, not all of them also confer legitimacy on the resulting action. For example, tossing a coin, consulting an astrologer, or examining the entrails of a sacrificial animal are ways of determining what action to take. Each of these ways is, or has been, appropriate in some contexts. They are not currently considered appropriate in many situations. In a society that honors rules, however, the use of internal or external rules (which may be rules about how to make decisions, such as voting rules) has the advantage of both limiting the frame of reference and, for reasons discussed above, often conferring legitimacy on the result. It is not the only source of such legitimacy, but it is a central one in our culture.

Any means of decision making must narrow the frame of reference. A coin toss requires two options (or a series of options that can be counterpoised); internal procedures require a definition of the situation, so that the appropriate procedure can be applied; even a vote requires a defined set of options. Our cases suggest that the law narrows the frame of reference and limits what is relevant to decision making in at least three specific ways. It limits the issues that are under consideration. It specifies procedures for introducing information as relevant to an issue. It establishes definitions that constrain all claimants. These three are described in the following paragraphs.

Since issues must have certain characteristics before they can be brought before the court (e.g., there must be relevant law; there must be someone who has been harmed and has "standing"), some claims are more likely to be resolved by law than others. The likelihood of lawsuits may be higher for some claimants than for others. Decisions may, as a result, be made so that these claimants have nothing to sue about. This dynamic can be seen in the case of commercial solicitation. In this case the people most likely to sue are the vendors, who may be deprived of the right to compete fairly against other vendors. As a result the decision is made primarily on the basis of how the university can deal with vendors without being sued by them.

Once a lawsuit is brought, procedures of the court and the constraints of the issue specify what information is relevant. Only information directly relevant to the question before the court is permissable. Introducing tangential information can only be accomplished through "laying a foundation" or creating a bridge from the directly relevant to the tangential information. Thus, in the asbestos case, the issue of harm to health has been central to virtually all court cases. In other cases universities have been held liable for health risks from both known and unknown physical hazards. It seems likely that future cases concerning asbestos and universities will revolve around whether the physical conditions of the university could have contributed to the long-term health problems of students, faculty, or staff. The EPA regulations and previous court cases define a standard against which the university can be compared. The overwhelming influence on decision making is to avoid the possibility of a large settlement against the university by engaging in asbestos removal at a level that will equal or surpass any known standard.

The third way in which the legal context for decision making narrows the frame of reference is that the court can simply establish what definitions will be used in making future decisions. To some extent this has happened in the asbestos removal cases. The courts have established a definition of liability in the judgments that have been made. This power of courts is perhaps even better illustrated in the speech code case. Two federal district judges and the Supreme Court have declared that First Amendment rights are primary and that restrictions on speech may only be based on the doctrine of "fighting words." Such action by the courts reduces some of the equivocality

in the speech code issue. It clearly defines certain actions as unacceptable and restricts the university from making those decisions.

The Appearance of Perversity

Some of the decisions in the cases we have described may appear
to be perverse. A decision based on a legal judgment (or the threat
of a legal judgment) may appear to be perverse to the extent that it
differs from an outcome that would be consistent with any substantive agreement. For example, one perspective on asbestos suggests
that the right answer is to leave nondeteriorating asbestos in place.
People holding this view claim that this plan produces the least harm
for the least cost. The only alternative that produces less harm is to
abandon the buildings, either permanently or for a considerable period,
while asbestos is removed and the asbestos dust settles. This alternative is extremely costly. The alternative that is apparently promoted
by court settlements and the threat of legal suits is complete removal
of asbestos without clearing the buildings for long enough periods
for all of the dust to settle. This alternative produces neither least
harm nor least cost, nor some balance of the two. Thus, it appears to
be perverse. While our cases rely on the law as a set of rules external
to the organization, similar "perversity" is possible when internal
procedures are the mechanism for decision making.

This appearance of perversity stems from our notion that decisions
should be based on agreement on the substance of the issue. This is
one form of what Weber referred to as "legal legitimacy." It is based
on "a voluntary agreement of the interested parties" (Weber, 1978,
p. 36). In this case as in many others, however, there is no basis for
agreement. Therefore, there is no rational basis for the decision. The
legal basis provides an alternate legitimacy. This form of legitimacy
"is imposed by an authority which is held to be legitimate and therefore
meets with compliance" (Weber, 1978, p. 36). In a legal-rational
society, the rules themselves are the authority, providing that they
are made in accordance with the rules for rule making and executed
in accordance with the rules of execution, and so forth. The legitimacy
provides a basis for action, though it does not necessarily "make sense."

Another version of perversity is cynicism. According to this argument, perverse outcomes will occur because they are in the interest
of one or another powerful claimant. While we do not deny the
dynamics of power, the fact that organizations use the law to help

produce decisions should not be taken to imply that the organization necessarily uses the law to achieve the substantive outcome that it wants. Certainly claimants are strategic. They use the law to assert their own claims, and they use their power to achieve the outcome they believe is in their best interest. That is not all there is to the situation, however. First of all, there are the traditional problems of determining what it means for an organization to want an outcome (Cyert & March, 1963; March & Simon, 1958), which is more complicated under conditions of multiple claims (March & Olsen, 1989). More to our point, however, in the condition of multiple claims we have been examining, the ability to act may at times be more important than the specific action. Our primary claim is that the legal context provides a legitimate context for action and frees the organization from potential paralysis.

Multiple Claims

In this chapter we have repeatedly suggested that multiple claims on a decision complicate decision making and increase the likelihood that the law will influence the resulting decision. We have not specified the source of the multiple claims beyond the comment that the claims may come either from inside the organization or from relevant outsiders. If the importance of law and legalistic mechanisms is on the rise in organizations (Sitkin & Bies, this volume), then our argument suggests that one of the reasons this may be true is that decision makers are confronting a broader array of perspectives that are relevant to the decision-making process. One of the reasons this may occur is that there is a greater diversity of people in positions that can influence decision making. While pressures to conform are no doubt still high, the day of the "homosocial reproduction" that Kanter describes in *Men and Women of the Corporation* (1977) may be diminishing. As women, people of color, gays and lesbians, and other heretofore marginalized groups become more common in organizations, issues that were previously unproblematic (because everyone in the homogeneous group agreed about them) or that were nonexistent (because they did not affect anyone in the homogeneous group) have become issues about which there are multiple perspectives. Sitkin and Roth (1993) have shown, for example, how such issues as productivity and interdependence have become problematic when organization members have HIV/AIDS and related ailments, rather than the more traditional heart disease and cancer. New organizational members bring new organizational issues and new perspectives to old issues. The consensus that derived from homosocial reproduction is no longer possible. One response is to adopt "legalistic remedies" (Sitkin & Roth, 1993). Whether this response is long-term or short-term, and how widespread it is, are questions for further research.

Summary

In the preceding paragraphs the effects of the legal context have been simplified, and probably exaggerated, to make a point. Organizational decision making is often extremely difficult, because of the multiple sources of ambiguity and equivocality associated with many issues about which organizations must make decisions. The legal context sometimes provides a means of focusing attention on issues that are perceived to be relatively simpler to resolve, and it sometimes provides ways of perceiving issues that favor certain decisions. In settings in which people must act in the face of many competing claims, organizational members may attend to the legal context in part because it helps to make decision making possible.

■ Notes

1. For a discussion of the differences between these two concepts and the reasons for using them interchangeably see Feldman (1989, pp 19-20).

2. See Stone (1988, pp. 1- 4) and Schön (1983, pp. 187-203) for additional examples.

3. See Stith Thompson's *Motif Index of Folk Literature*, section J2072 (1985), for several examples of this category of folk tale.

4. There are many technical, scientific, and academic examinations of environmental risk assessment, which this paper makes no effort to systematically review. For a brief nontechnical and very critical analysis of how the EPA and other parts of the federal government deal with risk assessment, see Jeremy Main, (1991).

5. There is a sense that college students are especially vulnerable because they are operating independently, in most cases for the first time, with the ability to make spending decisions not previously available to them. A recent example that is attracting national attention has to do with issuance of credit cards to full-time college students. Many credit card companies, as their other markets have become saturated, have turned to college students as a relatively untapped large population of ostensibly upwardly mobile consumers, who, surveys indicate, already spend considerable sums in such areas as expensive travel, electronics, and entertainment. College campuses have been flooded with solicitation by credit card companies, much of which takes place in residence halls and student unions; students have responded with a 37% increase in credit card accounts for the 3-year period of 1988 to 1990. Financial aid and dean's offices are reporting increasing numbers of students who use the credit

cards as loan instruments for tuition and other big-ticket items and then are over-whelmed by debt and monthly payments; in the most extreme cases, credit card abuse results in students having to leave school. How far can or should the institution step in to mitigate this sort of problem?

6. A brief overview of the issues involved in access by nonresidents to residence halls is discussed in Fields (1984).

■ References

ACLU says U-M policy limits free expression. (1989, May 26). *Ann Arbor News*.

Allison, G. T. (1971). *The essence of decision: Explaining the Cuban missile crisis*. Boston: Little, Brown.

Appellate court holds CGL exclusion does not free insurer from defense in asbestos suits. (1992, March 14). *Insurance Advocate*.

Askari, E. (1990, September 11). EPA says asbestos scare wasted millions. *Detroit Free Press*.

Barr, M. J. (1988). *Student services and the law*. San Francisco: Jossey-Bass.

Benveniste, G. (1972). The politics of expertise. Berkeley, CA: Glendessary.

Brunsson, N. (1985). *The irrational organization*. New York: John Wiley.

Bush, G.H.W. (1991, May/June). Commencement address. *Michigan Alumnus, 97*(5).

Cohen, M. D., March, J. G., & Olsen, J. P. (1972). A garbage can model of organizational choice. *Administrative Science Quarterly, 17*, 1-25.

Cyert, R. M., & March, J. G. (1963). *A behavioral theory of the firm*. Englewood Cliffs, NJ: Prentice-Hall.

Discrimination and discriminatory harassment by students in the university environment. (1988, April 18). *University Record*.

Downs, A. (1957). *An economic theory of democracy*. New York: Harper & Row.

Doe v. University of Michigan 721 F. Supp. 852 (1989).

Energy and Environmental Policy Center. (1989). Summary of symposium on health aspects of exposure to asbestos in buildings. *Report of the international symposium on the health aspects of exposure to asbestos in buildings*. Cambridge, MA: Harvard University, working paper.

Environmental Protection Agency. Managing asbestos in the workplace. Washington, DC: Government Printing Office.

Feder, B. J. (1990, December 13). The disputed deal at Eagle-Picher. *The New York Times*.

Federal court rules against ban on hate speech at Wisconsin U. (1991, October 13). *The New York Times*.

Feldman, M. S. (1989). *Order without design*. Stanford, CA; Stanford University Press.

Feldman, M. S. (1990, April 20). *Alternate uses of information for decision making*. Paper presented at the Conference on Understanding and Improving Public Decision-making; Institute of Government and Public Affairs, University of Illinois, Urbana.

Feldman, M. S., & March, J. G. (1981). Information in organizations as signal and symbol. *Administrative Science Quarterly, 26*, 171-186.

Fields, C. M. (1984, July 5). Access to dorms could become an issue of free speech. *Chronicle of Higher Education*.

Galbraith, J. R. (1973). *Designing complex organizations*. Reading, MA: Addison-Wesley.

Gehring, D. D. (Ed.). (1992). *Administering college and university housing: A legal perspective* (2nd ed.). Asheville, NC: College Administration Publications.

Gibbs, A. (1986). Solicitation on campus: Free speech or commercialization? *Journal of College Student Personnel, 27*(1).

Greenhouse, L. (1992, June 23). High court voids law singling out crimes of hatred. *The New York Times.*

Health Effects Institute/Asbestos Research. (1991). *Asbestos in public and commercial buildings.* Cambridge, MA: Author.

International symposium cites hazards of improper removal of asbestos. (1989, August 19). *Insurance Advocate.*

Kanter, R. M. (1977). *Men and women of the corporation.* New York: Basic Books.

Lindblom, C. E. (1959). The science of muddling through. *Public Administration Review, 19,* 79-88.

Luna, G. (1987). Regulating commercial speech in public college and university residence halls. *Journal of College and University Student Housing, 17*(2).

Magner, D. K. (1990, March 7). Lawsuits claim 2 universities knowingly allowed exposure to asbestos. *Chronicle of Higher Education.*

Main, J. (1991, May 20) The big cleanup gets it wrong. *Fortune.*

Manning, P. K. (1977). *Police work.* Cambridge: MIT Press.

Manning, P. K. (1980). *The narc's game: Organizational and informational limits on drug law enforcement.* Cambridge: MIT Press.

March, J. G. (1972). Model bias in social action. *Review of Educational Research, 42,* 413-429.

March, J. G., & Olsen, J. P. (1976). *Ambiguity and choice in organizations.* Bergen, Norway: Universitetsforlaget.

March, J. G., & Olsen, J. P. (1989). *Rediscovering institutions: The organizational basis of politics.* New York: Free Press.

March, J. G., & Sevon, G. (1984). Gossip, information and decision making. In L. S. Sproull & P. D. Larkey (Eds.), *Advances in information processing in organizations* (Vol. 1). Greenwich, CT: JAI Press.

March, J. G., & Simon, H. A. (1958). *Organizations.* New York: John Wiley.

Miller, T. E., & Arnone, J. R. (1988). Liability risk management. In J. H. Schuh (Ed.). *Educational programming in college and university residence halls.* Columbus, OH: Association of College and University Housing Officers International.

Mossman, B. T., Bignon, J., & Corn, M. (1990). Asbestos: Scientific developments and implications for public policy. *Science, 247,* pp. 294-301.

Oppat, S. (1992, May 29). Asbestos suit settled out of court. *Ann Arbor News.*

Pfeffer, J. (1981). *Power in organizations.* Marchfield, MA: Pitman.

Reynolds, R. T. (1989, August 26). Judge rules U-M harassment policy violates first amendment. *Ann Arbor News.*

Schön, D. A. (1983). *The reflective practitioner.* New York: Basic Books.

Simon, H. A. (1956). Rational choices and the structure of the environment. *Psychological Review, 63,* 129-138.

Sitkin, S. B, & Roth, N. L. (1993). Explaining the limited effectiveness of legalistic remedies for trust/distrust. *Organization Science, 4*(3), 367-392.

Skowron, S. (1992, July 14). 6 companies negligent in asbestos case. *Ann Arbor News.*

Steinbruner, J. D. (1974). *The cybernetic theory of decision: New dimensions of political analysis.* Princeton, NJ: Princeton University Press.

Stevens, W. K. (1991, September 26). Study asserts intact asbestos poses little risk for most inside buildings. *The New York Times*.

Stevens, W. K. (1989, September 5). Despite asbestos risk, experts see no cause for "fiber phobia." *The New York Times*.

Stone, D. A. (1988). *Policy paradox and political reason*. Glenview, IL: Scott, Foresman.

Thompson, S. (1955). *Motif index of folk literature*. Bloomington: Indiana University Press.

Tversky, A., & Kahneman, D. (1974). Judgement under uncertainty: Heuristics and biases. *Science, 185*, pp. 1124-1131.

Tyack, D., & Hansot, E. (1990). *Learning together*. New Haven, CT: Yale University Press.

Van Maanen, J. (1973). Observations on the making of policemen. *Human Organization, 32*(4), 407-418.

Weber, M. (1978). *Economy and society*. (G. Roth & C. Wittich, Eds.). Berkeley: University of California Press.

Weber, M. (1946). Bureaucracy. In H. H. Gerth & C. W. Mills (Eds.). *From Max Weber*. New York: Oxford University Press.

Weick, K. E. (1979). *The social psychology of organizing*. New York: Random House.

Wilensky, H. L. (1967). *Organizational intelligence: Knowledge and policy in government and industry*. New York: Basic Books.

Will, G. F. (1989, November 5). Limits on speech freedom inappropriate on university campuses. *Ann Arbor News*.

Part III

Legalistic Criteria in Decision Making

6

Stigma as a Determinant of Legalization

Nancy L. Roth

Sim B Sitkin

Ann House

■ Legalization, Institutionalization, and the Choice of Control Mechanisms in Organizations

Law, Legalism, and Legalization

As a form of social control, law specifies the "normative life of a state and its citizens" by defining "deviant behavior and the response to it, such as prohibitions, accusations, punishment and compensation" (Black, 1989, pp. 1-2). By recognizing "unofficial" norms and practices and granting them legal status, law tends to foster the formal, the explicit, and the deliberately instituted (Selznick, Nonet, & Vollmer, 1969) over the informal, tacit, and traditional. These attributes of law are designed to minimize arbitrariness in decision making, to legitimate power, to protect the rights of citizens, and to specify their responsibilities (Lieberman, 1981; Selznick et al., 1969; Shklar, 1964).

AUTHORS' NOTE: We wish to gratefully acknowledge support while portions of this chapter were prepared from the National Center in HIV Social Research, University of New South Wales, Australia (where Roth was a visiting research fellow), and from the Graduate School of Industrial Administration, Carnegie-Mellon University (where Sitkin was a visiting faculty member).

The importance of formal control mechanisms is central to Shklar's (1964, p. 1) definition of legalism as "the ethical attitude that holds moral conduct to be a matter of rule following, and moral relationships to consist of duties and rights determined by rules." The danger inherent in such a strong emphasis on formal control is highlighted by Selznick (Nonet & Selznick, 1978; Selznick et al., 1969) when he observes that law degenerates into legalism when the integrity of formal legal procedures is maintained at the expense of the ends the legal process was designed to serve.

Comparable phenomena are found in organizations. For example, bureaucratic organizations similarly rely on such formal controls as written rules and procedures, job specifications, quality control standards, and contracts. Even though formal controls may be adopted to achieve rationality, efficiency, and evenhandedness (Weber, 1947), "goal displacement" can lead to features that resemble the legalisms described by Shklar and Selznick. The emergence of these dysfunctional characteristics in organizational settings has been referred to as "legalization" (Meyer, 1983; Yudof, 1981). Legalization in organizations mimics the law in many ways: It is adversarial and formalistic, uses legalistic procedures and criteria, employs legal terminology, and emphasizes reconciliation through litigation or ultimate reliance on some sort of judicial review (Sitkin & Bies, 1993). However, it goes beyond mere compliance with legal requirements to include the adoption of excessively cumbersome or inappropriate administrative control processes (Jasanoff, 1985; Meyer, 1983) that exceed what the law requires.

Sitkin and Bies (this volume) define legalization in terms of "the diffusion of legalistic reasoning, procedures and structures as a means of sustaining or enhancing the legitimacy of the organization (or an organizational subunit) with critical internal or external constituencies." According to Sitkin and Bies (1993), "legalization is most often used to legitimate proposed changes . . . or to avoid undesired change." While legalization is often initially proposed to assure fair treatment of employees or to improve organizational achievement of goals such as efficiency, much of the literature on organizational legalization focuses on how formalized procedures and decision criteria are instead adopted to enhance the organization's institutional legitimacy.

Institutional Theory and Legalization

The observation that organizations increase legalization as a way to enhance their legitimacy with internal and external constituencies is consistent with recent theoretical trends in the organizational literature. Tracing its roots to the earlier work of Selznick (Selznick, 1949; Nonet & Selznick, 1978; Selznick et al., 1969), institutional theorists suggest that much organizational activity can be understood as efforts to establish and sustain legitimacy (see Powell & DiMaggio, 1991; Scott, 1987). However, according to DiMaggio and Powell (1991), the "new institutionalism" in organizational analysis departs from the "old institutionalism" in terms of the relative emphasis each places on the legitimating function played by formal versus informal control mechanisms:

> [T]he old institutionalism highlighted the "shadowland of informal inter-action" (Selznick, 1949, p. 260)—influence patterns, coalitions and cliques, particularistic elements in recruitment or promotion— . . . The new institutionalism, by contrast, locates irrationality in the formal structure itself, attributing diffusion to certain departments and operating procedures . . . (DiMaggio & Powell, 1991, p. 13)

Research on legalization draws heavily on both the new and the old schools. Consistent with old school, it stresses legitimacy, practicality, and habit as driving forces behind organizational action. Consistent with the new school, it focuses on legalization as formal change in the ongoing structuring of the organization.

In this chapter, we wish to explicitly push the debate toward a revitalization of aspects of the old institutionalism that DiMaggio and Powell suggest have been left behind. We would suggest that it is not so much that recent institutional research has ignored the role of informal control as a mechanism of legitimacy attainment as it is that recent work has implicitly assumed the coincidence of formal cultural symbols with the adoption of symbolically acceptable formal structures.

The presumption that both formal and informal structural features can and will be used to enhance the perceived legitimacy of the organization, profession, or other social entity is in direct contrast with the recent formulation of the legalistic form of institutional theory of Sitkin and Bies (1993, this volume). They contend that the adoption of highly formal, law-like features will drive out informal practices, because the apparent objectivity of the law could be undermined by the use of more informal, symbolic features. One implication of this alternative perspective on institutional theory is that formal and informal claims to institutional legitimacy may be alternatives that can be used contingently, but not concurrently. In the exploratory research reported here, we examine the relationship between the use of formal and informal control mechanisms in response to threats to decision and decision-maker legitimacy as a way of joining these issues.

■ Stigmatized Catastrophic Illnesses as Threats to Institutional Legitimacy

To explore these theoretical issues empirically, we will examine the extent to which decision makers rely on an organization's formal and informal control mechanisms in making decisions about employees who have catastrophic illnesses that vary in their level of stigmatization. The focus of this approach rests on the idea that decision makers might be influenced by the tacit threat represented by that which is stigmatized, and that their decisions concerning stigmatized employees would, therefore, be a useful way to differentiate the relative use of formal and informal control mechanisms as potential legitimating tools.

Stigma as an Example of Institutional Threats

The literature defines stigmas as extreme negative infractions of norms or expectations (Goffman, 1963; Jones, Farina, Hastorf, Marcus, Miller, & Scott, 1984; Page, 1984) that are perceived as uncertain and potentially dangerous (Douglas, 1966; Sontag, 1979) and threaten to tarnish people or organizations associated with them (Page, 1984). Stigmatization represents a potentially fundamental threat to organizations not only because it can undermine the formal authority structure of the organization but also because it can unravel the carefully woven threads of legitimacy that connect an organization with its internal and external constituencies (Sitkin & Roth, 1993a; Sutton & Callahan, 1987).

HIV/AIDS is an example of a stigmatized illness because it manifests the five features associated with stigmatization (fatality, uncertainty, attributed marginality, voluntarism, and communicability) identified by Sitkin and Roth (1993b). Although recent research indicates that

HIV/AIDS is not communicable in ordinary workplace settings, and may soon be a long-term manageable illness, the stigmas associated with HIV/AIDS are communicable not only to coworkers but to the organization as a whole (see Sitkin & Roth, 1993a, 1993b). Thus, the mere presence of people with HIV/AIDS in the workplace is often perceived as a threat to coworkers and managers (Gray, 1989; Rowe, Russell-Einhorn, & Baker, 1986). Because of the association of HIV/AIDS with these stigmatized features, we suggest that the mere presence of an employee known to have HIV/AIDS would have a potential impact on the organization's sense of legitimacy.

Influences on Decisions Concerning Catastrophic Illness Cases

Use of Formal and Informal Controls to Guide Decision Making. Organizations can rely on formal or informal controls in deciding how to handle an employee with a catastrophic illness. If an organizational decision maker perceives the ill employee's case as representing a potential threat to the organization—for example, because the disease is stigmatized—that decision maker may use the organization's formal and informal controls differently than if the case were not seen as stigmatized and thus represented no perceived threat. For example, Sitkin and Bies (1993) and Sitkin and Roth (1993a) have suggested that organizations respond to legitimacy-threatening situations by increasing their reliance on formal policies and procedures to increase the legitimacy of any action taken by shielding the organization from later accusations of preferential or discriminatory treatment. Similarly, Kirp (1989) and Kirp, Epstein, Franks, Simon, Conaway, and Lewis (1989) describe how the informal norms and practices of an organization can play a critical role in providing an accepting and supportive environment for ill employees—or a harsh, exclusionary situation in which the ill employee is treated like an unworthy outsider.

Legal Guidance Concerning the Handling of Catastrophic Illness Cases. In deciding how to handle such cases, it would be logical for managers to look to the law for guidance with respect to hiring/firing, benefits, or confidentiality in handling cases where employees have a catastrophic illness. For example, hiring and firing is one area where there is clear legal guidance. Federal employment statutes stipulate that hiring and firing decisions must be made based on an individual's current ability to carry out the responsibilities of a position. The courts have also found that a person who is physically impaired by some diseases (e.g., HIV/AIDS) may be construed as "handicapped" under the Federal Vocational Rehabilitation Act of 1973 (as well as many state and local laws), and thus protected against discrimination.

Legal guidance about such organizational concerns as confidentiality and employee benefits is less clear—or completely nonexistent. Therefore, informal controls might be expected to play a larger role in guiding decisions about confidentiality and benefits for employees with HIV/AIDS. While federal law protects the legal confidentiality of physician records (e.g., the comprehensive Alcohol Abuse and Alcoholism Prevention, Treatment and Rehabilitation Act Amendments of 1974 protect individual confidentiality concerning medical treatment for alcoholism), the confidentiality of workplace records depends upon state law. Some states require insurance companies to maintain confidentiality; but law, regulation, and litigation in most states are silent on the issue of how work organizations (especially non-insurance firms) are to handle the confidentiality of such records. Similarly, with respect to employee benefits, there is no statutory or case law requirement that employers provide employees with sick leave, insurance, disability, or other benefits. However, there is some legal protection for employees who exercise their rights under a benefit plan, and employees cannot be fired because their insurance claims increase organizational benefit costs.

■ Hypotheses

Theoretical work on legalization, institutionalization, and organizational control suggests that there might be discernable patterns in the relationship between an organization's typical use of control mechanisms and its response to a situation that involves stigma. To the extent that organizations respond to the threat posed by stigma by adopting legalistic controls, Sitkin and Bies (1993) suggest that legalistic features (e.g., the use of formal controls) will tend to drive out other equally useful organizational controls. Their untested assertion raises two questions. First, is there evidence that legalistic features are actually used as "remedies" (Sitkin & Roth, 1993a) for institutional threats to organizational legitimacy? Second, when legalistic control mechanisms are used as remedies, is their use associated with the reduced use of other control mechanisms? Neither question has received much attention in the literature to date. The goal of this chapter is to provide a preliminary empirical examination of these ideas through an experimental study of human resource management (HRM) decisions that involve differing levels of institutional threat in the form of stigma.

Control Theory and Inertial Tendencies in Organizational Response Patterns

Organizations can be distinguished by the degree to which two basic types of control mechanisms are used to influence how decisions are made and implemented by organizational members. Burns and Stalker (1961), Ouchi (1979, 1980), Hofstede (1980), and Lebas and Weigenstein (1986) offer categorization schemes for distinguishing organizations based on the degree to which they rely on two primary mechanisms of control: formal bureaucratic controls or informal cultural controls. For example, Ouchi (1979, 1980) identified three types of controls used in organizations, contrasting formal control (*hierarchies*) with more informal forms of control that rely on shared values, beliefs, cultural norms, and traditions (*clans*) and forms of control that minimize both the formal and the informal to rely on free market controls (*markets*).

While the specifics vary from theory to theory, all of these works reflect an underlying control-based, configurational approach to categorizing organizations that can be captured by a two by two matrix, in which organizations are differentiated, based on the extent to which they rely upon informal control mechanisms (such as values, beliefs, traditions, and norms) or formal control mechanisms (such as written policies and procedures). As shown in Table 6.1, the organizations represented by the four cells are labeled *legalistic* (high formal, low informal), *normative* (low, high), *market* (low, low), or *integrative* (high, high).

Legalistic Control Orientation

In classic bureaucratic hierarchies, concern for task-related goals and performance reliability fosters the adoption of formal policies, such as those that standardize the procedures for handling cases where employees become catastrophically ill. These formalized workplace HRM policies and procedures can help employers cope with the

Table 6.1

Dominant Organization Control Mechanisms
as the Basis for Defining Organizational Types

		Reliance on Formal Policies and Procedures	
		Low	High
	High	**Normative Organizations** Decisions based to a great extent on informal mechanisms (values, beliefs, norms) and to a smaller extent on formal mechanisms	**Integrative Organizations** Decisions based to a great extent on formal and informal mechanisms
Reliance on Informal Cultural Norms and Traditions	Low	**Market Organizations** Decisions based to a smaller extent on both formal and informal mechanisms	**Legalistic Organizations** Decisions based to a greater extent on formal mechanisms (formal policies and procedures) and to a smaller extent on informal mechanisms

needs of workers who have catastrophic illnesses through the use of standardized, formal, and familiar mechanisms that convey that this is a routine organizational matter and that everything is under control.

Normative Control Orientation

In contrast, when organizations stress shared values and group solidarity, then selection, promotion, and other HRM decisions are likely to be driven more by the organization's tacit cultural values and traditions than its formal policies. To the extent a catastrophic illness does not directly challenge core cultural values, cultural responses may encourage coworkers or supervisors to respond in supportive, culturally appropriate ways. If, however, a catastrophic illness challenges strongly held cultural values (e.g., as is often the case for HIV/AIDS), a more highly insular, exclusionary response to HIV/AIDS may result in sick employees being literally and figuratively expelled from the organization's cultural "family."

Market Control Orientation

When an organization has agreement about neither a core set of cultural values nor common set of task-related goals, responses to HRM issues are left by default to the discretion and contractual negotiation skills of the individual manager. Such organizations may be more like a portfolio of independent contractors than a monolithic social unit. In addition to Ouchi's (1979, 1980) work on such organizations, recent attention to this type of control configuration (Miles & Snow, 1978; Pfeffer & Baron, 1988) has acknowledged that such forms rely on neither traditional formal bureaucratic nor informal cultural mechanisms of control.

Integrative Control Orientation

Some organizations are able to rely simultaneously on both formal and informal controls due to broad task agreement and widely shared core norms and values. Such an approach, at least in its prototypical form, explicitly recognizes that the collectivity which forms the foundation for an organization relies both on coordinated activities that promote task performance and on cultural concerns that encourage more than minimal, partial inclusion of employees. As illustrated by Kirp's (1989) study of Pacific Bell, organizations that implement an integrative response approach appear to combine formal guidelines (that can protect against exclusionary cultural abuses) with the capacity to draw upon the organization's culture to tailor responses to situation-specific needs.

The Effect of Inertia on Individual Decision Making

Building on the idea that the fundamental purpose of organizational control is to make individual actions more reliable and congruent with overall organizational goals and standards, Ouchi's control theory (1979, 1980) suggests that individual organizational members should exhibit the prototypical response patterns of their organization in carrying out their daily activities. Thus, individual decision makers in Ouchi's "bureaucratic" organizations would be predicted to be characterized by their high level of reliance on formal rules and procedures in making decisions.

Configurational organizational theories (Miles & Snow, 1978; Mintzberg, 1977) also posit that certain key organizational attributes tend to occur in bundled configurations that are relatively resistant to changing environmental pressures. A strict interpretation of the inertial argument suggests that even when faced with changing environmental pressures, organizations and their individual members tend to persist in their traditional ways of perceiving, interpreting, and addressing problems. While such a strong inertial argument may seem somewhat extreme, research on commitment (Salancik, 1977; Staw & Ross, 1987) and perception processes (e.g., Daft & Weick, 1984; Kiesler & Sproull, 1982) suggest that defensiveness, selective attention, competency traps, and habitual routines can make it difficult to overcome inertial tendencies.

Hypothesis 1: As perceived threat (stigma) increases, decision makers' reliance on formal and informal control criteria to make and legitimate their decisions will continue to be determined by their organization's prototypical control orientation.

The New Institutional Theory and the Reliance on Formal Controls to Ameliorate Threats to Legitimacy

In contrast to the inertial predictions of control theorists, a number of scholars have noted that organizations and their decision makers do respond differently when threatened—and that threat may lead to departures from prototypical response patterns. For example, Meyer (1982) described how several hospitals responded to the "jolt" of a doctor's strike by altering their traditional control patterns. Staw, Sandelands, and Dutton (1981, p. 513) proposed a "threat-rigidity effect," in which both individuals and organizations respond to threat with a "mechanistic shift in which there is increased centralization of authority, more extensive formalization, and standardization of procedures . . . [to enhance] control and coordination of organizational action" (Burns & Stalker, 1961).

"New" institutional theorists make similar predictions, stressing that organizations adopt well-accepted formal structures and procedures so they appear to conform to social norms (Meyer & Rowan, 1977; Scott, 1987). The adoption of readily recognizable and normatively proper formal control mechanisms is an especially important tool when organizations are threatened and need to foster the perception that they are acting rationally and legitimately (Edelman, 1990; Feldman & March, 1981), such as when controversial decisions or questionable activities may be viewed as violating social norms or organizational goals (Elsbach & Sutton, 1992; Sitkin & Roth, 1993a).

The focus of institutional theorists on the importance of sustaining the organization's legitimacy, in the eyes of internal and external constituencies, centers around formalization as the prototypical legitimacy-enhancing response to real and perceived threats. While institutional theory suggests that institutional pressures can foster stable response patterns when organizations face stable environmental pressures, it also highlights the degree to which organizations respond to internal and external threats by adopting legitimate formal structures that will simultaneously ameliorate legitimacy concerns and permit questionable activities to proceed unimpeded.

One cluster of recent empirical work on institutionalized organizational responses focuses on the adoption of formalized HRM procedures to minimize the potential conflict and controversy surrounding fair hiring and firing practices, comparable worth, and sexual harassment (Abzug & Mezias, 1993; Dobbin, Edelman, Meyer, Scott, & Swidler, 1988; Edelman, 1990; Gutek, 1993). These studies suggest that organizations have cloaked controversial decisions, discriminatory practices, and the like in the acceptable guise of procedures (e.g., due process), language, and decision criteria that mimic the legal system, as a means of appropriating the legitimacy of the law. That is, like other forms of institutional formalization, organizational legalization is used as a shield when the organization's legitimacy is threatened. Thus, "new" institutional theory suggests that organizations will respond to potential threats to their legitimacy (e.g., stigma) by increasing their reliance on formal control mechanisms. This leads us to hypothesize:

Hypothesis 2: As perceived threat (stigma) increases, decision makers will rely increasingly upon formal control mechanisms in making decisions.

Reliance on Informal Controls to Ameliorate Threats to Legitimacy

"Old" Institutional Theory. Although "new" institutional theorists focus on the legitimating function of formal controls, recent work (e.g., Elsbach & Sutton, 1992; Oliver, 1991) draw attention to the comparable use of informal mechanisms such as norms, symbols, or traditions. The notion that informal cultural controls could serve

such an institutionally legitimating role is consistent with the definition of institutional legitimacy as "the degree of cultural support for an organization . . . [resulting from] cultural accounts [that] provide explanations for its existence" (Meyer & Scott, 1983, p. 201). Moreover, an emphasis on the institutional function of informal ceremonies, symbols, and rituals can be traced to the cornerstones of the old institutional approach (e.g., Berger & Luckmann, 1967, Meyer & Rowan, 1977; Selznick, 1949).

Elsbach and Sutton (1992, pp. 714-715) illustrate this point in their description of how an activist environmentalist organization (Earth First!) was able to legitimate spiking trees being cut by lumber companies by claiming it followed specific organizational norms in marking the trees and notifying authorities of its actions. In addition, the group was able to diffuse blame when loggers were injured by claiming the injury could not have been caused by an Earth First! spike since it did not conform to the organization's informal traditions.

Thus, from a traditional institutional perspective, threats should also lead to claims of legitimacy that invoke informal cultural norms and traditions. That is, legitimacy can be maintained by adhering to such informal cultural norms as: coworkers coming to the aid of a fellow member of the organization's "family" by doing extra work so that an employee can take time off for a personal family emergency; coworkers shunning an employee who has violated informal norms concerning how assertive junior employees should act in staff meetings; or workers accepting unpaid leave to ensure that an informal norm of "no layoffs" is upheld. As illustrated by these examples, this perspective implies:

> Hypothesis 3a: As the perceived threat (stigma) increases, decision makers will rely increasingly upon informal control mechanisms in making decisions.

The Legalistic Perspective

Comparable to "new" institutionalists, the legalistic perspective stresses that an emphasis on legalistic legitimacy (e.g., formal rules and procedures) serves two functions: (a) masking the potentially controversial or unacceptable behind formal routines to enhance legitimacy; and also (b) distancing the organization from any controversy or illegitimacy that does leak out. However, with respect to the role of informal controls, the legalistic approach to institutional theory

(Sitkin & Bies, this volume; Sitkin & Roth, 1993a) departs from that of traditional institutional theorists. Whereas the traditional institutional view highlights the legitimacy-enhancing potential of invoking informal norms or traditions to mask or justify potentially controversial actions, the legalistic perspective suggests that decision makers who confront threats to firm legitimacy will reduce their reliance on informal control criteria (the differences between the two perspectives are illustrated in Figure 6.1).

Many organizations rely on informal norms—such as the previously mentioned example of coworkers supporting "members of our corporate family" by informally covering for an individual who has a family emergency. However, if the emergency were stigmatized (e.g., the illness involved a same gender spouse), the legalization perspective suggests that reliance on informal norms or organizational traditions (e.g., the use of the "corporate family" metaphor) would be abandoned as a tool of institutional legitimation and would be replaced by legalistic controls to legitimate whatever response to the situation was chosen.

The legalization perspective reflects that reliance on informal controls in the face of threat (e.g., stigmatization) can be ineffective in protecting the organization's legitimacy, because it strengthens the organization's apparent link to that which threatens perceived legitimacy. By invoking normative controls to legitimate a controversial action, an organization ties its image to that illegitimate action by suggesting that the action is consistent with how that organization operates. Rather than distancing the organization from the threat by isolating its significance or salience, the use of informal controls can thus suggest that the apparent institutional violation does not contravene the organization's informal norms, and thus can threaten to taint the organization's legitimacy more broadly. Imagine, for example, Union Carbide trying to justify the Bhopal accident by suggesting that "our firm traditionally worries less about safety when operating in Third World countries." Thus, the legalistic perspective suggests an alternative prediction concerning the use of informal control mechanisms to legitimate potentially controversial decisions:

Hypothesis 3b: As threat (stigma) increases, decision makers will rely less upon informal control mechanisms in making decisions.

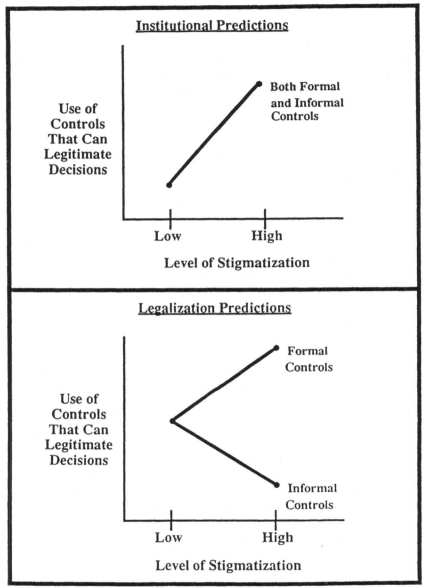

Figure 6.1. Visual Comparison of Institutionalization and Legalization Predictions

■ Methodology

Procedure

Subjects completed a brief questionnaire about an organization for which they had worked, including questions about the types of controls routinely relied upon in the organization. They were then given an HRM in-basket exercise for which they were asked to assume the role of a decision maker in a fictitious organization. To mask the actual focus of the study, the decision issues included vacation requests, salaries and budgets, as well as handling several health insurance problems concerning employees who were HIV infected, had alcoholism-related illnesses, or had lung cancer. All subjects were given identical roles and firm descriptions, except that the dominant type of control mechanisms used in the fictitious firm were manipulated to match each subject's prior organizational control experience by creating four conditions.

Subjects were asked to make decisions about several employee cases in order "to help a committee to develop new organizational policies for handling catastrophic illness." The description for each case provided a standardized performance and health summary, which described the employee as an "above average performer" who posed an "above average risk" of incurring high insurance costs. For each case, subjects were then asked to indicate the extent to which they would base their decisions about firing, confidentiality, and benefits on two factors: (1) formal policies and procedures, and (2) informal norms and values.

Once the in-basket exercise was completed, subjects were asked to respond to a brief questionnaire that included manipulation checks, demographic information, and additional information about their prior work experience. The entire procedure took approximately 30 minutes, after which subjects were debriefed.

Sample

Seventy-two members of a required upper-level undergraduate business class participated in the experiment as part of an in-class exercise in human resource management decision making. Although the subjects were undergraduates, 75% reported 2 or more years of experience (45% reported at least 5 years of work experience), primarily in organizations of more than 1,000 employees. In addition, the types of organizations for which they had worked were distributed across the four types shown in Table 6.1 (i.e., their organizations varied in the extent to which they relied on formal and informal controls to guide their daily actions).

Design

Each subject was asked to make three HRM decisions (e.g., whether to fire an employee) concerning each of two employees whose cases presented one high level and one low level of stigmatization. For each HRM decision, subjects were asked to indicate the extent to which their decision would be influenced by their (simulated) organization's formal policies or informal cultural norms. Thus, the design calls for each subject to provide 12 repeated measures: 3 HRM decisions (firing, confidentiality, benefits) × 2 levels of stigmatization (low, high) × 2 sources of influence (formal, normative). A repeated measures MANOVA was used to test the hypotheses (experience as a covariate was also examined, but since it had no effect and did not alter the results, it was not retained in the analyses reported here).

The primary purpose of this study is theory testing, rather than the prediction of specific managerial behaviors. Therefore, a carefully constructed simulated environment seemed to be the most appropriate approach since it provides some measure of external validity while assuring the control necessary to fairly test competing theories (Wood & Bandura, 1989). Clearly, field research in this area is important, but because it is premature to move to the field before key theoretical relationships have been established under more controlled conditions, our goal here was to conduct an experiment that could yield a clearer theoretical foundation that could serve as a more focused basis for designing future field research.

In addition, an exploratory factor was introduced to enhance external validity. Specifically, based on an extension of Ouchi's (1979, 1980) conceptual framework, the subjects were asked to characterize their own most substantial organizational work experience (i.e., the organization they had worked for the longest or knew the best) in terms of the type of control mechanisms used in that organization. Subjects were then placed in a simulated organizational condition that matched the dominant control characteristics each had personally experienced previously.

Measures

Influences on HRM Decisions

The dependent variables in this study concern the extent to which decisions made about ill employees (whose illnesses varied in level of stigmatization) rely on formal policies or informal norms. Subjects, in the role of organizational decision makers, were asked to rate the extent to which they would base three HRM decisions (about firing, confidentiality of medical records, and insurance benefits) on two types of controls (formal and informal). Examples of *formal* criteria included the existence of written rules, the strict enforcement of written rules, the development of policies and procedures, and the resolution of conflict through structured/formal mechanisms. Examples of *informal* criteria included intense family-like relationships, personal involvement and concern about coworkers, knowing informally what is considered appropriate and acceptable, and the use of stories to reinforce informal norms. Excluding filler questions, each subject provided a total of 12 ratings for the study (3 HRM decisions × 2 levels of stigmatization × 2 influences on their decision).

Organizational Conditions

To ensure that each subject was able to imagine what it would be like to make decisions within an experimentally assigned type of organizational setting, subjects were assigned to one of four organizational control conditions, based on their own description of the controls used routinely by an organization with which they had worked and were most familiar. Their organizations were categorized based on two four-item indices that measured their organization's reliance on formal controls (items adapted from Glick, Huber, Miller, Doty & Sutcliffe, 1990) and informal controls (items adapted from Price & Mueller, 1986). Subject ratings of their organization's use of each type of control were categorized as "low" if the score was 16 or lower (out of a maximum possible score of 28) and "high" if the total score was 17 or higher. Organizations that scored "high" on formal controls and "low" on informal controls were categorized as Legalistic Organizations. Organizations high on informal and low on formal were considered to be Normative Organizations. Organizations that were low on both the formal and informal control dimensions were categorized as Market Organizations, while those organizations high on both were categorized as Integrative Organizations.

Subjects were assigned to organizational conditions based on the type of organization with which they were familiar. Subjects were not informed of their organizational type, rather they were instructed to select a specific packet color for their in-basket exercise, based on their organization's scores. Each color-coded set of materials included different descriptions of the organization within which decisions were being made. For the Legalistic Organization type, we drew upon Nonet and Selznick's (1978, p. 108) characterization of legalization as "the proliferation of rules and procedural formalities" to focus on written rules and procedures and capture those aspects of legalization that stress the use of formal controls (Sitkin & Bies, 1993). The firm was described as:

> . . . a rapidly growing competitor in the high-tech components industry. It began with a small, closely knit staff, but rapid expansion has required a tenfold increase in personnel in a very short time. *A comprehensive policies and procedures manual serves as the basis for most decisions.*

Only the italicized portion of the preceding description was varied between subjects to manipulate organizational type. For Normative, Market, and Integrative Organizations the italicized words were replaced as follows:

> *The firm does not have many formal policies, and decisions are generally influenced by the firm's cultural norms and values.* (Normative)
> *The firm does not have many formal policies or broadly shared cultural norms and values. As a result, individual managers have considerable free-dom in decision making.* (Market)
> *Decisions are based on both the formal policies and procedures manual, and also on being consistent with the company's cultural norms and values.* (Integrative)

Stigmatization of Catastrophic Illnesses

To vary the degree of stigmatization, three catastrophic illnesses that affect workers in organizations were identified, based on previous research (Douglas, 1966; Ross, 1988; Sontag, 1988; Weiner, Perry, & Magnusson, 1988). Illnesses were selected to present two cases with distinct levels of stigmatization on which our analysis would focus— one for an illness that was considered high on stigmatization (HIV/ AIDS) and one for an illness low on stigmatization (lung cancer). An additional third case (involving an alcoholism-related illness) was also included as filler, to make the focal contrast less stark by representing a more ambiguous level of stigmatization. The order of the three illnesses was randomized.

■ Results

Manipulation Checks

Stigmatization of Catastrophic Illnesses

Because different catastrophic illnesses were used as proxies for stigmatization, a manipulation check was required to ascertain the perceived level of stigmatization associated with each of the illnesses. Subjects were asked to assess the extent to which employees of the simulated organization "would be comfortable working with a co-worker who had [each of the illnesses]." The same question was repeated concerning the organization the subject originally reported having worked for. Finally, subjects were asked how comfortable they themselves would be in working with this person. The three questions formed reliable scales for each illness (α = .84, .85, and .83 for HIV, alcoholism-related illnesses, and lung cancer, respectively). Stigmatization scales were formed for each illness, and multivariate analysis of variance and planned contrasts was then used to check the relative stigmatization of the three illnesses. Differences were significant (T^2 = 2.71, F = 93.50, df = 2,69, p<.001) and strongly support the use of HIV/AIDS as a proxy for high stigmatization (M = 3.09, SD = 1.45) and lung cancer as a proxy for low stigmatization (M = 5.24, SD = 1.21), with alcoholism providing a middle-range, mixed case. Differences in stigmatization between each pair of illnesses were found to be significant at the p<.05 level using the Newman-Keuls procedure.

Organization Control Types

A second manipulation check concerned the degree to which subjects perceived their assigned organizational conditions to have been characterized by the formal and normative controls intended. Subjects were asked at the end of the study to rate the simulated organization in terms of the extent to which "formal policies and procedures" were important in decision making and to similarly rate the importance of "cultural norms and values." Subjects were also asked six factual questions about aspects of the in-basket exercise (e.g., concerning the importance of certain tasks) that did not vary across the four organizational conditions. As expected, perceived organizational characteristics differed significantly in terms of both formal policies and procedures ($F = 47.70$, $df = 3,71$, $p<.001$) and cultural norms and values ($F = 8.44$, $df = 3,71$, $p<.001$), but did not differ for any of the nonmanipulated characteristics.

Order Effects and External Validity Checks

To check for an order effect, subjects were randomly assigned within each condition to different illness orders. The overall order effect was nonsignificant. In addition to finding no overall effect for order, the effect of order was examined for each of the 12 dependent variables, of which none were significant and one was found to be marginally significant. Based On these results, order was not included in further analyses.

We were concerned about the ability of undergraduates to place themselves realistically in an organizational decision-making context. To check this concern, we examined differences in responses, based on the subjects' levels of prior work experience. Specifically, analyses were repeated for the subset of subjects who had 5 or more years of work experience (45%). Virtually identical patterns were found, suggesting not only that the anticipated inexperience of an undergraduate sample had less of an impact than expected, but also that variations in work experience did not adversely affect the external validity of the results.

Hypothesis Tests

Hypotheses were tested using a 2×2 repeated measures multivariate analysis of variance with two within-subject factors—stigmatization (high, low) and organizational controls (formal, informal)—and three dependent variables (HRM decisions concerning firing, benefits, and confidentiality). Results indicated that there was a significant main effect for stigmatization ($T^2 = 0.15$; $F = 3.40$, $df = 3,68$; $p = .023$), a nonsignificant effect for organizational controls ($T^2 = 0.01$; $F = 0.17$; $df = 3,68$; $p = .92$), and a significant interaction effect ($T^2 = -.19$; $F = 4.30$; $df = 3,68$; $p = .008$). Results are illustrated in Figure 6.2.

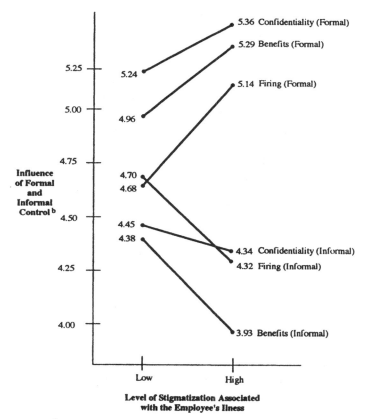

Figure 6.2. The Effect of Stigmatization on Decision Making: Reliance on Formal and Informal Controls

The organizational inertia perspective (Hypothesis 1), which predicted the stable reliance on particular control configurations, was not supported in that no main effect for control types was found.

The pattern of results concerning use of formal control criteria is consistent with the predictions of the two institutional perspectives. Both approaches were consistent in predicting that the reliance on formal control criteria would be higher for high levels of stigmatization than for low levels (Hypothesis 2). Examining each of the three HRM decisions separately, the results provide uniformly consistent support of this prediction for decisions concerning firing ($t = 2.17$, $df = 70$; $p = .033$) and benefits ($t = 2.09$, $df = 70$; $p = .04$), and are nonsignificant but in the predicted direction for confidentiality ($t = 0.69$).

The two theoretical approaches diverged in predicting the effect of stigmatization on the reliance on informal controls, with the traditional institutional approach predicting a positive association (Hypothesis 3a) and the legalistic institutional approach predicting a negative association (Hypothesis 3b). Results support the legalistic perspective over the traditional institutional perspective in that reliance on informal control criteria was uniformly lower when stigmatization was greater. Specifically, reliance on informal cultural control criteria was significantly or marginally significantly lower for decisions concerning firing ($t = -1.97$, $df = 70$; $p = .053$) and benefits ($t = -2.46$, $df = 70$; $p = .034$), and nonsignificant but in the predicted direction for confidentiality ($t = -0.34$).

Exploratory Examination of Different Organizational Types

To further explore the apparent legalistic institutional pattern of responses to stigmatization, we compared the responses of subjects who had been placed in different organization conditions. For subjects in all four organizational conditions, the results show that reliance on formal controls increases and reliance on informal controls decreases for higher levels of stigmatization. As shown in Figure 6.3a, the overall pattern described above was replicated for subjects in legalistic, market, and integrative organizational control types. Although these data are just exploratory, they also suggest that formal decision criteria were relied upon to a greater extent than were informal decision criteria for legalistic ($t = 2.06$, $p = .069$), market ($t = 3.31$, $p = .006$), and integrative organizational conditions ($t = 2.96$, $p = .008$). In contrast, the theoretically predicted pattern (increased use of formal criteria and decreased use of informal criteria) is just as clearly apparent for normative organizations as for the other types (see Figure 6.3b), but the pattern of relative reliance on informal control criteria versus formal criteria was reversed, although not

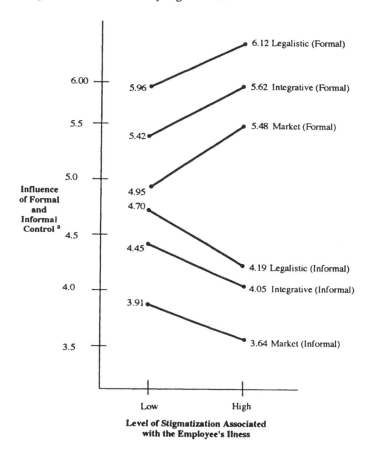

6.12 Legalistic (Formal)

5.96

5.62 Integrative (Formal)

5.42

5.48 Market (Formal)

4.95

4.70

4.45

4.19 Legalistic (Informal)

4.05 Integrative (Informal)

3.91

3.64 Market (Informal)

Influence
of Formal
and
Informal
Control [a]

6.00
5.5
5.0
4.5
4.0
3.5

Low   High

**Level of Stigmatization Associated
with the Employee's Illness**

[a] Influence of formal rules and the influence of informal norms were
each rated on seven point scales, with higher numbers indicating
greater reliance on formal/informal controls in decisionmaking.

Figure 6.3a. Illustration of Common Legalistic Patterns Across Legalistic,
Integrative, and Market Organizations

significantly ($t = -1.01$, ns). While these results provide additional
support for the pattern of responses predicted in Hypotheses 2 and
3b, future research will be required to verify whether these organizational types can be differentiated, based on the patterns of formal and
informal control criteria use found in this exploratory analysis.

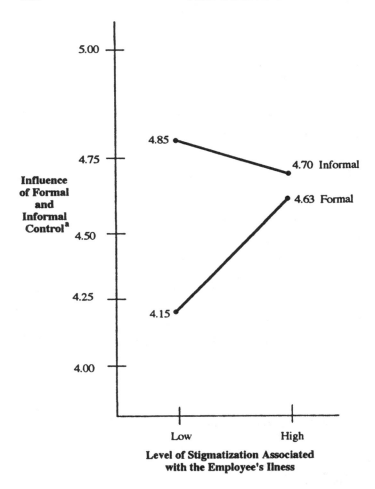

[a] Influence of formal rules and the influence of informal norms were
each rated on seven point scales, with higher numbers indicating
greater reliance on formal/informal controls in decisionmaking.

Figure 6.3b. Illustration of Similar Legalization Effect in Normative
Organizations

■ Discussion

The results of this study advance our understanding of how a threat
to institutional legitimacy—in this study operationalized as the stig-

matization of HIV/AIDS—might lead to the increased use of formal, legalistic responses (i.e., legalization). Stigmatization was found to increase the reliance on formal control mechanisms and to decrease the reliance on informal controls (see Figure 6.2) across organizational conditions (see Figures 6.3a and 6.3b), supporting both new institutional theory (Hypothesis 2) and legalistic theory (Hypothesis 3b).

First, our results provide preliminary empirical support for a legalistic approach to institutional theory, over a more traditional institutional approach or inertial theories. It also provides some guidance for relatively unexplored areas for future research. For example, specific types of institutional responses may need to be compared more systematically than has been recognized. Much of the literature has examined a single type or cluster of legitimacy-enhancing responses that were predicted to move in tandem. Our approach suggests that institutional research could benefit from focusing on the bundling and unbundling of alternative response option sets, since it appears that the use of legitimating responses to institutional threats is not simply additive, but may also involve tradeoffs, complementarities, and contingencies that need further exploration. For example, we found that as threat (stigma) increased, there was a tradeoff between reliance on formal and informal control mechanisms. While this idea has not received much attention in the institutional literature to date, it merits further attention. In addition to using the work reported here as a springboard, future research can build on the earlier work of Ashforth and Gibbs (1990) and Elsbach and Sutton (1992).

Second, legalization is often a positive, protective response to threats to the organization or to individual employees, but it can also have dysfunctional effects for both. On one hand, legal mandates and formal requirements are often designed to ensure fair treatment for workers in difficult circumstances and, thus, are likely to be an important determinant of managerial choice when HRM decisions concern legally protected classes (such as persons with HIV/AIDS). However, when faced with stigmatized issues that could negatively affect the organization itself, decision makers might be more inclined to act in ways that are illegal and/or infringe upon employee rights. Paradoxically, even when adopted to protect employees, reliance on formal mechanisms does not ensure that managers will avoid infringing upon employee rights. Indeed, by adhering to the letter of the law, managers may avoid committing outright illegal acts, but still discriminate against sick employees. For example, managers may carefully watch sick employees' behavior for violations of organization policy and cite those infringements when firing them, even though their initial motivation for firing was illness-related (Sitkin & Roth, 1993b). Thus, the actual uses to which legalistic responses are put needs much closer scrutiny.

Exploratory Results Concerning Organizational Types

As an ancillary part of our focus on the effect of institutional threats (i.e., stigmatization) on legalistic responses, we found that each of the four different types of organizations examined supported the overall pattern found in the data. However, a closer look at this result (see Figures 6.3a and 6.3b) also provides potentially interesting avenues for further investigation. Specifically, we found that subjects representing three of the four organization types used formal control mechanisms to a significantly greater extent than they used informal control criteria—where the only exception was for Normative Organizations.

The argument that there are systematic differences between these types of organizations is supported by the data (see Figure 6.3a) in that the relative ranking of the organization types remained constant across the two types of control and for both routine and stigmatized conditions. These results provide generally supportive evidence for the typologies proposed by Ouchi (1979; 1980) and Lebas and Weigenstein (1986) in the context of HRM decisions concerning catastrophic illness, although future research clearly needs to check these exploratory findings. In particular, our sample reported that their work experience was relatively low in the organization's hierarchy and involved large organizations, both of which could skew the results toward a heavy reliance on formal controls (due to the subjects' relative inexperience, lack of authority, and degree of organizational bureaucratization).

It is also possible that HRM decision making may tend to be more bureaucratic than other types of decision making because HRM decisions are often subject to labor laws, affirmative action requirements, and various contracts that constrain decision makers to rely on (or at least justify their decisions in terms of) formal control mechanisms. Thus, future research could contrast HRM decisions with other types of organizational decisions (for example, marketing, financial, purchasing) to see if our finding of relatively high reliance on formal control mechanisms across organization types generalizes to other types of organizational decisions.

Institutional Organizational Responses to the Threat of Stigma

Expanding the Types of Stigmatization Considered

Future research might explore reliance on formal and informal control mechanisms in decision making about other stigmatized issues. HIV/AIDS is not the only carrier of stigma that organizations confront, and it will be interesting for future studies to examine the dimensions of organizational responses to other types of stigmatization. Relatively little work has been done to date on the topic, but we can speculate on fruitful areas, including the stigmatizing effects of poor performance, sex in the workplace, and criminal or unethical acts.

Sutton and Callahan (1987) have pointed to negative organizational performance (in their case, corporate bankruptcy) as a potentially stigmatizing event. An extension of our analysis to the likely stigmatizing effect of poor organizational performance also would be consistent with the formal, rigid, defensive maneuvers described as the prototypical response to the stigma of failure by Argyris (1985), Hambrick and D'Aveni (1988), Sitkin (1992), and Staw et al. (1981).

Another possible avenue for future research on stigmatization in organizations would be to examine romance and sexual relations in the workplace, which has in recent years begun to draw more scholarly attention (e.g., Hern, Sheppard, Sheriff-Tancred, & Burrell, 1989). The (largely negative) publicity and vague sense of scandal that surround sexual liaisons in the workplace suggest that some degree of personal and institutional stigmatization may be present. As the Mary Cunningham/William Agee case at Bendix (Cunningham, 1984) suggests, although such affairs may not be fatal in a literal sense, the sullying of a professional reputation or the termination of employment that often follows the revelation of an office liaison can be fatal for the career aspirations of a would-be fast-tracker.

Stigma research could also be extended to examine corporate crimes and ethics breeches that can sometimes exhibit stigma-like characteristics. In fact, an emphasis on publicity as a deterrent to corporate crime (Fisse & Braithwaite, 1983) suggests the potentially tainting effect of being identified with criminal actions.

Other Considerations in Studying Stigma in Organizations

In addition, future research might investigate actual organizational behavior, rather than relying on experimental data. Although this study was designed to maximize external validity by linking experimental manipulations to individual work experience, nonetheless the results should be viewed as preliminary until additional research examines how such decisions are made in organizations that have encountered stigma-related decisions, such as how to respond to employees with HIV/AIDS. Although there have been a number of surveys of how businesses have responded to AIDS in the workplace (Mitchell, 1990; Myers & Myers, 1987), these surveys have been too general to be useful for theory development or theory testing. An essential next step is examine the effect of key organizational, decision maker, and situational characteristics on how specific cases are being handled.

For example, it is possible that Meyer's (1982) analysis of "jolts" would only be applicable to contexts for which HIV/AIDS or other stigmatized issues actually represent a jolt-like threat to the organization's viability, since under other circumstances the potential impact of the threat may be construed as minor, and therefore treated as routine. Thus, future research should look for environmental or organizational attributes that would lead the threat to be more or less of a jolt for a particular organization or set of organizations. Following this logic, we might examine whether an organization has to take into account the concern of its employees, customers, or regulators in dealing with threatening issues.

Implications of HIV/AIDS for Organization Effectiveness

As HIV/AIDS becomes more widespread, and improved drug therapies increase the number of years that infected employees are able to work, more organizations will be faced with the issues associated with catastrophic illness and the stigmas associated with HIV/AIDS. Our research suggests that although organizations differ somewhat in their responses to employees with this illness, many will rely to a great extent on legalistic responses designed to protect the organizations from lawsuits and the employees from discrimination.

Are such legalistic responses the most effective? Legalistic responses to employees with catastrophic illness have several liabilities (Sitkin & Roth, 1993a, 1993b), including: (a) they do not address the emotional needs of sick employees or their coworkers; and (b) in the presence of stigma, loopholes can be found to circumvent the protective intentions of the formal policies and procedures—with the potential effect of hurting both affected employees and the organization as a whole. However, our results suggest that formal mechanisms may be used in conjunction with informal mechanisms. To the extent that informal mechanisms provide a supportive rather than an exclusionary environment, informal responses, when used *in conjunction* with highly formalized, legalistic responses, may provide the best possible response for both employees and the organization. If organizations can recognize and counteract the tendency to increase legalization *at the expense of* informal support, perhaps the harmful effects of stigmatization can be ameliorated—at least in organizational contexts. While it is unfortunate that scholars cannot at this time offer many specifics about the effects of stigmatization or how to alter them, recent attention to this issue at least provides hope that in the future we will more fully understand the role of stigma as a determinant of legalization, and perhaps be able to tailor organizational responses to maximize the benefits and minimize the liabilities of legalization.

■ References

Abzug, R., & Mezias, S. J. (1993). The fragmented state and due process protections in organizations: The case of comparable worth. *Organization Science, 4*(3), 433-453.

Argyris, C. (1985). *Strategy, change and defensive routines*. Boston: Pitman.

Ashforth, B. E., & Gibbs, B. W. (1990). The double-edge of organizational legitimation. *Organization Science, 1*(2), 177-194.

Berger, P. L., & Luckmann, T. (1967). *The social construction of reality*. Garden City, NY: Anchor Books.

Black, D. (1989). *Sociological justice*. New York: Oxford University Press.

Burns, T., & Stalker, G. M. (1961). *The management of innovation*. London: Tavistock.

Cunningham, M. (1984). *Power play: What really happened at Bendix*. New York: Simon & Schuster.

Daft, R. L., & Weick, K. E. (1984). Toward a model of organizations as interpretation systems. *Academy of Management Review, 9*, 284-295.

DiMaggio, P. J., & Powell, W. W. (1991). Introduction. In W. W. Powell & P. J. DiMaggio (Eds.), *The new institutionalism in organizational theory* (pp. 1-38). Chicago: University of Chicago Press.

Dobbin, F. R., Edelman, L., Meyer, J. W., Scott, W. R., & Swidler, A. (1988). The expansion of due process in organizations. In L. G. Zucker (Ed.), *Institutional patterns and organizations: Culture and environment* (pp. 71-98). Cambridge, MA: Ballinger.

Douglas, M. (1966). *Purity and danger: An analysis of the concepts of pollution and taboo*. New York: Penguin.

Edelman, L. (1990). Legal environments and organizational governance: The expansion of due process in the workplace. *American Journal of Sociology, 95*, 1401-1440.

Ellsbach, K. D., & Sutton, R. I. (1992). Acquiring organizational legitimacy through illegitimate actions: A marriage of institutional and impression management theories. *Academy of Management Journal, 35*(4), 699-738.

Feldman, M. S., & March, J. G. (1981). Information in organizations as signal and symbol. *Administrative Science Quarterly, 21,* 171-186.

Fisse, B., & Braithwaite, J. (1983). *The impact of publicity on corporate offenders.* Albany: State University of New York Press.

Glick, W. H., Huber, G. P., Miller, C. C., Doty, D. H., & Sutcliffe, K. M. (1990). Studying changes in organizational design and effectiveness: Retrospective event histories and periodic assessments. *Organization Science, 1,* 293-312.

Goffman, E. (1963). *Stigma: Notes on the management of spoiled identity.* Englewood Cliffs, NJ: Prentice-Hall.

Gray, A. (1989). The AIDS epidemic: A prism distorting social and legal principles. In P. O'Malley (Ed.), *The AIDS epidemic: Private rights and the public interest* (pp. 227-249). Boston: Beacon.

Gutek, B. A. (1993). Sexual harassment: Rights and responsibilities. *Employee Responsibilities and Rights Journal, 6*(4), 325-340.

Hambrick, D. C., & D'Aveni, R. A. (1988). Large corporate failures as downward spirals. *Administrative Science Quarterly, 33,* 1-23.

Hearn, J., Sheppard, D., Sheriff-Tancred, P., & Burrell, G. (Eds.). (1989). *The sexuality of organizations.* Newbury Park, CA: Sage.

Hofstede, G. (1980). *Culture's consequences: International differences in work-related values.* Beverly Hills, CA: Sage.

Jasanoff, S. (1985). The misrule of law at OSHA. In D. Nelkin (Ed.), *The language of risk: Conflicting perspectives on occupational health* (pp. 155-177). Beverly Hills, CA: Sage.

Jones, E. E., Farina, A., Hastorf, A. H., Marcus, H., Miller, D. T., & Scott, R. A. (1984). *Social stigma: The psychology of marked relationships.* New York: Freeman.

Kiesler, S., & Sproull, L. S. (1982). Managerial response to changing environments: Perspectives on problem sensing from social cognition. *Administrative Science Quarterly, 27*(4), 548-570.

Kirp, D. L. (1989, May/June). Uncommon decency: Pacific Bell responds to AIDS. *Harvard Business Review,* 140-151.

Kirp, D. L., Epstein, S., Franks, M. S., Simon, J., Conaway, D., & Lewis, J. (1989). *Learning by heart: AIDS and schoolchildren in America's communities.* New Brunswick, NJ: Rutgers University Press.

Lebas, M., & Weigenstein, J. (1986). Management control: The roles of rules, markets and culture. *Journal of Management Studies, 23*(3): 259-272.

Lieberman, J. K. (1981). *The litigious society.* New York: Harper & Row.

Meyer, A. D. (1982). Adapting to environmental jolts. *Administrative Science Quarterly, 27,* 515-537.

Meyer, J. W. (1983). Organizational factors affecting legalization in education. In J. W. Meyer & W. R. Scott (Eds.), *Organizational environments: Ritual and rationality* (pp. 217-232). San Francisco: Jossey-Bass.

Meyer, J. W., & Rowan, B. (1977). Institutionalized organizations: Formal structure as myth and ceremony. *American Journal of Sociology, 83,* 340-363.

Meyer. J. W., & Scott, W. R. (Eds.). (1983). *Organizational environments: Ritual and rationality.* San Francisco: Jossey-Bass.

Miles, R. E., & Snow, C. C. (1978). *Organizational strategy, structure, and process.* New York: McGraw-Hill.

Mitchell, J. (1990). The management of the AIDS crisis in the workplace: A survey of employers in New York City. *Industrial Crisis Quarterly, 4,* 63-74.

Mintzberg, H. (1977). *Structure in fives*. Englewood Cliffs, NJ: Prentice-Hall.

Myers, P. S., & Myers, D. W. (1987, April). AIDS: Tackling a tough problem through policy. *Personnel Administrator*, 95-108.

Nonet, P., & Selznick, P. (1978). *Law and society in transition: Toward responsive law*. New York: Harper.

Oliver, C. (1991). Strategic responses to institutional processes. *Academy of Management Review, 16*(1), 145-179.

Ouchi, W. G. (1979). A conceptual framework for the design of organizational control mechanisms. *Management Science, 25*(9), 833-848.

Ouchi, W. G. (1980). Markets, bureaucracies and clans. *Administrative Science Quarterly, 25*, 129-141.

Page, R. M. (1984). *Stigma*. London: Routledge & Kegan Paul.

Pfeffer, J., & Baron, J. M. (1988). Taking the workers back out: Recent trends in the structuring of employment. In B. M. Staw & L. L. Cummings (Eds.), *Research in Organizational Behavior* (Vol. 10, pp. 257-303). Greenwich, CT: JAI Press.

Powell, W. W., & DiMaggio, P. J. (Eds.). (1991). *The new institutionalism in organizational theory*. Chicago: University of Chicago Press.

Price, J. L., & Mueller, C. W. (1986). *Handbook of organizational measurement*. Marshfield, MA: Pitman.

Ross, M. (1988). Components and structures of attitudes towards AIDS. *Hospital and Community Psychiatry, 39* (12), 1306-1308.

Rowe, M. P., Russell-Einhorn, M., & Baker, M. A. (July-August, 1986). The fear of AIDS. *Harvard Business Review*, 28-36.

Salancik, G. R. (1977). Commitment and the control of organizational behavior. In B. M. Staw & G. R. Salancik (Eds.), *New directions in organizational behavior* (pp. 1-54). Chicago: St. Clair Press.

Scott, W. R. (1987). The adolescence of institutional theory. *Administrative Science Quarterly, 32*(4), 493-511.

Selznick, P. (1949). *TVA and the grassroots*. New York: Harper.

Selznick, P. H., Nonet, P., & Vollmer, H. (1969). *Law, society, and industrial justice*. New York: Russell Sage.

Shklar, J. N. (1964). *Legalism*. Cambridge, MA: Harvard University Press.

Sitkin, S. B. (1992). Learning through failure: The strategy of small losses. In B. M. Staw & L. L. Cummings (Eds.), *Research in Organizational Behavior* (Vol. 14, pp. 231-266). Greenwich, CT: JAI Press.

Sitkin, S. B, & Bies, R. J. (1993). The legalistic organization: Definitions, dimensions, and dilemmas. *Organization Science, 4*(3), 345-351.

Sitkin, S. B, & Roth, N. L. (1993a). The limited effectiveness of legalistic remedies for trust/distrust. *Organization Science, 4*(3), 367-392.

Sitkin, S. B, & Roth, N. L. (1993b). Legalistic organizational responses to catastrophic illness: The effect of stigmatization on reactions to HIV/AIDS. *Employee Responsibilities and Rights Journal, 6*(4), 291-312.

Sontag, S. (1979). *Illness as metaphor*. New York: Vintage/Random House.

Sontag, S. (1988). *AIDS and its metaphors*. New York: Farrar, Strauss, & Giroux.

Staw, B. M., & Ross, J. (1987). Behavior in escalation situations: Antecedents, prototypes, and solutions. In B. M. Staw & L. L. Cummings (Eds.), *Research in organizational behavior* (Vol. 9, pp. 39-78). Greenwich, CT: JAI Press.

Staw, B. M., Sandelands, L. E., & Dutton, J. E. (1981). Threat-rigidity effects in organizational behavior: A multilevel analysis. *Administrative Science Quarterly, 26*, 501-524.

Sutton, R. I., & Callahan, A. L. (1987). The stigma of bankruptcy: Spoiled organizational image and its management. *Academy of Management Journal, 30,* 405-436.

Weber, M. (1947). *The theory of social and economic organization.* New York: Free Press.

Weiner, B., Perry, R., & Magnusson, J. (1988). An attributional analysis of reactions to stigmas. *Journal of Personality and Social Psychology, 55,* 738-748.

Wood, R., & Bandura, A. (1989). Social cognitive theory of organizational management. *Academy of Management Review, 14,* 361-384.

Yudof, M. G. (1981). Legalization of dispute resolution, distrust of authority, and organizational theory: Implementing due process for students in the public schools. *Wisconsin Law Review, 1981*(5), 891-923.

7

The Threat of Legal Liability and Managerial Decision Making:
Regulation of Reproductive Health
in the Workplace

Donna M. Randall

Douglas D. Baker

I magine that you were a manager in the Bunker Hill Company, a large mining firm in Kellogg, Idaho, which operated a zinc refinery, fertilizer plant, and lead smelter. In mid-April 1975, a physician on contract with your company attended a lead industries conference and was advised by a small number of nationally known experts to encourage the company to remove female employees from smelter jobs. If a female employee became pregnant, the fetus might be exposed to lead. However, the exact level and length of exposure necessary to cause damage was unknown. You also did not know if the substance affected the reproductive abilities of male workers. If you restricted the employment of pregnant women or women of childbearing age, you might have been accused of interfering with their right to equal employment, opening the firm to charges of discrimination. Conversely, if you allowed fertile women to continue to work around the substance, and reproductive damage did occur, a child harmed from fetal exposure to toxic substances could bring a personal injury suit against the company. You were told that parents could not legally waive the right of a fetus to sue for damages in the future, and a deformed child, alleging the cause of a congenital deformity as workplace exposure of the mother, might be awarded a multimillion-dollar judgment.

Managers in such complex and dynamic decision environments, as portrayed above, were confronted with a host of rather amorphous and nonquantifiable ethical, economic, legal, political, social, and medical issues. The looming threat of legal liability demanded that they somehow grapple with those issues. How can managers, at the same time, meet the seemingly contradictory goals of providing equal employment opportunities for female workers, protecting the privacy of employees' reproductive status, safeguarding fetal health, and protecting the economic viability of the firm? How can the interests of the fetus, male and female employees, the organization and its stakeholders, and larger society simultaneously be met?

Faced with the situation described above, managers of the Bunker Hill Company felt great pressure to take immediate action and decided to implement a "fetal protection policy." This policy required all female employees of childbearing age, who wished to work in areas of the company with toxic exposures, to either be surgically sterilized or medically demonstrate infertility (Randall, 1985). The data for the case study were gathered through personal interviews, mail surveys, and telephone interviews with Bunker Hill managers, local and national union leaders, male and female employees of the Bunker Hill Company, interest group members, and federal and state regulatory agencies (see Randall, 1982, 1985, for further information on the case study and the methodology used).

In the following section, we first provide a background on the complex and uncertain decision environment faced by the Bunker Hill managers. We then use this case to illustrate how managers dealt with this complexity at the individual and institutional level. The inherent problems with these micro- and macro-level solutions to complexity are then examined. Finally, we discuss implications for managerial decision making and offer tentative prescriptions for managers faced with the threat of legal liability in complex and dynamic environments.

■ The Bunker Hill Company Case Study

Scientific and Regulatory Environment

Toxic workplaces contain occupational hazards that are known to be, or are suspected of being, detrimental to the health of workers (e.g., lead, cotton dust, ionizing radiation, and coal dust). Over the past two decades, managers in toxic workplaces have been faced with an increasingly salient problem: how to react to the threat of legal liability for reproductive damage due to toxic exposures in the workplace. The problem is reaching crisis proportions. In 1985, the federal Centers for Disease Control called reproductive failure a widespread and serious problem and labeled it one of the 10 most prevalent work-related diseases (Marshall, 1987). In addition, the government estimated that 15 to 20 million jobs in the United States expose workers to chemicals that might cause reproductive injury (Marshall, 1987).

Despite the seriousness of the problem, the National Research Council estimated that only 6% of all chemicals in commercial use have been tested for their effects on reproduction (Marshall, 1987). Due to a lack of clear medical evidence, the Occupational Safety and Health Administration (OSHA) developed regulations for only 53 of the 145 chemicals listed as carcinogenic in the National Toxicology Program's annual report. Standards for 36 of these 53 chemicals were developed 15 years earlier, and without consideration of their carcinogenic effects ("OTA Blasts OSHA," 1987).

Moreover, the relative susceptibility of male and female workers to toxic exposure is unclear. While there is a relative abundance of animal studies on the effects of toxins on the development of the embryo/fetus due to the exposure of females, there is a dearth of information on male exposure (U.S. Congress, 1985). Similarly, the research on the human reproductive effects of occupational exposure is much more extensive on women than men (Bertin & Henifin, 1987; Walsh & Kelleher, 1987).

Despite the relative lack of research on the effect of toxins on the male reproductive system, an OSHA study concluded that of the 26 chemicals identified as dangerous for women of childbearing age, 21 may also cause male infertility or genetic damage (Marshall, 1987). Exposure of men to toxic chemicals may cause mutations in sperm; sperm deformities; and reduction in sperm numbers, movement, and sexual behavior (Bertin, 1986). Dr. Anthony Robbins, director of the National Institute for Occupational Safety and Health contended, "There is no reason a priori to believe that the genetic material of a male worker is in any way more resistant to toxic occupational injury than that of a female" (Rawls, 1980, p. 29).

In addition to scarce epidemiological evidence on the effects of toxins on both male and female employees, there was uncertainty about the position of regulatory agencies. In some cases, existent regulations even appeared to be contradictory. For instance, the Occupational Safety and Health Act of 1970 charged employers with the responsibility for providing a safe and healthy workplace. To protect the reproductive capabilities of female employees, an employer could elect to exclude fertile female employees to protect potential offspring. Yet, in doing so, employers might violate Title VII of the Civil Rights Act of 1964, in which workers are given a right to equal employment opportunity (Hyatt, 1977).

Bunker Hill Actions

In mid-April 1975, Bunker Hill managers had no conclusive evidence that a serious problem existed at its smelter or that the company would be held liable for fetal damage. However, within days of being advised by the company physician not to employ women of childbearing capacity around lead, Bunker Hill managers, in consultation with legal counsel, designed and announced a fetal protection policy. The policy required all female employees of childbearing age (from 15 to 45) in toxic work areas, who desired to keep their position, to be surgically sterilized or to medically demonstrate infertility (Randall, 1985). At least three women underwent sterilization procedures within the following 3 months so that they would be allowed to return to their jobs (Randall, 1985).

Male employees were allowed to stay in toxic work areas. Bunker Hill managers maintained that while there had been research on the effects of lead on the female reproductive system, there was "no clear evidence one way or the other on whether lead affects the reproductive abilities of men" (Randall, 1982, p. 107). A vice president of the company explained, "I'm waiting for the 'great white phantom' to tell me what to do about lead exposures to male workers. When the medical evidence comes in showing that lead is harmful to men, the company will do something" (Randall, 1982, p. 107). Further, a manager at Bunker Hill explained that the company could not very convincingly deny a maternal link to the damaged child (as the maternal link is incontestable), but could call into question, or at least cast doubt on, the paternal linkage to the child. Managers maintained that this extra burden of proof would weaken the chances of a lawsuit initiated by a male worker being successful (Severo, 1980).

The fetal protection policy at Bunker Hill was adopted without extensive consideration of alternatives. Yet, a number of other options, though each with certain limitations, were available at the time. For instance, employers could have sought to reduce exposure to suspected hazards, eliminate those hazards, introduce technological improvements, introduce engineering controls, provide protective clothing for employees, implement job rotation to nonexposed or lower-exposed jobs, monitor female workers for pregnancy, use voluntary medical removal and transfer programs, offer medical disability leave during pregnancy, or could have simply taken no action.

Few of these alternatives to fetal protection policies were explored in any depth by Bunker Hill managers. For instance, technological modifications were quickly dismissed by Bunker Hill managers as infeasible (Randall, 1985). Yet, critics of fetal protection policies contended that technology existed at the time to economically engineer jobs so that they were not hazardous; the only problem was that the technology was perceived to be expensive to implement (Hyatt, 1977; Weiksnar, 1976).

Bunker Hill's fetal protection policy was met with significant resistance. In April 1975, female employees contacted a civil rights lawyer and, through their local union, requested an investigation by the International Office of the United Steel Workers of America (USWA). These actions proved to be ineffectual. In the fall of 1975, the Idaho Human Rights Commission investigated Bunker Hill's policy and drew up a "Memor-andum of Understanding" (which the company reportedly refused to sign). Eighteen female employees of Bunker Hill then filed sex discrimination charges with the Equal Employment Opportunity Commission (EEOC) and, in March of the following year, the EEOC nego-tiated a settlement for all women affected by the policy (in which the women were reimbursed for lost wages).

In April 1980 an OSHA representative investigated the Bunker Hill policy and in September of that same year issued a citation against the company for maintenance of the policy. The citation was dismissed in July 1981 (Randall, 1985). Despite the number and variety of complaints from employees, interest groups, and regulatory agencies, Bunker Hill managers did not review any of the other plausible options, nor did they reconsider or revise the fetal protection policy.

Using the Bunker Hill case as a backdrop, we now turn to an exploration of some of the inferential strategies that may have led managers to react as they did to the perceived threat of legal liability.

■ Managerial Inference Strategies

As described in the case above, managers in toxic work environments were faced with a variety of vague, incomplete, and seemingly contradictory stimuli. When confronted with such a complex environment, as that presented to Bunker Hill managers, it is unlikely that individuals will be able to perceive, attend to, and appropriately weigh all the environmental cues (Simon, 1947). Further, it is unlikely that decision makers will explore a full range of alternative courses of action and develop a complete utility ordering for the consequences of those actions (Hogarth, 1980). Instead, individuals will rely on judgmental heuristics and implicit theories to help them reduce complex, inferential tasks to simple, judgmental operations (Tversky & Kahneman, 1974). However, these cognitive mechanisms used to reduce complexity, when misapplied, can lead to erroneous conclusions (Nisbett & Ross, 1980). Some of these inferential problems are examined below.

Judgmental Heuristics

Judgmental heuristics are cognitive strategies that allow individuals to solve a variety of inferential tasks, such as deciding what environmental stimuli to attend to and how to weight the importance of those stimuli (Nisbett & Ross, 1980; Tversky & Kahneman, 1974). For example, people tend to employ an availability heuristic. That is, they perceive, remember, and employ information that is easily accessible. Potentially, the use of this heuristic can be overextended and can lead individuals to overestimate the importance of easily available information. Further, individuals often do not search for representative information once they have received easily available information. Thus, their estimates of sample characteristics or causal relations may be biased.

A factor affecting the use of the availability heuristic is the vividness of the information (Nisbett & Ross, 1980; Taylor & Fiske, 1978). Vivid information tends to be emotionally interesting, concrete, and image provoking, as well as temporally and spatially proximate. Thus, vivid information may be overrepresented when managers are making decisions because it is more likely to be cognitively available, while aggregate, statistical data may be ignored because such data often lack concreteness and emotional interest. Such vivid information may affect the decision frames managers employ as they identify problems and search for solutions (Beach & Mitchell, 1990).

The attention of organizational decision makers at Bunker Hill was drawn to the vivid possibility of astronomically large civil or criminal lawsuits for corporate actions. This was due to both how the problem was presented to them and by U.S. society's "litigation mentality" (Bies & Tyler, 1993). Media coverage of lawsuits, personal knowledge of legal actions, and pending legal action all made the threat highly concrete and proximate in both the memory and perception of managers (Fischhoff, Lichtenstein, Slovic, Derby, & Keeney, 1981). Extensive publicity had been given to personal injury verdicts in product liability cases (U.S. Congress, 1985). As Wildavsky (1988) noted, corporations have been confronted with personal injury lawsuits involving billions of dollars in claims; many of these have been won outright, while others have been settled with substantial compensation. One court has suggested, "In today's litigious society, the potential for litigation rests in almost every human activity" (*Hayes v. Shelby Memorial Hospital*, 1984).

While the threat of litigation may be overstated, and a "liability paranoia" may exist in the United States (Robinson, 1979), managers are still well advised to look both within and beyond the boundaries of their firms to assess legal consequences of their decisions before taking action. As such, legalistic concerns exert an increasing influence on internal organizational processes (Sitkin & Bies, 1993).

As the case of Bunker Hill illustrates, the threat of legal liability for fetal harm through maternal exposure, raised by a physician on contract to the company, presented a highly vivid cue to management. The possibility of a deformed child in front of a jury, alleging maternal exposure to toxic chemicals, was an image-provoking possibility. At Bunker Hill, as elsewhere, managers were highly fearful of lawsuits due to the toxic exposure of fertile women in the workplace (Robinson, 1979). Yet, by being so focused on this vivid cue, they appeared to be blinded to other potential legal threats (e.g., stemming from gender discrimination or from genetic harm to the male reproductive system) and thus failed to search for alternative solutions (e.g., cleaning the environment or monitoring actual lead levels) (Randall, 1987). Concerned about the immediate protection of the firm from legal liability, such temporally distant outcomes as sex discrimination lawsuits may be devalued or discounted by management (Kahneman & Tversky, 1979).

Managers at Bunker Hill adopted the fetal protection policy within days of learning of potential corporate liability (Randall, 1985). The rapid adoption of such policies may indicate that decision makers had preexisting belief systems, which they used to filter data and to make causal inferences. The effects of such knowledge structures are discussed below.

Knowledge Structures

Knowledge structures, like judgmental heuristics, are an inferential tool that allow individuals to process information. A knowledge structure contains preconceptions, beliefs, and ideologies about the environment (Nisbett & Ross, 1980) and allows individuals to define and interpret their physical and social world. The schemas contained in knowledge structures provide interpretive knowledge that helps to frame experiences and to anticipate events (Cantor, 1990). These preexisting beliefs and theories influence what individuals perceive and remember. For example, information that matches current beliefs is perceived and added to memory to bolster existing theories, while disconfirming evidence is not often sought, or is filtered out if presented (Hogarth, 1980). As with any human knowledge structures, these underlying belief systems are resistant to change (Nisbett & Ross, 1980).

When confronted with ambiguous stimuli, such as that presented by the threat of legal liability for fetal exposure to toxic chemicals, managers can rely upon these knowledge structures to guide their perceptions, to help them define problems, and to help them build standardized solutions. Moreover, if those ideologies and beliefs are firmly held, managers can seek out and create data to support their convictions (Beyer, 1981).

At the Bunker Hill plant, as at other mining enterprises, equal employment legislation helped open doors for the employment of women in jobs traditionally filled by men. Yet, a lingering belief remained among both Bunker Hill miners and managers that women simply did not belong there (Randall, 1982).

Traditionally, there were few women production workers at Bunker Hill. Women were viewed as too weak for the difficult work, and their employment was viewed as taking work away from men who needed it. For years, special protective legislation restricted the employment of women across a number of U.S. corporations, justified on the basis of women's "special role as childbearers and guardians of home and family" (Bertin & Henifin, 1987, p. 105). Similar to managers in other companies, Bunker Hill managers expressed reservations about hiring women to work around toxic substances and strongly resisted their employment (Randall, 1985).

In 1972 the company opened production jobs to women in response to pressure from the EEOC. Between 1972 and 1976, 45 women were hired as production workers out of a total work force of approximately 2,100. Thirty of these women were assigned to the lead smelter, and

15 to the zinc smelter, where they also were exposed to lead. During the early 1970s newly hired women at Bunker Hill reported significant resistance by coworkers and management to their employment (Randall, 1982). They continued to be excluded from certain positions, such as underground mining operations, due to their gender and the nature of the work.

Thus, although the development of fetal protection policies was rationalized as being driven solely by a fear of legal liability, characteristics of fetal protection policies hint at an underlying theme of sexism. As "cultural outsiders" (Sitkin & Roth, 1993), women were stigmatized in this setting, and legalistic influences provided management greater protection. Preconceptions may have led to the policy's narrow concern about the female reproductive system, to limited information and choice given to women affected by the policy, and to a refusal to accept alternative forms of birth control over sterilization.

Indeed, management may have conveniently framed the problem (Kahneman & Tversky, 1979) as a concern with legal liability, because such a concern is clearly a more respectable guise for the exclusion of women from toxic work environments. Just as "scientific objectivity" often conceals the values embedded in many diagnostic tests (Nelkin & Tancredi, 1989), a concern for legal liability may also have masked certain values. Critics of fetal protection policies claimed such policies are "a smokescreen laid down by male workers to obscure their self-interest in maintaining full employment for men" ("Do Protective Laws," 1980, p.1).

Critics of fetal protection policies also contended that once gender-based discrimination became illegal, fetal protection policies represented a form of "new protectionism," focused on the fetus (Bertin & Henifin, 1987). Fetal protection policies, like new technologies, are "usually applied in ways that reinforce old convictions and support existing institutional practices" (Nelkin & Tancredi, 1989). Williams (1981, p. 643) questioned, "To what extent will women's recent gains in employment be eroded by new, 'scientifically based' exclusions, which may be a reemergence of the old women's protective legislation in a new and 'respectable' guise?"

Clauss and Bertin (1981, p. 13) noted the stereotypical assumptions underlying such policies: Women are always potentially pregnant and thus must be treated as if they are always actually pregnant; women are unable to prevent pregnancy; women alone are responsible for the health of their offspring; and harm to future children can only occur through maternal exposure. Whatever the label, it appears that existing belief systems played a prominent role in affecting the adoption of the fetal protection policy at Bunker Hill.

When individuals find themselves threatened, they become rigid and risk-averse (Staw, Sandelands, & Dutton, 1981). Despite feedback that beliefs in their knowledge structures might have been questionable, Bunker Hill managers failed to reassess initial assumptions guiding their actions, to view the complaints lodged by stakeholders as at least partially valid, to evaluate the costs that would accrue if messages from these parties turned out to be correct, and to actively search for evidence about the probabilities that messages might prove to be correct.

■ Institutional Environment

In the previous section, we examined a number of individual-level explanations for the adoption of fetal protection policies. We explored how the limits of human cognition in the face of complex decision environments may have led to the adoption of questionable policies. A number of authors have suggested that structural or institutional-level responses also occur in reaction to complexity.

In regard to institutional pressures, DiMaggio and Powell (1983) argued that, when faced with ambiguous goals, uncertainty about the relationship between means and ends, and limitations in knowledge and problem-solving skills, corporations often adopt the organizational structure and policies of those in their immediate environment. More specifically, DiMaggio and Powell identified three forces that lead organizations to have similar structures and policies: mimetic pressures (associated with organizations modeling themselves on other organizations), coercive pressures (resulting from both formal and informal pressures exerted on organizations and by cultural expectations), and professional pressures (stemming from professionalization).

Institutional theorists have argued that environmental complexity and uncertainty are powerful forces that encourage imitation. Modeling provides solutions for organizations, with little immediate inferential energy expense (DiMaggio & Powell, 1983).

Bunker Hill, and many other organizations working with toxic substances, were faced with a complex regulatory environment. Given that governmental regulations (or what DiMaggio and Powell [1983] would call coercive control) were uncertain and sometimes contradictory, organizations had to enact their own policies. Because of the difficulty in developing policies in the ambiguous legal environment, many organizations merely mimicked other companies' fetal protection policies.

When the Bunker Hill Company introduced its fetal protection policy in 1975, it was not the first company to do so, and over the next 15 years, a number of other major companies operating toxic workplaces implemented similar policies. Those companies included Johnson Controls, American Cyanamid, Olin Corporation, Kleberg County Hospital, Shelby Memorial Hospital, Digital Equipment Corporation, Firestone Tire and Rubber, Union Carbide, Monsanto, General Motors, Gulf Oil, Sun Oil, B-F Goodrich, Dow Chemical, DuPont, BASF Wyandotte, Allied Chemical, St. Joseph Zinc, and Eastman Kodak (see Randall, 1985). A spokesperson for Gulf Resources, the owner of the Bunker Hill Company, contended that it was typical in the industry to prevent women who can bear children from working in areas with lead exposure (Harris, 1980).

Many of these policies were not changed until a Supreme Court decision involving Johnson Controls' fetal protection policy (*International United Auto Workers of America et al. v. Johnson Controls, Inc.*, 1991) clarified the legal environment. The 1991 Supreme Court decision dealt with what Judge Frank Easterbrook called "likely the most important sex-discrimination case in any court since 1964." In the case, the United Auto Workers union sued Milwaukee-based Johnson Controls for barring women from holding jobs at 15 car battery plants, where they were exposed to lead, unless they could medically document infertility. Ultimately, the Supreme Court found these policies to be illegal. Thus, mimetic processes seem to have had a powerful effect in ambiguous environments, while coercive forces may be more effectual when the ambiguity has been reduced.

The influence of mimetic and coercive processes was in operation at Bunker Hill. However, it leaves open the question as to why the third type of influence—professional norms—identified by DiMaggio and Powell (1983) had so little influence on the policy outcome. The policy represented the economic and legal interests of the company to the exclusion of ethical and moral concerns. Those ethical and moral concerns are often reflected in professional norms in a way that can ground legal influences into a more balanced view of situational requirements (Sitkin & Sutcliffe, 1991).

The answer may partially lie in Weber's early writings on the ubiquitous characteristics of bureaucracies. In describing the development and inherent problems of bureaucracies, Weber (1930) traced the rise of capitalism and the concomitant bureaucratic structures to the Protestant Reformation. He argued that Protestantism led sect members to dutifully pursue economic gain in their vocational callings. Over time their efforts led to the accumulation of wealth and laid the foundation for the rise of the Industrial Revolution. Ultimately, the wealth created by these activities eroded the ascetic, religious underpinnings of the Protestant organizations. However, the normative religious control systems were no longer needed because they had been supplanted by the rational-legal authority systems of bureaucracies. Such authority systems relied on formal, standardized procedures and policies.

Because of this, Weber warned that modern bureaucracies are largely devoid of any ethical guiding principles. Such a commitment to a legal-rational form of authority tends to depersonalize the world, and workers become content to pursue wealth in their "iron cage" of bureaucracy (Weber, 1930). Quoting from Goethe, Weber (1930, p. 182) warned that a society dominated by bureaucracies will be populated with "specialists without spirit, sensualists without heart . . . this nullity imagines that it has attained a level of civilization never before achieved." Thus, the focus of capitalist organizations shifted. The efficient accumulation of wealth was now seen as the end, rather than the means to a higher moral goal.

Bureaucratic structures, with formalized rules and specialized roles, continue to dominate modern capitalist organizations. The world is inherently complex, and humans must put boundaries upon that to which they attend and upon how they make resultant decisions (March & Simon, 1958). As Nelkin and Tancredi (1989) observed, organizations operate in a constant tension between their economic needs and the rights of employees. Without interpersonal ties to build trust and a common morality framework to guide behaviors, organizations rely on contracts, bureaucratic procedures, and legal requirements as control mechanisms (Sitkin & Roth, 1993). Such control mechanisms provide specific guidance to individuals in uncertain and complex environments. Furthermore, it is often more rewarding for employees to allow the organization to bind their rationality, and simply comply with the prescribed activities (Milgram, 1965). For example, organizational members may increase their power by obediently fulfilling their prescribed roles, thereby proving their loyalty and justifying a future increase in their power (Biggart & Hamilton, 1984).

Thus, faced with an uncertain and complex environment, mimetic influences led Bunker Hill to rely upon a fetal protection policy until coercive influences prevented its use. Professional norms, which could have provided a check on these influences by representing moral and ethical concerns, had little influence on managers at Bunker Hill. Managers were merely following formalized, standardized procedures that have evolved in contemporary bureaucracies to protect their economic interests.

■ Discussion

As the case of Bunker Hill illustrates, the development and implementation of fetal protection policies in toxic work environments can be understood as a function of managers' attentiveness to vivid cues of legal liability, a knowledge structure incorporating certain beliefs about the role of women, an institutional environment promoting impersonal decision making, and a highly uncertain environment encouraging mimetic policy making.

The case also illustrates that, while inferential tools and imitation unquestionably help managers cope with complex and uncertain environments by minimizing computing time and effort, such strategies have their price. Due to the vividness of the threat of legal liability and the prevalent existing belief structures, more abstract and less emotionally involving cues, such as the social, ethical, and psychological impact of such policies, were not given extensive consideration by Bunker Hill management.

The exclusive focus on economic issues and legal threats overshadowed other, equally important concerns (Sitkin & Bies, 1993). "There are a myriad of delicate decisions, made within complex organizations, that require carefully measured judgments, and that are not realistically amenable to formalization—at least not if reasonable decisions are to be made" (Yudof, 1981, pp. 922-923). Selznick (1969, p. 77) warned that bureaucracies are not in the business of dispensing fairness and that "legal decisions may be rigorously controlled by internal criteria of validity, yet substantive justice, as defined by society, may be wanting."

At Bunker Hill, little attention was paid to the social, ethical, and psychological issues. Each of these issues will be briefly considered below.

Social Concerns

If widely adopted, fetal protection policies as developed by Bunker Hill would have a major social impact, particularly in traditionally male-dominated industries such as the lead trade. If women of child-bearing age are not allowed to work where there is lead exposure, almost two of every three female applicants for an estimated 1.3 million jobs would be turned away (Hricko, 1978). As a result of the fetal protection policies that were implemented, women not only lost employment possibilities, but they were also terminated from their jobs, demoted to lower-paying jobs, and lost promotional and career development opportunities. When faced with a substantial cut in income or loss of a job, some women chose to be sterilized in order to remain in those jobs (Brandt-Rauf & Brandt-Rauf, 1986).

As is common in making safety and risk decisions (Wildavsky, 1988), the prohibition of fertile and pregnant women from toxic work environments ignored the potential benefits of allowing women to work in mildly hazardous situations. That is, improved prenatal health care, better housing, and better food associated with continued employment may offset their threats (U.S. Congress, 1985).

Ethical Concerns

The development and use of fetal protection policies also raised thorny ethical issues not fully explored by management, in part because the law provided a sense of confidence and legitimation of their actions. Should a corporation be exerting such direct influence over the reproductive decisions of its workers? Who should determine how the threat of reproductive risk is handled—the mother, the father, the corporation, regulatory agencies, interest groups, or society? Issues such as confidentiality, privacy, workers' rights to know, individual autonomy, and paternalism were overlooked or downplayed by Bunker Hill management in the design of fetal protection policies. Lacking moral guides, managers in bureaucracies stepped in to dictate highly personal decisions regarding fetal health. As a result, fetal protection policies presented women with an Orwellian choice between their reproductive capabilities and their economic security.

Psychological Concerns

Fetal protection policies, such as the one developed by Bunker Hill, also appeared to have significant psychological consequences not addressed by management. The policy was not perceived as fair by a number of stakeholders and had a particularly chilling effect on co-worker and subordinate-superior interactions. Some women at Bunker Hill reported that they felt like "fish in a goldfish bowl"; they experienced a loss of personal control and a loss of trust in management; and they felt coerced to succumb to a sterilization procedure to keep their jobs (Randall, 1982). For those women consenting to sterilization, the policy had an even more exacting price when the plant closed less than 5 years later due to a fall in the price of metals. Thus, the impersonality reflected by fetal protection policies undermined the degree to which organizational goals were aligned with human needs.

In addition to their social, ethical, and psychological problems, fetal protection policies resulted in a formalization paradox (Sitkin & Bies, 1993), in which the effort to reduce legal liability through fetal protection policies appears to have actually contributed to a growing adversarial climate. As Platt (1973) noted, the legal system represents a kind of social trap, in that while it provides numerous short-term benefits, it also poses long-term hazards and unanticipated side effects. If these are ignored, then further litigation may be forthcoming, because informal norms have been transgressed and employees will participate in an increasingly adversarial climate (Sitkin & Bies, 1993). The emphasis of formal rules in superior-subordinate relations may introduce a vicious cycle of legalization and distrust (Shapiro, 1987; Sitkin & Roth, 1993).

For instance, male employees initiated lawsuits. While Bunker Hill managers quickly reacted to the vivid image of lawsuits due to fetal exposure of female workers, they appeared to ignore potential legal threats from male workers. A number of men in various companies, not covered by reproductive risk policies and facing health risks, have subsequently sought relief in court—for a lack of protection (Bertin, 1986). Suits have been filed by men, alleging reproductive damage due to herbicides, pesticides, solvents, and other industrial chemicals (Centers for Disease Control, 1981; Shabecoff, 1979). By developing policies that sought to protect the organization only from lawsuits by offspring of female workers, managers have opened themselves to future litigation from male workers. Fetal protection policies have been subject to court challenges on the grounds of sex discrimination (U.S. Congress, 1985).

In the Bunker Hill case, it is particularly ironic that there was no real threat of legal liability from the fetus and that the development of fetal protection policies actually led to increased litigation. In spite of its vivid possibilities, there was no legal precedent for corporate liability for fetal damage due to exposure of female employees to toxic substances. Indeed, as of 1985, the Office of Technology Assessment (U.S. Congress, 1985, p. 17) contended that "there are no records of any lawsuits brought by the children of exposed women workers." Because workers cannot themselves sue for fetal damage, the Office of Technology Assessment (U.S. Congress, 1985, p. 14) concluded: "Therefore, for the most part, reproductively damaged workers have very limited access to redress against their employers through the courts."

■ Implications

The Bunker Hill Company, like many other firms, adopted fetal protection policies in response to a complex and uncertain environment. When confronted with the threat of legal liability, the firms developed and implemented fetal protection policies. We argued that the reasons for this response can be traced to both the individual and institutional level. What can managers do to minimize the negative consequences of such policies?

At an individual level, managers clearly need prescriptions for overcoming inferential errors. Formal decision tools to aid in information scanning, sampling, data collection, and data analysis, as proposed by writers such as Hogarth (1980) and Nisbett and Ross (1980), should be helpful. While managers at Bunker Hill did not seek to apply such tools, the use of formal decision tools can help overcome problems related to judgmental heuristics such as overattentiveness to vivid cues.

However, the utilities of such formal decision tools are limited by management's knowledge structure. The knowledge structure will continue to dictate how organizational problems are perceived, defined, and resolved. The knowledge structure provides a single-loop learning system, which is "only adequate enough to enable the organization to implement its existing policies and meet its stated objectives" (Argyris, 1978, p. 29). Such a learning system inhibits the detection and correction of errors, and the use of formal decision tools cannot compensate for the use of such learning patterns.

To change management's knowledge structure, managers will need to break away from single-loop learning patterns. They will need to use double-loop learning patterns, which permit questioning and examining of underlying norms, assumptions, and goals behind policies and decisions (Argyris, 1982).

In dealing with issues such as reproductive risk, use of a double-loop learning system would encourage the generation of valid information and make the ethical, social, economic, legal, medical, and political dilemmas raised by the threat of reproductive damage recognizable. Ideologies and beliefs embedded in managers' knowledge structures could be exposed and scrutinized. This, in turn, could create the tension needed to reexamine those structures.

Furthermore, given the inherent complexity of modern organizations, limits to human cognition, and the current institutional environment, organizational decision makers will continue to make mistakes. Often they will resist feedback and related change. What is needed is an organizational structure and culture in which mistakes are tolerated (Sitkin, 1992). Within this context, incremental steps toward problem resolution can be pursued, their effect carefully assessed, and corrective action can ensue (Wildavsky, 1988). It is hoped this will forestall the escalation of commitment to decisions with large-scale, hazardous implications. Yet, even with such an adaptive style, care must be taken in the initial decision making to avoid the occurrence of grievous inferential errors, as discussed in this chapter.

Even if organizations employ formal decision tools and engage in double-loop learning to overcome decision-making flaws at an individual level, the institutional environment of organizations may still exert uncontrollable pressure on decision makers. Organizational decision makers will need to reach beyond their policies and examine the relevant institutional environment.

In complex environments, such as that facing Bunker Hill managers, mimetic pressures encouraged the adoption and spread of fetal protection policies. The case of Bunker Hill illustrated that such policies were ultimately controlled through coercive pressure. Due to the recent Supreme Court decision on the use of fetal protection policies (*International United Auto Workers of America et al. v. Johnson Controls, Inc.*, 1991), which banned the broad use of fetal protection policies, managers in toxic work environments are now being encouraged to craft solutions that take into account the complex web of issues related to reproductive health.

At Bunker Hill, professional norms played a minimal role in influencing the policy outcome. The decision makers were apparently minimally influenced by professional codes of conduct. However, such norms can be powerful. For example, Sitkin and Sutcliffe (1991) provided evidence that professional pharmacists experience competing pressure from both professional and organizational factors. Pharmacists are placed in the dual roles of independent professional practitioner and organizational agent. While individually oriented legal sanctions influenced pharmacists' behavior, legal sanctions aimed at the organization did not significantly influence their behavior. Thus, in uncertain and complex environments, professional organizations have the potential to ensure that ethical and moral issues are addressed in such policy decisions as faced by Bunker Hill managers.

While managers in the current case were responding to the threat of legal liability for reproductive risk, the overwhelming influence of vivid legal cues will likely be felt, in some form, in other controversial decision environments, such as those dealing with sexual harassment suits (Terpstra & Baker, 1992) and the threat of AIDS in the workplace (Napier, 1991; Sitkin & Roth, 1993). Managers in bureaucracies, with high degrees of formalization and specialization, may give little consideration to the ethical and moral implications of policy decisions involving sexual harassment and AIDS. Further, mimetic pressures may encourage firms to adopt and spread less than optimal policies in the uncertain and complex environments surrounding these issues.

To understand policy outcomes in such decision environments, it is important to consider both cognitive limitations of decision makers and institutional level pressure. For instance, Sitkin and Pablo (1992) argued that characteristics of the individual decision maker, characteristics of the organization, and characteristics of the problem are key predictors of risk behavior, mediated by risk perception and risk propensity. Therefore, until a clear regulatory and legal landscape is developed, until individual decision makers seek to employ formal decision tools, and until professional norms incorporate consideration of relevant ethical and social issues, organizational decision makers in highly complex and uncertain environments may continue to develop, enforce, and spread policies that protect the organization legally while ignoring the more amorphous and qualitative ethical, psychological, and social issues.

■ References

Argyris, C. (1978, Spring). Is capitalism the culprit? *Organizational Dynamics*, 21-37.
Argyris, C. (1982). *Reasoning, learning, and action: Individual and organizational*. San Francisco: Jossey-Bass.

Beach, L. R., & Mitchell, T. R. (1990). Image theory: A behavioral theory of decision making in organizations. *Research in Organizational Behavior, 12,* 1-41.

Bertin, J. E. (1986). Reproduction, women, and the workplace: Legal issues. In Z. A. Stein & M. C. Hatch (Eds.), *Reproductive problems in the workplace* (pp. 497-508). Philadelphia: Hanley & Belfus.

Bertin, J. E., & Henifin, M. S. (1987). Legal issues in women's occupational health. In A. H. Stromberg, L. Larwood, & B. A. Gutek (Eds.), *Women and work: An annual review* (Vol. 2, pp. 93-115). Beverly Hills, CA: Sage.

Beyer, J. M. (1981). Ideologies, values, and decision making in organizations. In P. Nystrom & W. Starbuck (Eds.), *Handbook of organizational design* (pp. 166-202). Oxford, UK: Oxford University Press.

Bies, R. J., & Tyler, T. R. (1993). The "litigation mentality" in organizations: A test of alternative psychological explanations. *Organization Science, 4*(3), 352-366.

Biggart, N. W., & Hamilton, G. G. (1984). The power of obedience. *Administrative Science Quarterly, 29,* 540-549.

Brandt-Rauf, P. W., & Brandt-Rauf, S. I. (1986). Ethical aspects of reproductive health in the workplace. In Z. A. Stein & M. C. Hatch (Eds.), *Reproductive problems in the workplace* (pp. 509-515). Philadelphia: Hanley & Belfus.

Cantor, N. (1990). From thought to behavior: "Having" and "doing" in the study of personality and cognition. *American Psychologist, 45,* 735-750.

Centers for Disease Control. (1981). Epidemiologic notes and reports: Reproductive abnormalities in male chemical workers—Kentucky. *Morbidity and Mortality Weekly Report, 30*(17), 199-200, 205.

Clauss, C. H., & Bertin, J. E. (1981). *Brief of the American civil liberties union women's rights project et al., amici curiae.* New York: American Civil Liberties Union Foundation.

DiMaggio, P. J., & Powell, W. W. (1983). The iron cage revisited: Institutional isomorphism and collective rationality in organizational fields. *American Sociological Review, 48,* 147-160.

Do protective laws hinder women on job? (1980, October 26). *Idaho Statesman,* p. 1.

Fischhoff, B., Lichtenstein, S., Slovic, P., Derby, S. L., & Keeney, R. L. (1981). *Acceptable risk.* Cambridge: Cambridge University Press.

Harris, W. (1980, September 16). OSHA fines Bunker Hill on sterility policy. *Metals Daily,* pp. 1, 2.

Hayes v. Shelby Memorial Hospital, 726 F.2nd 1543 (1984).

Hogarth, R. M. (1980). *Judgement and choice: The psychology of decision.* Chichester, UK: John Wiley.

Hricko, A. (1978). Social policy considerations of occupational health standards: The example of lead and reproductive effects. *Preventive Medicine, 7,* 394-406.

Hyatt, J. (1977, August 1). Work safety issue isn't as simple as it sounds. *Wall Street Journal,* p. 1.

International United Auto Workers of America et al. v. Johnson Controls, Inc. 499 U.S. 187 (1991).

Kahneman, D., & Tversky, A. (1979). Prospect theory: An analysis of decisions under risk. *Econometrica, 47,* 263-291.

March, J. G., & Simon, H. A. (1958). *Organizations.* New York: John Wiley.

Marshall, C. (1987). An excuse for workplace hazard. *The Nation, 244,* pp. 532-534.

Milgram, S. (1965, February). Some conditions of obedience and disobedience to authority. *Human Relations,* 57-76.

Napier, B. (1991). AIDS suffers at work and the law. In M. Davidson & J. Earnshaw (Eds.), *Vulnerable workers: Psychosocial and legal issues* (pp. 139-158). New York: John Wiley.

Nelkin, D., & Tancredi, L. (1989). *Dangerous diagnostics: The social power of biological information.* New York: Basic Books.

Nisbett, R., & Ross, L. (1980). *Human inference: Strategies and shortcomings of social judgment.* Englewood Cliffs, NJ: Prentice-Hall.

OTA blasts OSHA as lax in cancer agent control. (1987). *WOHRC News, 8*(4), 1.

Platt, J. (1973). Social traps. *American Psychologist, 28,* 641-651.

Randall, D. M. (1982). *The dynamics of social problem careers: The case of Bunker Hill.* Unpublished doctoral dissertation, Washington State University, Pullman.

Randall, D. M. (1985). Women in toxic work environments: A case study and examination of policy impact. In L. Larwood, A. H. Stromberg, & B. A. Gutek (Eds.), *Women and work: An annual review* (Vol. 1, pp. 259-281). Beverly Hills, CA: Sage.

Randall, D. M. (1987). Protecting the unborn. *Personnel Administrator, 32*(9), 88-97.

Rawls, R. (1980, February 18). Reproductive hazards in the workplace. *Chemical and Engineering News,* p. 29.

Robinson, G. (1979). The new discrimination. *Environmental Action, 10*(20-21), 4-9.

Selznick, P. (1969). *Law, society, and industrial justice.* New York: Russell Sage.

Severo, R. (1980, September 24). Should the firm screen the workplace or the worker? *The New York Times,* p. E22.

Shabecoff, P. (1979, November 9). Union, citing birth defects, asks ban on a herbicide. *The New York Times,* p. A16.

Shapiro, S. P. (1987). The social control of impersonal trust. *American Journal of Sociology, 93,* 623-658.

Simon, H. A. (1947). *Administrative behavior.* New York: Macmillan.

Sitkin, S. B. (1992). Learning through failure: The strategy of small losses. *Research in Organizational Behavior, 14,* 231-266.

Sitkin, S. B, & Bies, R. J. (1993). The legalistic organization: Definition, dimensions, and dilemmas. *Organization Science, 4*(3), 345-351.

Sitkin, S. B, & Pablo, A. L. (1992). Reconceptualizing the determinants of risk behavior. *Academy of Management Review, 17,* 9-38.

Sitkin, S. B, & Roth, N. L. (1993). Explaining the limited effectiveness of legalistic "remedies" for trust/distrust. *Organization Science, 4*(3), 367-392.

Sitkin, S. B, & Sutcliffe, K. M. (1991). Dispensing legitimacy: The influence of professional, organizational, and legal controls on pharmacist behavior. *Research in the Sociology of Organizations, 8,* 269-295.

Staw, B. M., Sandelands, L. E., & Dutton, J. E. (1981). Threat-rigidity effects in organizational behavior: A multilevel analysis. *Administrative Science Quarterly, 26,* 501-524.

Taylor, S. E., & Fiske, S. T. (1978). Salience, attention, and attribution: Top of the head phenomena. *Advances in Experimental Social Psychology, 11,* 249-288.

Terpstra, D., & Baker, D. D. (1992). Outcomes of federal court decisions on sexual harassment. *Academy of Management Journal, 35,* 181-190.

Tversky, A., & Kahneman, D. (1974). Judgment under uncertainty: Heuristics and biases. *Science, 185,* 1124-1131.

U.S. Congress, Office of Technology Assessment. (1985). *Reproductive hazards in the workplace.* Washington, DC: Government Printing Office.

Walsh, D. C., & Kelleher, S. E. (1987). The "corporate perspective" on the health of women at work. In A. H. Stromberg, L. Larwood, & B. A. Gutek (Eds.), *Women and work: An annual review* (Vol.2, pp. 117-142). Beverly Hills, CA: Sage.

Weber, M. (1930). *The Protestant ethic and the spirit of capitalism.* London: George Allen & Unwin. (Original work published in 1904/5).

Weiksnar, M. (1976). To hire or fire: The case of women in the workplace. *Technology Review, 79*(1), 16-18.

Wildavsky, A. (1988). *Searching for safety.* New Brunswick, NJ: Transaction Books.

Williams, W. W. (1981). Firing the woman to protect the fetus: The reconciliation of fetal protection with employment opportunity goals under Title VII. *Georgetown Law Journal, 69,* 641-704.

Yudof, M. G. (1981). Legalization of dispute resolution, distrust of authority, and organizational theory: Implementing due process for students in the public schools. *Wisconsin Law Review, 5,* 891-923.

8

Law, Privacy, and Organizations:
The Corporate Obsession to Know Versus the Individual Right not to Be Known

Mary J. Culnan

H. Jeff Smith

Robert J. Bies

Today, whenever individuals use a credit card, call a toll-free number, enter a sweepstakes, run their "frequent shopper" cards through the scanner at a local grocery store or engage in many other routine activities, they leave their electronic footprints as every detail of these transactions is recorded by one or more computers. This information is often combined with information compiled from public records that reveals, among other things, whether we drive a luxury car or a clunker; our age, height, weight, and marital status; and the purchase price and current assessed value of our home. Advances in computer technology facilitate the collection, use, and widespread sharing of all of this information. For managers working in the competitive global economy, detailed knowledge about individual preferences is increasingly valuable for building relationships with existing customers, targeting prospective customers efficiently, or minimizing the financial risks in establishing a new relationship with a consumer.

As a result, individuals are begining to sense a decline in personal elbowroom, based on perceiving we are unable to control the secondary use of personal information. Secondary information use occurs when information collected for one purpose is used for another purpose. It may be viewed as a privacy invasion when it occurs without the knowledge or the consent of the individual. Recently, these privacy concerns have become the center of a public debate which has at its center conflict between a firm's need to know and the individual's desire not to be known. Consider the following examples:

- Citicorp POS Information Services abandoned a plan to create a massive database of purchase behavior for 25 million to 40 million households. Privacy concerns were cited as one reason for the program's failure, as consumers were unwilling to supply demographic information on themselves (Jaffee, 1992).
- The Lotus MarketPlace: Households was expected to revolutionize the mailing list industry by making names, addresses, summarized demographic, and prior purchase behavior data for 120 million U.S. consumers available on CD-ROM. Some of the data originated in consumer credit reports. Public opposition to the product began building after the product's announcement. Prior to its release, Lotus Development Corporation and Equifax, Inc., announced they were canceling the project, citing the "substantial, unexpected additional costs to address consumer privacy concerns" (Culnan & Smith, 1992).
- American Express announced an agreement with the New York State Attorney General's office, whereby it agreed to inform its customers that it tracked their buying habits and used these data to compile mailing lists that it sold to other companies. Since 1974, American Express had a longstanding policy of notifying its customers of their right to remove their names from any mailing lists (Crenshaw, 1992).
- Citing tough privacy protections imposed by state regulators, Pacific Bell recently announced that it would not offer Caller-ID in California. The State Public Utilities Commission had ruled that the 40% of California households with unlisted telephone numbers would automatically have their numbers blocked from being displayed on the Caller-ID system. Pacific Bell felt that allowing such a substantial number of households to block display of their telephone numbers eroded the value of the service to the point where it was no longer economically viable (Lazzareschi, 1992).

All of these examples share a common theme. That is, they illustrate public concerns about secondary information use and reflect the fundamental tension between personal privacy and legitimate business interests.

■ Forces Making Privacy an Issue

Privacy exists when an individual can make autonomous decisions without outside interference and/or can control the release and subsequent circulation of personal information (Bennett, 1992; Stone & Stone, 1990; Westin, 1967). People often perceive a loss of privacy when their autonomy or control appear to be lost or reduced (Laufer & Wolfe, 1977), or when people's actions are unknowingly structured (Simitis, 1987). As this chapter deals with consumer privacy, privacy is defined as the ability of individuals to control the access others have to personal information about them. Underlying any definition of privacy is an implicit understanding that the individual's interests are balanced with those of society at large. Individuals are willing to surrender a measure of privacy by disclosing personal information in exchange for some economic or social benefit, based on the "calculus of behavior," an assessment of their ability to manage any of the consequences of today's choices in the future (Laufer & Wolfe).

Fair information practices define procedural guarantees, similar to fair trade and labor practices, which allow individuals to balance their privacy interests with an organization's need to gather personal information to support its targeted marketing programs (Bennett, 1992). Fair information practices are based on the following principles: (a) Individuals should have the right to know how organizations use personal information, to inspect their records, and to correct any errors; (b) individuals should have the right to prevent secondary use of personal information if they object to such use; and (c) organizations which collect or use personal information must take reasonable precautions to prevent misuse of the information.

Prior research suggests that, in general, individuals are less likely to perceive information practices as privacy-invasive when (a) information is collected in the context of an existing relationship, (b) they perceive that they have the ability to control future use of the information, (c) the information collected or used is relevant to the transaction, and (d) they believe the information will be used to draw reliable and valid inferences about them (Clarke, 1988; Stone & Stone, 1990; Stone, Gardner, Gueutal, & McClure, 1983; Tolchinsky, McCuddy, Adams, Ganster, Woodman, & Fromkin, 1981; Woodman, Ganster,

Adams, McCuddy, Tolchinsky, & Fromkin, 1982). Medical information and financial information have been documented as being more sensitive than some other types of information (Louis Harris and Associates, Inc., 1990; Stone et. al., 1983; Woodman et. al., 1982). There is, however, no general theory of the specific attributes or characteristics of an information practice and whether that practice is privacy-invasive.

In their dealings with organizations, individuals may first question an organization's motives when they are asked to provide personal information, particularly when the information is perceived as irrelevant to the transaction at hand. The 1990 Equifax survey reported that 90% of the public felt that consumers being asked to provide excessively personal information was a problem. Forty-two percent of the public has refused to provide information to a company because it thought the information was not needed or was too personal, while 30% of the public has decided not to apply for something because it did not want to provide certain kinds of personal information (Louis Harris and Associates, Inc., 1990).

Even if the principle of minimization—collecting only necessary information—applies when individuals are asked to provide information, other problems can emerge during the processing, storage, and use of personal information. These can include both deliberate or accidental errors, unauthorized or improper use, or secondary use without the individuals' knowledge or consent (Culnan, 1993b; Smith, 1993), which are also illustrated by some of the examples at the beginning of this chapter. The 1990 Equifax survey found that 93% of the public believes inaccuracy and mistakes were problems for consumers, 82% believes the sharing of information by companies in the same industry was a problem, and nearly 75% of the public felt that individuals had lost all control over how personal information is circulated and used by companies. Figure 8.1 illustrates the secondary use of personal information for marketing.

■ Historical Perspective

Concerns about privacy are not new and often emerge when the public perceives that information technologies with enhanced capabilities for surveillance, storage, retrieval, and communication of personal information threaten privacy (Clarke, 1988; Gentile & Sviokla, 1990; Mason, 1986; Miller, 1971; Westin, 1967). In their landmark article,

Information
Processing
Activity:

Acquire	1. Profile own customers based on existing transaction data.	2. Acquire new information about existing customers from a third party.	3. Acquire information about prospective customers from a third party.
Use	4. Target own customers for new or repeat business.	5. Market research or cross-market own customers for new business.	6. Target prospective customers for new business.
Transfer	7. Transfer information about own customers within organization.	8. Transfer information about customers to a third party.	9. Transfer information about prospects to other third parties.
	Customer (Internal Info)	Customer (External Info)	Prospect

Relationship with Consumer

NOTE: Information transferred or acquired may include demographic information

Figure 8.1. Dimensions of Secondary Information Use for Marketing

"The Right to Privacy," Warren and Brandeis (1890) first articulated the need to secure for the individual "the right to be left alone." They wrote in reaction to the loss of privacy experienced by the nineteenth-century equivalent to paparrazi—instantaneous photographs and newspapers—but they also expressed concern that numerous mechanical devices were threatening to make true the prediction that "what is whispered in the closet shall be proclaimed from the housetops" (p. 195).

The perceived threats posed by new computerized record-keeping systems helped to bring privacy to the public's attention beginning again in the 1960s (Bennett, 1992). In anticipation of some of the challenges to privacy that these systems would bring, two seminal books were published during this period: Alan Westin's (1967) *Privacy and Freedom,* and Arthur Miller's (1971) *The Assault on Privacy.* In addition, two landmark pieces of legislation, the Fair Credit Reporting Act and the Privacy Act of 1974, were enacted during the 1970s. The Privacy Act established the Privacy Protection Study Commission

(PPSC) to assess the privacy implications associated with the use of computers to process credit reports, banking, insurance and medical records, and mailing lists (PPSC, 1977). A number of western European countries also passed data protection legislation during this period (Bennett, 1992).

In the late 1980s, information privacy again became a public issue, fueled by the coming of age of both database marketing and telemarketing. Media attention to Caller ID/Automatic Number Identification; new applications for Point-of-Sale (POS) systems; and other technologies that promote the collection, analysis, and exchange of detailed personal information, and facilitate the compilation of detailed personal profiles; has caused the public once again to focus its attention on privacy (See for example Buchwald, 1992; Cohen, 1991; Miller 1991). In the 1991 Equifax Survey, 79% of the public expressed concern about threats to personal privacy, compared with 64% of the public in 1978. Nearly 75% of the public felt that individuals had lost all control over how personal information is circulated and used by companies, while a majority of the public often views telemarketing solicitations as an invasion of privacy (Louis Harris and Associates, Inc., 1991).

Consumer privacy has also emerged as a major issue for global firms. The European Community has issued a revised draft directive on data protection that is stricter than the voluntary protections currently implemented by many American companies. As a result, the ability of American firms to continue to either trade openly or establish new business relationships with the European Community after 1992 may be jeopardized if, in the eyes of the Europeans, U.S. laws do not provide an adequate level of privacy protection (Commission of the European Communities, 1990; Flaherty, 1989).

While the majority of industrialized countries have enacted data protection laws, the approaches to data protection vary (Bennett, 1992; Flaherty, 1989). In the United States, privacy laws aim primarily to protect citizens from the government; protecting individuals from abuses by private-sector record holders has been legislated in a very targeted or sectorial manner (Reidenberg, 1992). This is in direct contrast to the European approach, where omnibus data protection laws have been enacted to provide individuals with a set of rights related to private sector record-keeping practices and to provide a basis for the government to protect citizens from abuses in the private sector (Plesser & Cividanes, 1991).

■ Responding to Growing Public Concerns About Privacy: The Case of Direct Marketing

Direct marketing is an example of the escalating tension between an individual's right to privacy and the organization's need to gather and use personal information to more effectively market goods and services. For nearly two decades, the Direct Marketing Association (DMA) has attempted to defend its members against legislation through programs of industry self-regulation.

In 1977 the Protection Study Commission, which was established following passage of the Privacy Act of 1974, issued its final report. The Privacy Protection Study Commission (PPSC) addressed a range of privacy issues across industries, including the privacy issues raised by mailing lists. At the same time, the DMA launched a large-scale "Freedom to Mail" public relations campaign and testified before the commission that privacy concerns could best be addressed through existing programs of self-regulation. The commission concurred with the industry position and, in its 1977 report, recommended against legislation to require an organization engaged in interstate commerce to remove an individual's name from a mailing list upon request. In the mid-1970s, the DMA instituted its Mail Preference Service (MPS) and collected names of consumers who wished to have their names removed from all national mailing lists. The DMA encouraged but did not require its members to match the MPS file against their own mailing lists and remove any names where a match occurred. A 1992 survey of members revealed that about half used MPS (Culnan, 1993a).

Privacy once again became an issue for the DMA in the late 1980s, fueled in part by the entry of the three largest credit bureaus into the list business, by an increase in the amount of unwanted mail received by consumers, and by increasing media and legislative scrutiny of these and other list practices. In 1992 the DMA reported that it was tracking more than 1,000 privacy bills at the state level and 10 proposals for new federal legislation. Much of this pending legislation was characterized as a direct assault on the industry's right to commercial free speech. Privacy was identified as one of the top public policy issues facing the industry, along with environmental and postal concerns.

The DMA launched a number of initiatives to address the privacy issue. In 1988 it formed a Privacy Task Force, which developed a Privacy Action Plan that was announced in 1992. The plan consisted of formal

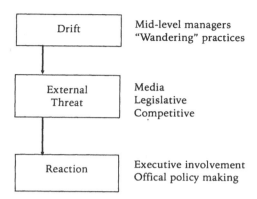

Figure 8.2. Cycle of Organizational Responses

procedures for members to use to assess their own privacy practices, programs for more aggressive self-regulation to ensure member compliance with industry guidelines, member education, and increased lobbying efforts.

In the next section, we review research findings that how organizations in different industries respond to similar public concerns about privacy and the use of personal information for marketing purposes.

■ Organizational Responses to the Privacy Issue: Drift, Threat, and Reaction

In this section, we review the findings of Smith (1993), who used grounded theory methodology (Glaser & Strauss, 1967) to investigate how organizations develop information privacy policies in response to growing public concerns about privacy. His research focused on seven different organizations in four industries: two health insurers, one life insurer, three banks, and one credit card issuer. From the data, Smith observed a three-phase cycle of organizational responses to these public concerns about privacy. These phases are *drift, external threat,* and *reaction,* as can be seen in Figure 8.2.

In the *drift* phase, executives abdicated responsibilities to midlevel managers, who crafted their own sets of practices based on their localized interpretations. This was a time in which pragmatic approaches were taken: If something did not work, it was changed. Even though the issues were value-laden ones, they were usually not viewed that way. Instead, they were perceived as operational or economic in nature.

In the second phase, organizations responded to a perceived *external threat* concerning their collection and use of personal information. This threat often took the form of excessive negative publicity about a marketing practice, as in the case of Lotus MarketPlace: Households (Culnan & Smith, 1992), or legislative scrutiny, as in the case of the hearings held by the House of Representatives on the Fair Credit Reporting Act between 1989 and 1992.

The third phase took the form of an immediate and forceful *reaction* from top executives, who then focused attention on the development of policies and procedures related to personal privacy to which they had previously given short shrift. At this time, an attempt was made to codify existing practices, to give the appearance of having responded to public concerns in a formal, legalistic way.

Depending on the industry, the time frame for this three-phase cycle could be as short as several months—in the case of one life insurer's approach to handling of AIDS test data—or of a length that is still undetermined. For example, at the time of Smith's study, the banks had yet to experience their external threat, so they had not entered their period of reactive policy making and were still engulfed in a period of drift. This three-phase cycle was observed in each of the four industries studied by Smith (1993), as described below. The results of Smith's study are summarized in Table 8.1.

Health Insurance

The experience of both of the health insurance organizations was similar: They had omnibus privacy policy statements—officially codified documents of from two to eight pages, which provided specific guidelines for almost all uses of personal information in the organization—from the early 1980s but had, in the words of one executive, "outgrown [them]." This growth had taken place during the drift stage, as various organizational units had addressed specific items with their own practices. Different work groups perceived societal changes in different ways, and each had modified its own work procedures to accommodate those changes. However, this had not been done in a consolidated fashion—with most decisions being made by midlevel

Table 8.1

Policy Making Cycle

Type of Organization	Drift Stage	External Threat	Reaction
Health Insurance	Disclosure to employers Collection of claim information	Legislative	Task force to create new omnibus policy
Health Insurance	Disclosure to employers Collection of claim information Customer service unit procedures	Legislative	Task force to create new omnibus policy
Life Insurance	AIDS test results	Media Legislative	Industry task forces New internal, official policies
MIB[1]	Database codes for handling AIDS test results	Media Legislative	Task forces Deleted database code Official policies
Credit Cards	Customer data used for marketing, credit decisions Customer data shared with other firms	Media Legislative Competitive	Policy statement circulated for consensus Changes in data use
Bank	Customer data used in targeted marketing Purchasing data about customers Access to customer data	None	None
Bank	Customer data used in targeted marketing Purchasing data about customers Access to customer data	None	None
Bank	Customer data used in targeted marketing Access to customer data	None	None

NOTE: [1]Although not one of the corporate sites in the study, included here for the sake of completeness. See endnote for more information.

managers—so that consistency between units was rarely found. Only when an external threat was perceived did a reactive policy-making process, supported by senior management, come into being.

Drift. A trend toward more competitive marketing of health insurance and an increasing focus on reducing health care costs were complicating the drift stage at both health insurers. The combination of these two forces led to pressures from employers—who served as the insurers' primary customers—to learn more about their employees' medical claims, since their success in reducing their employees' medical costs would ultimately be reflected in lower insurance premiums. Since the insurers were trying to woo the employers in an increasingly competitive environment, there was an incentive to respond positively to the employers' requests for information about their employees' medical conditions and treatments.

Yet the boundaries on such releases of information were not immediately clear. The story of the 1980s had been one of progressive liberalization at both insurers—from a policy of no release of medical information to one in which, with certain accounts at one insurer, employee medical information was exchanged rather freely. The path through the 1980s had not been a smooth one at either health insurer. At one insurer, in a spirit of "improving our responsiveness to [accounts'] concerns," according to one executive, a number of reports were being provided to employers on a monthly basis. But the reports had undergone several iterations of changes, based on their sensitive content, and had created a large amount of confusion. One interviewee, who was close to the process of report refinement, said:

> We have changed the content of these reports so many times that I cannot always remember what is in them. First, we were only going to tell employers the total charges for their companies. Then, we decided it was okay to do it by division, but we would never put any [sensitive medical information] on the reports. But now we're giving out totals in small categories that sometimes only include a few claims, so employers can figure out which employees had which charges, even if we don't explicitly tell them. So, we say we don't give out diagnoses, but I think it could sometimes be figured out. It's been a confusing experience, and I'll be glad when we finally get it all straightened out.

The wandering nature of the drift stage had also led to repeated friction between different groups in the organization. Since boundaries on acceptable and unacceptable uses of data were unclear, different groups had made different interpretations.

External Threat. Although senior management was aware that practices in various units were evolving, there had not been a focus on an overall reevaluation of the omnibus policy until the health insurers perceived an external threat. In late 1989 a state law regarding the handling of AIDS information in the health insurance industry went into effect in one of the states served by both insurers. Although it did not directly affect all of the practices at the health insurers, it served as a shock to force an across-the-board executive reaction. An executive at one of the health insurers remarked:

> We knew then that we would have to reconsider the overall policy in light of the new law . . . not because the law itself was onerous, but because it signalled a shift to us that we needed to think about: What if other states, or the federal government, were to pass more laws? It just kind of shook us up, [and] it also reminded us that there were several organizational units that had developed procedures . . . that were not addressed by our overall policy. We needed to get in a room together and consider where we were all going. The policy needed attention. In fact, it probably needed it several years earlier, but we didn't focus on it until the law was passed.

Reaction. Consequently, task forces of high-ranking executives had been formed to rewrite the policies—which would turn the relatively freewheeling environment of the drift stage into a more legalistic one, with a stronger orientation on new, codified rules. All of the various organizational practices, which had evolved over the past 7 years, were to be considered, and the perceived threat of new laws was to be addressed. As an illustrative example, one of the health insurers found that its task was especially complex because its business operations had expanded geographically since its earlier policy and it had become a quite aggressive marketer of its insurance plans. Since that aggressiveness often led to a greater number of case-by-case decisions, most of which were somewhat liberal in their interpretation of the rules regarding information disclosure, it appeared that its reconsideration of the privacy policies would be quite difficult. The objective of both organizations' efforts was a new omnibus policy statement that reflected an official interpretation of appropriate practices for all organizational areas: underwriting, claims processing, marketing, and so on.

Life Insurance

The same issue, AIDS data, prompted a reaction in the life insurance industry just as it did for health insurers. However, it was the issue of AIDS test data, and not medical claims, that caused the concern.

Drift. The life insurance underwriting process entails the gathering of medical information regarding each applicant for life insurance, so that, based on the individual's health risk, the application can be accepted or rejected and, if accepted, the appropriate premium can be calculated. When tests for the AIDS virus became available, many life insurance companies understandably wished to include those tests in their underwriting process, to store the results in their databases, and to share the results with other life insurers through the industry's shared database, the Medical Information Bureau (MIB).[1] But this testing occurred without a clear set of formalized rules, so that implementation was quite uneven.

External Threat. Only a matter of months after the study's life insurer began performing AIDS tests, the life insurance industry had to confront the issue of negative public and legislative reaction to the collection and storage of AIDS test information. When this happened, the life insurer in the study learned that it had not read the public sentiment correctly. The underwriting director said:

> The stigma of AIDS was very large. People were being fired because they had AIDS. We were attacked on the right to do testing, to use the results in the underwriting process, and to share positive results [with other insurance companies]. . . . A lot of gay advocates started attacking us, and the media picked up on their charges. It was claimed that we were "blacklisting" gay people on the basis of this [test] information. . . . We made a mistake in our early responses. We said "We have handled confidential information for over 100 years, and inappropriate disclosure has never been a problem. Why are you making such a fuss now?" This was thrown back at us with the challenge, "If you say AIDS is like any other disease, you don't understand AIDS."

Calls for additional legislation were made. Various advocacy groups—many, but not all, with roots in the gay community—became more and more aggressive in their tactics.

Reaction. As a result of significant public pressure and legislation—largely based at the state level—the life insurance industry had recrafted its policies regarding handling of AIDS test data. Most of the new policies had been created in industry-wide task forces, in which industry executives and representatives from other interested organizations—health care professionals and gay activists, for example—worked together to consider an acceptable solution to the questions surrounding AIDS test information. "Once we saw what we were up against, we tried to be responsive so as to head off any future problems," said an executive. At the life insurer, new policies were instituted immediately, which some executives deemed "an overreaction." For example, AIDS test results were now hand-delivered to a special doctor at LifeIns, and all the AIDS case files were kept in a special locked cabinet. Special procedures for informing applicants of positive test results had been developed—"an area of special concern," noted an executive, "since the applicant [usually] doesn't know that he or she has the problem."

At MIB, the task forces had resulted in the removal from the database of a code that was used to report "two or more different types of antibody tests indicating exposure to HTLV-III (AIDS) virus." Instead of this code, life insurers were to use a more general code, which meant only an "abnormal blood test for which there is no specific code." MIB's documentation said that this change was made "so that the insurer's need for MIB information can be balanced against the applicant's right to confidentiality."

Credit Cards

Drift. The credit card issuer's approaches to marketing to its cardholders had also evolved during its drift stage, as it had tried to balance an enlightened approach to targeted marketing with a responsiveness to consumers' concerns. The major issues with which the organization had grappled were (a) the proper extent to which cardholders' transaction histories (i.e., what they had purchased) should be used in determining whether to target them for new offers or make credit decisions and (b) to what extent the information about cardholders should be shared with other organizations. The creation of information-handling procedures for such efforts—including questions regarding the appropriate and inappropriate uses of cardholder transaction information—had occurred on a case-by-case basis. Coupled with existing product offerings—sometimes internally and sometimes through selected third parties—the customer base was quickly becoming a source of vast strategic advantage. Managers in this study realized this and had also become aware of consumers' concerns about the use of personal information in some marketing practices. However, no cohesive statement regarding information privacy had been formulated or debated.

External Threat. Until, that is, the organization perceived an external threat: In 1989-1990, media attention to targeted marketing began to increase; the U.S. House subcommittee hearings on the Fair Credit Reporting Act focused on various uses of credit information; and another credit card issuer began to advertise a "privacy protection plan" for its cards, under which it promised, "We will never give your name and number to one of those telemarketing firms." None of the actions seemed to be targeted directly toward the credit card issuer in the study. It was, instead, the "sense of a shift in the overall environment," according to one executive, that prodded an examination of the practices. "The signs are all there," he said shortly thereafter, "and we will only hurt ourselves by ignoring them. Public image, legislation, you name it. Even if we are only on the periphery right now, the *threat* [emphasis added] of our being directly confronted has gotten our attention."

Reaction. The organization assigned to a vice president the responsibility for creating a privacy policy for the organization, and reduced its telemarketing and targeted mailing activities. It also discontinued some sharing of customer names and addresses with outside parties and increased the visibility of its "opt out" campaign, by better informing customers about some marketing practices and giving a toll-free number that cardholders could call to avoid those practices.

Banks

Unlike the insurance companies and the credit card issuer, the banks had not yet encountered an external threat, so they had not yet entered a period of privacy policy making. Even so, the drift stage had been under way for some time.

Drift. The drift was especially visible with respect to the sharing of customer names, addresses, and telephone numbers outside the organization. All of the banks were trying to increase their targeted marketing efforts by choosing small sectors of current or prospective customers for particular offers of products or services. Some early telemarketing efforts at one bank had resulted in a large number of privacy complaints from customers, and new practices had been embraced. Creative uses of existing customer information and purchases of additional demographic information regarding existing customers were also underway.

Also creating some confusion at banks was the level of access to customer data that should be granted to various employees. New computer applications were providing information to tellers and customer service representatives that previously had been available only to specialized bank employees, such as loan officers. In other cases, employees of some departments were being given access to files that were arguably outside the bounds of their responsibilities. A manager said, "Quite frankly, in most cases, a supervisor's saying that an employee needs access is all that is required." Another manager said:

> We are not really consistent on how we manage this. It ebbs and flows. In general, I can say that we do not control access at the level we perhaps could or should. For example, if someone from a certain department (say, loan) says they need to see the checking account information for their customers, they probably wind up with access to all the checking account data for *all* customers. They don't really need that much information, but we don't control their access to customers who aren't their own. . . . There definitely are some privacy implications here.

No attempts to create new, cohesive policies for either targeted marketing or access were evident because the banking industry was receiving little media or legislative attention regarding privacy at the time of the study. Thus, the drift stage was continuing without interruption, with a decidedly nonlegalistic approach to privacy practices. At the time of this study, the bank had yet to enter the threat or reaction stages of policy making.

■ Managing the Privacy Issue Strategically: A Move Toward Legalization

As defined by Sitkin and Bies (1993), legalization is the "diffusion of legalistic reasoning, procedures, and structures to sustain or enhance the legitimacy of the organization . . . with critical internal or external constituencies." The organizational responses identified in the previous section correspond to key dimensions of legalization.

First, the research findings presented in the previous section suggest an increasing development of and reliance on formal, standardized policies and procedures to handle personal information about individuals—a cornerstone of the legalization process (Sitkin & Bies, 1993). For example, in the health insurance industry, organizations created new "codified rules" to handle AIDS information. Legalistic procedures also emerged in the life insurance industry—hand-delivered AIDS test results, AIDS test results kept in locked cabinets, and formalized procedures of how to communicate positive AIDS test results. Finally, one credit card company created a formal mechanism for consumers to "opt out" of its mailing list, as a way to reduce the likelihood of future consumer lawsuits or government regulation.

Second, the data suggest that the privacy issue is beginning to shape managerial actions and decisions as suggested by the formal legalized procedures described above. But even more compelling, these legal ramifications were beginning to influence directly the corporate "mentality" about possible litigation (Bies & Tyler, 1993) and the emergence of new laws that might further constrain organizational freedoms. For example, Smith (1994) found that managers engage in "anticipatory legalization." All uses of information, as described by corporate interviewees, revealed a remarkable respect for the legal boundaries around their business processes. Although some at the banks were unsure at times about the legal prohibitions on certain uses of customer information—and at times even asked the interviewer whether he could tell them about the law—all expressed a desire to adhere to the law, and many framed their arguments about their policies and practices in terms of their legal prerogatives (e.g., "It's legal for us to buy that information, of course").

It is interesting to note that the corporate commitment was not merely to existing law, but also to the concept of avoiding new laws. On numerous occasions, corporate interviewees noted that they wanted to temper their actions so that "we don't get a lot of new legislation" or "wind up with some onerous regulations." One high-ranking bank executive said:

> If you could tell me which of our current activities would lead to a clamoring for new laws, I'd walk downstairs right now and say, "Stop the project, it's not worth it!" The last thing we need are a bunch of new privacy

regulations on top of the stuff we already have to deal with for [capitalization and real estate guidelines]. I'd give up half of our marketing to avoid having to deal with another OCC-like [entity] picking over everything we do.

An insurance executive said:

> Probably the smartest thing we could do as a company and an industry is to behave so that the legislators think we are the finest, privacy-respecting organizations they have ever seen. I'm not saying that we're doing that today, mind you, but it would be our smartest move. We should act as though our every move could contribute to a legal backlash.

What the corporate interviewees often missed in looking at present and potential laws, however, was the fact that when it comes to information privacy, adhering to the law is only a *necessary* condition for societal acceptability; it is by no means a *sufficient* condition. The law has not kept up with the technical possibilities, and consumers are applying their own sense of right and wrong, which often goes beyond the legal dictates. For example, the bankers in the study often argued that buying information about their customers was acceptable because it was legal.

But Smith (1994) also explored the views of consumers via focus groups and interviews. Consumer stakeholders brushed across the legal questions and added their own analysis:

> Maybe there are companies out there that legally sell this demographic information, but I would be pretty mad if I found out my bank was buying information about me. I'm not sure [that I would move my account], but I would certainly complain if I knew they were doing it. It doesn't seem like they're respecting me and my business. There have got to be some banks that realize I don't give them my account so that they can go snoop around behind my back. If I can figure out which banks those are, I might move there. (Smith, 1994)

So, the commitments of corporate executives—to existing law and to the avoidance of additional legislation in their industries—differ greatly from those of many other stakeholders.

■ Conclusion

The pressures on organizations to gather information about consumers is great and growing. For example, organizations need accurate

and in-depth information to make decisions about the creditworthi-
ness of customers and improving the effectiveness of marketing
practices. Indeed, the need for personal information about consumers
is argued to be even greater today, as organizations are under increasing pressure to succeed in a competitive, global marketplace.

Against the backdrop of these pressures on organizations to collect, store, and use greater amounts of information about consumers,
consumers expect their privacy to be protected (Stone & Stone, 1990).
It is an expectation as simple and fundamental as that. This expectation of privacy is also consistent with the norms of society (Bies, in
press).

The opposing forces surrounding the privacy issue highlight the
broader political and social implications of how personal information
is handled. Privacy issues are political in the sense there is the
question of what is the proper balance of individual and organizational interests in the gathering and disclosure of personal information
about consumers. Determining what is the proper balance of interests is not a straightforward rational process; for the balancing of
interests is not only shaped by the push and pull of negotiation by
managers internal to the organization, but also by court cases and
legislative mandates in the larger political-legal environment.

Privacy issues are also political in the sense that they carry implications for organizational governance. From the balancing of interests
and resolution of ensuing conflicts comes the emergence of formalized
procedural safeguards and establishment of rights for individuals
(Selznick, 1969), with correspondent managerial responsibilities and
obligations (Folger & Bies, 1989). The fulfillment of those managerial
responsibilities often requires those in power to make judgments that
attempt to balance the rights-based concerns of individuals with the
organizational interests of efficiency and control, thus further highlighting the political aspects of justice issues. Indeed, as one executive stated: "Where do you draw the line? That's the question. It takes
good judgment and a sense of fair play" (DeGennaro, quoted in Zalud,
1989, p. 40).

Finally, and in a more fundamental social sense, the concern for
privacy follows from the assumption that an individual has an "in-
violate personality . . . (and) the individual's independence, dignity
and integrity" is violated when one's privacy is invaded (Bloustein,
1964, p. 971). Human dignity represents a radical criterion to judge
the strategic processes and outcomes of organizations. However, for
those of us theorists and researchers who adopt human dignity as a

core assumption of organization and management information theory, our role is that of a social critic: on the margin, not in the mainstream, motivated by what Beaney (1966) calls "a never-ending quest to increase the respect of all . . . for the essential values of human life" (p. 271).

■ Notes

1. A nonprofit incorporated trade association of about 750 life insurance companies formed to conduct a confidential exchange of underwriting information among its members as an alert against fraud. Life insurance companies submitted brief computer records for each person who applied for insurance, noting any medical conditions uncovered during the underwriting process. If the person later applied for life insurance at another company, the second company would query the MIB database and would retrieve the record filed by the original company.

■ References

Beaney, W. M. (1966). The right to privacy and American law. *Law and Contemporary Problems, 31*, 253, 271.

Bennett, C. J. (1992). *Regulating privacy: Data protection and public policy in Europe and the United States.* Ithaca, NY: Cornell University Press.

Bies, R. J. (in press). Privacy and procedural justice. *Social Justice Research.*

Bies, R. J., & Tyler, T. R. (1993). The "litigation mentality" in organizations: A test of alternative psychological explanations. *Organizational Science, 4*(3), 352-366.

Bleakley, F. R. (1991, April 3). Citicorp's folly? How a terrific idea for grocery marketing missed the mark. *Wall Street Journal,* p. A1.

Bloustein, E. J. (1964). Privacy as an aspect of human dignity: An answer to Dean Prosser. *New York University Law Review, 39*, 962-1007.

Buchwald, A. (1992, June 25). Credit card sharks. *Washington Post,* p. C1.

Clarke, R. A. (1988). Information technology and dataveillance. *Communications of the ACM, 31*(5), 498-512.

Cohen, R. (1991, April 21). The rebellion of Private Cohen. *Washington Post Magazine,* p. 5.

Commission of the European Communities. (1990, September 13). *Proposal for a council directive concerning the protection of individuals in relation to the processing of personal data.* SYN 287. Brussels.

Crenshaw, A. B. (1992, May 14). Credit card holders to be warned of lists. *Washington Post,* p. D11.

Culnan, M. J. (1993a). *Consumer attitudes toward direct mail, privacy and name removal: Implications for direct marketing.* Paper presented at the Symposium on Consumer Privacy, Chicago/Midwest Direct Marketing Days, Chicago.

Culnan, M. J. (1993b). "How did they get my name?": An exploratory investigation of consumer attitudes toward secondary information use. *MIS Quarterly, 17*(3), 341-363.

Culnan, M. J., & Smith, H. J. (1992). *Lotus MarketPlace: Households. Managing information privacy concerns (A) & (B)*. Case study. Washington, DC: Geogetown University, School of Business Administration.

Direct Marketing Association. (1992). *1991/92 statistical fact book: Current information about direct marketing*. Dubuque, IA: Kendall/Hunt.

Flaherty, D. (1989). *Protecting privacy in surveillance societies*. Chapel Hill: University of North Carolina Press.

Folger, R., & Bies, R. J. (1989). Managerial responsibilities and procedural justice. *Employee Responsibilities and Rights Journal, 2*, 79-90.

Gentile, M., & Sviokla, J. J. (1990). *Information technology in organizations: Emerging issues in ethics & policy*. Boston: Harvard Business School Note.

Glaser, B., & Strauss, A. (1967). *The discovery of grounded theory*. Chicago: Aldine.

Jaffee, L. (1992, October 26). Citicorp POS Inc. Phasing out supermarket scanner database. *DM News*, 61.

Laufer, R. S., & Wolfe, M. (1977). Privacy as a concept and a social issue: A multi-dimensional developmental theory. *Social Forces, 33*(3), 22-42.

Lazzareschi, C. (1992, December 23). Pacific Bell hangs up its offer on caller ID. *Los Angeles Times*, p. D1.

Louis Harris and Associates, Inc. (1990). *The Equifax report on consumers in the information age*. Atlanta: Equifax Inc.

Louis Harris and Associates, Inc. (1991). *Harris-Equifax consumer privacy survey 1991*. Atlanta: Equifax Inc.

Mason, R. O. (1986). Four ethical issues of the information age. *MIS Quarterly, 10*(1), 4-12.

Miller, A. (1971). *The assault on privacy: Computers, data banks and dossiers*. Ann Arbor: University of Michigan Press.

Miller, M. W. (1991, March 14). Hot lists: Data mills delve deep to find information about consumers. *Wall Street Journal*, p. A1.

Plesser, R. L., & Cividanes, E. W. (1991). *Privacy protection in the United States: A 1991 survey of laws and regulations affecting privacy in the public and private sector*. Washington, DC: Piper & Marbury.

Privacy Protection Study Commission (PPSC). (1977). *Personal privacy in an information society*. Washington, DC: Government Printing Office.

Reidenberg, J. R. (1992). Privacy in the information economy.: A fortress or frontier for individual rights? *Federal Communications Law Journal, 44*(2), 195-243.

Selznick, P. (1969). *Law, society, and industrial justice*. New York: Russell Sage.

Simitis, S. (1987). Reviewing privacy in an information society. *University of Pennsylvania Law Review, 135*, 707-746.

Sitkin, S. B, & Bies, R. J. (1993). The legalistic organization: Definitions, dimension, and dilemmas. *Organization Science, 4*(3), 345-351.

Smith, H. J. (1993). Privacy policies and practices: Inside the organizational maze. *Communication of the ACM, 36*(12), 105-122.

Smith, H. J. (1994). *Managing privacy: Information technology and corporate America*. Chapel Hill: University of North Carolina Press.

Stone, E. F., & Stone, D. L. (1990). Privacy in organizations: Theoretical issues, research findings, and protection mechanisms. In *Research in personnel and human resources management* (Vol. 8, pp. 349-411). Greenwich, CT: JAI Press.

Stone, E. F., Gardner, D. G., Gueutal, H. G., & McClure, S. (1983). A field experiment comparing information-privacy values, beliefs, and attitudes across several types of organizations. *Journal of Applied Psychology, 68*(3), 459-468.

Tolchinsky, P. D., McCuddy, M. K., Adams, J., Ganster, D. C., Woodman, R. W., & Fromkin, H. L. (1981). Employee perceptions of invasion of privacy: A field simulation experiment. *Journal of Applied Psychology, 66*(3), 308-313.

Warren, S. D., & Brandeis, L. D. (1890). The right to privacy. *Harvard Law Review, 4*(5), 193-220.

Westin, A. F. (1967). *Privacy and freedom.* New York: Atheneum.

Woodman, R. W., Ganster, D. C., Adams, J., McCuddy, M. K., Tolchinsky, P. D., & Fromkin, H. (1982). A survey of employee perceptions of information privacy in organizations. *Academy of Management Journal, 25*(3), 647-663.

Zalud, B. (1989). The conflicts of privacy. *Security, 26*(10), 38-41.

9

The Changing Legal Environment:
A Review and Recommendations for Today's Corporate Directors

Idalene F. Kesner

Jeffrey B. Kaufmann

The legal environment for today's corporate board members is changing. Gone are the days when directors could avoid legal interference by subjectively arguing that their decisions were made in good faith and with loyalty to their company. In its place is an environment where corporate directors must perform certain specified actions in order to demonstrate such good faith and loyalty.

While there are many reasons for the change, two in particular signal long-term consequences for directors. First, boards are facing increased attention from regulatory bodies. Because regulatory oversight is expensive, government agencies have found that they can minimize costs by making officers and directors individually responsible for corporate actions. The result is an ever-increasing set of regulations, requiring boards to take some actions and forbidding them from taking others. A second reason for the change is that outside parties (e.g., shareholders, creditors) are more willing to sue directors than ever before. These lawsuits, in turn, have produced an ever-changing set of judicial standards by which to judge the actions of boards and their members.

Although the reasons behind this changing environment are clear, the impact of the change is less obvious. The goal of this chapter, therefore, is to explore the effects of environmental changes on individual directors and on the board as a whole. Toward this end, we begin with a brief review of the role of directors. Next, we provide an overview of the components making up the general legal environment for U.S. boards, and a review of recent changes and trends as they affect directors. We continue with a look at the current litigation explosion, by discussing what is happening, the consequences of this trend, and the impact it has on corporate boards. Following this, we explore options directors have for protecting themselves. And finally, we offer some recommendations to assist directors as they balance their strategic and legal obligations and make their way through this complex and dynamic environment.

■ The Role of Directors and Corporate Boards

In order to fully understand the effects of legal changes on modern day directors, it is important to first review the role of directors. Shareholders, as owners of companies, elect a board of directors to represent them in the management of their organization. These directors, in turn, have various responsibilities. According to Vance (1983), directors are responsible for: (a) the control and oversight of management, (b) ensuring that the corporation adheres to all legal obligations and responsibilities, (c) looking after the interests of the organization's stakeholders, and (d) advancing the interests of the stockholders. Table 9.1 contains a partial list of how these general functions translate into the specific duties of corporate directors.[1]

As this list of duties suggests, the board of directors has considerable power. Yet its power is as a unit; individual directors may be relatively powerless. The analogy can been made between an individual director and a representative in Congress. Both may exert tremendous influence over the actions of the organization, but neither has any official power when acting alone. Unlike members of Congress, however, individual directors may be held legally accountable to others for both their own actions and those of the corporation.

Types of Directors

Continuing with this analogy, there are different types of directors, just as there are different members of Congress (i.e., senators and representatives). Most boards in the United States are composed of three types of directors: outsiders, insiders, and affiliates. Each plays a unique role on the board, and each is described in turn.

Table 9.1

Control and Oversight of Management

Select the CEO
Assure managerial competency
Evaluate management's performance
Set management's compensation
Chart corporate course
Devise/revise policies to be implemented by management

Legal Prescriptions
Keep abreast of changes in the legal environment
Ensure that the organization fulfills every legal requirement
Pass bylaws and related resolutions
Select new directors
Approve capital budgets
Authorize borrowings, new stock issues, and so on

Stakeholder Interests
Monitor product quality
Review labor policies and practices
Improve the customer "climate"
Keep community relations at the highest level
Use influence to better external contacts
Maintain a good public image

Stockholder Rights
Preserve the stockholders' equity
Stimulate corporate growth
Provide articulate and equitable stockholder representation
Keep shareholders informed
Declare proper dividends
Guarantee corporate survival

SOURCE: From *Corporate Leadership: Boards, Directors, and Strategy* by S. C. Vance, 1983, New York: McGraw-Hill. Copyright © 1983 by McGraw-Hill. Reprinted by permission.

Outside Directors

Outside directors are those who have no connection with the management of the organization other than their role as directors. In short, these individuals are not employed by the firm. Nevertheless, they play a particularly important role in fulfilling Vance's (1983) list of board responsibilities. Foremost among these roles is the oversight of management. Because outsiders are neither intimately involved with management's decision-making process nor dependent on other members of management for employment, compensation, or promotion, they are thought to bring a certain amount of objectivity to their evaluation of top management. It has long been argued that because insiders work for the chief executive officer (CEO) on a daily basis, they cannot properly exercise their duties in monitoring and controlling his or her performance (Mace 1971; Mintzberg, 1983; Pfeffer, 1972). According to Louden (1982, p. 92), "It is unreasonable to think that a subordinate director can successfully challenge the chief executive at board meetings."

Outsiders are less likely to be affected by this relationship. Moreover, the importance of outsider independence is magnified when the chairman of the board is also the CEO (Rechner & Dalton, 1989). The chairman has the primary responsibility to evaluate management's performance in light of shareholders' interests. The CEO, on the other hand, is the leader and key representative of management. Thus, there is a potential conflict of interest in uniting both roles in one person (Kesner & Johnson, 1990a). The scope of this problem is enormous. According to a recent Korn/Ferry International survey (1987) of more than 500 firms, 77.3% of the responding CEOs also chaired their boards. As such, this potential conflict exists for most U.S. boards. Beyond overseeing the CEO's performance, inside directors are also placed in the difficult position of evaluating their own performance as members of management. This clearly makes objective oversight impossible.

Outside directors also play the role of boundary spanners for the organization. More importantly, this may involve securing scarce resources from external sources (Pfeffer, 1972; Pfeffer & Salancik, 1978). An additional resource brought into the organization by outside directors is their own skills and experience. While insiders bring depth to the board with their specialized knowledge of the company, outsiders bring breadth. Nonmanagement directors often have experiences that span various companies and industries (Kesner & Johnson, 1990a). These experiences may prove invaluable to the organization in understanding its environment or when faced with a new situation.

The advantages of outside directors have prompted some to suggest that most, if not all, board members be outsiders (Securities and Exchange Commission, 1980). Empirical studies, however, have failed to find any connection between the percentage of outsiders and firm financial performance (Chaganti, Mahajan, & Sharma, 1985; Schmidt, 1975; Vance, 1964; Zahra & Stanton, 1988), social performance (Kohls, 1985) or the firm's commission of illegal acts (Kesner, Victor, & Lamont, 1986).

Inside Directors

At the other extreme are those directors who are full-time employees of the organization. Known as inside directors, these individuals are usually members of the organization's top management team. The role played by inside directors is very different from the one played by outside directors. First, inside directors often have superior technical backgrounds in areas that are vital to the success of the organization. They tend to be more familiar with the industry and the key competitive factors present. As such, their participation on the board makes this information available during all discussions involving the strategic decisions of the organization. Second, insiders have greater familiarity with the company, its history, its culture, and its future goals and objectives. Like their industry knowledge, this company-specific information can be invaluable in charting the firm's future course. Third, inside directors are immediately available for both routine and emergency meetings of the board. As such, insiders play a vital role in handling both short-term and long-term issues. Fourth, inside directors often have a keener appreciation of the problems and desires of certain organizational stakeholders (i.e., employees, customers, and the like). This ensures that some balance is offered to the representation of shareholders by outsiders. Finally, inside directors are likely to have greater dedication to the organization. Unlike outsiders, insiders lose their livelihood if the organization fails. As such, they may go to great lengths to ensure organizational stability.

Despite the important role played by insiders, there are clear legal disadvantages to having too many inside directors on the board. These disadvantages include a greater propensity to be sued by your own shareholders and the greater scrutiny of board decisions by the courts (Kesner & Johnson, 1990a).

Affiliated Directors

Not all directors can be classified as insiders or outsiders. Between these two categories is a group of directors who are not employees of the organization, but who have some relationship with management. This relationship has the potential to affect decision making. Included in this category are those directors who are former employees of the organization, those who are related to members of management, and those who derive a significant portion of their income from dealings with the institution. The Securities and Exchange Commission requires that directors who have such a relationship with the organization be identified in proxy statements.

From a practical standpoint affiliated directors can be considered insiders for some purposes and outsiders for others. Affiliate status has no effect on the director's skills and experiences, or on his or her ability to act in a boundary-spanning capacity. For these issues, affiliated directors can be considered the same as outsiders. On the other hand, their financial and emotional ties to management may affect their ability to oversee management. Therefore, for matters of oversight, affiliated directors may be regarded as insiders. This is especially relevant, given the greater scrutiny of board decisions by the courts in cases where too few directors are considered sufficiently objective.

The Board's New Activism

While in theory there has been little change in the roles and responsibilities of corporate directors over the years, there has been tremendous change in practice. Up until the 1980s, many corporate boards were regarded as "rubber stamps." Rather than actively fulfilling their responsibilities, they simply ratified management's decisions. Yet, within the past decade, we have seen a tremendous change in how corporate boards operate. Today's boards are more active than ever before ("Taking Charge," 1989).

Signs of this new activism include the forced removal of the CEO by the boards of Alcoa, Pillsbury, Mellon Bank, and Oak Industries. In the Alcoa situation, for example, directors wanted the organization to refocus on aluminum. Toward this end, they engineered the ouster of CEO Charles W. Parry in 1987 and installed a fellow director in his place. Boards have also begun to intervene in the composition of top management teams. At Control Data, for example, directors bolstered management in 1988 by engineering their own choice for chief operating officer and charging him with the recovery of Control Data's ailing computer business. Still other boards have rejected director nominations. At General Motors (GM), for instance, directors vetoed Chairman Roger Smith's plan to seat three new directors drawn from management. One director explained the rejection by stating that such a move would send the wrong message to the corporation's stakeholders ("Taking Charge," 1989).

An even more dramatic revolt by outside directors at GM occurred in April 1992. Outsiders became frustrated with management's seeming inability to address the firm's declining performance. Led by John Smale, former chairman of Proctor & Gamble, the outside directors removed GM Chairman Robert Stempel from his role as the head of the board's executive committee. Smale was appointed in Stempel's place, and the committee then demoted and replaced GM's President, Lloyd Reuss, and its chief financial officer, Robert O'Connell ("The Board Revolt," 1992). The message to management was clear: The board was not going to sit idly by while performance suffered. If GM's key executives were unable to fix the situation, the board would find others who could and would.

It is also worth noting that independent directors who assert control during such crisis situations are often afforded hero status in the business press. Directors Carl Pohlad and Peter Ueberroth, for example, have been praised for their intervention in the crises at Texas Air (Eastern Airlines) and E. F. Hutton, respectively ("Taking Charge," 1989). Both of these outside directors assumed de facto leadership of the board when it became apparent that management was failing to solve the problems facing the organization.

This new stance by directors is due in large part to the changes in our legal environment. Yet, before we can understand these changes, we must first review how the law affects directors in general.

■ The General Legal Environment

The legal environment surrounding corporate boards of directors in the United States consists of rules and regulations arising from three basic sources: the common law, state law, and federal law.[2] From the standpoint of an individual director's activities, any of these sources can create liability for any action. The sources differ, however, in two important respects. First, each draws its legitimacy from a distinctive source. Second, these sources are hierarchical in nature, so that one overrules another when a conflict occurs.

Although any one of the three sources can regulate the actions of a director, each source relies on different authority for making rules. As such, each new rule must address the activity from the perspective of its source's mandate. The common law's authority, for example, focuses on the relationship between parties to a social or contractual agreement. Common law rules are created when the court settles the disputes of parties appearing before it. These court decisions are made in the absence of any statutory laws on the subject, and they are based heavily on earlier court decisions. The cumulative result of these decisions is an evolving set of standards and duties that speak to almost any agreement. Examples of relationships covered by the common law include those between a principle and agent, a landlord and tenant, and two or more parties to a contract. From the standpoint of an individual director, the common law defines the responsibilities arising from his or her relationship with the corporation itself, shareholders, creditors, and third parties.

In contrast to common law, state law authority most often stems from the state's power as the creator of corporations. As this implies, corporations are not natural entities. Rather, they are legal fictions or artificial creations of the state, empowered to engage in certain enumerated acts. A corporation's existence depends on compliance with the rules and regulations of its state. Thus, state law literally defines what a corporation is, and creates the context for relationships between the corporation, its components, and those with whom it deals. From the standpoint of a director, the board and its members are components of the corporation and, as such, they exist only as defined by state law. Any action outside of this definition may be treated as the director acting as a private individual and, therefore, personally liable for his or her actions.

The third body of law is federal law. Here, authority to intervene in corporate affairs stems from the federal government's constitutional power to tax and to regulate interstate commerce. Of these powers, the regulation of interstate commerce has been used most often to form what has been described as the "federal law of corporations" (Hamilton, 1987). From the standpoint of a director, almost any action can be interpreted to be part of interstate commerce. As such, the federal government has a wide range of authority to regulate and impose liability.

These three sources of law stand in a hierarchical relationship. When two or more sources regulate the same activity, federal law preempts state law, which rules over common law. The conflict must be direct, however. If two or more sources regulate different aspects of the same activity, the laws are cumulative, and directors must obey both. Finally, when state law is stricter than federal law, directors must obey both the federal law and the stricter standard.

Before we continue with a more detailed look at the effects of each source of law for boards of directors, it is important to note that the board as a unit is never liable. Liability for board actions falls on the corporation as a whole. Individual liability for board decisions is based on the actions of individual directors. As such, if individual directors act in a legally reasonable manner, they will not be held liable for unreasonable board actions. With this principle in mind, let us continue with a more detailed examination of the relationship between the three sources of law and corporate boards of directors.[3]

Common Law

As noted earlier, the term *common law* refers to the body of law created by the judgments and decrees of the courts. Although the concept of common law dates back to the Norman invasion of England in 1066, it is actually very dynamic in nature. Each new decision is based on applying or interpreting prior decisions in order to resolve current conflicts. Duties and responsibilities under the common law evolve as a result of this constant expanding and contracting of prior decisions.

Originally, the common law courts did not interfere in corporate affairs or specifically address the responsibility of directors, other than requiring that a director be competent to contract.[4] In 1742, however, this legal philosophy of noninterference with corporate affairs changed when the English courts heard the case of *The Charitable Corporation v. Sir Robert Sutton & others.*[5] In this case, a corporation sued its directors for breach of trust, fraud, and the failure of the directors to oversee the management of the company. In imposing liability for negligence, the court laid down general principles of director responsibility. These principles have evolved into the current duties of care, loyalty, and obedience as well as the fiduciary duty owed to shareholders and others. Even today, these principles serve as the foundation of director behavior. Each is discussed in turn.

The Duty of Care

The *duty of care* is the first of the duties owed by the director, and it is owed to the corporation itself rather than its shareholders. Simply stated, the duty of care requires that a director be active in board decisions, stay informed as to relevant data in making these decisions, and above all else, act in good faith and as an ordinarily prudent person would act in similar circumstances.[6] Essentially this means that a director must bring his or her own skills and experiences to the situation. If these skills and experiences are ignored, a board member may be found liable for failing to act with good faith.

Until recently, it was generally believed that the courts would not find directors liable under the duty of care absent a showing of self-dealing, bad faith, or fraud. This changed in 1985, however, when the Delaware Supreme court decided the case of *Smith v. Van Gorkom*.[7] In that case, the directors of Trans Union Corporation were found liable for making an uninformed decision regarding the sale of their company despite the absence of self-dealing, bad faith, or fraud. The court set out the facts in *Van Gorkom* in great detail. Briefly, the case involved a cash-out merger, approved by the board after only a 2-hour meeting called by Trans Union's CEO, Van Gorkom, to discuss the proposal. At the meeting the board heard a 20-minute presentation from Van Gorkom; an oral statement by the chief financial officer, who had learned of the proposal only that day; and a statement by an attorney retained by Van Gorkom to render advice to the board on the legal aspects of the merger. After completing this agenda, the board voted unanimously to approve the merger. Moreover, 5 months after the board's vote, the shareholders, too, voted overwhelmingly to approve the proposal.

In spite of this shareholder approval, the Delaware court found the directors grossly negligent and liable for the difference between the fair value of the company at the time of the merger minus the actual money received.[8] The court cited numerous acts by the board that contributed to this negligence. These acts can be summed up as follows: The directors did not ask the right questions of the right people; they did not have adequate time to consider the merger (i.e., too little time between when they first learned of the proposal and when they voted on it); they accepted Van Gorkom's statements too uncritically; and no member of the board was trained to understand the merger (i.e., the board contained no investment bankers or trained financial analysts).

There can be little doubt as to the significance of this case for today's directors. The principles laid down by the Delaware court apply not only to situations involving mergers and acquisitions but also to virtually all strategic activity. Directors making strategic decisions must seek out all relevant information, take sufficient time to consider this information, ask questions, and seek outside advice from experts when appropriate.

The Duty of Loyalty

The second duty owed to the corporation is the *duty of loyalty*. According to this duty, directors are required to place the interests of the corporation and its shareholders above their own. This duty currently arises in three situations: (a) conflicts of interest, (b) corporate opportunities, and (c) confidentiality. Each is discussed in turn.

A conflict of interest transaction is one in which a corporate board member has a direct or indirect interest. The fear is that directors will make decisions based on their own interests rather than those of the corporation. The duty of loyalty, therefore, requires that directors be conscious of the potential for such conflicts, and that they act with candor and care in dealing with such situations.[9]

The second situation in which the duty of loyalty arises concerns corporate opportunities. A corporate opportunity occurs when a director engages in a transaction that he or she reasonably should know may be of interest to the corporation. In such cases the director must disclose the transaction to the board of directors far enough in advance and in sufficient detail to enable the board to act or decline to act on the opportunity.

Although the circumstances surrounding corporate opportunities seem clear, courts have yet to agree on a single, specific test to define when a corporate opportunity occurs. The absence of uniform standards, however, may leave directors in an uncomfortable position. Transactions which may be acceptable in one jurisdiction may be actionable in another. As such, directors are left in a position where they must ensure that the transaction is acceptable under any and all standards currently being followed.

The final situation where a director's duty of loyalty arises concerns the confidentiality of corporate information. Simply stated, directors may not disclose information about their company's legitimate activities unless they are already known by the public or are a matter of public record. The duty of safeguarding a firm's secrets usually arises in one of two situations. First, the director may not use or disclose a corporation's trade secrets to the detriment of the organization. This situation usually arises when directors use inside information to buy or sell stock or property, where the value of the stock changes once the information is made public. In these so-called "insider trading" situations, the director is often required to give back any profits made on the transaction. In addition, the director may be liable for any additional expenses the organization incurred as a result of the breach. A recent case exemplifying this situation is *Anheuser Busch Inc. v. Thayer*.[10] Here, a former director tipped off his friends to an upcoming acquisition by the company. Anheuser Busch sought to recover damages resulting from the additional costs it incurred when the stock price of the target company rose after this disclosure. In this instance, the SEC took the unusual step of filing a brief with the court, urging the court to find that this action was indeed a breach of the duty of loyalty.

These situations clearly illustrate that a director's duty of loyalty is expanding. Directors must take care to ensure that their actions are guided by the spirit, and not just the letter, of the law regarding the duty of loyalty. To do otherwise is to invite possible liability under the changing boundaries of this duty.

The Duty of Obedience

A third duty owed by a director to the corporation is the *duty of obedience*. Under this duty, a director is responsible for ensuring that the corporation obeys all relevant laws and regulations. The rationale behind this duty is that the board of directors is ultimately responsible for the actions taken by a company. If the firm breaks the law, directors may be liable under one of two rationales. First, they may be liable because they were actively involved in guiding the corporation toward the illegal activities. Second, they may be liable for failing in their responsibilities of monitoring the organization. As such, they "allowed" the illegal activity to occur. In this case, the law views the director as actively failing in his or her duty to oversee management.

The impact of this duty on directors is enormous. First, both judicial and regulatory bodies may hold board members directly responsible for the illegal actions of a corporation. This means that directors charged with such actions may be required to pay any damages out of their own pockets.[11] Second, the duty of obedience can also lead to indirect liability for directors. In cases where illegal conduct is found, and the corporation is held liable for damages, it is possible for the company to turn around and sue its directors for failing in their duties.

The Fiduciary Duty to Shareholders and Creditors

While the primary duties of a director are toward the corporation, directors also owe a *fiduciary duty* to shareholders and creditors. A fiduciary duty means that the director must act for the benefit of another in matters connected with his or her undertakings. Stated differently, a board member who deals directly with, or acts in some way which injures the economic interests of shareholders, or creditors, may be liable. An obvious problem occurs when the interests of shareholders and creditors conflict with each other or with the interests of the corporation. Under these circumstances the director must act carefully to safeguard all interests to the greatest extent possible.

The Business Judgment Rule

While the common law imposes numerous duties and standards on directors, the courts also realize that the director must be given some room to make decisions. In an effort to provide directors with this leeway, the courts have developed the *business judgment rule*. The rationale behind this rule can be summed up in the following three statements: (a) Directors should be granted discretion with respect to the management of the corporation; (b) this discretion, in general, should not be subject to judicial review; and (c) most judges are not business people; as such, they are generally not capable of second-guessing the effective exercise of a director's discretion.

Essentially, the business judgment rule states that decisions made in good faith, upon reasonable information, and with some rationality will not give rise to director liability, even if those decisions turn out badly or disastrously from the standpoint of the corporation. While the rule may seem somewhat vague, the courts have used the following three-part test to determine when it applies: (a) The director must not be interested in the transaction; (b) the director must be reasonably informed as to the subject matter of the transaction; and (c) the director must reasonably believe that his or her business judgment is in the best interests of the corporation.

Courts have traditionally given directors a broad area in which to act under the protection of the business judgment rule. In *Gries Sports Enterprises, Inc. v. Cleveland Browns Football Co., Inc.,*[12] for example, the Ohio Supreme Court stated that "[t]he rule is a rebuttable presumption that directors are better equipped than the courts to make business judgments and that directors acted without self-dealing or personal interest and exercised reasonable diligence and acted with good faith." As this statement clearly illustrates, directors are allowed a reasonable degree of flexibility and freedom with this rule. Unless proven otherwise, directors are assumed to have used their best business judgment. A recent study of lawsuits filed against corporate directors, whose companies were involved in mergers and acquisitions, confirms that the rule is firmly in place (Kesner & Johnson, 1990b). According to the authors, "board members' decisions will not be questioned where directors can demonstrate they have been well informed and involved" (p. 33). Nevertheless, prudent directors cannot rely blindly on the protection of this rule. Rather, to avoid liability under the common law, they must ensure that their actions do not violate any of the common law duties described above.

Summary

The dynamic nature of common law makes it essential that directors stay current with its developments. Directors should not be lulled into a false sense of security because the terminology used in common law has remained virtually unchanged over the years. While the terms are the same, the meanings of the words are constantly changing. Although the duty of care has been around since the mid-1700s, for example, the scope of this duty was radically altered in 1985, with the ruling in *Smith v. Van Gorkom*. As this case illustrates, each new decision has the potential to alter dramatically the scope of directors' responsibilities.

A second reason for understanding the common law is that much of it has been codified by either the state or the federal government. Therefore, directors must understand the essence of the common law if they wish to perform their duties effectively. Actions that fall within the technical requirements of the state or federal law may still be challenged as a violation of the more subjective common law. With this in mind, let us turn now to consider the effects of state law on the legal environment of the board of directors.

State Law

As previously discussed, state law derives its authority for the regulation of corporate directors from its role as the creator of the corporate entity. State law itself is a creation of each individual state legislature. It is theoretically possible, therefore, to find 50 different rules concerning the same action. This has not been the case, however, when it comes to laws affecting corporate boards. Most states base their laws on either the Delaware state law or on the Revised Model Business Corporations Act (RMBCA). In the sections that follow, both of these options are discussed.

Delaware State Law

The influence of Delaware state law began in the early 1900s, when states realized that the incorporation of businesses could be a profitable business in itself. Having a firm incorporate in one's state brought tax revenues, provided jobs for the populace, and created a market for other related businesses. In an effort to attract businesses into their states, legislatures began to loosen restrictions on corporations. As one state altered its laws to be more attractive to potential businesses, other states would imitate these changes. Justice Brandeis referred to this competition as a race "not of diligence but of laxity"[13] while others have referred to it as a "race to the bottom" (Hamilton, 1987). Delaware was generally considered to be the winner of this "race."

Reacting to the perception of Delaware as a place conducive to their operations, corporations began to incorporate there in droves. As a result, approximately 56% of all *Fortune* 500 companies and 45% of all New York Stock Exchange firms are incorporated in Delaware (Kesner & Johnson, 1990b). Other states, seeing these results, began to emulate Delaware law. This point is illustrated by the following statement issued in an Indiana court case: "Indiana takes its cues in matters of corporation law from the Delaware courts, which are more experienced in such matters since such a large fraction of major corporations is incorporated in Delaware."[14]

While Delaware remains the leading state in numbers of incorporations, this status may be changing. Modern Delaware corporate law is no longer considered more lax than that of other states. The main reason for this is the increasing standards of director behavior in Delaware. The *Van Gorkom* case is an example of such an increase. Clearly, this case raised the standards and potential liabilities of corporations and their directors.

The effects of Delaware's changes cannot be judged at this time. Other states may accept the status quo (i.e., the distribution of incorporations across states) and raise their legal standards regarding corporate directors up to the new Delaware standard. Conversely, states may retain their current (lower) standards or even reduce standards further in an effort to attract more in-state incorporations. The relaxing of corporate restrictions by other states is exemplified by the spate of legislation throughout the 1980s, which was designed to enable corporations greater latitude in the defense of takeover attempts.[15] Judicial influence changes slowly, however, and Delaware is still considered very influential in the shaping of corporate law throughout the nation.

The Revised Model Business Corporations Act

The other major influence on state corporate law has been the Committee on Corporate Laws of the American Bar Association. This committee has worked to standardize state law by offering a model version for states to follow, known as the Model Business Corporation Act. The Model Act was originally offered in 1950 and was significantly revised in 1984. Despite this broad revision, the Revised Model Business Corporation Act (RMBCA) continually undergoes reevaluation and alteration. In 1990, for example, the committee amended the RMBCA to allow corporations to limit the liability of corporate directors. As these changes suggest, the RMBCA should be considered a dynamic document. In addition, adoption of the RMBCA is neither immediate nor complete. Adoption of the provisions from the 1984 revision, for example, has been a gradual process, with state legislatures picking and choosing the provisions they wish to implement. Yet, even when states adopt the RMBCA in its entirety, they may (and often do) alter or amend existing laws to cover new or different contingencies. The result of all this is that state laws throughout the United States are quite varied.

Although the major function of the RMBCA is to codify the common law rules regarding the duties of directors, it also establishes the basic structure of the board, creates a hierarchy for governing rules internal to the organization, and regulates various activities of the board. As such, it is imperative that directors be aware of any changes in the RMBCA itself or in the adoption of any existing provision by their state of incorporation.

Summary

No area of the legal environment surrounding corporate directors is in a greater state of flux than that created by the state. First, the stability offered by Delaware's leadership in corporate law has been seriously reduced, with recent decisions such as *Van Gorkom*. These decisions raise the applicable standards of director conduct. This change in judicial philosophy by the Delaware courts has created tremendous uncertainty in state law. While it is still too early to tell how this uncertainty will be resolved, early indications are that at least some states are competing in a "downward spiral." If this is indeed the case, directors may face dramatic shifts in terms of their duties and responsibilities. Second, the increasing acceptance of the

RMBCA also adds to the current uncertainty in the law. So far, more than two-thirds of the state legislatures have adopted provisions of the RMBCA, and it is likely that they will still be adopting various provisions well into the 1990s. This current uncertainty in state law requires prudent directors to stay abreast of legislative developments. Directors who fail to do so may unwittingly stray over the legal line, and face liability for their actions.

Federal Law

Liability of a director under federal law originates from the federal government's power to regulate interstate commerce. This federal regulation of, and the subsequent intervention into, corporate affairs starts with an act of Congress, which addresses a particular problem in a general way. The act often authorizes a federal agency to administer the law through the creation of necessary rules and standards. In general, the agency that drafts the rules is charged with the investigation and adjudication of any alleged violations. Penalties for failing to abide by agency regulations include injunctions of the prohibited activities, sanctions restricting the conduct of the board or its members, monetary fines, or even criminal prosecution resulting in incarceration. Penalties for noncompliance are determined by the regulation itself and by the circumstances surrounding the prohibited activities.

Over the past half century, federal intervention has branched out into all areas of corporate life. The reason for this extensive intervention can be traced to the expansion of the definition of interstate commerce. Originally, under the 1933 Securities Act, interstate commerce was defined as "trade or commerce in securities or any transportation or communication relating thereto among the several states." This definition was gradually expanded by the courts and agencies. Today's definition includes all activities that utilize the *means* of interstate commerce. Therefore, any company that uses the telephone or the mails in its business may be judged to be involved in interstate commerce.

Along with this expansion in the scope of federal intervention in corporate affairs has come an increase in agency attention to corporate directors. This increased attention can be traced back to 1982, when then-President Reagan issued Executive Order 12,291, requiring federal agencies to perform a cost-benefit analysis on all major draft rules. Agencies are now legally mandated to try to ensure that their rules are cost-effective.[16] From the perspective of these agencies, one relatively easy means of ensuring cost-effectiveness is to make individuals responsible for organizational actions. Individuals who are being held responsible have an incentive to ensure that the organization does not violate the regulations in question. This greatly simplifies agency oversight and enforcement, thereby making it cheaper. When federal agencies regulate corporate actions, their attention focuses on directors—they are, of course, the legal heads of the organization. As such, directors know that if they shirk their responsibilities to either the organization or the government, they will be prosecuted.

One agency that has been instrumental in the expansion of federal corporate law is the Securities and Exchange Commission (SEC). Through rule making and adjudication, the SEC has created numerous rules regarding boards of directors and director conduct. Examples of these rules include requiring the presence of certain committees (e.g., audit committees), prescribing a minimum number of outside directors, and restricting when and how a director may sell his stock in the organization. In the following two sections we discuss the federal intervention, described above, as it applies to directors.

Liability Based on a Director's Actions as an Individual

Generally, under federal law, a corporate officer is not vicariously liable for wrongdoing without some participation on his or her part. In the case of directors, however, participation can be found on the basis of direct action, ratification, or knowing acquiescence of a prohibited action. The ramifications of the above policy on directors are serious and may be shown in the example of U.S. antitrust laws. These laws are geared toward the protection of trade and commerce from unlawful restraints, price discriminations, price fixing, and monopolies. Persons injured by an antitrust violation of the company can sue for treble damages.[17] As such, any board member who acted directly, ratified, or acquiesced in the prohibited activity may be named as a defendant. The fact that the director may not have intentionally violated the statute, or the fact that he or she acted in good faith or with good intentions, is irrelevant. Moreover, even if the director is not named in the original suit, a corporation found liable for antitrust violations may seek to recover its money by suing a director for breaching the duty of obedience.

Identifying what constitutes a violation of the antitrust laws is difficult, because there is no clear distinction between aggressive but permissible corporate actions and violations of the antitrust laws. As such, directors may find themselves in an uncomfortable position. Even a prudent director of an aggressive company may stray into this gray area and find himself or herself liable. Board members may find that their choices are difficult ones. If they push their company to act less aggressively, they risk losing market share and profits to those who are more aggressive. Conversely, if they act more aggressively, they may face the possibility of liability under the antitrust laws.

Federal law also regulates the actions of directors as individuals (i.e., above and beyond their actions on behalf of the organization). The Securities Exchange Act, for example, restricts the discretion of directors to buy and sell securities in their company. Any profit made by a director through the sale and purchase (or purchase and sale) of such a security within a 6-month period belongs to the corporation.[18] Traditionally, the mere fact that there was a matching purchase and sale within 6 months was all that was needed for liability. Some modern courts, however, appear willing to look into the circumstances of the transactions, refusing to impose liability when there appears to be no abuse of insider information. While on the one hand, this suggests an atmosphere of greater leniency for directors, there is a negative side to this as well. With greater court discretion comes greater uncertainty and unpredictability. Therefore, prudent directors may choose to act conservatively in such cases.

Finally, it should be noted that, although the above examples concern the civil liability of directors, federal law may also impose criminal liability.[19] Individual criminal liability may arise in three situations. First, directors may be liable for crimes they personally commit. This is based on the idea that a director is responsible for his or her own actions and should not be able to hide behind the corporate entity.[20] Second, a director may be criminally liable if he instructs, counsels, or aids someone else to do a criminal act. Under federal law an accomplice is liable as if he had committed the crime himself.[21] Finally, a director may be criminally liable if he had a "responsible relation" to the situation. This type of relation exists when the director has the ability to control or alter the action, and in many ways it is a variation of the common law duty of obedience to the organization. Examples of this latter rationale include the Federal Hazardous Substances Act and the Occupational Safety and Health Act.

The above rationales for imposing criminal liability are not limited to the federal government. States may also impose criminal liability on corporate directors. While the first two rationales are general principals of law, the third rationale (i.e., responsible relation to the situation) requires special legislation. So far only California has passed such a statute. The 1991 corporate crime law holds officers and directors liable for workplace conditions or product defects that cause harm to employees or consumers. Penalties include up to 3 years in jail. The California statute has yet to be tested in court, although it is currently being used as the basis for a criminal probe into the actions of Dow Corning with regard to its silicone breast implants.

Still another, more ominous, instance of corporate heads being held criminally liable occurred in Illinois. In this case, the former president and part-owner of Film Recovery Systems, along with two of its officers, was convicted of murder for the death of an employee. The employee died of cyanide poisoning while leaching silver from used X-rays. The court blamed the death on unsafe working conditions. According to reports, employees worked in a slippery-floored shed crammed with open vats of sodium cyanide. Protection for the workers consisted of only surgical masks and cotton gloves. State safety investigators examining the death noted that the corporation's employees regularly coughed, gasped, and stumbled outside for fresh air. At the trial, the judge himself described the working conditions as "totally unsafe." The executives were found guilty of murder and were sentenced to 25 years in prison. Although the convictions were reversed in 1990 on a legal technicality,[22] the appeals court found sufficient evidence of guilt on the part of the officers to justify a retrial.

The criminal prosecution of corporate officers and directors is at a critical juncture. Successful convictions under the California statute and the *Film Recovery* case may signal a new era of holding officers and directors criminally responsible for corporate actions.

Liability Based on a Director's Status as a Member of the Board

In addition to liability based on directors' actions as individuals, federal law also contains one example of a director being held liable simply for being a member of the board. Section 11 of the Securities Act imposes liability on directors for misstatements in registration materials filed with the SEC prior to the original issue of securities. In this case, the person suing need only show that there has been a misstatement or absence of material facts. There is no requirement that the plaintiffs relied on the misstatement, just that they acquired a security subject to a defective registration. Here, director liability is based on the individual's status as a member of the board when the statement becomes effective.[23] Plaintiffs who prove their case can recover any damages suffered as a result of a decline in value of the securities. Moreover, directors found liable under Section 11 are jointly and severally liable.[24] At a minimum, this aspect of federal law reinforces the need for directors to stay involved with every aspect of the registration process.

Summary

Federal law affecting the legal environment of corporations has expanded to include all aspects of a director's life. Yet, in addition to this increase in the scope, there is also a trend toward placing greater responsibility on directors for the actions of their corporations. These two trends combine to make it difficult to advise prudent directors as to what they should do. For some boards, this dilemma encourages directors to check every action with an attorney who is knowledgeable about federal regulation, in an effort to avoid potential legal costs. However, this approach is costly, time-consuming, and stifling. It is clear that in today's environment, prudent directors may attempt to minimize their exposure, but they cannot eliminate it.

■ Implications of the Changing Legal Environment

In the previous sections of this chapter we discussed the changes in the laws regulating the conduct of corporate directors. Yet, the number or types of laws in a society only tell us which actions could lead to a potential lawsuit and subsequent liability. To fully understand the current threat facing corporate boards, we must consider not only the laws themselves, but also the extent to which they are applied.

Shareholder Suits: Reality in Today's Legal Environment

Corporate directors face a greater risk of being sued than ever before. (Kesner & Johnson, 1990a, 1990b). The 1990 Wyatt Survey of major U.S. corporations reveals that 51% of directors' claims to their insurance companies originated with suits filed by shareholders. This figure represents an increase from 40% in 1987. Whether this trend will continue to rise at this pace remains to be seen. Nevertheless, it reinforces the fact that shareholders are utilizing their rights to file suit against companies and their directors.

The increase in the number of lawsuits filed against directors stems from two main sources. First, as discussed earlier, the federal government has been focusing more attention on corporate boards as a way to reinforce accountability for corporate actions. The actual number of actions brought against corporate directors by the government is difficult to determine due to the nature of governmental enforcement. Federal agencies may either file suit against directors in federal court or they may (and usually do) proceed against directors in internal adjudications. Furthermore, many instances of potential director liability are settled through negotiations with the agency and are not adjudicated at all. Yet, even if we look at only the instances of known cases against corporate directors by the government, the numbers are increasing dramatically.

An even greater source of lawsuits against the board involves actions initiated by the company's own shareholders. The number of shareholder suits against directors is increasing at an almost geometric rate. During the 1960s, a director of a major U.S. corporation had a 1 in 20 chance of being sued. By the late seventies, the rate had increased to 1 in 9. Finally, by the mid-eighties the chances were 1 in 5 that a director would be involved in some kind of shareholder suit (Kesner & Johnson, 1990b).

Thomas M. Jones of the University of Washington has studied the trends in shareholder suits, and he offers the following conclusions. First, while the number of shareholder suits is increasing (Jones, 1980), the increase is not equal across all firms. There is a connection between firm size and chance of being sued. Larger organizations are sued more often, due in part to their deeper financial pockets (Jones, 1981, 1985). In other studies, Jones examined the relationship between board structure and number of shareholder suits. Here he found that boards of medium size (i.e., more than 12 but fewer than 17 members) are linked to fewer suits (Jones, 1979, 1986). Presumably, this is because they are small enough to function efficiently and work closely together, yet large enough to capitalize on a broader resouce and knowledge base. In addition, Jones also found that boards dominated by outsiders (i.e., 60% or more outside directors) are also associated with fewer suits. Jones states that this may be due to the greater "objectivity and independence [of] the board" (Jones, 1986, p. 348).

Another study of shareholder suits was conducted by Kesner and Johnson (1990a). Like Jones, these authors found that shareholder suits against corporate boards were more likely when firms had a high percentage of directors who were also members of management (i.e.,

Table 9.2

Corporate Board Resignations
Because of Loss of Adequate Directors' Liability Coverage

Company	Number of Resignations
Armada	8
Continental Steel	7
Control Data	6
DeltaUS	7
Enterra	3
GCA	4
Seiscom Delta	6
Sykes Datatronics	5
Tipperary	3
Verna	4

SOURCE: Data taken from "The Job Nobody Wants," *Business Week*, 1986 (September 8), pp. 56-61.

insiders). They concluded that shareholders may be more suspicious of the motives of directors who are members of management. Therefore, they may be more willing to take legal action when they perceive that directors are guilty of wrongdoing.

In a separate study, however, involving only firms active in mergers and acquisitions, Kesner and Johnson (1990a) found only modest support for Jones's earlier findings linking firm size to shareholder suits. Moreover, in contrast to their own earlier study, these authors found that shareholder suits against directors were not associated with the composition of the board. Their results also failed to show support for the often discussed link between incidence of shareholder suits and other commonly cited boardroom reforms (e.g., separating the positions of CEO and chairperson, requiring that directors hold substantial amounts of stock, and decreasing board size). According to the authors, the difference between these findings and earlier results suggests that the context or situation in which directors make their decisions may be a better predictor of shareholder suits than structural characteristics.

The Impact of Shareholder Suits on Today's Boards

The above discussion concerning the current legal environment facing directors paints a bleak picture for a number of reasons. First, with increased liability, directors are forced to put their personal financial health at risk. As a result, individuals may begin to decline service ("Willing Directors," 1992). Joseph Barr, former director of Control Data Corporation, for example, gave the following reason for resigning from the company's board: "I didn't want to risk my personal net worth for the $35,000 to $50,000 I'd get from the board." Five directors joined Joseph Barr in leaving Control Data's board in the months following the firm's suspension of its liability policy. In a more extreme example, when DeltaUS, a Texas-based oil and gas drilling company, could not get insurance due to its mounting losses, seven of its nine directors resigned. A company spokesperson was quoted as saying, "We looked a little bit for new directors but who would want to join a board where there is no liability insurance" ("The Job," 1986). As Table 9.2 demonstrates, director resignations can be especially acute when a corporation drops its director liability insurance.

Outside directors are often more likely to defect than inside directors due to the escalation in shareholder suits. Yet, as was discussed earlier, outside directors play a vital role in the functioning of the organization. If outsiders step off boards, not only do their organizations lose the objectivity of these directors, but they also lose access to their boundary-spanning capability. Consequently, the performance of many U.S. corporations may suffer as a result.

A second consequence of the increasing trend in suits against directors is that potential liability may act as a Damoclean sword. As noted earlier, directors facing possible financial ruin may act, or require the corporation to act, so passively and conservatively that market share and profits are lost to more aggressive competitors. The rewards of an aggressive strategy for the individual director may be slight when compared with the potential legal costs of such acts. In fact, one of the only rewards may be for members holding stock in the firm. Yet, at this level, ownership tends to be so slight for the average director that the potential gains (or losses) resulting from stock appreciation (or depreciation) tend to be scant (Kesner, 1987). A strategic action, such as a corporate merger or acquisition, for instance, may net the corporation millions of dollars. For a director holding only a minimum number of shares, however, this same action may represent only a small financial gain. Instead, it is the costs of this decision that may loom more heavily for the director. As in the *Van Gorkom* case, directors may be personally required to compensate shareholders for any loss due to poor decisions. As this situation so clearly illustrates, an imbalance exists between potential personal gains and losses—an imbalance few directors can afford to ignore.

Third, directors who face possible financial ruin may resign from the board when the corporation is facing a problem or a major decision. Take, for instance, firms facing financial distress. A recent study indicates that directors frequently step off their boards as companies approach Chapter 11 bankruptcy (Gales & Kesner, in press). While the authors acknowledge the time demands of reorganizing under Chapter 11 and the stigma of being associated with a bankrupt company as two key reasons for the exodus, a third significant factor is the threat of shareholder suit. The study goes on to note that resignation may seem the best solution from the perspective of the individual director, yet the organizational consequences may be quite severe. Resignation of one or more board members sends a very strong signal, both internally and externally, that the organization faces potentially insurmountable problems. Moreover, the board is left short of resources and skills at the very time these elements are most needed. As we have seen before, a type of paradox emerges, where trends oriented toward strengthening corporate boards actually have the reverse effect.

Three additional effects of these environmental changes on corporate boards are worth noting. First, as the frequency of lawsuits against directors increases, greater emphasis is placed on avoiding liability by meeting the applicable legal standards of conduct. To help ensure that this takes place, corporate boards often formalize the minimum legal standards by incorporating them into a decision-making checklist. Over time, board behavior converges on the minimum/maximum standard, as boards acting below the standard raise their standards accordingly, while those acting with higher standards tend to lower theirs. This phenomenon creates a dilemma for those creating the standards in the first place. The goal of setting standards is to create a floor, below which directors are liable. No judge or legislature has ever stated that the standards presented should act as a maximum; yet over time, this seems to be the case.

Second, as the minimum/maximum standard is formalized, it may become the only part of the decision that is documented. Consequently, even though decisions may be based on additional factors outside the formal standard, these issues or factors may not be documented. The result is that the decision-making process becomes more closed to the persons affected by the decision. By contrast, in the absence of concrete minimal standards, more of the decision-making process may be documented as directors attempt to avoid potential liability. It is ironic, therefore, that by creating standards, we may have reduced the level of documentation and information available to the public.

Finally, directors facing new situations may rely on the minimum/maximum standard to guide them in determining the appropriate decision-making process. The problem is that directors may never consider whether these standards are adequate, or whether more action is needed. Given the constantly changing legal and business environment, what was appropriate 5 or 10 years ago may not be appropriate today. The possible detrimental effect of this is twofold. First, the outdated decision-making process may lead to decisions that are not in the best interests of the organization. Second, directors may be liable, based on what should be the appropriate standard, not on whether they meet the requirements of outdated and inappropriate standards. Again, this result seems to run counter to the spirit behind the setting of minimal standards.

In sum, the above suggests that the creation of minimal standards has caused board members to use them in place of their own judgment. This result is dangerous; standards change and board members are usually held to the standard at the time of trial.[25]

Director Protections

While the above points illustrate that the risks of board service are increasing, three solutions have emerged recently that reduce these risks and protect the personal wealth of directors. These solutions are indemnification, insurance, and state statutes limiting director liability. Each is discussed in turn.

Indemnification

Indemnification refers to the reimbursement of directors by the corporation for expenses incurred as a result of being named as defendants in litigation. Under the common law, rights of indemnification are limited to those situations where the director's defense is successful.[26] Some courts further limit a director's right to indemnification by requiring proof that the litigation is beneficial to the corporation.[27]

The RMBCA addresses the issue of director indemnification direct-ly. Section 8.52 gives a director indemnification when he is "wholly successful, on the merits or otherwise, in the defense of any proceed-ing to which he was a party because he is or was a director of the corporation." "Wholly successful" means that the entire proceeding was disposed of in favor of the director. A director who disposes of some charges through plea bargaining (or other means), but is found liable on the remaining charges, is not entitled to partial indemnifica-tion. The second part of the phrase, "on the merits or otherwise," is placed in the statute so that a director who has a valid procedural defense does not have to undergo a prolonged and expensive trial in order to become eligible for indemnification.

Although section 8.52 covers indemnification when a proceeding is disposed of in favor of the director, section 8.51 allows the corpora-tion to indemnify a director on grounds other than complete success. The corporation may indemnify a director if he or she: (1) acted in good faith, and (2) believed that the actions were in the best interests of, or at least not opposed to the best interests of, the corporation.[28] Such permissive indemnification by the corporation is limited, however. Indemnification is not permitted when the suit is brought by the corpor-ation (or in its name) and there is a finding of improper conduct on the part of the director. Indemnification is also not permitted when a director is found to have improperly received a personal benefit as a result of his or her misconduct.

Rights of indemnification are not exclusive to the RMBCA. Forty-one states have expanded the rights granted by the RMBCA by enacting statutes that allow corporations to contract with their directors to provide indemnification in situations not covered. Different states pro-vide different degrees of freedom to corporations for granting addi-tional indemnification. As such, there are no single standards. An individual serving on two separate boards in two separate states can receive significantly different levels of protection. As this point illus-trates, great variability and uncertainty face today's directors on this issue. The only limitation consistent with all of the expansion statutes is that indemnification is not permitted when doing so would violate the law or public policy.

Finally, indemnification is only the right to reimbursement from the corporation. This right is worthless if the corporation has no money. If the organization is insolvent and declares bankruptcy, a director's claim of indemnification places him or her in the group of general creditors. The result is that directors who have legal or contractual rights to indemnification may receive either no reimbursement or only partial reimbursement.

Director and Officer (D&O) Liability Insurance

The second method of protecting directors from personal financial loss is through the purchase of director and officer (D&O) liability insurance. The typical D&O insurance policy is composed of two parts. The first part insures the corporation and reimburses it for indemnification payments made to officers and directors. The second section reimburses individual directors and officers for losses that are not indemnified by the corporation.

Until the 1980s, D&O insurance provided minor coverage at minimal cost. Then, as corporate directors found themselves facing increased liability exposure, due in large part to the *Smith v. Van Gorkom* case, there was a realization that the typical D&O policy was inadequate. The insurance companies faced with this increased exposure responded by quickly and substantially raising their rates. Policy rate increases have generally been in the 500% to 1,000% range, although increases as high as 9,000% per year have been reported (Kesner & Johnson, 1990b). The result was an "insurance crisis," as policies became an important and expensive requirement to keep directors on the board.

Yet, raising the premiums was not the cure-all for the insurance crisis. Insurance companies also tried to cope by increasing deductibles and adding more aggressive limits to their policies. Even with these restrictions, claims made against D&O insurance carriers continue to rise. A recent survey by the Wyatt Company (Wyatt Survey, 1988) estimates that the rate of claims will continue to increase between 10% and 25% per year. In addition, the survey estimates that the average costs for claims made in 1988 will be in excess of $3 million. As these trends show, increasing rates and decreasing coverage are facts of life for modern directors.

Given the trend toward increasing shareholder suits and the rising costs of D&O insurance, it is not surprising to find that director indemnification and director liability were the most common issues addressed in management resolutions during the late 1980s.[29] According to a study by the Investor Responsibility Research Center, by the last half of 1986, shareholders in more than half the 1,200 companies surveyed approved management proposals limiting the personal financial liability of directors and officers for breaches of the fiduciary duty of care. Moreover, most of these firms also adopted provisions that provided broader indemnification for directors (Marcil & O'Hara, 1987).

Today, virtually all major U.S. firms have acted on similar proposals. And while these resolutions are clearly in the best interests of directors, their protections should not be regarded as all-encompassing. They do not, for example, affect the duty of loyalty or the duty of obedience. Furthermore, while most limit some forms of liability, they do not eliminate liability altogether. Directors may still find shareholder suits (and the settlements or judgments associated with these suits) to be costly from both a financial and a personal perspective.

State Statutes Which Limit Director Liability

The final method used to protect the personal financial health of directors is state statutes limiting director liability. These statutes came into being recently and were in response to the D&O insurance crisis. These statutes either restrict the personal liability of directors generally, or modify the applicable standards of director conduct, or increase the number of factors directors may consider under the business judgment rule. In addition, the RMBCA was amended in 1990 to allow a provision in the articles of incorporation limiting director liability.[30] Currently, 44 states have laws on the books limiting director liability.

Within the past few years there has been considerable discussion about placing a cap on the amount of damages that can be collected in certain actions. So far, only Virginia has enacted such a statute regarding director liability. Under the Virginia statute, director liability may be capped by the articles of incorporation or bylaws. Otherwise, liability is limited to the greater of $100,000 or the amount of the cash compensation received by the officer or director during the 12 months immediately preceding the act for which liability was imposed. Even so, certain actions are not covered by the statute (e.g., knowing violation of the criminal law or liability imposed under the securities laws). The constitutionality of these caps on liability were upheld by the Virginia Supreme Court.[31] The Washington Supreme Court, on the other hand, overturned a similar statute. The Washington court ruled that such statutes interfere with the jury's traditional role in setting damages.[32] Given this split in state supreme court decisions, it is too early to tell whether Virginia is the start of a trend, or an anomaly.

Summary

While the above measures (i.e., indemnification, D&O insurance, and state statutes limited director liability) offer a degree of financial protection for modern directors, each suffers from limitations that leave a director partially exposed. In addition, the boundaries of these limitations are in a state of flux. Each has undergone dramatic change in the past few years. Prudent directors, therefore, are afforded some protection, but they must still work to ensure that their actions conform to the various standards discussed earlier. Otherwise, they may find themselves unprotected and forced to pay damages out of their own pockets.

■ Recommendations for Directors and Researchers

As we have noted throughout the chapter, the changes in the legal environment have greatly complicated the lives of modern-day directors. If today's directors act in a manner deemed adequate 10 years ago, they may suffer financial consequences or worse. In order to guide directors in their attempt to limit potential liability, while still fulfilling their strategic responsibilities to the corporation, we offer the following recommendations.

First and foremost, individual directors must take the responsibility to protect themselves from liability, and not rely on others to look out for their best interests. Individual liability is generally based on individual actions. Directors who do not seek information on the applicable standards affecting their roles in the decision-making process may dramatically increase their chances of facing liability for that decision.

One source of information for directors on the applicable standards of conduct is the corporation's general counsel. The prudent director understands that such counsel represents the corporation and not the individual director. Therefore, a director should ask specific questions of counsel and seek outside advice if, for any reason, the director is not satisfied with the answers received.

Second, at least one member of the board of directors should be an attorney who is knowledgeable in the area of business law. The role of this director is not to render legal advice; that is the role of the general counsel. Not only will the specifics of the legal question often fall outside the director-attorney's legal expertise, but the necessary objectivity of the director-attorney may be subject to greater scrutiny when he or she is intimately involved in making decisions. Instead, the role of the attorney-director is to spot potential legal issues that arise through board activities. In an effort to ensure that this role is fulfilled, the director should be asked for possible legal issues, as a matter of course, in every major or nonroutine board decision. Prudent directors should not rely completely on attorney-directors. Corporate counsel should still be consulted regularly to ensure that potential legal pitfalls are not overlooked. In addition to these unique roles played by corporate counsel and the director-attorney, these individuals should also take a lead in establishing guidelines for director conduct. In this manner a corporation can spell out its expectations regarding each of the director's main duties.

While seeking legal advice is important, directors faced with a nonroutine decision, which raises potential liabilities, should also seek external expert advice. This recommendation flows directly from RMBCA section 8.30, which allows board members to rely on such advice. Directors considering the sale of one of the corporation's divisions, for instance, should seek the advice of a financial analyst in valuating such divisions, a tax accountant to render advice on the tax consequences of the sale, and an investment banker regularly involved in similar transactions. Even so, directors should not blindly follow such advice. Questions must be asked of the expert, and unsatisfactory answers should be followed by more probing questions. A director who is still not satisfied should insist that further advice be obtained from another expert.

A fourth recommendation is that boards of directors should make extensive use of committees. First, section 8.30 of the RMBCA affords directors who rely on these committees the same types of protections as when they rely on outside experts. As such, the board should create oversight and special issue committees (e.g., audit, compensation, nominating, public affairs/environmental) and staff them with directors knowledgeable of the issues at hand. Still another benefit of using committees is that they allow the board to consider important issues in more depth. Any board decision that is complicated, or takes an inordinate amount of time to collect and digest relevant information, should be delegated to a standing or ad hoc committee for initial deliberation. In short, extensive use of committees not only allows the board to consider issues with greater depth and breadth, but also affords directors who rely on such committees a large degree of protection from liability.

The third and fourth recommendations raise an interesting question of just how much reliance directors can place on the advice of others.[33] The general standard is that a director may rely on information or guidance provided by outside experts, corporate officers, or employees if, and only if, the director reasonably believes that this person is reliable and competent in the matters presented. However, a director may not ignore what is going on around him or her in the conduct of the business. If a director learns of suspicious circumstances or has any reason to doubt the advice given, such inquires must be made as an ordinarily prudent person would make under the same or similar circumstances. Whether the director acted prudently is a question of fact to be decided by the court.

Fifth, directors must become more involved in board activities and corporate decisions. As we saw in the section on the duty of care, directors who act passively face potential liability for their nonaction. At a minimum, modern day directors should follow the suggestions presented earlier. Specifically, directors should insist on receiving adequate information; they should take sufficient time to consider this information; they should ask questions and play the role of devil's advocates when considering the advice of others; and they should seek outside expert advice when appropriate. As this list suggests, being a director today is more time-consuming than ever before. As such, directors should also consider limiting the number of boards on which they serve. Directors are opening themselves up to problems if and when they join boards they cannot adequately serve. In addition to following the above advice, prudent directors should also leave an explicit paper trail of all actions taken. More important, those who follow the applicable legal standards described in this chapter may still be liable unless they can prove that the standards were met. A paper trail provides this objective "proof."[34]

For researchers, the current legal environment raises many interesting and important issues. One potential topic concerns the effect of legal changes on board stability, and the resulting impact of this on firm performance. Will changes in the legal environment continue to result in director turnover? In addition, researchers may want to study shifts in director characteristics, and changes in the format and structure of boards, that result from this dynamic environment. Another possible research topic would be exploration of the role organizations play in creating or enacting their own legal environment. In the case of state statutes limiting director liability, for example, it is not known how active corporations have been in lobbying for these changes. Nevertheless, such moves may have dramatic implications for firm performance. Still another area for future research may lie in the area of boardroom processes. As legal accountability is increased, we may see directors taking greater responsibility and more active roles in day-to-day operations. This, in turn, may alter how the courts and regulatory agencies view boards. These examples represent only a few of the many issues open to researchers in this area. Moreover, given the dynamic nature of the law, there is little doubt that directors can benefit greatly from such research.

■ Conclusion

As this chapter has shown, the legal environment surrounding corporate boards of directors is changing. Laws regulating director conduct are becoming more pervasive. Attention from regulatory agencies is on the rise. Also on the rise is the willingness of outside parties to use these laws and regulations to bring directors into the legal system through lawsuits and regulatory agency adjudication. Yet at the same time, the methods available to protect the personal financial health of directors are in a state of flux. While some protections are increasing (e.g., state statutes), others (e.g., D&O insurance) are decreasing. More important, the protections offered are incomplete. Directors who must defend themselves against legal action often face significant financial risks (only some of which may be offset by insurance or indemnification). The price seems especially high when added to the huge time commitments, stress, personal embarrassment, and opportunity costs involved.

The job of corporate director is an extremely difficult one, and this difficulty is increasing due to the changes in the legal environment. While we can offer suggestions on how to act, and describe some of the minimal legal standards, there is no substitute for responsible, ethical, and informed behavior. Above all else, directors must remember that it is their responsibility to protect themselves from liability. In today's legal environment, not doing so is a risk directors can ill-afford to take.

■ Notes

1. The actual execution of these policies is most often conducted by individuals (i.e., professional managers) hired by the board for that purpose. The board, for example,

is directly responsible for hiring the chief executive officer (CEO) who, in turn, hires other top managers.

2. The exception is Louisiana, which uses Napoleonic Code instead of the common law.

3. Two additional points concerning the law are worth noting. First, the law is filled with exceptions and qualifications to the rule. Because this chapter deals with general aspects of the law, we ignore most of these exceptions and qualifications. Second, the law necessarily defines a set of minimally acceptable behaviors. These behaviors may be defined either as those which are required or those which are prohibited.

4. A person competent to contract must be at least a certain age and not mentally ill or incapacitated.

5. 2 Atk. 400 (1742).

6. See, for example, *Selheimer v. Manganese Corporation of America*, 224 A.2d 634 (Pa. 1966).

7. 488 A.2d 858 (1985).

8. With 20 million shares of Trans Union stock outstanding, this measure of damages could have been catastrophic for the directors. The case, however, was settled for $22 million. The majority of this amount was paid by the acquiring company and through the director's liability insurance.

9. Ideally, recognition of conflicts will occur prior to any discussion by the board on the transaction in question. The issue of disclosure timing is currently being debated within the legal community. A committee of legal scholars, working on a Restatement of the Law of Corporate Governance, has included a section in their report which mandates that approval be obtained before a particular transaction takes place. If accepted, this section would greatly alter the legal environment of directors.

10. C.A. 3-85-0794-R (N.D. Tex. 1986).

11. Financial liability is not the only punishment that directors may face for corporate wrongdoing. Some statutes, such as the Foreign Corrupt Practices Act of 1977, have provisions allowing courts to apply jail terms to directors of convicted organizations.

12. 496 N.E.2d 959 (1986).

13. *Liggett Co. v. Lee*, 288 U.S. 517 (1933) (Justice Brandeis, dissenting).

14. *Dynamics Corporation of America v. CTS Corporation*, Fed. Sec. L. Rep. (CCH), p. 92, 768 (1986).

15. These laws made it easier for directors and managers to keep their jobs. Among the many states which have enacted these statutes are Pennsylvania (1990) and Wisconsin (1990).

16. For a more detailed discussion of the role of cost-benefit analysis on federal regulation, see Heimann et al., 1990.

17. Clayton Act § 4, 15 U.S.C. § 15 (1982).

18. A director who purchases 100 shares of his company's stock on January 1 for $10/share and then sell 50 shares on May 25 for $13/share, for instance, must give his or her profit of $150 to the company.

19. Examples of federal statutes that include possible criminal liability for directors include the Foreign Corrupt Practices Act, the Racketeer Influenced and Corrupt Organizations Act (a.k.a. RICO), as well as sections of securities, environmental, and tax laws.

20. *United States v. American Radiator & Standard San. Corporation*, 433 F.2d 174 (3rd Cir. 1970) *cert denied* 401 U.S. 948 (1971).

21. 18 U.S.C. § 2 (a.k.a. The Complicity Statute).

22. *People v. O'Neil,* N.E.2d 1090, leave to appeal denied, 534 N.E.2d 400 (1990).

23. A person who is not currently a director, but who is mentioned in the registration statement as someone who is about to become a director, may also be liable.

24. Joint and several liability means that the penalty must be paid by the defendants, regardless of how the defendants divide up their contributions. Under joint and several liability, if the corporation becomes bankrupt and the other defendants have no money, a lone solvent director may be legally responsible for the entire judgment.

25. For example, see *Van Gorkom* where the applicable interpretation of the standards of behavior was developed at the trial for behaviors that had occurred previously.

26. The belief is that directors who breached their duty should not pass the loss on to the corporation.

27. Recent court decisions have gotten around this requirement by holding that a policy of indemnification, on its own, benefits the corporation by encouraging people to undertake the responsibilities of a director.

28. When the director faces potential criminal liability, there is an additional requirement that the director had no reasonable cause to believe that his or her conduct was unlawful.

29. A management resolution is a proposal submitted by management for inclusion in a firm's annual proxy statement. Management is asking shareholders to consider and support proposed changes in existing corporate policies via their proxy vote.

30. This limitation applies except in cases where (a) the director received a financial benefit to which he or she was not entitled, (b) harm was intentionally inflicted, (c) distributions were unlawful, or (d) there was an intentional violation of criminal law.

31. *Etheridge v. Medical Center Hospitals,* 376 S.E.2d 525 (Va. 1989).

32. *Sofic v. Fiberboard Corporation,* 112 Wash. 2d 636 (1989).

33. It is interesting to note that in the *Van Gorkom* case, the attorney who addressed the board of Trans Union advised the directors that they might be sued if they *failed* to accept the offer, and that a fairness opinion was not required as a matter of law. The board vote came after, and in partial reliance on, this advice.

34. The primary vehicle for this paper trail will be the board minutes. Therefore, care should be taken to ensure that all applicable standards are reflected within these documents.

■ References

Chaganti, R., Mahajan, V., & Sharma, S. (1985). Corporate board size, composition and corporate failures in retailing industry. *Journal of Management Studies, 22,* 400-416.

Gales, L., & Kesner, I. (in press). An analysis of board of director size and composition in bankrupt organizations. *Journal of Business Research.*

Hamilton, R. (1987). *The law of corporations in a nutshell.* St. Paul, MN: West.

Heimann, C. M., Bennett, D., Binzer, M., et al. (1990). Project: The impact of cost-benefit analysis on federal administrative law. *Administrative Law Review, 42,* 545-654.

Jones, T. (1979). Stockholders and the corporation: A new relationship. *The Journal of Contemporary Business, 8*(1), 93-102.

Jones, T. (1980). What's bothering those shareholder plaintiffs? *California Management Review, 22*(4), 5-19.

Jones, T. (1981). Shareholder suits: Good news and bad news for corporate executives. *California Management Review, 23*(4), 77-86.

Jones, T. (1985). The shareholder litigation threat. In E. Matter & M. Ball (Eds.), *Handbook for corporate directors.* New York: McGraw-Hill.

Jones, T. (1986). Corporate board structure and performance: Variations in the incidence of shareholders suits. In L. Preston (Ed.) *Research in corporate social performance and policy* (Vol. 8, pp. 345-359). Greenwich, CT: JAI Press.

Kesner, I. (1987). Directors' stock ownership and organizational performance: An investigation of Fortune 500 companies. *Journal of Management, 13*(3), 499-507.

Kesner, I., & Johnson, R. (1990a). An investigation of the relationship between board composition and stockholder suits. *Strategic Management Journal, 11,* 327-336.

Kesner, I., & Johnson, R. (1990b). Boardroom crisis: Fiction or fact. *Academy of Management Executive, 4*(1), 23-35.

Kesner, I., Victor, B., & Lamont, B. (1986). Board composition and the commission of illegal acts: An investigation of Fortune 500 companies. *Academy of Management Journal, 29*(4), 789-799.

Kohls, J. (1985). Corporate board structure, social reporting and social performance. In L. Preston (Ed.), *Research in corporate social performance and policy* (Vol. 7, pp. 165-189). Greenwich, CT: JAI Press.

Korn/Ferry International. (1987). *Board of directors: Fourteenth annual study.* Los Angeles: Author.

Louden, J. (1982). *The director, a professional's guide to effective board work.* New York: American Management Associations.

Mace, M. (1971). *Directors: Myth and reality.* Boston: Division of Research, Graduate School of Business Administration, Harvard University.

Marcil, S., & O'Hara, P. (1987). *Voting by institutional investors on corporate governance issues in the 1987 proxy season.* Washington, DC: Investor Responsibility Research Center's Corporate Governance Survey.

Mintzberg, H. (1983). *Power in and around organizations.* Englewood Cliffs, NJ: Prentice-Hall.

Pfeffer, J. (1972). Size and composition of corporate boards of directors, the organization and its environment. *Administrative Science Quarterly, 17,* 218-228.

Pfeffer, J., & Salancik, G. (1978). *The external control of organizations: A resource dependence perspective.* New York: Harper & Row.

Rechner, P. L., & Dalton, D. R. (1989). The impact of CEO as board chairperson on corporate performance: Evidence vs. rhetoric. *Academy of Management Executive, 3*(2), 141-143.

Schmidt, R. (1975). Does board composition really make a difference? *Conference Board Record, 12*(10), 38-41.

Securities and Exchange Commission (SEC). (1980). *Staff report on corporate accountability* (Printed for the use of the Committee on Banking, Housing, and Urban Affairs—United States Senate). Washington DC: Government Printing Office.

Taking charge: Corporate directors start to flex their muscle. (1989, July 3). *Business Week,* pp. 66-71.

The board revolt: Business as usual won't cut it anymore at humbled GM. (1992, April 20). *Business Week,* pp. 30-36.

The job nobody wants: Outside directors find that the risks and hassles just aren't worth it. (1986, September 8). *Business Week*, pp. 56-61.

Vance, S. (1964). *Boards of directors: Structure and performance*. Portland: University of Oregon Press.

Vance, S. (1983). *Corporate leadership: Boards, directors, and strategy*. New York: McGraw-Hill.

Willing directors are hard to find. (1992, July 22). *Wall Street Journal*.

Wyatt Survey. (1988). *Directors and officers liability survey—1988*. Chicago: The Wyatt Company.

Wyatt Survey. (1990). *Directors and officers liability survey—1990*. Chicago: The Wyatt Company.

Zahra, S., & Stanton, W. (1988). The implications of board of director's composition for corporate strategy and performance. *International Journal of Management, 5*, 229-236.

Part IV

Legalistic Rhetoric

10

Communication Under Conditions of Litigation Risk:
A Grounded Theory of Plausible Deniability in the Iran-Contra Affair

Larry D. Browning
Robert Folger

> *"All you have to remember," one executive says, "is . . . let the language be ambiguous enough that if the job be successfully carried out, all credit can be claimed, and if not, a technical alibi be found. . . . "*
>
> Whyte (1952, p. 52).

Adding to previous organizational analyses about the account- ability of conduct (e.g., Browning, 1988; Folger & Bies, 1989; Hamilton & Sanders, 1992; Tetlock, 1985), this chapter looks at account- ability in a particular context: when actions are taken deliberately because the risk of litigation has been considered. *Plausible deniability*, a term used by participants in the Iran-Contra affair, adds a new per- spective on accountability by stressing the dilemmas that stem from anticipating risks associated with litigation. Iran-Contra participants had anticipated such risks. They consciously acted in advance to minimize the President's accountability, taking actions that subsequently would add credibility when he denied knowledge of decisions or endeavors allegedly under- taken on his behalf. Referring to meetings with Ronald Reagan, for example, John Poindexter reported having made "a very deliberate decision not to ask the President" about diverting funds to the Contras so Reagan would have "future deniability . . . if it ever leaked out" (Rowley, 1988). Poindexter also once noted that: "We've built a wall around the President to provide him 'deniability' " (Hitchens, 1987).

The Iran-Contra tactics of plausible deniability illustrate management practices that emerge when lower-level decision makers willingly protect higher-level decision makers from litigation risk and work to keep the latter from being held accountable by the public. When anticipating possibly adverse litigation, managers of such risky projects face the challenge of satisfying internal (corporate) demands for accountability and yet reconciling those demands with the need to avoid external (legal) demands for accountability. Plausible deniability represents a way of dealing with this accountability challenge—the problem of reconciling the need for subordinate accountability with the leader's need for protection from legal liability.

Analyzing the Iran-Contra case, which few would hold up as embodying virtuous organizational practices, thus helps emphasize the possible tension between the goal of encouraging subordinates' responsibility for problem solving and the goal of avoiding litigation (Browning & Shetler, in press; Sitkin & Sutcliffe, 1991; Tamuz & Sitkin, 1992). This case on avoiding legal constraints thereby adds to the literature on managerial discretion (Feldman,1992; Hambrick & Finkelstein, 1987). One of the few remaining advantages of bureaucracy—clear lines of authority—is undermined at a time when researchers are showing the benefits of flat organizations and leaderless teams (Larsen & LaFasto, 1989; Peters, 1992). The Iran-Contra material illustrates the difficulty of assigning responsibility in an organization of shrewd and independent participants.

Making *legal* responsibility (liability) hard to assign was the goal of these actors. From a legal standpoint, the less someone knows about a problem and the less one is directly involved in receiving or sending earlier information about a problem, the less one is at risk (Allen, 1987; Tamuz & Sitkin, 1992). The establishment of innocence becomes complex when there are multiple players in regular, job-related contact with one another. Accountability becomes problematic in an organizational hierarchy because role obligations are reciprocal: "the subordinate's duty is to carry out orders, while the authority's reciprocal obligation is to oversee subordinates" (Hamilton, 1986, p. 120). These obligations of communication make innocence especially important at a later unfortunate time when the problem springs out of control, as it did when the Challenger exploded (Browning, 1988). The most compelling argument protecting NASA leadership following the explosion was that, according to the Challenger report, they had not known about the launch decision, and if they had known, would certainly have made a different decision. This chapter tells the story of practices designed to make that type of defense believable.

The chapter is organized into the following sections: (1) Grounded theory is justified as a procedure for analyzing plausible deniability; (2) a data section makes explicit the rule system for plausible deniability that Iran-Contra participants used implicitly; (3) distinctive features of plausible deniability are highlighted; (4) comparative material illustrates similarities and differences with other organizational instances in which denying culpability has been a goal; and (5) a summary of this analysis provides the basis for concluding commentary.

■ Grounded Theory Methodology

The method of grounded theory (Browning, 1978; Glaser, 1978; Glaser & Strauss, 1967; Strauss, 1987) is a content analysis procedure for managing large amounts of disparate, qualitative data. It can be applied to an array of qualitative data, including diaries, letters, interviews, and observations (Strauss, 1987). It allows the formation of a set of "rules" for plausible deniability from the Iran-Contra hearing transcripts and from the print and television media surrounding the hearings. It departs from content analysis procedures that assume categories are mutually exclusive. Instead, grounded theory encourages multiple meanings in data and hence overlapping categories. The most important criterion for data is theoretical saturation, meaning that the corpus of data contains as many instances and types of the phenomenon under study as possible. A single system is examined until the data become repetitive (e.g., asking questions in interview research until no outlying or novel examples are uncovered).

This study responded to the requirement for theoretical saturation by conducting a DIALOG search on *plausible deniability*. DIALOG is a commercial information-retrieval service subsidiary of the Knight-Ridder Communications company. The DIALOG search, which covered more than 350 databases, indicated that the term *plausible deniability* (or *deniability*) was used 237 times in hearings and media commentary during the Iran-Contra hearings in the summer of 1987. The senior author generated a manuscript for analysis by searching for the word "deniability" in the DIALOG files and adding two sentences before and after the 237 uses of the term to build in context for the term.

When these four sentences failed to provide enough clarity to sort the incident, he read the entire text before making an assignment.

The strength of grounded theory is its attention to details and its progression from details to abstraction. Single units of data or *incidents*, which range in length from a sentence or two to a paragraph, are marked, separated, and numbered to prepare them for coding (Browning, 1978). Single incidents are continuously sorted into an emerging set of categories until every incident has been analyzed. Glaser and Strauss (1967), who developed this procedure, call it *constant-comparative analysis*. The method calls for units of the qualitative data to be sorted into a category system by the inductive selection of a label or phrase to collections of similar examples until a smaller, abstract representation of the data has been generated.

The method was applied to the data on plausible deniability by reviewing the 237 incidents and sorting them into an emerging coding scheme. For example, a statement by Elliott Abrams of the State Department was contained in a paragraph on plausible deniability: "I think most of us were careful not to ask lots of questions other than once in a while to say 'Is this okay? Is this stuff legal?' " (Hitchens, 1987). This quote was sorted into a category called *Avoid Identifying Specific Details* because Abrams consciously avoided asking questions. Another example in this category comes from the Iran-Contra hearings, when Senate committee counsel Arthur Liman asked Poindexter: "What you are really saying to me is that if an [administrative official] didn't want to know, [he'd] have to make an effort not to know?" "Yes," Poindexter replied (Hasson, 1987).

These two examples of coding were typical of the analysis of plausible deniability. This research was unusual because the match between data and categories required fewer inferential steps than customary for grounded theory analysis. There were few marginally applicable examples in this data set. This was true because the texts—from the media and the hearings—were focused and had little incidental information surrounding their presentation. This was a study of sophisticated and conscious performers—writers, lawyers, and actual participants—who created a direct and pointed text. This methodological artifact will later appear as an organizational achievement. In the Iran-Contra initiative, organization members carried out their roles with high consensus on who should say and do what. Ideology notwithstanding, there is very little conflict among the texts. There is no missing piece; there is no smoking gun.

The analysis did create some uncertainty about which categories provide the best placement for particular incidents. Because grounded theory deconstructs a text into relatively small pieces and then reconstructs a model from the bits, the research method generates differentiated categories whose differences are sometimes subtle. For example, all the categories in *The Limits on Written Records Core* focus on limiting or avoiding data. Although these categories are different, as the description that follows each presentation demonstrates, the assignment of some data pieces went into more than one of the categories. During the final shaping of the constant comparative analysis, overlapping incidents were assigned to the category that increased the comprehensiveness of data and created a richer description (Fielding & Fielding, 1986; Geertz, 1973). In instances where data could be used in more than one category, it was assigned to the category it bolstered the most. This subjective choice is offset by the transparency of the relationship between data and theory, which allows the reader to monitor the research with two questions: Do the examples fit the category listed? Are there enough differences in the categories offered to justify the distinction?

Grounded theory analysis continues to move to a more abstract textual representation of the data. The final step moves to integration—the "ever increasing articulation of the components of the theory" (Strauss, 1987, p. 21)—after completion of the category analysis of the qualitative data. Integration involves searching for the underlying uniformities in the set of categories produced by the qualitative data and formulating a theory with a smaller set of high-level concepts. This step "elaborates upon the category system by abstracting from it" (Glaser & Strauss, 1967, p. 110) by identifying the core categories that account for most of the variation in a pattern of behavior, while maximizing the parsimony and scope of the theory (Strauss, 1987). Because grounded theory seeks to generate interpretations, the core categories are tied to theoretical literature to increase the abstractness and widen the application of the findings. The theoretical core of this research focused on the problem of reconciling the need for subordinate accountability with the leader's need for protection from liability. Under conditions of risk, this problem leads to the use of innovative management practices, rather than overtly legalistic practices.

This coupling of theory and data occurs after analyzing the data, which collectively serve as a sensitizing device (Bacharach & Lawler, 1980) for recalling and adding theory to the data. Adding theory to the data is particularly important in single-case analyses, such as this one, because adding multiple theoretical interpretations to a single case increases the "degrees of freedom" for interpreting the research (Campbell, 1975). The data were compared and coded until all examples of plausible deniability were included.

■ A Grounded Theory of Plausible Deniability

This section provides analysis by listing the rules for accomplishing plausible deniability extracted from the DIALOG files. These rules are interwoven with examples from the DIALOG files and an explanation of how the rules operate. The term *rules* functions as an organizing device because the discourse included in this analysis has high occurrences of justification and purpose. Rules differ from laws in that the participants are not required to follow these practices, but they tend to do so with great regularity across players; they follow a comprehensive, yet largely unspoken set of cultural rules (Harre & Secord, 1972). Because grounded theory seeks continual division of data into larger categories, the rules are arranged into core sets of organizing and communication practices, which are explained in the section following the presentation of data.[1]

The term *plausible deniability* subsumes the specific categories identified below because it reflects the single purpose underlying all rules for action: *To insulate a leader from responsibility.* Plausible deniability was seen as justifiable because leaders "confront the necessity of directing actions that they would, in normal circumstances, be inclined to call immoral" (Friedrich, 1986a). Because the purpose of deniability is to protect the leader, underlings have to make judgments on the appropriateness of a topic for the dignity of the office their leader holds. Donald Gregg, a national security adviser to (then) Vice President George Bush, exemplified this point in describing why he withheld information from Bush during the Iran-Contra Affair: "I had no sense of illegality . . . I had a sense of corruption. . . . I frankly did not think it was vice presidential level" (Friedrich, 1986b; Roland & Mianowany, 1987). This first instance hints at how a practice, which was later scorned, was used in the name of honor for the exalted reason of protecting a leader.

To insulate leaders, people acting as buffers must make decisions with protection in mind. Poindexter was aware of both the risk of controversy and of his authority to approve Oliver North's request:

But because it was controversial, and I obviously knew that it would cause a ruckus if it were exposed, I decided to insulate the President from the decision and give him some deniability . . . I decided at that point not to tell the President. . . . I didn't tell Col. North that I was not going to tell the President. . . . I recognize that it would be a lot easier on me now if I had told him, but honestly, the facts are I did not tell him. (Drinkard, 1987)

Plausible deniability protected the leader from a disastrous outcome. Subordinates accomplished this overall objective by using specific tactics. Coding of the Iran-Contra material (see Table 10.1) revealed that those tactics fell into two major sets. Those classified under the heading of "Organizing Categories" involved tactics affecting the way various participants organized themselves for action, particularly according to methods that enhanced autonomy and minimized accountability; those under the heading of "Communication Categories" indicate the way communication practices also facilitated the objective of deniability.

■ Organizing Categories

Autonomy (Core, I)

Organizations take risks, despite expectations for order in traditional bureaucracies, by emphasizing innovation and individual autonomy (cf. Peters & Waterman, 1982, chap. 7). The actions of the Iran-Contra participants mirror this entrepreneurial practice by focusing on the performance of a small unit of people who are part of a larger organization. Four practices of plausible deniability support individual autonomy.

Rule I.A., Assign responsibility to a selected, single, low-level volunteer. This rule points to the role played by Oliver North and is exemplified in his famous statement that he agreed to "go on the spear." He became "the switching point that made the whole system work" and, according to Poindexter, "the kingpin to the Central American opposition once the CIA was restricted" (Knutson, 1987). North's role as the locus of responsibility for the task was widely affirmed (Magnuson, Muller, & Van Voorst, 1986). In return for this autonomy, North freely accepted the responsibility to take blame after the risk turned to failure. When asked who he was accepting responsibility for, North's reply was

Table 10.1

Outline of a Primer for Plausible Deniability

Purpose: Insulate Leader From Responsibility

Organizing Categories	I. The Autonomy Core.
	  A. Localize responsibility on a selected, single, low-level volunteer.
	  B. Formulate organizational structure through action.
	  C. Move commitments to action from top-down to bottom-up.
	  D. Develop bonds of trust in commitments.
		II. The Uncertain Membership and Resources Core.
		  A. Obtain resources—free of formal accountability.
		  B. Select members who are free of organizational role expectations.
		  C. Develop a staff outside direct responsibility chains.

Communication Categories	III. The Limits on Written Records Core.
	  A. Avoid identifying specific details.
	  B. Avoid written record of the organization.
	  C. Destroy evidence.
	  D. Delay providing details.
		IV. The Obfuscation Core.
		  A. Have vague recollections or be completely forgetful.
		  B. Have multiple, ambiguous estimations of wrong-doing to avoid focus.
		  C. Use passive voice in acknowledging wrongdoing.
		  D. Have low-level members accept blame for wrongdoing.
		  E. Use conceptual diversions to insulate the leader from responsibility.
		  F. Prefer truth and be satisfied with dishonesty.

unequivocal: "For whoever necessary; for the administration, for the President, for however high up the chain that they needed someone to say, 'That's the guy that did it, and he's gone. And now we've put that behind us and let's get on with other things,' " (Hitchens, 1987). Thus, North participated willingly in adopting the role of a scapegoat. In Kenneth Burke's terms, North became the " 'representative' or 'vessel' of certain unwanted evils, the sacrificial animal upon whose back the burden of these evils is ritualistically loaded" (Burke, 1973, pp. 39-40).

The Iran-Contra initiative's dependence on low-level performers is theoretically consistent with innovative management strategies in organizations. Innovation is often accomplished by single individuals, freed from organizational control (Pelz, 1969, 1976; Souder, 1983) to act out a distinctive personality openly—riding a motorcycle through the laboratory, for example—while pursuing unique definitions of organizational goals. The paradoxical requirements of an innovative structure are simultaneously to provide stability and to allow individuality. There is a tendency for stability to be placed in the system and for novelty to "be placed in the members, often one or two individuals" (Smith & Berg, 1987, p. 648).

Rule I.B., Formulate organizational structure through action. This rule is represented widely in the transcripts. Rather than operating from a plan, which is difficult to keep from circulation in a culture where news leaks are likely, actions often occurred instead of plans. People were known for what they did, and action spoke louder than words, indicating a "bias for action" (Peters & Waterman, 1982). Action created the Iran-Contra organization. For example, Richard Secord was known as "a guy who can go to key people in foreign countries and get things done," an expert expediter. "He can move things from one place to another almost immediately . . . the heart of special operations" (Chaze, 1986, p. 26)

This emphasis on the immediacy of action is consistent with the available evidence suggesting that diversion of the arms-sale money to the Contras was unplanned—events began to unfold spontaneously within the space of a few minutes after Oliver North had proposed the action during a meeting of the two men in Poindexter's White House office (Parry & Barger, 1986). Formulating organizational structure through action means placing top priority on getting things done, and done quickly, rather than on following procedures. In the case of Iran-Contra, the ends justified the means. A statement by the late Grace

Hopper, the Navy's grand speaker for innovation, illustrates that justification of the means can become an afterthought when action precedes plans: "And remember, it is easier to ask for forgiveness than to ask for permission" ("The Grand Lady of Technology," 1986). Such actions may seem careless or irresponsible, even adolescent and playful— unlike the seasoned judgment expected of a high-level official. Because this testing of the boundaries of decorum is done in the Iran-Contra case by a low-level performer, it is a less surprising role violation and less embarrassing to the organization (Einhorn & Hogarth, 1986).

Rule I.C., Shift direction of risky commitments to action from top-down to bottom-up. This rule is consistent with the teamwork practice of making use of the knowledge of innovators when they are young and impassioned with ideas (Larson & LaFasto, 1989). Poindexter's and North's words tie the risk they took to a world of imperfection. Poindexter: "I frankly don't find that [selling arms to Iran] distasteful . . . I think that we live in a very imperfect world, a very dangerous world, and sometimes you don't have the best options or the ideal option, and you've got to do what's necessary" (Hitchens, 1987). North spoke similarly: "This is not the way things ought to be . . . but this was a high-risk venture. We had an established person to take the spear, and we had hoped we had established plausible deniability of a direct connection with the U.S. government" (Hitchens, 1987).

Having responsibility at lower levels is one way to manage the requirement for consistency in a world of contradiction and rapid change. "You frequently do limited things to achieve a specific result that may be inconsistent with your general policy. That's not that unusual" (Knutson, 1987). In the Iran-Contra affair, this scheme represented the difference between short- and long-term objectives.

Using a bottom-up development of commitments also allows for multiple approaches to a problem (Deleuze & Guattari, 1987). Because there are more people at lower levels, the range of ideologies is distributed across more individuals. An organization with a pool of ideologies increases its chances for effectiveness on any given task. Career bureaucrats can administer standard programs, and innovators can link ideology to practice in innovative programs. Innovation is fraught with failure (cf. Sitkin, 1992), however, and failures can be located at the level of the individual or sub-unit because of the catastrophic effects of organization-level failure (March, 1981).

Rule I.D., Develop bonds of trust. This rule identifies an ingredient required when action conveys shared values, despite a lack of formal support or predictable progress. Trust is reciprocated and reinforced when people provide support under conditions of risk (Deutsch, 1962; Fox, 1974; Sitkin & Roth, 1993) and the threat of litigation adds to the risk of covert activities.

> [Senator] Nunn asked one more question. "Is it fair to say that those who deal with covert activities in the world of deception, in the world of secrets, have to trust each other?" "Absolutely," the spy replied. "If you can't trust each other you are dead in this world." (Knutson, 1987)

Incidents and conversations including secrecy, action, and risk—which abound in these data—thus indicate varieties of in-group behavior requiring norms of shared trust among participants in the Iran-Contra affair.

Uncertain Membership and Resources (Core, II)

The rules in the uncertain membership and resources core illustrate the following principle: Ambiguities regarding membership and resources facilitate unconstrained action. Tolerance of ambiguity means not being constrained by rational means-ends connections identified and approved in a hierarchical system of allocation.

Rule II.A, Obtain external resources—free of formal accountability. This rule argues for the value of ambiguous (e.g., untraceable) resources. This rule illustrates a variation on the theme of industrial "skunk works," in which innovators often acquire resources by means outside of bureaucratic guidelines while toiling out of sight or inconspicuously (Peters & Waterman, 1982). Examples include North's recruitment of "Ross Perot to pay ransom for the release of a hostage in Lebanon" in spite of the U.S. policy against ransoming hostages ("Iran-Contra Arms Sale," 1986). The lack of formal accountability for resources meant that "more than half of the $27 million in nonlethal assistance approved by Congress last year for the Contras could not be tracked" (Parry & Barger, 1986).

Rule II.B., Select members who are free of organizational role expectations. This rule refers to the types of formal expectations central to classical views of authority. If actors' roles are not formally defined or detailed, their denial of direct knowledge can more easily withstand questioning. People who have no direct responsibilities are called "cutouts" (Parry & Barger, 1986). For example, North recruited former government employees who knew the undercover ropes but no longer had any formal relationship with the government, so that such denials would be more plausible ("School for Scandal," 1986).

Rule II.C., Develop a staff outside direct responsibility chains. This rule refers to defining job positions ambiguously. The U.S. advisor in El Salvador had "knowledge of supplies going to the Nicaraguan Contras, but he had deniability; he was (it is claimed) only an observer, not a supervisor" (Hitchens, 1987). This category includes the private groups President Reagan referred to, saying that "the administration has known of private groups and citizens aiding the Nicaraguan Contras, but not exactly what they were doing" (Magnuson et al., 1986). Remarks by CIA Director William Casey also fall into this category: "I don't know anything about diversion of funds," Casey told *Time.* "The NSC [National Security Council] was operating this thing; we were in a support mode" (Magnuson et al,, 1986).

Collectively, rules in these organizing categories maintained the autonomy of subordinates and fostered generally high levels of ambiguity for strategic reasons. Rules in the communication categories, described below, illustrate the way the desire to protect a leader also produces various communication practices. The organizing categories are a design for flexibility; the communication categories are the practice of flexibility.

■ Communication Categories

Limits on Written Records (Core, III)

This core's four rules avoid specificity and writing. They directly contradict Taylor's rational theory: "The work of every workman (*sic*) is fully planned out by the management at least one day in advance, and each man receives in most cases complete written instructions, describing in detail the tasks which he is to accomplish as well as the means to be used in doing the work" (Taylor, 1947, p. 39). Taylor, of course, placed great emphasis on the advantages of standardization and routine, whereas the details of the Iran-Contra operation were anything but ordinary.

Rule III.A, Avoid identifying specific details. This rule includes Elliott Abrams's comment cited earlier: "I think most of us were careful not to ask lots of questions other than once in a while to say 'Is this okay? Is this stuff legal?' " (Alterman, 1987). Similarly, Poindexter's affirmative response to Senate counsel Liman's question: "If [an administration official] didn't want to know, [he'd] have to make an effort not to know?" illustrates such avoidance (Hasson, 1987). Another example is Casey's comment: "I think we knew in a general way that money was being raised and probably would have put a report together on it if we wanted to, but we didn't" (Magnuson et al., 1986). No one, it appears, wanted to acquire knowledge about specific details of the operation, which made subsequent denial of such knowledge much easier and potentially more plausible.

Rule III.B, Avoid written records. This rule accomplishes plausible deniability by providing some organizational structure "without leaving a paper trail" (Magnuson et al., 1986). Poindexter's testimony shows he was annoyed that a supply plane to the Contras had considerable identifying material on board. "I didn't think it was very professional, that these guys needed to shape up in terms of maintaining deniability of the operation. . . . And carrying identifying information aboard the aircraft was just not acceptable" (Drinkard, 1987). Such comments illustrate how this rule functions as an implementing device to support other rules, including several in the "Organizing Categories." Having no paper trail of reporting relationships makes it easier to formulate organizational structure through action (Rule I.B.), for example, and to develop a staff external to direct responsibility chains (Rule II.C.).

Rule III.C., Destroy evidence. This rule is illustrated by the 10 days North used to destroy important documents. "Because of Lt. Col. Oliver North's shredding of White House documents, the extent of President Reagan's involvement in the Iran-Contra scandal may never be known" (Rowley, 1988). Some things are known, however, from North's (1991) own description of events. This description notes a clear connection between his increased shredding of documents and the type of objectives central to achieving plausible deniability. In particular, North wrote that he "began to shred more than the routine excess paperwork from the office" as a direct response to instructions from Casey to "Shut it down [covert operations] and clean it up."

Based on those instructions, "during my final weeks at the NSC I shredded more than ever" (North, 1991, pp. 297-298).

As in the previously cited instance of Poindexter's concern with participants' identifiability over possible wrongdoing, such actions are of at least questionable legality. They also imply an underlying attitude about morality that gives greater weight to personal expediency and individual choice than to the consensually validated norms of a moral community. The lack of control by authority or by adherence to procedural rules and regulations, in other words, seemed to foster arbitrary and capricious actions—or at least actions that prevent individual judgment from being subject to checks and balances by outside review. Further discussion of this attitude appears in conjunction with rule IV.F., below.

Rule III.D., Delay providing details. This rule means leaders operate via the hope that present actions will either credibly align with future specific outcomes or be forgotten. This rule is illustrated by action aimed at "Keeping Congress in the dark about the arms sales for 14 months" (Richards, 1987). A standard for negotiation practice is to initiate bargaining with broad goals, to allow possible agreement with contenders to develop over time (Bowers, Gilchrist, & Browning, 1980; see also Shapiro & Kolb, this volume). If compromises or negotiated agreements are reached only after considerable time has passed, a chance exists that initial demands will ultimately be excluded or modified beyond the extent of revealing liability. The logic of delay assumes that if deniability is initially problematic, it may become easier to achieve later. This is a hopeful, even optimistic, cultural rule.

Obfuscation (Core, IV)

The six rules in the obfuscation core are verbal practices that match the instability of a loose and indirect organization. An organization with low accountability corresponds with low accountability language. Collins, Warnock, Aiello, and Miller (1975) show how easily individuals accept ambiguous data:

> It does not trouble people much that their heads are full of incomplete, inconsistent, and uncertain information. With little trepidation they go about drawing rather doubtful conclusions from their tangled mass of knowledge, for the most part unaware of the tenuousness of their reasoning. The very tenuousness of the enterprise is bound up with the power

it gives people to deal with a language and a world full of ambiguity and uncertainty. (p. 383)

These statements by Collins et al. attest to the power of language as a substitute for structure. The following rules illustrate how diffuse and dissipative language adds to the practices cited above in contributing to plausible deniability.

Rule IV.A., Have vague recollections or be completely forgetful. This rule includes Poindexter's repeated loss of memory. Although he has a reputation for a photographic memory, he used: "I don't remember" and "I don't recall" in public questioning at least 184 times. This category also fits Casey, whose intelligence was known to diminish quite conveniently when he was giving testimony. As one old friend noted, "His mumble becomes decidedly worse when he has to talk to Congress," (Magnuson et al., 1986). Rule IV.A. is invoked when a post hoc evaluation attempts to sort confusing details. As Lyotard (1984) notes, a narrative cannot be obtained from someone who chooses not to offer it. Thus, despite its simplicity, claiming a loss of memory is powerful because it is almost hopeless to ask questions that expose this strategy. Neither "I do not believe you" nor "It is impossible that you are that forgetful" can be stated in legal hearings.

Rule IV.B., Have multiple, ambiguous estimations of wrongdoing to avoid focus. This rule includes the judgment as to whether staff people were incompetent or dishonest: "Are the staff members lying? Are they incompetent? Any one of those possibilities ain't good for the people involved" (Parry & Barger, 1986). This estimation was applied to Poindexter. His " 'management style' was so loose, his judgment so lamentable, that one was left with the choice of either giving him the benefit of the doubt by assuming he was lying or being dumbstruck that such a dummy could have been a national security advisor" (Parry & Barger).

Rule IV.B means that when one is charged with being either devious or stupid, additional choices create protective confusion. Connecticut Democrat Samuel Gejdenson contended: "If Casey really knows as little as he tried to portray, he ought to be fired for incompetence. And if he knew more, he ought to be fired because the President instructed his people to be forthcoming" (Magnuson et al., 1986). The yes/no possibility for each of the two: (a) devious, but not stupid; (b) stupid, but not devious; combined with (c) an indeterminate middle ground, gives the evaluator three choices instead of either a yes or no that is crucial for the assignment of blame. Although the potential for multiple condemnation may not seem very appealing, the willingness to evoke a bad impression can help prevent more serious consequences. The strategist has won when the either/or categories of blame versus innocence are transformed into a more slippery conclusion of multiple, uncertain possibilities.

Rule IV.C., Use passive voice in acknowledging wrongdoing. This rule includes the "mistakes were made" line, first articulated by George Bush and later Reagan himself (Hitchens, 1987). Rule IV.C. is intended to emphasize "having our hearts in the right places—and permit us to move on" (Richards, 1987). Reagan referred to the Iran-Contra scandal as "a policy that went astray," but his address to the American people on the affair left many crucial questions unanswered (Richards). The passive acknowledgement "mistakes were made" has the effect of acknowledging wrongdoing while softening the responsibility for ownership of action; this accomplishes plausibility by changing the objectivity of a specific attribution ("x" did "y") into a vague, open-ended attribution ("y" was done), thereby introducing greater subjectivity into conclusions about the sources of deeds. As Senator Nunn, one of the most powerful and incisive of the evaluators, asserts: "The final judgment probably will be individual judgments and they'll be subjective" (Mianowany, 1987). When an evaluator acquiesces to subjectivity, the person trying to avoid blame for an unacceptable action has used this defensive tactic successfully.

Rule IV.D., Have low-level members accept blame for wrongdoing. For example, one of Vice President Bush's aids "acknowledged he was 'derelict' in failing to tell Bush of reports that Lt. Col. Oliver North was relying on unseemly people to arm the Contras" (Walker & Hasson, 1987). This rule parallels one in the Organizing Categories that argues for moving risk-taking down to lower levels in the organization (Rule I.C.). The difference is that the former rule represents advice about how to assign responsibility in the first place (establishing role requirements); the latter refers to communications delivered to external audiences after wrongdoing has been detected. Subordinates following this rule, for example, could choose to accept responsibility afterward, even though it had not been assigned to them in advance.

Rule IV.E. Use conceptual diversions to insulate the leader from responsibility. This rule exemplifies the use of the term *deniability* between Admiral Poindexter and his legal examiner. When the examiner asks why Poindexter did not tell the President, and Poindexter responds with: "To protect his deniability," and the examiner replies with: "What do you mean by deniability?", the questioner stops questioning the Admiral's actions and begins to explore the conceptual rationale underlying those actions. When the questioner uses this strategy, he or she loses control of the interview. When actions are murky, talking about concepts is preferable. Justification of concepts via argument indicates a delay that takes attention away from the direct defense of an action itself, and occasionally leads to a complete tabling of the defense of that particular action. Justifications of concepts, as messages being communicated, can be modified and aligned (Bies, 1987; Staw, McKechnie, & Puffer, 1983); done deeds for which there is proof are harder to manipulate. It is easier to change concepts than to change historical events.

Rule IV.F., Prefer truth but be satisfied with dishonesty. This rule is the boldest of all rules; it acknowledges the weakness of ideals in a world of pragmatics. Plausibility, rather than truth, is a criterion under uncertain conditions—a form of apparently necessary "satisficing" rather than presumably infeasible optimizing. Douglas and Wildavsky (1982) testify to the importance of plausibility when uncertain conditions are interpreted in conjunction with self-interest by a group of like-minded people: "Plausibility is more important than belief. Plausibility depends on enough people wanting to believe in the theory, and this depends on enough people being committed to whatever moral principle it protects" (p. 38). Relying upon plausibility is not inherently evil (e.g., science may advance by such means), but with the Iran-Contra participants, it amounted to a pact of dishonesty. It was a justified allegiance (Douglas, 1992). Thus it overshadowed other rules of the undercover operation because dishonest pacts create bonding and commitment (Meyrowitz, 1985). Significantly, the nature of truth itself becomes tangled in pragmatics, preferences, and deception:

> You may deal in truth, in lies, in coloration. . . . As a standard operating procedure we try to deal with truth. Truth is an easier thing to defend. We don't like to deal in lies (or) even disinformation because you get caught up in it. . . . That doesn't mean we won't. But by and large our preference is to deal in truth. It (a covert operation) is a deception designed to deceive

the recipient of the action or the viewer of the action. But to call it a lie in itself is only true in some regard, with respect to its deniability. (Knutson, 1987)

This statement, which itself ends in a confused and convoluted fashion, implicitly acknowledges the insight of poet Sir Walter Scott, when he noted: "Oh what a tangled web we weave when first we practice to deceive." Plausible deniability thus requires some degree of willingness from the outset to depart from the truth, because of the effort that disingenuous explanations might require. Indeed, an emphasis on the plausible rather than the truthful may have been the genesis of other practices that emerged during the Iran-Contra affair. Now that the practices have been described in some detail, the following sections consider their implications.

■ Distinctive Features of Plausible Deniability

The phenomenon of plausible deniability focuses attention on otherwise neglected issues related to accountability. The following discussion highlights several distinctive features of plausible deniability as revealed in the Iran-Contra material.

Advance Face-Work

Tetlock (1985) pointed out that organizational decision makers must act as implicit politicians to manage the dilemmas associated with accountability. Similarly, Greenberg (1990) noted that in addition to using self-presentation tactics defensively to mend spoiled identities and to escape identity-threatening predicaments (cf. Sutton & Callahan, 1987), managers may also use various tactics assertively to establish desired images and identities in advance. The Iran-Contra practices represent a hybrid of Greenberg's two categories: The task was defensive, to avoid identity spoilage, but the tactics were assertive and proactive.

In contrast, the impression-formation literature frequently portrays saving face as something of an afterthought (activities prompted in a reactive, defensive manner after an image- or identity-threatening event has occurred): An action takes place, consequences occur that reflect negatively on the actor, and then the actor looks for means of damage control. Increased levels of litigiousness in society, however, make it more likely that organizational actors may engage in conscious attempts at building barricades to defend against impending attacks. In other words, the anticipated possibility of litigation creates a situation in which actions are conducted with that possibility in mind, thus encouraging the use of proactive tactics as a means to protect the organization's good name by marshaling defensive resources in advance (Sitkin & Bies, this volume). Iran-Contra actors illustrated such advance preparation by taking actions before accusations occurred—this made deniability easier once the accusations did occur.

These proactive practices involve much more than merely blind obedience to authority. This analysis thus contrasts with the way that Hamilton and Sanders (1992) characterize the thinking process of Iran-Contra subordinates: "Surprisingly, one thing that may be absent from their thoughts is cool, calculating self-interest" (pp. 52-53). On the one hand, Hamilton and Sanders rightly stress that Iran-Contra participants such as Oliver North place their superiors' interest above their own. On the other hand, the suppression of self-interest does not necessarily entail parallel suppression of "cool, calculating" thoughts. The practices we reviewed show evidence of calculated planning.

Obedience to authority need not be mindless and unthinking. Although loyal obedience may seem singularly focused and hence narrow-minded, such phrases only suggest that the mind of the obedient servant is closed, not that he or she is an automaton. Obedience does not necessarily engage automatic behaviors elicited like conditioned responses. Rather, obedience can involve cunning and guile (cf. Biggart & Hamilton, 1984; Barney, et al., cited in Sitkin & Bies, this volume). We must remember that the follower's narrowed focus refers to desired ends, not necessarily to the means of accomplishing those ends. Our focus on plausible deniability suggests that when the ends threaten risk of litigation, a compliant servant can become very creative in finding ways to ensure that the master will not be implicated.

We suspect that the current litigious environment will foster many other types of preplanned means for protecting organizations against charges of wrongdoing. The Iran-Contra material highlights a set of tactics within only one domain of defensive preparation, namely the defense of denying responsibility. Looking for examples of tactics illustrating other defensive domains (e.g., actions taken in advance to make subsequent justification easier) should prove an interesting exercise for future investigations.

Specifics of Denial as a Defensive Strategy

Although denial of responsibility is only one of a variety of means of saving face, the Iran-Contra material shows that this strategy by itself provides a number of different types of defenses against accusations of wrongdoing. Such denials fall within the general area of excuses, but they represent particular types of excuses. For instance, other literature on excuses (e.g., Bies, 1987) emphasizes the way accused actors refer to mitigating circumstances. These self-excusing circumstances can be external (e.g., references to coercion, influence of the social situation) or internal (e.g., temporary incapacitation by physical condition, emotional state). Schlenker (1982) added to those two types of mitigating circumstances the excuse categories of "denying one did it" and "denying foreseeability or intent" (p. 207). Similarly, Elsbach and Sutton (1992, p. 718—based on Scott & Lyman, 1968) described as "defenses of innocence" the categories of "defenses of noncausation ('it wasn't my fault')" and "defenses of nonoccurrence" ('it really didn't happen').

Iran-Contra actors seized on the notion of plausible deniability to defend Reagan's innocence against any subsequent charges. The noncausation defense, in other words, sought to demonstrate that Reagan was not at fault and could not be held accountable, because actions of his subordinates allegedly took place without his knowledge. The subordinates in this case developed a variety of tactics to implement this defense. In addition, as Tamuz and Sitkin (1992) show, the absence of a classical bureaucracy's formalism (e.g., avoiding the written record) and the presence of proactive methods to hide evidence (e.g., destroying materials) both illustrate means for accomplishing a nonoccurrence defense (if no evidence can be found that an event occurred, the response that "it really didn't happen" becomes more plausible). Thus the Iran-Contra material proves a rich resource of details about excuses using defensive tactics other than mitigating circumstances.

Organizational Structures for Risky Ventures

Tactics of plausible deniability include particular ways of organizing and operating. Some of these stand in marked contrast to the methods chosen by other organizations facing the threat of potential litigation. Indeed, other organizations often exhibit methods of legalization differing sharply from the approach that the Iran-Contra participants adopted. This contrast may make sense, considering that Iran-

Contra actors deliberately chose to operate illegitimately, whereas organizations prone to legalization may focus on legal operations— even to the detriment of other criteria (e.g., efficiency, profitability).

Sitkin and Bies (this volume) describe legalization's defining properties and indicate why it often occurs in response to the threat of litigation. A key feature is formalization/standardization, which can include cumbersome administrative processes, an emphasis on written documentation, and other hallmarks of bureaucracy. Yet within the otherwise highly bureaucratic confines of government, the Iran-Contra actors sought increased autonomy for a risky venture by forming structures and using practices that moved in the opposite direction from the bureaucratic tradition. Indeed, many of those structures and practices resemble approaches espoused by proponents of nontraditional management.

The following theme, therefore, emerges from analysis of Iran-Contra materials: When subordinates pursue objectives that potentially provoke litigation, their actions actually share many similarities with practices designed to encourage organizational creativity and innovation. Plausible deniability is a crafty practice universally chosen by the Iran-Contra participants, who thereby gained extraordinary autonomy and flexibility of action. The conditions of risk encouraged abandonment of traditional systems of authority; the practices of plausible deniability that emerged were almost identical to the practices of innovative management in vogue during the 1980s.

Consider, for example, the Peters and Waterman (1982) book about "excellence" in "America's best run companies," which remained at the top of *The New York Times* best-sellers list for a year and in the top 10 for the following 2 years. The book is an antibureaucratic, antirational tome that encourages flexibility and achievement through fluid operating systems. The chapters of the book emphasize a bias for action, autonomy and entrepreneurship, simplified organizational systems, and simultaneously loose-tight properties. Although some of Peters and Waterman's points are not congruent with the findings of this chapter (e.g., their discussion of the customer), many of the other management principles they espoused closely match the innovative practices used in the Iran-Contra affair.

Key components of plausible deniability thus stand in direct contrast to classic rational authority. Classic authority emphasizes written rules, clear instructions, clear lines of responsibility, common goals, and centralized control (Katz & Kahn, 1966). We instead found, within material generated by the Iran-Contra affair, evidence for practices such as the following: (1) an emphasis on oral communication that leaves little or no trace of action; (2) instructions based on estimations of what a leader wants derived from his general ideology; (3) indirect and diffuse rather than clear and direct lines of communication maintained to avoid direct responsibility; (4) goals that are altered as conditions change, and finally (5) local, rather than vertical, responsibility for the action. Once traditional forms of organizational authority are replaced by such practices, the Iran-Contra affair begins to look like an innovative and risky venture—a general mode of operation actively encouraged by top entrepreneurial firms, sometimes touted as the wave of the future.

The Iran-Contra material provides fresh grounds for additional theorizing that builds upon the analysis by Sitkin and Bies (this volume), because the contrast between legalization tendencies and entrepreneurial management tendencies reflects contrasting responses to litigiousness. Sitkin and Bies note that from the perspective of resource-dependency theory, increasingly litigious environmental contingencies might seem to call for an increasingly legalistic form of organization, which is suppported empirically in such studies as Edelman (1990) and Roth, Sitkin, and House (this volume). Why, then, did decision makers facing potential litigious challenges to Iran-Contra activities turn instead in nonlegalistic directions? Speculative hypotheses and new investigations might pursue grounds for reconciling these otherwise seemingly contradictory tendencies.

For example, a single underlying process may produce different tendencies, depending upon the circumstances. Conceivably, organizations might adopt increased legalization in the face of litigious possibilities when the likelihood of the possibilities stabilizes at a relatively predictable level; that is, a stable, new structural form matches the stable, new environmental characteristic. Iran-Contra participants, on the other hand, may have perceived their environment in less stable terms, and hence adopted more flexible structures as the appropriate mechanism for coping with strategic contingencies. Litigation and accusations of wrongdoing may have been seen as probable enough to engage defensive tactics proactively, and yet lacked the certainty of a stable environment because many of the arenas of action—such as the domain of military operations—still offered some cover-up potential as a function of national security and other related considerations. Thus the relative certainty of litigation may make a difference: Beyond a critical level of certainty, the best preparations for one's defense consist in having acted as legitimately as possible. When conditions have sufficient uncertainty, the temptation exists for pursuing illegitimate activities that offer greater flexibility (i.e., less formalism), and a concomitant defensive eye toward preparations for plausible deniability if caught.

Although this thesis is speculative, one parallel case provides it with at least some tentative and partial support—an analysis of defensive tactics used by two radical social movements (Elsbach & Sutton, 1992). In the following section, we note both the parallels between Iran-Contra and the social movements, and their differences. This juxtaposition further highlights some unique features of plausible deniability, especially as manifested in the specific circumstances surrounding the Iran-Contra operation.

■ Elsbach and Sutton as an Illustrative Comparison

Using data from two social movement organizations, Elsbach and Sutton (1992) analyzed methods of maintaining organizational legitimacy, despite illegitimate actions conducted on behalf of the organization. The analysis integrated two theoretical perspectives, institutional theory (addressing aspects of organizational structure) and impression management (addressing the verbal accounts offered by organizational actors). A parallel example emerged from Iran-Contra data in terms of major categories of analysis: One cluster of thematic content focused on how the organization structured its operations (e.g., the nature of reporting relationships), whereas another cluster focused on the content of utterances by officials (verbal defensive tactics).

Although our analysis parallels Elsbach and Sutton's in overall orientation (see Table 10.2), a key difference exists with regard to the use of legitimating structures.

Elsbach and Sutton (1992) note that their application of institutional theory emphasizes ways of "adopting visible and institutionalized structures and practices that mask or distract attention from controversial activities" (p. 700). The organizations they studied stood to gain by having such institutionalized forms and activities, and by making them highly visible, precisely because of their broad social acceptability or *legitimacy*. In other words, the social movements in question followed the strategy Sitkin and Bies (this volume) identify as useful in the face of litigation, namely incorporating legalistic features into the organization. By contrast, Iran-Contra participants structured their activities in nonlegalistic and virtually antibureaucratic ways to

Table 10.2
Comparison of Elsbach and Sutton (1992) Social Movement Characteristics With Those of Iran-Contra

Characteristics	Social Movements	Iran-Contra
Legalistic Blame Management		
Formalization:	increase	decrease
Perception of litigation prospects:	stable	uncertain
Adoption of legitimating legal forms:	yes	no
Discretion for authorities:	decrease	increase
Interactional Blame Management		
Public attention:	sought	avoided
Blame deflected away from:	organization	leader
Blame focused on:	outsiders	lower echelon
Prospects for decoupling harm doers:	easy	difficult
Types of accounts used:	justifications and excuses	excuses

maintain utmost flexibility. Consistent with the thesis suggested above, the social movements operated in a relatively stable environment, with respect to the strong probability of legal actions being taken against them (e.g., ranging from arrests to covert actions by the FBI). Furthermore, the media attention they sought virtually guaranteed attention from legal authorities as well. The Iran-Contra operation instead shunned publicity. It faced greater uncertainty regarding attention from legal authorities, and hence geared its structures toward escaping that attention, rather than concentrating on structural appearances of legitimacy created in case illegitimate acts were detected.

The social movement organizations did not rely exclusively on procedural formality and legitimacy of structures as defenses against charges of illegitimate activities. Rather, they also relied on decoupling: When confronted, these radical social organizations denied responsibility by disassociating the formal organization from individuals that the organization claimed were responsible for the wrongdoing (e.g., overzealous sympathizers). The principle of plausible deniability formulated by Iran-Contra participants also relied on affixing blame to a particular target and deflecting it from others, but two differences stand out. First, the target from which blame was being deflected— by using plausible deniability tactics—consisted not of the organization itself but rather its leader, namely, Reagan. Second, the blame was not deflected outside the organization, but rather to lower-echelon members of the organization, such as North.

Keeping the focus of blame within the organization presented particular difficulties, especially because leaders often get held accountable for their subordinates' actions. Wrongdoing by subordinates generally calls for more complete explanations of why they were not brought under control; whereas an organization cannot be held as responsible for the actions of wrongdoers outside the organization, and presumably less under its control. Within the governmental structure associated with the Iran-Contra affair, the agents conducting illegitimate activities could not be easily decoupled (with some exceptions, such as the use of Ross Perot), and thus the Iran-Contra structures eschewed legalistic formalism in favor of a style more suited to entrepreneurial ventures. The data from this study in contrast to the social movements examined by Elsbach and Sutton suggest that formalistic structures will more likely be used when decoupling opportunities are readily available; whereas much looser and more entrepreneurial structures will be preferred when decoupling is more difficult to accomplish. In general, comparing the Iran-Contra material with other naturalistic material on excuse-making lends itself to formulating various research hypotheses of this type for future investigation.

An illustration of such potential hypotheses emerges from yet another juxtaposition of social movements and Iran-Contra activities. Because Iran-Contra participants relied on plausible deniability as an overall defensive strategy, they offered excuses for their behavior, rather than justifications for the ends they sought. Their defensive preparations focused almost exclusively on denying responsibility. In contrast, the social movement organizations apparently were in a better position than the Iran-Contra participants to use both excuses and justifications. The major defense against charges of illegitimate actions in the social movement organizations was the excuse that the organization had not been responsible for those actions; instead, the actions represented the deeds of those whom the organization could not control. At the same time, the organization's own activities could be justified by pointing to the implementation of legitimating structures and other trappings of legalism.

A hypothesis from this analysis, therefore, can be proposed along the following lines: When agents of wrongdoing are completely decoupled from an organization, which is then able to deny responsibility completely, the organization gains access to additional sources of justification and may capitalize on them through "legalistic rhetoric" (Sitkin & Bies, this volume). When agents of wrongdoing deliberately operate within the sanctuary of an organization, however, attempts at justification by adopting legalistic structures and processes will run contrary to the autonomy necessary for covert action taken on the organization's behalf (purportedly, although problematically, in the organization's best interest).

■ Summary and Conclusions

The Iran-Contra data provide an illustration of plausible deniability as a method for deflecting blame when being held accountable. Being held accountable—and hence potentially liable, if litigation ensues—may motivate organizational actors to develop defensive strategies for protecting the organization's reputation. In the Iran-Contra case, the good name of the leader was to be protected at all cost. Careful, deliberately chosen actions contributed to that objective. Those actions helped Reagan deny responsibility while simultaneously maintaining the highest credibility possible.

In developing themes that elaborated on the analysis of categories coded from Iran-Contra data, we suggested several ways that plausible deniability differs from other defensive strategies, as well as instances where such strategies have been used. First, we noted the advance preparation that went into efforts at constructing the basis for excuses denying Reagan's responsibility in the most plausible ways possible. Second, we differentiated the tactics of plausible deniability from those pertaining to other defensive orientations. In particular, our discussion noted qualities associated with this specific approach to denying responsibility (namely, tactics for denying that an event occurred or for denying one's own causal connection to an event), as contrasted not only with the major defensive alternative of justification accounts but also with other subcategories of excuses (e.g., mitigating circumstances). Finally, we pointed out that when plausible deniability is adopted as a strategic orientation, its implementation typically calls for organizational structures and practices more similar to entrepreneurial ventures than to bureaucratic standardization, formalization, and related characteristics of legalization otherwise seen in organizations coping with potential litigation liability.

In addition, we compared the Iran-Contra material with material from an analysis of defensive tactics adopted by radical organizations acting on the fringe of legality. Our discussion illustrated that the actions of Iran-Contra participants do not exhaust potential tactics relevant to the strategy of plausible deniability; the radical social movements also sought to deny responsibility for illegal activities, yet they used different methods from those adopted in the Iran-Contra affair. Whereas our earlier discussion placed plausible deniability within the context of general categories of alternative approaches to preserving an organization's positive identity (generic strategies), the comparison with social movement organizations showed that the specific strategy of plausible deniability may be implemented in a variety of ways. We also suggested that tactics of implementation vary with the circumstances, and provided tentative speculation about the types of different circumstances that may be important.

The inquiry has been descriptive, not prescriptive. A normative comment in conclusion, however, is warranted, lest this text be mistakenly identified as having offered prescriptive advice. Scientific description has an "if . . . then" character easily misread as offering advice in the form of "If you want to accomplish these ends, here are the means." We hope the readers of our analysis will not conclude we want to make people more capable of using plausible deniability by knowing how to make preparations for its use.

We are troubled by this dilemma and know no easy way to resolve it. In hopes of encouraging others to join us in pursuing some form of resolution, therefore, we close with a warning and a challenge. The warning resolves the dilemma incompletely at best, because being forewarned in and of itself does not always mean being sufficiently forearmed—hence the challenge as an addendum. Our warning: Organizations that nourish entrepreneurial risk-taking (Sitkin, 1992) can also unwittingly allow the parallel growth of opportunities for people to skirt the edge of moral choice. This observation makes for an interesting counterpart to some of the paradoxes of legalization noted by Sitkin and Bies (this volume), which describe how an otherwise positive feature (e.g., attention to due process) may have unanticipated negative consequences (those following from decreased attention to other worthwhile objectives). Therein lies the challenge: to find a way of capitalizing upon the advantages possible from entrepreneurial forms of organization and management, without simultaneously providing an internal climate in which mismanagement can flourish unchecked.

■ Note

1. We owe thanks to the editors of this book for suggesting the format used in presenting these rules. We also owe thanks to Joanne Gilbert and Debra France for assistance in editing the final draft of this paper.

■ References

Allen, M. (1987, December). Cleaning house: U.S. Companies pay increasing attention to destroying files. *Wall Street Journal*, pp. 1, 18.

Alterman, E. (1987, May). *Washington Monthly*, p. 19.

Bacharach, S. B., & Lawler, E. J. (1980). *Power and politics in organizations*. San Francisco: Jossey-Bass.

Bies, R. J. (1987). The predicament of injustice: The management of moral outrage. In L. L. Cummings & B. M. Staw (Eds.), *Research in organizational behavior* (Vol. 9, pp. 289-319). Greenwich, CT: JAI Press.

Biggart, N. W., & Hamilton, G. G. (1984). The power of obedience. *Administrative Science Quarterly, 29*, 540-549.

Bowers, J. W., Gilchrist, J. G., & Browning, L. D. (1980). A communication course for high-powered bargainers: Development and effects. *Communication Education, 89*, 10-20.

Browning, L. D. (1978). A grounded organizational communication theory derived from qualitative data. *Communication Monographs, 45*, 93-109.

Browning, L. D. (1988). Interpreting the Challenger disaster: Communication under conditions of risk and liability. *Industrial Crisis Quarterly, 2*, 211-227.

Browning, L. D., & Shetler, J. (1992). Communication in crisis, communication in recovery: A postmodern commentary on the Exxon Valdez disaster. *International Journal of Mass Disasters and Emergencies, 10*, 477-498.

Burke, K. (1973). *The philosophy of literary form* (3rd ed.). Berkeley: University of California Press.

Campbell, D. T. (1975). "Degrees of freedom" and the case study. *Comparative Political Studies, 8*, 178-193.

Chaze, W. L. (1986, December 15). Inside the shadow network. *U.S. News & World Report*, p. 26.

Collins, A., Warnock, E., Aiello, N., & Miller, M. (1975). Reasoning from incomplete knowledge. In D. G. Bobrow & A. Collins (Eds.), *Representation and understanding: Studies in cognitive science*. New York: Academic Press.

Deleuze, G., & Guattari, F. (1987). *A thousand plateaus: Capitalism and schizophrenia* [B. Massumi, Trans.]. Minneapolis: University of Minnesota Press.

Deutsch, M. (1962). Cooperation and trust: Some theoretical notes. In M. R. Jones (Ed.), *Nebraska symposium on motivation* (pp. 275-320). Lincoln: University of Nebraska Press.

Douglas, M. (1992). *Risk and blame: Essays in cultural theory*. London: Routledge.

Douglas, M., & Wildavsky, A. (1982). *Risk and culture: An essay on the selection of technological and environmental dangers.* Berkeley: University of California Press.

Drinkard, J. (1987). AP story tag: Poindexter-Iran-Contra. DIALOG.

Edelman, L. (1990). Legal environments and organizational governance: The expansion of the choice process in the workplace. *American Journal of Sociology, 95,* 1401-1440.

Einhorn, H. J., & Hogarth, R. M. (1986). Judging probable cause. *Psychological Bulletin, 99,* 3-19.

Elsbach, K. D., & Sutton, R. I. (1992). Acquiring organizational legitimacy through illegitimate actions: A marriage of institutional and impression management theories. *Academy of Management Journal, 35,* 699-738.

Feldman, M. S. (1992). Social limits to discretion: An organizational perspective. In K. Hawkins (Ed.), *The uses of discretion.* New York: Oxford University Press.

Fielding, N. G., & Fielding, J. L. (1986). *Linking data.* Beverly Hills, CA: Sage.

Folger, R., & Bies, R. J. (1989). Managerial responsibility and procedural justice. *Employee Responsibilities and Rights Journal, 2,* 79-90.

Fox, A. (1974). *Beyond contract: Work, power, and trust in relationships.* London: Faber.

Friedrich, O. (1986a, December). The devilish doctrine of deniability. *Time,* p. 98.

Friedrich, O. (1986b, December). Presidential responsibility for covert operations. *Time,* p. 98.

Geertz, C. (1973). Thick description: Toward an interpretative theory of culture. In C. Geertz, *The interpretation of cultures.* New York: Basic Books.

Gerstel, S. (July, 1987). UPI story tag: Iranarms-Byrd. DATELINE WASHINGTON.

Glaser, B. (1978). *Theoretical sensitivity.* Mill Valley, CA: Sociology Press.

Glaser, B., & Strauss, A. (1967). *The discovery of grounded theory.* Chicago: Aldine.

Greenberg, J. (1990). Looking fair vs. being fair: Managing impressions of organizational justice. In B. M. Staw & L. L. Cummings (Eds.), *Research in organizational behavior* (Vol. 12, pp. 111-157). Greenwich, CT: JAI Press.

Hambrick, D. C., & Finkelstein, S. (1987). Managerial discretion: A bridge between the polar view on organizations. In B. M. Staw & L. L. Cummings (Eds.), *Research in organizational behavior* (Vol. 9, pp. 369-406). Greenwich, CT: JAI Press.

Hamilton, V. L. (1986). Chains of command: Responsibility attribution in hierarchies. *Journal of Applied Social Psychology, 16,* 118-138.

Hamilton, V. L., & Sanders, J. (1992). Responsibility and risk in organizational crimes of obedience. In B. M. Staw & L. L. Cummings (Eds.), *Research in organizational behavior* (Vol. 14, pp. 49-90). Greenwich, CT: JAI Press.

Harre, R., & Secord, P. (1972). *The explanation of social behavior.* Oxford: Basil Blackwell.

Hasson, J. (1987, July, 15). AP story tag: Iranarms-analysis. DIALOG.

Hitchens, C. (1987, May 23). Minority report: Iran-Contra hearings. *Nation, 244,* p. 673.

Iran-Contra arms sale. (1986, December). *New Republic,* p. 7.

Katz, D., & Kahn, R. L., (1966). *The social psychology of organizations.* New York: John Wiley.

Knutson, L. L. (1987, August). AP story tag: Iran-Contra. DIALOG.

Larson, C. E., & LaFasto, F. M. (1989). *Teamwork: What must go right, what can go wrong.* Newbury Park, CA: Sage.

Lyotard, J. F. (1984). *The postmodern condition.* Minneapolis: University of Minnesota Press.

Magnuson, E., Muller, H., & Van Voorst, B. (1986, December). Plumbing the CIA's shadowy role; what Bill Casey didn't know and when he didn't know it. *Time,* p. 26.

March, J. G. (1981). Footnotes to organizational change. *Administrative Science Quarterly, 26,* 563-577.

Meyrowitz, J. (1985). *No sense of place: The impact of electronic media on social behavior.* New York: Oxford University Press.

Mianowany, J. (1987, July). UPI story tag: Iranarms. DIALOG.

North, O. L. (1991). *Under fire: An American story*. New York: HarperCollins.

Parry, R., & Barger, B. (1986, November). Reagan's shadow CIA: How the White House ran the secret "Contra" war. *New Republic*, p. 23.

Pelz, D. C. (1969, December). The climate of communication in problem solving organzations. Invited lecture on *The management of technical organizations*. The American Psychological Association, Washington, DC.

Pelz, D., & Andrews, F. M. (1976). *Scientists in organizaitons* (rev. ed.). Ann Arbor, MI: Institute for Social Research.

Peters, T. (1992). *Liberation management*. New York: Random House.

Peters, T., & Waterman, R. (1982). *In search of excellence: Lessons from America's best run companies*. New York: Harper & Row.

Richards, C. F. (1987, August). UPI story tag: Iran-Contra. DIALOG.

Roland, R., & Mianowany, J. (1987, September 8). UPI story tag: Iran-Contra. DIALOG.

Rowley, J. (1988, July 9). UPI story tag: Iranarms-excerpts. DIALOG.

Schlenker, B. R. (1982). Translating actions into attitudes: An identity-analytic approach to the explanation of social conduct. In L. Berkowitz (Ed.), *Advances in experimental social psychology* (pp. 193-247). New York: Academic Press.

School for scandal. (1986, December 29). *New Republic, 195*, p. 7.

Scott, M. B., & Lyman, S. M. (1968). Accounts. *American Review, 33*, 46-48.

Sitkin, S. B. (1992). Learning through failure: The strategy of small losses. In B. M. Staw & L. L. Cummings (Eds.), *Research in organizational behavior* (Vol. 14, pp. 231-266). Greenwich, CT: JAI Press.

Sitkin, S. B, & Roth, N. R. (1993). Explaining the limited effectiveness of legalistic remedies for trust/distrust. *Organization Science, 4*(3), 367-392.

Sitkin, S. B, & Sutcliffe, K. M. (1991). Dispensing legitimacy: Professional, organizational, and legal influences on pharmacist behavior. In P. Tolbert & S. Barley (Eds.), *Research in the sociology of organizations* (Vol. 8, pp. 269-295). Greenwich, CT: JAI Press.

Smith, D. D., & Berg, D. N. (1987). A paradoxical conception of group dynamics. *Human Relations, 40*, 633-658.

Souder, W. E. (1983). Organizing for modern technology and innovation: A review and synthesis. *Technovation, 2*, 27-44.

Staw, B. M., McKechnie, P. I., & Puffer, S. (1983). The justification of organizational performance. *Administrative Science Quarterly, 28*, 582-600.

Strauss, A. (1987). *Qualitative analysis for social scientists*. Cambridge, UK: Cambridge University Press.

Sutton, R. I., & Callahan, A. L. (1987). The stigma of bankruptcy: Spoiled organizational image and its management. *Academy of Management Journal, 30*, 405-436.

Tamuz, M., & Sitkin, S. B. (1992). *The invisible muzzle: Organizational and legal constraints on the disclosure of information about health and safety standards*. Manuscript under review.

Taylor, F. W. (1947). *Scientific management*. New York: Harper.

Tetlock, P. E. (1985). Accountability: The neglected social context of judgment and choice. In B. M. Staw & L. L. Cummings (Eds.), *Research in organizational behavior* (Vol. 7, pp. 297-332). Greenwich, CT: JAI Press.

The grand lady of technology. (1986, August). *The Boston Globe*, p. 17.

Walker, D., & Hasson, J. (1987, September 10). UPI story tag: Iran-Contra. DIALOG.

Whyte, W. H. (1952). *Is anybody listening? How and why U.S. business stumbles when it talks to human beings*. New York: Simon & Schuster.

11

The Consequences of Language:
A Metaphorical Look at the Legalization of Organizations

Randall K. Stutman

Linda L. Putnam

The legalization of organizations is becoming a common practice for many managers and workers. Organizations are moving toward formal and adversarial procedures for handling problems and are employing legal criteria in making routine decisions (Sitkin & Bies, 1993). Individuals who are adept at using legal terminology for personal influence engage in a rhetoric that has led several scholars to exclaim that a "litigation mentality" currently pervades every aspect of organizational life (Bies & Tyler, 1993; Lieberman, 1983; Meyer, 1983; Yudof, 1981). One concern that continues to interest researchers and theorists is the role of legalistic language in an organization. The question that lies at the heart of this inquiry is: How does language both reflect and perpetuate the growing legalization of organizations? This chapter will advance the concern that a litigation mentality can be found in the ordinary language used within organizations and will argue that, as a metaphor for thinking about disputes within relationships, this legalization of the organization could have detrimental effects.

Researchers often employ language analysis to identify the shared experiences of group members and the organizational performances that construct a cultural reality (Chaika, 1982; Pacanowsky & O'Donnell-Trujillo, 1983; Smircich, 1983). In this view, language practices reveal how organization members create, maintain, and change culture through language use in everyday interaction.

One particular language pattern that has captured the attention of interpretive scholars is metaphors. Metaphors play a critical role in developing paradigms of organization theory (Manning, 1979; Morgan, 1986) as well as in understanding the way organizational reality is socially constructed (Deetz & Mumby, 1985; Koch & Deetz, 1981; Nielsen, 1991; Pondy, 1983; Smith & Eisenberg, 1987).

This chapter applies the concept of metaphor to the debate regarding the legalization of organizations. In particular, we treat litigation and negotiation as contrasting metaphors and contend that the litigation metaphor transforms or reframes the nature of organizational relationships. To explicate this argument, we compare the actual processes of litigation and negotiation, present the definition and functions of metaphors, delineate the characteristics of litigation and negotiation as metaphors, and contrast the two metaphors as competing approaches to conceptualizing organizational relationships. Throughout the chapter, we maintain that litigation as a way of thinking and talking in organizations constrains how problems are conceived, and may alter the way flexibility, trust, and shared meanings govern the essence of organizational relationships.

■ Managing Conflict: Litigation Versus Negotiation

Conflict is an inevitable component of social life. Within organizations two typical means for addressing conflict are negotiation and litigation. The two processes differ markedly, as displayed in Table 11.1.

As a formal action, litigation makes a dispute public and brings in a third party who has control over the outcome. This control gives the judge or jury coercive power over the individuals. Negotiation may be formal or informal and allows the parties to keep a dispute private while maintaining control of the process and outcome through the give-and-take of interaction. Power is naturally distributed between the parties who have a variety of power resources.

Litigation puts the participants in a competitive situation where the outcome will inevitably result in a winner and a loser. Negotiation gives participants motivation to cooperate as well as compete, a mixed-motive situation. All parties compete in order to look out for personal interests but cooperatively recognize their interdependence. The open-ended nature of negotiation allows participants to control their

Table 11.1

Characteristics of Litigation and Negotiation

Litigation	Negotiation
Public	Private
Third-party control	Interactively controlled through bids and counterbids
Coercive power	Distributed power
Competitive; win-lose	Mixed motive; win-win
Legally defined issues	Disputants define issues
No concern for underlying relationships	Concern for ongoing relationships

own outcomes and, through creativity and cooperation, potentially arrive at a mutually beneficial outcome, a win-win situation.

In litigation the law defines the issues. In contrast, in negotiation the participants define and even haggle over what the issues are. Litigation contains a dispute within standardized boundaries, while negotiation is a forum for the participants to set the boundaries.

In litigation, the parties are concerned with judgment, a settlement that reflects the moral order of who is in the right and who is in the wrong. Relational concerns, when they are apparent at all, take a secondary position behind the third-party decision. The cooperation inherent in negotiation reflects a concern for the underlying relationship. Negotiation embodies an implicit concern for what the other believes, values, and stands for. Even more salient, negotiation is grounded in the belief that the ongoing relationship must be safeguarded or protected from dissolution.

As alternatives for responding to disputes, each process has its own place. Litigation may be desirable when one party lacks the power or resources to bring an issue to negotiations, when the disputed action involves grave damages, or when a clear violation of legally binding rules or laws occurs. Conversely, negotiation enables participants to preserve their relationship and to respond well to situations in which expectations or rules are unclear, or their application to a particular situation is unclear. Negotiation responds to dynamic situations and ongoing relationships. Litigation results in *an* outcome; negotiation can result in a *series* of outcomes, which can build upon the groundwork laid by previous agreements. Litigation responds to a particular problem, offers recompense for damages, and serves as a chilling warning to other potential violators. But litigation does not address or show concern for the relationship between disputants. Because of the cooperation required in the give-and-take process and the mutual definition of issues in negotiation, the relationship between the participants is significant to the process and may be beneficially redefined. Negotiation sends a message of working together to improve a situation and sets the groundwork for future negotiations within the relationship.

While negotiation and litigation are two specific processes that can be used to address conflict, they are also conventional ways to think about conflict management. We will argue that they represent conventional, competing metaphors in organizational life that serve to structure our thinking and limit our options. To develop this argument we must first examine the significance of metaphors in everyday life.

■ On Defining Metaphor

The word *metaphor* is derived from the Greek term *meta*, meaning "over," and *pherein*, meaning "to carry." Accordingly, Hawkes (1972) defines metaphor as a particular set of linguistic processes whereby aspects of one object are transferred to another object, so that the second object is spoken of as if it were the first. Thus, a metaphor is a linguistic expression that treats an experience, a set of practices, or an abstraction as a different concept or object. For some theorists, metaphors link abstract constructs to concrete things (Lakoff & Johnson, 1980) and provide a cognitive bridge between two dissimilar domains (Ortony, 1979). Although technical differences exist among metaphors, similes, and analogies, in this chapter we employ Cooper's (1986) use of metaphor, which encompasses analogy, simile, metaphorical idioms, and metaphorical clichés that establish the relationship between primary and secondary subjects.

But metaphors may be best understood as systems of beliefs, not individual "things" (Black, 1962). To interpret a metaphor, an individual constructs a set of beliefs about a principle subject (the man in "man is a wolf") parallel to a set of beliefs about a secondary subject (the wolf). Thus, assertions about the principle subject are correlated with similar statements about the secondary subject (Black, 1962). In interpretation, however, the two sets of beliefs interact to highlight some features of the principle subject while suppressing others. For instance, the metaphor of "argument as war" highlights the competitive nature of conflict while it hides the view of "argument as collaborative problem solving" or as a logical construction. The interaction between the principle and the secondary subject also induces reciprocal changes in the secondary subject (Black, 1962). If argument is cast as war, then war is also put in a new light. War is different when it is linked to argument. The interaction of the two sets of beliefs, then, produces a new meaning.

Functions of Metaphors and Language Use

This chapter adopts a social construction view of metaphor. That is, it adheres to Lakoff and Johnson's (1980) position that metaphors are a pervasive part of everyday life and are fundamental to thought and language use. Metaphors shape how we see and make sense of the world. They influence thought by orienting "the perception, conceptualization, and understanding of one object or event in terms of another" (Koch & Deetz, 1981, p. 5). Langer (1957) even contends that new ideas are understood through metaphors, that is, through linking a new thought to some familiar thing. They influence not only what we understand as reality, but also our behavior: what we create as knowledge, what we experience, and what we do. Metaphors "sanction actions, justify inferences, and help us set goals" (Lakoff & Johnson, 1980, p. 142). The primary function of metaphor, then, is to structure reality (our perceptions and beliefs) and behavior.

In addition, metaphors aid in expressing abstract ideas, conveying vivid images, making language succinct and crisp, and transferring large chunks of information (Ortony, 1979; Paivio & Begg, 1981). Metaphors enable us to talk about experiences that have no literal equivalent and to make experiences emotionally arousing and memorable. Use of metaphors, then, may facilitate communication effectiveness through enhancing flexibility and organizational learning (Broms & Gahmberg, 1983; Coffman & Eblen, 1987).

Metaphors are revealed through everyday language use. That is, we employ words and phrases that embody metaphorical connections and serve as evidence of such conceptual systems. These connections often appear as structurally coherent systems through identifying clusters of metaphors that reveal the way rules, roles, and strategies fit into an internal complex (Deetz, 1986; Lakoff & Johnson, 1980). For example, the military metaphor, as a pervasive metaphor of organizational life (Weick, 1979), structures our views of bureaucracy through the use of such phrases as "chain of command," "waging campaigns," "gathering intelligence," "conferring with the brass," and "assessing the rank and file." In such an organization, bypassing the chain of command may be viewed as "insubordination," and criticism is met with defensiveness and counterattack (Deetz, 1986).

External structure refers to the relationship between different metaphorical systems. The external structure of the military metaphor differs from one that treats organizations as machines. Frequent use of such phrases as "wearing down," "getting the company running," "cranking out a report," and "throwing a wrench in the works" signifies a machine metaphor (Deetz, 1986; Koch & Deetz, 1981). Coaching and sports activities surface as metaphors of organizations through terms like "best available athlete," "end run," "touchdown," "all-star team," and "practicing for the big game" (Koch & Deetz, 1981). Because metaphors infiltrate routine language use, organizational members may neither recognize links between the principle and secondary subjects nor identify them as metaphors. As the link between first and second object becomes taken for granted, a metaphorical statement is typically perceived as simply a statement of the way things really are, a conventional rather than figurative statement.

Conventional refers to metaphors that are commonplace and are used unconsciously in everyday talk. Neither the speaker nor the listener is aware of the secondary subject of the metaphor, or of the conceptual structures implied in the metaphor's use. In a specific context, conventional metaphors may become root metaphors that provide rich summaries of worldviews and subsume other metaphors (Smith & Eisenberg, 1987). These symbols become emotionally significant or highly charged universes of meaning that are taken for granted (Pondy, 1983). For example, conceiving of a business as a family may become a root metaphor that could clash with other expressions of organizational life (Smith & Eisenberg, 1987). If employees lose sight of the metaphorical comparison between their organization and a family, and instead perceive that their organization *is* a family, then they may resist practices that make good business sense because they are inconsistent with the love, support, and understanding that should typify a family.

The structuring function of conventional metaphors is not necessarily arbitrary. By virtue of what metaphors hide, they can lead to human degradation. Specifically, when human labor becomes a "natural resource" that is "tapped," "invested," and "measured," the distinctions between meaningful and meaningless work are erased (Lakoff &

Johnson, 1980). The effect of such conventional metaphors is that people accept and support the status quo by treating human labor as fixed or natural, rather than as mutable and situated within an historical context. As Lakoff and Johnson (1980) note, these are metaphors we live by.

The use of multiple metaphors, especially to refer to complex experiences, highlights different aspects of these events. Multiple metaphors may provide complementary or competing views of reality. For example, the expression "argument is a game" retains some features of the war metaphor by highlighting competition and strategy, but it implies that arguments are also cooperative and fun. In the absence of a central root metaphor, competing metaphorical expressions may signal struggles between changing ideologies (Pondy, 1983; Smith & Eisenberg, 1987), subculture or individual differences (Coffman & Eblen, 1987), or covert practices that mask power relationships between novel metaphors at the surface level and conventional ones at a deeper structure (Deetz & Mumby, 1985). Use of multiple or mixed metaphors within the same context may reveal that no one metaphor can capture all the nuances of social reality and that sense making evolves as a response to prior frameworks, and as the precursor of future conceptions (Smith & Eisenberg, 1988).

Even though litigation and negotiation have been described as actual practices, these practices themselves are based within metaphorical views of organizations and conflict. In addition, the familiarity with these two processes has led to their acceptance as conventional metaphors for thinking about any conflict situation.

Legalism and Metaphor

The increasing reliance upon the legal system in our culture has led to legalistic thinking and structuring of situations (Meyer, 1983; Selznick, 1969; Sitkin & Bies, 1993; Yudof, 1981). The legal process not only is an option for addressing problems but has also become a metaphor for how to think about them. The process is circular: Recourse to legal means in our society leads to an infiltration of legal language into organizations; the language creates a conventional metaphor, which then structures how individuals think about situations in the workplace and increasing reliance on legal or legalistic processes.

Even when official legal channels are not used, other channels for managing problems are modeled after them. This tendency to view conflict and means to addressing problems within the legal frame represents a spreading conventional metaphor in our culture. Legalistic means involve "mechanisms that are institutionalized, mimic legal forms and exceed legal regulatory requirements" (Sitkin & Bies, 1993; Sitkin & Roth, 1993). The metaphor then structures thinking about how to address problems and affects actions and sanctions. Further, we would add it begins to pervade people's thinking about relationships independent of any particular bureaucratic structures. Consider events such as children suing or "divorcing" parents, or a state legislature considering passing laws requiring teachers to assign homework at least once a week in grades 1 through 12. Such newsworthy events work to structure our thinking about how to address problems, and influence how we think about relationships.

■ Metaphors of Conflict and Organizational Disputes

Conflict has played a critical role in organizational theory. Although several scholars review the changing models of conflict in organizational theory (Burrell & Morgan, 1979; Kolb & Putnam, 1992; Morgan, 1986), only a few theorists center on metaphors or images of conflict (e.g., Beisecker, 1988; Hocker & Wilmot, 1991; Sergeev, 1991). To understand how litigation and negotiation function metaphorically in organizations, we briefly review the literature on conflict metaphors and organizational theory.

Early theories of organizations, such as classical management and the human relations approaches, treated conflict as a disease to be eradicated or healed through managerial action. Basically, conflict disrupted the harmonious order or the health of the organism. Deviants and troublemakers infected the organization with germs that could spread and disrupt the unity of the system (Burrell & Morgan, 1979). In the 1960s conflict surfaced as an inevitable feature of organizational life, determined by differences in specialization, hierarchical level, and the need for interdependence. Conflict had to be integrated into the organizational order through socializing members, inculcating values and premises, enhancing organizational commitment, and promoting integration. In the 1970s and 1980s, organizations with this orientation developed strong cultures to unify disparate forces and bring members into the fold. Conflict became an organizational crusade in which the true believers engaged in a symbolic struggle to inculcate the organizational doctrine and defend the faith. Both the disease and the crusade metaphors of conflict espoused a unitary model of organizations and viewed conflict as disruptive to the dominant values of the system. This model assumed that all members shared common goals, and that individual goals were inconsistent with organizational goals.

Other metaphors that surfaced in the 1960s treated organizations as pluralist systems rather than unitary structures (Morgan, 1986). In the pluralist model, conflict was not only inevitable but also functional. As an outgrowth of divergent interests among groups and individuals, conflict surfaced through an inevitable competition for scarce resources, and disagreements on the nature of organizational goals and effectiveness (Notz, Starke, & Atwell, 1983). Conflict was functional in that it promoted change and achieved unity through uncovering alternatives that satisfied all parties.

With a political metaphor of organizations, conflict was a game in which both sides developed optimal strategies through a system of rules aimed at winning (Beisecker, 1988). Motivated by self-interest, participants employed a game plan with sets of options, specific utilities, and particular strategies to reach mutually acceptable outcomes. Contingent on the relative skills and resources of the participants, outcomes were short termed and often fluctuated in the next match, trial, or contract.

The game metaphor of conflict dominates perceptions of bargaining and conflict management in organizations (Putnam, 1985; Putnam & Poole, 1987). It underlies a number of theories of conflict, including zero-sum games, social exchange, bilateral monopoly, joint decision making, and coalitions. More specifically, it forms a root metaphor for two different approaches to dispute management in organizations: litigation and negotiation. These two approaches serve as different types of metaphors for managing relationships in organizational disputes. Because they stem from a common root metaphor, these two systems seem complementary. A comparison of their functions, structures, and interrelationships, however, suggests that the two metaphors represent competing ideologies with diverse domains of experience, rules of operation, forms of control, and sets of beliefs.

Several caveats frame our discussion of these two types of metaphors. First, to contrast diverse systems of organizational relationships, negotiation and litigation are treated as distinct systems. Nonetheless, since both draw from the same root metaphor, negotiation may resemble litigation, particularly in its focus on rules, procedures, and outcomes for maximizing self-gain. Yet, important differences exist in the way each metaphor casts organizational reality, influences understanding, and shapes organizational behavior. The two types of metaphors also differ in their language patterns and internal structures.

Second, even though negotiation constitutes a metaphor for managing relationships in organizational disputes, scholars differ as to the exact nature of the bargaining process (Sergeev, 1991). While some scholars center on the social exchange aspects of negotiation (Roloff, 1987; Tutzauer, 1991), others stress joint problem solving, debate, ritual, dance, or social drama as alternative perspectives for understanding the bargaining process (Friedman, 1989; Pruitt, 1981; Putnam, Van Hoeven, & Bullis, 1991; Trice & Beyer, 1984; Walcott, Hopmann, & King, 1977). This chapter, however, focuses on negotiation and litigation as metaphors for managing organizational disputes, rather than as ways of depicting the internal processes of conflict.

Third, in this chapter we reify negotiation and litigation as institutional systems. Although we realize that most organizations mix these metaphors or draw from both systems to process disputes, we contend that the two cast distinct organizational visions, as revealed through different ontological frames. Yet we acknowledge that neither is a pure, coherent, or static mode of managing organizational relationships.

■ The Legal Infiltration of Organizational Life

Recourse to the judicial system for handling disputes is as American as baseball and apple pie. As a regulated system of social conflict, the courts aim to preserve cherished values, such as fair and impartial treatment, equality, and protection from abuses of power. This system also reflects basic beliefs about communication: Problems are to be solved through logical arguments supported with evidence and adjudicated by an impartial third party. This regulated system also reinforces our cultural drive to be competitive, rugged individualists. Therefore, turning to the court system as a model for handling organizational disputes is not surprising.

The law has entered organizational life in innumerable ways, including regulating relationships between business and the public (e.g., disclosure and warning laws), between organizations and potential employees (e.g., codification of recruitment and hiring procedures), between management and labor (e.g., union contracts defining work assignments, evaluation and grievance procedures), and even interpersonal relationships (e.g., definitions and sanctions concerning sexual harassment). Litigation has infiltrated organizational life, not only as a formal system for guiding and enforcing behaviors but also as a way of managing informal relationships.

Litigation as a Metaphor for Organizational Disputes

This infiltration is evident in the language of organizational disputes. Relationships are "contractual." When expectations are violated, members claim, "You broke our agreement." Members react to "accusations" by claiming that they are not "the guilty party." Organizational disputes are legitimate if they are "grievable." They are evaluated in the following ways: "You don't have a case." "You need to document the problem." "What are the facts?" And a disagreement may only be "alleged" until all the facts are in. Consequences of ill-begotten behaviors are expressed as "damages." Actions may be taken for "damage control." If a "contract is broken," then "punitive measures" may be taken or a "deal may be cut."

Communication is also structured by the legal metaphor. Individuals are "cross-examined"; "statements" are "on [or] off the record"; and decisions are described as "impartial." Decisions may be put off until someone has a chance to "deliberate," and until that time, the "jury is still out." Labels for behaviors can become threatening in and of themselves due to their legal connotations: "That's 'sexual harassment.' "

These language patterns can be clustered into a coherent system of shared meanings and behaviors that orient perceptions and interpretations of organizational events. If we treat organizational relationships as litigation, a coherent structure emerges based on the following entailments: (a) Behavior can be objectively defined (e.g., "You need proof." "Get the facts." "Your evidence better be sound."); (b) relationships are adversarial (e.g., "Your defense better be good." "If I'm for it, he's against it."); and (c) socially accepted standards of behavior, such as fairness and equality, emanate from consistent application of the law (e.g., "The precedent indicates that this decision is wrong." "All such violations of the contract must be handled in the same way.").

Implications of the Legal Metaphor

Thus, a legal metaphor for dispute management highlights particular domains of experience, rules of operation, forms of control, and sets of beliefs. Even when the "law" has not been invoked, the litigation metaphor implies that disputes are socially sanctioned, open to public scrutiny, and shaped by adversaries who seek to "win" their cases (Rieke & Stutman, 1990). In other words, the situation is legalistic (Sitkin & Bies, 1993). Procedures become the rules or guardians of fairness (Tyler & Bies, 1990). Disputants must follow these rules in communicating proofs and arguments, by focusing on issues in the immediate dispute and by presenting a "case" with specific evidence. These rules are not aimed at preserving the underlying relationship between disputants; rather they strive to document the "alleged" behavior, to uphold standard definitions for appropriate behavior, and to redress past actions (e.g., "Did X take place?" "What harm was done?" "Is Mary guilty of violating a rule or legal principle?"). Control over the outcome of the dispute is manifested externally by an impartial third party who "judges" each party's case and his or her adherence to legal procedures.

Litigation is not only a domain of experience that prescribes behaviors, but also a set of beliefs or a way of conceiving the correspondence between organizational life and social reality. Like science, law posits a correspondence between a relatively stable world and clear measures of that world. Correspondence involves a relationship among three points: the real world, the perception of that world, and the statement of that perception (O'Connor, 1975). The law presumes that the world is stable, though it recognizes that perceptions lack the same degree of stability and accuracy. Even when perceptions of the world are "correct," statements about them may misrepresent the perceptions to others. The law approaches this problem of correspondence by attempting to elicit sound data and eliminate bad data, by probing the motives and competence of perceivers, and by asking if each piece of data is relevant to the event in question and to the larger argument that the advocates make.

An example of the litigation metaphor is a dispute about the use of employer records in performance evaluation. Teachers in a union system complained that principals were using information collected in their personnel files as evidence in teacher evaluation reports. An infraction such as being late for lunchroom duty would appear on the evaluation form without informing the teacher that this data was in his or her file. Teachers viewed this practice as an abuse of the current appraisal policy, a lack of openness in superior-subordinate interaction, and ineffective downward communication.

If the teachers adopt a legal metaphor to manage this dispute, they might treat the principal as their adversary and highlight the "violation" of the contract, obtain "facts" and "proof" that the notes were used in evaluation sessions, link the proof to the "right to know," decry the lack of "due process" in evaluating employees, and seek "redress" for past actions and for "breaking contractual obligations." They would set up a public dispute process with a verdict determined by a jury of peers or by an impartial judge selected by both sides. Ironically, many collective bargaining approaches to dispute management follow this legal metaphor in processing grievances and in designing dispute systems (Ury, Brett, & Goldberg, 1988). Collective bargaining, however, may also be based on a negotiation metaphor of dispute management.

■ Negotiation and the Social Construction of Organizational Life

Many scholars from different fields use negotiation as a metaphor to explain how people develop a shared understanding of each other and their social environment. Specifically, negotiation is a process for socially constructing reality (Berger & Luckmann, 1967; Bullis & Putnam, 1985; Putnam, 1985; Putnam et al., 1991) and for shaping social order and organizational culture (Strauss, 1978). Communication theorists suggest that the purposes and procedures of interaction episodes are negotiated (Cronen, Pearce, & Harris, 1982; Newell & Stutman, 1988, 1989/1990, 1991; Pearce & Cronen, 1980). Other theorists describe the development and maintenance of interpersonal relationships as an ongoing negotiation of identities, roles, situations, and rules (Adams, 1985; Fisher, 1987; Wood, 1982). In effect, when two or more people interact with one another they bring to the conversation their own views of self, others, and the situation. Over time shared meanings develop through revised expectations and interpretations in the give-and-take of interaction.

Negotiation as a Metaphor for Organizational Disputes

As a metaphor for dispute resolution, negotiation embodies a different set of language patterns and metaphorical structure than does litigation. Organizational members form agreements through "making deals" or "driving a hard bargain." These agreements imply that disputants find a "middle ground" or a "compromise" from their initial positions. Negotiators regard each other as "fitting opponents" or "skillful players," rather than as adversaries who must be defeated.

The process of negotiation also adheres to rules and procedures; however, unlike litigation, the rules are normative and negotiated between the disputants. Disputants engage in an "exchange of offers" that may follow a "tit for tat" pattern. Norms of "reciprocity" imply that both sides are expected to "trade offers," and that one party's actions are adapted to the moves and expectations of the other side. The parties indicate their desire to negotiate through a willingness "to meet at the table" and adherence to "bargaining in good faith." These standards form a normative base for appropriate behavior, one determined by the participants, rather than by objective legal criteria.

If we treat organizational relationships as negotiation, a coherent structure emerges, with the following entailments: (a) behavior as co-constructed and subjectively defined (e.g., "tit for tat," "I can match and alter your bid"); (b) relationships as interdependent (e.g., "I need you to get what I need," "win-win"); and (c) normative standards for behavior (e.g., "reciprocity," "bargaining in good faith"). Negotiation, then, differs from the litigation metaphor in domains of experience, rules of operation, forms of control, and sets of beliefs. Through the give-and-take process of negotiation, participants can develop shared definitions of situations, issues, and behaviors within the context of their relationship and their organization. Negotiation involves confrontation or a direct management of problems, an activity that superiors and subordinates value in the workplace (Lawrence & Lorsch, 1967; Wheeless & Reichel, 1988). By directly confronting one another, disputants reveal their expectations and make them open for affirmation or denial, negotiation or change (Morris & Hopper, 1980; Newell & Stutman, 1988, 1989/1990, 1991).

In negotiation, rules of operations are not legal procedures or objective criteria for proof and precedent action. Rather, negotiation relies on normative standards of reciprocity, good faith bargaining, and collaborative exchange. These norms are defined intersubjectively through social behavior. Although bargainers develop agendas based on key items, the issues in dispute are socially constructed and may be splintered, multiplied, reframed, and dropped (Putnam, 1990). Hence, the issues may extend beyond the immediate concerns in a dispute, and beyond simply redressing past actions. In forms of control, participants in negotiation take personal responsibility for addressing shared problems. Emphasis is placed on establishing a working consensus for an ongoing relationship.

Implications of the Negotiation Metaphor

Negotiation both requires and fosters trust and internal control of the dispute. Negotiation rejects the notion of a stable world and the need to seek a correspondence between organizational life and social reality. Instead, organizations are in various states of flux and change.

A negotiation metaphor for managing disputes would follow a different approach in the teacher evaluation example than was previously cited. Rather than treat the principal as an adversary, the teachers might view him or her as someone who may have ignored, misunderstood, or misinterpreted the contract, or as someone who had different concerns that could be met in alternate ways. In this approach, the contract is not an objective document; rather, it is an agreement open to interpretation. The principal's actions may violate the initial agreement between the teachers and administration, but both the violation and the interpretation of the contract are open for discussion.

The teachers might confront the principal about what he or she sees as the problem and try to negotiate a change in the practice. If this approach is unsuccessful, the teachers might take the problem to formal negotiations. In both instances, the teachers would make arguments about the harms or disadvantages of putting notes into their files. They might offer alternatives for attaining the principal's goals without placing notes in files. The principal might counter the teachers' proposals. This argumentation process, however, differs from rules for providing evidence, making legal claims, and sticking to the issues in dispute.

In the negotiation metaphor, argumentation is a way of co-constructing problems, issues, and alternatives (Putnam, 1990). It is a means of acquiring knowledge or information about the other person's interests, perceptions, and goals (Keough, 1992). Through argumentation the issue might shift to questioning the nature of personnel files, or altering the teacher evaluation procedures (Putnam & Geist, 1985), or other issues that go beyond the exact dispute. Finally, the negotiation would occur privately, to allow for collaborative problem solving as well as competitive argument. The disputants would control the agreement and determine the outcomes of the process through generating proposals and reacting to each other's proposals.

■ Contrasting the Two Metaphors

The differences between the two approaches indicate that even though litigation and negotiation stem from the same root metaphor of conflict, the two differ dramatically in their assumptive ground and actual practice, as illustrated earlier in Table 11.1. These differences have direct bearing on the way organizational relationships are managed.

It is difficult to classify the two types of metaphors. In everyday language, both metaphors are conventional. We speak of organizational disputes as "grievances" and cast agreements as "contracts." In some organizations, boards of directors "deliberate" decisions, and managers proclaim "verdicts" or decide "if the jury is still out." Since the litigation metaphor is so commonplace in social situations, it is not surprising to regard it as natural, fixed, and immutable in organizations. In like manner, negotiation is a conventional metaphor, one that is even more prevalent in everyday use than litigation. Budget negotiations entail "trading offers" and "meeting at the table to hammer out agreements." Interdepartmental disputes seek "win-win settlements" to facilitate future coordination and preserve interdependence. Subordinates "negotiate" roles and "bargain" for raises and job assignments. Negotiation is so commonplace that we rarely treat it as a metaphor for organizational relationships.

Organizational Vision of the Two Metaphors

Although both metaphors are conventional and appear complementary, the two clash when litigation moves into the informal and interpersonal domain previously dominated by negotiation. As the legal realm expands its terrain, organizational members may regard this vision as the appropriate way to handle all problems. As the litigation metaphor begins to structure organizational disputes, other ways of managing problems become masked (Sitkin & Bies, 1993). The negotiation metaphor, in contrast, highlights a number of elements that foster positive attitudes in the workplace and benefit ongoing relationships.

Through examining the implications of each metaphor for organizational relationships, two different visions of organizational life emerge. Table 11.2 contrasts the way both metaphors sanction actions and justify inferences (Lakoff & Johnson, 1980). The litiga-

Table 11.2
Organizational Vision of Litigation and Negotiation Metaphors

Relationship by Litigation	Relationship by Negotiation
Relationships as regulated	Relationships as managed
External control	Internal control—self-determination
Objective definitions of behavior	Inter-subjective definitions
Fairness established by consistent application of the law	Fairness defined by unique goals and needs of participants
Trust in the system	Trust in one another
Adversaries	Partners
Emphasis on redressing past behaviors and setting precedent for future	Emphasis on working consensus (past/future vs. present)

tion metaphor regulates relationships by sanctioning what can and cannot be done.

Since laws and rules apply to different situations, they must be defined in a clear and objective manner. Consistent application of the law across a variety of situations ensures fairness. Moreover, an external authority or third party must enforce these laws and rules to assure consistent interpretation.

When organizational members turn to the law for managing disputes, they place their trust in the legal system rather than in each other. The litigation metaphor defines participants as adversaries and controls their behaviors through use of threats and punishment. These sanctions result in an organizational vision based on the inference that the other party is not to be trusted (Sitkin & Roth, 1993) and that the participants are not responsible for handling their own problems. Consequently, individuals become passive and claim little control over their organizational lives. Organizational members may follow the letter of the law, but not necessarily the spirit of it; hence, the law may conceal rather than resolve organizational disputes.

An example illustrates the potential ramifications of the litigation metaphor. Litigation places emphasis on whether a behavior is grievable—whether a case can be made (e.g. sufficient evidence, credible witnesses, and the like). In an instance of sexual harassment in which a credible, high-power individual harasses someone of lesser power, comments are typically made only in private. If participants feel constrained by the legal metaphor, one person may feel safe and the other individual may feel like a powerless victim. A person who feels that "this situation would not stand up in a court of law" may produce victim behaviors, while an individual who feels in control of the situation may confront and defend himself or herself. The "perpetrator" may not be aware of how his or her behavior is perceived, but might have been willing to modify it, if confronted. The litigation metaphor screens out differential perceptions from the objectivity of the law.

In addition, the standards that are supposed to guarantee fair treatment under the law may in fact be used to subvert the system. If "good" relations are defined by set standards, then individuals may meet the standards and still be treated unfairly. Furthermore, the standards for making a case may deter effective dispute management, because the case fails to meet the required "burden of proof." For example, in cases of sexual harassment, an individual may feel powerless to act because "it is simply one person's word against another's." In a system of litigation, individuals may not acquire the skills or experience to manage problems directly because they depend on third-party adjudication.

In contrast, relationships within the negotiation metaphor are managed. Individuals must take responsibility for their own lives and disputes. Expectations for relationships and the behavior of others are open for interpretation and negotiation. Through interaction, individuals develop intersubjective meanings that are contextually based. The relationship between disputants is one of partners who must work together to establish a consensus for now and into the future. The resulting organizational vision emphasizes active participation and control, flexibility to adapt to specific changes over time, and feelings of camaraderie.

■ Conclusion

An organization, even in its administrative manifestation, is a field of discourse. That is, an organization is composed of people who are responsible for performing logical operations grounded on specific assertions. These assertions are constituted and reconstituted through language practices. This chapter endorses the position that language and thought are fundamentally metaphorical. In this view, metaphor is not a riddle, an aberration, or an ornament of language, but rather it influences how we see and make sense of the world. Metaphors carry much of the data of everyday life in organizations. Language practices have a tremendous impact, not only on what gets done but also on how it gets done. This chapter contrasts two conventional metaphors for managing organizational disputes. It posits that the two images project different visions of organizational life, and that the litigation metaphor is slowly eroding the negotiation one as a dominant way of thinking and talking about organizational relationships. The litigation metaphor, in turn, may drastically change the nature of relationships by altering flexibility, trust, and the development of shared meanings.

■ References

Adams, K. (1985). *Communication as negotiation: A study of strategic interaction in social relationships.* Unpublished doctoral dissertation, University of Utah.

Beisecker, T. (1988). *Conflict metaphors: The importance of naming.* Unpublished manuscript, University of Kansas, Lawrence.

Berger, P., & Luckmann, T. (1967). *The social construction of reality.* Garden City, NY: Doubleday.

Bies, R. J., & Tyler, T. R. (in press). The "litigation mentality" in organizations: A test of alternative psychological explanations. *Organization Science, 4*(3).

Black, M. (1962). *Models and metaphors.* Ithaca, NY: Cornell University Press.

Broms, H., & Gahmberg, H. (1983). Communication to self in organizations and cultures. *Administrative Science Quarterly, 28,* 11-21.

Bullis, C. A., & Putnam, L. L. (1985, November). *Bargaining as social construction of reality: The role of stories and rituals.* Paper presented at the annual meeting of the Speech Communication Association, Denver.

Burrell, G., & Morgan, G. (1979). *Sociological paradigms and organizational analysis.* London: Heinemann.

Chaika, E. (1982). *Language, the social mirror.* Rowley, MA: Newburg House.

Coffman, S. L., & Eblen, A. L. (1987). Metaphor use and perceived managerial effectiveness. *Journal of Applied Communication Research, 1-2,* 53-66.

Cooper, D. (1986). *Metaphor.* Oxford: Basil Blackwell.

Cronen, V. E., Pearce, W. B., & Harris, L. M. (1982). The coordinated management of meaning: A theory of communication. In F. E. X. Dance (Ed.), *Human communication theory: Comparative essays* (pp. 61-89). New York: Harper & Row.

Deetz, S. (1986). Metaphors and the discursive production and reproduction of organizations. In L. Thayer (Ed.), *Organization—communication: Emerging perspectives* (Vol. 1, pp. 168-182). Norwood, NJ: Ablex.

Deetz, S., & Mumby, D. (1985). Metaphors, information and power. *Information and Behavior, 1,* 369-386.

Fisher, B. A. (1987). *Pragmatics of human communication.* New York: Random House.

Friedman, R. A. (1989). Interaction norms as carriers of organizational culture: A study of labor negotiations at International Harvester. *Journal of Contemporary Ethnography, 18,* 3-29.

Hawkes, D. F. (1972). *Metaphor.* London: Methuen.

Hocker, J. L., & Wilmot, W. W. (1991). *Interpersonal conflict* (3rd. ed.). Dubuque, IA: William C. Brown.

Keough, C. M. (1992). Bargaining arguments and argumentative bargainers. In L. L. Putnam & M. E. Roloff (Eds.), *Communication and negotiation* (pp. 109-127). Newbury Park, CA: Sage.

Koch, S., & Deetz, S. (1981). Metaphor analysis of social reality in organizations. *Journal of Applied Communication Research, 9,* 1-15.

Kolb, D. M., & Putnam, L. L. (1992). Introduction: The dialectics of disputing. In D. M. Kolb & J. M. Bartunek (Eds.), *Hidden conflict in organizations* (pp. 1-31). Newbury Park, CA: Sage.

Lakoff, G., & Johnson, M. (1980). *Metaphors we live by.* Chicago: University of Chicago Press.

Langer, S. (1957). *Philosophy in a new key.* Cambridge, MA: Harvard University Press.

Lawrence, P. R., & Lorsch, J. W. (1967). *Organization and environment: Managing differentiation and integration.* Cambridge, MA: Harvard University Press.

Lieberman, J. K. (1983). *The litigious society.* New York, NY: Basic Books.

Manning, P. K. (1979). Metaphors of the field: Varieties of organizational discourse. *Administrative Science Quarterly, 24,* 660-671.

Meyer, J. W. (1983). Organizational factors affecting legalization in education. In J. W. Meyer & W. R. Scott (Eds), *Organizational environments: Ritual and rationality.* Beverly Hills, CA: Sage.

Morgan, G. (1986). *Images of organizations.* Beverly Hills, CA: Sage.

Morris, G. H., & Hopper, R. (1980). Remediation and legislation in everyday talk: How communicators achieve consensus. *Quarterly Journal of Speech, 66,* 266-274.

Nielsen, S. (1991). Metaphor analysis and organizational reality. *Australian Journal of Communication, 18*(3), 73-80.

Newell, S. E., & Stutman, R. K. (1988). A model of the social confrontation episode. *Communication Monographs, 55,* 266-285.

Newell, S. E., & Stutman, R. K. (1989/1990). Negotiating confrontation: The problematic nature of initiation and response. *Research on Language and Social Interaction, 23,* 139-162.

Newell, S. E., & Stutman, R. K. (1991). The episodic nature of social confrontation. In J. A. Anderson (Ed.), *Communication yearbook* (Vol. 14, pp. 359-392). Newbury Park, CA: Sage.

Notz, W. W., Starke, F. A., & Atwell, J. (1983). The manager as arbitrator: Conflicts over scarce resources. In M. H. Bazerman & R. J. Lewicki (Eds.), *Negotiating in organizations* (pp. 143-164). Beverly Hills, CA: Sage.

O'Connor, D. L. (1975). *The correspondence theory of truth.* London: Hutchingson University Library.

Ortony, A. (1979). *Metaphor and thought.* Cambridge, UK: Cambridge University Press.

Pacanowsky, M. E., & O'Donnell-Trujillo, N. (1983). Organizational communication as cultural performance. *Communication Monographs, 50,* 126-147.

Paivio, A., & Begg, I. (1981). *Psychology of language.* Englewood Cliffs, NJ: Prentice-Hall.

Pearce, W. B., & Cronen, V. E. (1980). *Communication, action, and meaning: The creation of social realities.* New York: Praeger.

Pondy, L. R. (1983). The role of metaphors and myths in organization and in the facilitation of change. In L. R. Pondy, P. J. Frost, G. Morgan, & T. C. Dandridge (Eds.), *Organizational symbolism* (pp. 157-166). Greenwich, CT: JAI Press.

Pruitt, D. G. (1981). *Negotiation behavior.* New York: Academic Press.

Putnam, L. L. (1985). Bargaining as organizational communication. In R. D. McPhee & P. K. Tompkins (Eds.), *Organizational communication: Traditional themes and new directions* (pp. 129-148). Beverly Hills, CA: Sage.

Putnam, L. L. (1990). Reframing integrative and distributive bargaining: A process perspective. In B. H. Sheppard, M. H. Bazerman, & R. J. Lewicki (Eds.), *Research on negotiation in organizations* (Vol. 2, pp. 3-30). Greenwich, CT: JAI Press.

Putnam, L. L., & Geist, P. (1985). Argument in bargaining: An analysis of the reasoning process. *The Southern Speech Communication Journal, 3,* 225-245.

Putnam, L. L., & Poole, M. S. (1987). Conflict and negotiation. In F. M. Jablin, L. L. Putnam, K. H. Roberts, & L. W. Porter (Eds.), *Handbook of organizational communication* (pp. 549-599). Newbury Park, CA: Sage.

Putnam, L. L., Van Hoeven, S. A., & Bullis, C. A. (1991). The role of rituals and fantasy themes in teachers' bargaining. *Western Journal of Speech Communication, 55,* 85-103.

Rieke, R. D., & Stutman, R. K. (1990). *Communication in legal advocacy.* Columbia: University of South Carolina Press.

Roloff, M. E. (1987). Communication and conflict. In C. R. Berger & S. H. Chaffee (Eds.), *Handbook of communication science* (pp. 484-534). Newbury Park, CA: Sage.

Selznick, P. H. (1969). *Law, society, and industrial justice.* New York: Russell Sage.

Sergeev, V. M. (1991). Metaphors for understanding international negotiation. In V. A. Kremenyuk (Ed.), *International negotiation: Analysis, approaches, issues* (pp. 58-64). San Francisco: Jossey-Bass.

Sitkin, S. B, & Bies, R. J. (1993). The legalistic organization: Definitions, dimensions, and dilemmas. *Organization Science, 4*(3).

Sitkin, S. B, & Roth, N. L. (1993). The limited effectiveness of legalistic remedies for trust/distrust. *Organization Science, 4*(3).

Smircich, L. (1983). Concepts of culture and organizational analysis. *Administrative Science Quarterly, 28,* 339-358.

Smith, R. C., & Eisenberg, E. M. (1987). Conflict at Disneyland: A root-metaphor analysis. *Communication Monographs, 54,* 367-380.

Smith, R. C., & Eisenberg, E. M. (1988, August). *Root metaphor analysis: A heuristic method for studying organizational change.* Paper presented at the annual meeting of the Academy of Management, Anaheim, California.

Strauss, A. (1978). *Negotiations: Varieties, contexts, processes, and social order.* San Francisco: Jossey-Bass.

Trice, H. M., & Beyer, J. M. (1984). Studying organizational cultures through rites and ceremonials. *Academy of Management Review, 9,* 653-669.

Tyler, T. R., & Bies, R. J. (1990). Beyond formal procedures: The interpersonal context of procedural justice. In J. S. Carroll (Ed.), *Applied social psychology and organizational settings* (pp. 77-98). Hillsdale, NJ: Lawrence Erlbaum.

Tutzauer, F. (1991). Bargaining outcome, bargaining process, and the role of communication. In B. Dervin & M. J. Voigt (Eds.), *Progress in communication sciences* (Vol. 10, pp. 257-300). Norwood, NJ: Ablex.

Ury, W. L., Brett, J. M., & Goldberg, S. B. (1988). *Getting disputes resolved.* San Francisco: Jossey-Bass.

Walcott, C., Hopmann, P. T., & King, T. D. (1977). The role of debate in negotiation. In D. Druckman (Ed.), *Negotiation: Social-psychological perspectives* (pp. 193-211). Beverly Hills, CA: Sage.

Wheeless, L. R., & Reichel, L. S. (1988, May). *A reinforcement model of the relationships of supervisors' general communication styles and conflict management styles to task attraction.* Paper presented at the annual meeting of the International Communication Association, New Orleans.

Weick, K. E. (1979). *The social psychology of organizing* (2nd. ed.). Reading, MA: Addison-Wesley.

Wood, J. T. (1982). Communication and relational culture: Bases for the study of human relationships. *Communication Quarterly, 30,* 5-83.

Yudof, M. G. (1981). Law, policy, and the public schools. *Michigan Law Review, 79*(4), 774-790.

12

Reducing the Litigious Mentality by Increasing Employees' Desire to Communicate Grievances

Debra L. Shapiro

Deborah M. Kolb

T he theme of this book is the increasing legalization of thinking and action in organizations. It is interesting that while this claim is made for organizations, a major trend has been occurring that runs counter to this argument. During the past decade or so we have been witnessing a major shift in the ways our legal system and our society more generally deal with their disputes. This shift has been one away from litigation in the courts, executive edict in government, legislative hearing in communities, and authoritative decision making in organizations toward mediation, a process of consensual problem solving (Administrative Conference, 1987; Goldberg, Green, & Rogers, 1992). Mediation, in other words, is seen as an alternative to the accustomed ways we have of dealing with difference. It brings a different kind of process to the problems of overcrowded and unsympathetic courts, to changing and conflict-ridden communities, to the stalemates that accompany long and contentious struggles over public policy and international affairs, and more locally to silenced employees who lack ways to voice their grievances.

Likened by some to a social movement (Milner, Lavaas, & Adler, 1987), mediation is increasingly being used to resolve differences in our families and communities (Pearson & Thoennes, 1989), in the organizations in which we work (Kolb & Sheppard, 1985), and in our

303

relations with other countries (Bercovitch & Rubin, 1992). One reason for this growing popularity is that many believe mediation promises a better, more satisfying, more efficient, and more harmonious way for society to deal with its conflicts. In particular, mediation is seen as an antidote to the large caseloads and delays in court brought on by the "litigation explosion" (Galanter, 1983). As considerable evaluation studies attest, mediation delivers agreements that are reached sooner and at lower cost and leave parties satisfied and committed to implementation (McEwen & Maiman, 1984; Pearson & Thoennes, 1989).

In a somewhat analogous fashion, an alternative movement of sorts has been developing in organizations. Partially in response to the increasing legalization of the workplace (Sitkin & Bies, 1993), many organizations have installed complaint systems that are intended to give employees voice in the expression of their grievances (Edelman, 1990; Ewing, 1989; Rowe, 1987; Westin & Feliu, 1988; Ziegenfuss, 1988). The promise of an open door, an ombudsman, a peer complaint panel, and a multistep grievance procedure is put in place as a means to keep conflicts contained within the organization, and so keep the state out of an organization's human resource management affairs. While some of these systems resemble adjudicative rule-based procedures akin to those found in law (Near, Dworkin, & Miceli, 1993), practitioners and researchers find that the mediation-type processes comprising the latter systems (e.g., open doors and ombudsmen) are preferable to more legalistic procedures as ways of dealing with complaints (Rowe, 1987; Ury, Brett, & Goldberg, 1989).

Similar claims are made with regard to informal modes of conflict handling (Kolb & Putnam, 1992). Studies in field and simulated organizations suggest that people find mediation fairer and more satisfactory than arbitration and/or other forms of authoritative decision making (Brett & Goldberg, 1983a; Karambayya & Brett, 1989; Lewicki & Sheppard, 1985; Shapiro & Brett, in press).[1] The bases for these claims derive from a number of considerations. One concerns control. The argument is made that mediation, as distinguished from other forms of dispute resolution such as arbitration and adjudication, reserves the decision about settlement to the parties. Disputing parties have outcome control in mediation, and this difference has been identified as one reason why they prefer to have their conflicts mediated than dealt with in some other fashion. Mediation is also better suited to deal with underlying problems in the context of ongoing relationships (Fuller, 1971; Goldberg, Green, & Sander,

1985). Mediation, in other words, has become the preferred alternative to other forms of handling differences. If we want to resolve our disputes in the organizational house, then it is mediation that offers the most promise. Or does it?

The problem with this claim is that it is based on what has been labeled an essentialist definition of mediation. From this perspective, mediation is defined as a core set of attributes that presumably distinguish it from other forms of dispute handling. Thus, mediation is a process of persuasion, not decision making, that is oriented toward the relationship of the parties and not the law which governs them (Fuller, 1971). Rather than focus on rights or rules, mediators oversee a process that is designed to help disputing parties resolve the issues that separate them.

In contrast to this essentialist perspective, many who have studied mediation in practice conclude that it is often difficult to distinguish it according to any set of basic characteristics. This is because mediation seems to be a rather adaptive process that is quite variable, depending upon where it is conducted, when in the dispute process it occurs, and who is doing the mediation (Kolb & Kressel, 1994). Indeed, many argue that mediation in a particular setting has more in common with the legalistic alternative it replaces than it does with the way it is practiced in other domains (Kolb, 1989). The reasoning runs as follows. By the time mediators get involved in most disputes, parties have framed the issues as claims (Felstiner, Abel, & Sarat, 1980-1981). That is, mediation gets introduced in most dispute resolution channels rather late, after parties have pursued other avenues and exhausted other means (Merry, 1990). They are ready for justice and that tends to involve an adjudicatory process.

In this chapter we will argue that the language characterizing the mediation process encourages disputing parties to replace their initial "rights" (or adjudicative) orientation with an interests-oriented perspective. In this way, mediation serves to de-legalize the issues. Mediation, because it focuses on underlying interests rather than rights, promises to contain disputes within the organization and resolve them in ways that meet the joint interests of both employees and the organization. For this reason, mediation has the potential as an antidote to legalistic activity. But the need to deal initially with disputants' rights orientation means that even mediation occasionally resembles the more legalistic procedure it is designed to replace. When claims are made about the virtues of mediation, therefore, we need to look both at the process in relation to the broader dispute resolution system of which it is a part and at the specifics of that process, so that we can consider how mediation serves to de-legalize issues that disputants initially frame as matters of rights to be adjudicated.

The purpose of this chapter is to consider mediation as an organizational alternative open to employees who claim that their rights have been violated in some fashion. The first section considers these claims in the context of grievance mediation and suggests that the distinctions between dispute resolution procedures, as rights- versus interest-based, are not as clear as the claims made for them. Based on an in-depth study of a well-regarded mediator and arbitrator, William Hobgood, we will argue that in the case of grievance arbitration and mediation, the former influences the latter in such a way that it is difficult to untangle the two processes (See Kolb, 1989; 1994). This overlap creates different demands on a mediator that may undercut some of the perceived advantages, in terms of employee satisfaction of mediation relative to arbitration. Based on studies of managers and others in dispute resolution settings, we argue that it is only when mediators talk and act in ways that signal concern and consideration to disputants that the promise of a mediated approach can be realized (Shapiro, in press; Shapiro & Brett, in press). And when mediators use language and other actions that indicate employees' complaints are being considered, employees will be more likely to communicate disagreement and less likely to look for someone else (e.g., a court judge or arbitrator) for resolution. Ironically, it may be that organizations are likely to reduce employees' litigation mentality if they design procedures and reward behaviors that increase employees' desire to communicate differences, and so enhance the overall capacity of the organization to deal with its internal conflicts. The reason for this is that mediation has the potential to keep disputes close to the point of origin, and so helps managers, organizations, and employees retain flexibility and control over the disposition of problems that more formal, legalistic procedures preclude (Bies & Tyler, 1993; Sitkin & Bies, 1993). We conclude on a more pessimistic note. It is possible that mediators' efforts to resolve disputes inside, rather than outside, the organization may encourage them to address the narrow issues at the expense of broader, institutional ones. If so, then mediation may promote the communication of differences that exceed the organization's capacity to deal effectively with them.

■ Mediation and Its Alternatives

In most fields where mediation is used, it is part of a hierarchy or channel of procedures and is intended to be an alternative or complement to another already existing process for handling conflicts. The nature of these overlaps is considerable in the case of grievance arbitration and mediation. It is often said that the grievance procedure is at the very heart of a collective bargaining agreement because it provides workers and managers with a mechanism to interpret the contract in light of day-to-day operations (Slichter, Healy, & Livernash, 1960). The multistep grievance procedure with provision for arbitration is now a fixture in 98% of collective bargaining agreements, and some nonunion settings as well. It provides for a first step in which a grievant (sometimes accompanied by a shop steward) discusses the problem orally with the supervisor. Failing agreement, the grievance is put in writing and submitted to a higher level of line management. In the second step, a representative of the union and management meet and discuss the grievance. Typically, management's response is put in writing. In the third step, the grievance is appealed to higher line management and/or the industrial relations department. Local or international representatives of the union are also involved in this step. If there is no agreement, then the union must decide whether to submit the grievance to binding arbitration, the fourth and final step.

Arbitration is a quasi-judicial process in which the arbitrator renders a final and binding decision on an aspect of the contract that is contended by the parties. Arbitration is one of the great success stories of American labor relations (Kochan, 1980; Peach & Livernash, 1974). It removes the daily conflicts that arise in the workplace from the courts and gives authority to labor relations specialists, who can use their knowledge and expertise to take the culture of the shop floor into account. Often interpreted as the quid pro quo for the strike during the term of the agreement, arbitration has contributed substantially to industrial peace in many industries (Thomson, 1974). Indeed, historically arbitration was itself an alternative to the increasing legalization of labor problems (Kochan, 1980). When initially introduced, arbitrators were viewed not as judges but as "labor relations physicians" (Kochan, 1980). An arbitrator's role was to provide, not merely a "cure" (binding solution) for the problem ailing disputing parties, but also "preventative" (more long-term) conflict intervention, by helping disputants improve their relationships. The role of arbitrators over time has become increasingly judicial, because disputants generally seek arbitration after they have failed to resolve the dispute through other means (via negotiation or other problem-solving procedures, such as mediation), and consequently, after disputants feel a need for a binding decision. Despite the strengths of arbitration, there continues to be dissatisfaction with many aspects of the process, particularly with the failure of the procedure to be either speedy or inexpensive and to address the underlying source of problems in the workplace.

Critics note that delays and costs make timely resolution of disputes an impossible goal. Adding to delays and the increasing legality of the process is arbitration's formality, which makes use of rules of evidence, examination and cross-examination of witnesses, submission of written briefs, post-hearing briefs, and use of attorneys' written transcripts. The adjudicatory process that arbitration has become makes winning the end toward which the parties aspire (Ury et al., 1989). And, the win-lose framework often has unfortunate consequences in terms of the parties' satisfaction, perceptions about the fairness of the process, and willingness to comply with the decisions.

An interesting irony is that a procedure designed to avoid legalization itself became legalistic. It is the increasing legalization of arbitration that has made mediation seem a desirable alternative. Consider the words of William Hobgood, an experienced labor arbitrator and mediator, on the subject.

> The job of the arbitrator is to determine who is right or wrong. Even though you as an arbitrator may want to know about extenuating circumstances, most arbitrators will tell you that many times they walk away from a case without knowing the full facts because the parties chose not to bring them forward. Because what's the goal of the players in arbitration? It's to win. So you play it in a way that is going to achieve that and that's not to give the arbitrator the benefit of the extenuating circumstances. After all, you don't want to help the opposition build its case. So nothing about extent, frequency, fault, type, or other extenuating circumstances will come out. Rather, the issues come out in a mechanical, cut-and-dried manner. (Kolb, 1994)

Mediation is intended to correct this problem. When parties agree to mediate their grievances, a new step is inserted into the process. Prior to arbitration, the parties agree to use a mediator, who typically has extensive arbitration experience as well, to help them resolve their differences so that arbitration is not needed. (For extensive descriptions of the process, see Brett & Goldberg, 1983a, 1983b; Silbey & Merry, 1986; Ury et al., 1989). Mediation is presumed to be an improvement over arbitration because it allows the mediator to help the parties shift their focus from the rightness or wrongness of their position and concentrate instead on the interests underlying these positions, in the hopes that they may reach a settlement that accommodates these interests. Again, according to Hobgood:

> What are seen as extenuating circumstances in an arbitration case are the kinds of issues that you can deal with in the mediation process. Mediation gives you the capacity to either keep the agreement as narrowly defined as possible, or because an issue will come up again and again, you can broaden it to the policy question and see if it makes sense so that we can deal with it in a different way. (Kolb, 1994)

If parties fail to reach agreement, the mediator can offer them an oral advisory arbitration opinion, which, based on his best estimates, would reflect the likely decision of an arbitrator if the case went to arbitration.

While the formal definitions and claims of a well-known practitioner imply a clear distinction between the two procedures, observations from practice suggest that the boundaries are rather blurred (Kolb & Kressel, 1994). First, mediation is shaped by the previous steps in the grievance procedure. The parties have already worked at resolving their issues as they relate to the labor contract. Hence the kinds of right/wrong arguments that Hobgood decries are part of the framework that disputants bring to mediation.

> In mediation you are faced with the weaknesses of the multistep procedure. By the time the problem gets to the mediation process it has had what I call double reinforcement. The supervisor makes the initial decision and it's probably already been checked all the way up to the top. Then Step 2 reinforces Step 1, and Step 3 reinforces Step 2. By the time the mediator arrives on the scene, both parties have convinced themselves that they are right and can't back away from it because of the positions that have been taken all along the way. (Kolb, 1994)

Second, the provision for arbitration means that somebody may render either a formal or an advisory opinion about rightness or wrongness of positions. This possibility continues to infuse the mediation process with a rights-based or legal focus that is supported by the parties and reinforced by the mediator. In short, mediators work with disputants who are prepared with the arguments and evidence necessary to enhance their chance of receiving both a positive advisory opinion and, if necessary, a positive arbitration decision. When they come to mediation, parties speak in the language of the grievance steps just past and a projected future step in arbitration (Kolb, 1989). Consequently, parties have a legalistic orientation toward the mediation process. The implications of this for the process of mediation are explored below.

■ Blurred Boundaries and Blurred Roles: Facilitators and Forecasters

Disputants enter mediation fresh from their efforts to resolve a grievance at the previous step. Their language is one of contract violation (or not) and their stance is litigious, to prove that their position is the correct one. The challenge for the mediator is to encourage disputing parties to abandon this legal rhetoric (Sitkin & Bies, 1993), and so de-legalize their language, reframe their understanding of the issues, and alter the adversarial and litigious stance that has served them well previously. The mediator's objective is to transform the parties' approaches from a legalistic to a problem-solving orientation. This is not possible in all cases.

In many cases the parties frame the issues, explain them to the mediator, and present and argue their case in ways that reflect their experience in the grievance procedure. For example, to meet the contractual requirements for the earlier steps, the problem is presented in terms of contractual rights or custom that have been transgressed by management: that people were assigned jobs not according to the seniority clause, that a supervisor performed union work, that progressive discipline was not followed. Often these contractual interpretations of the issue dominate the discussion. The framing of the issues in terms of violation of contractual rights in preparation for the earlier steps and arbitration, however, makes it difficult for the mediator to refocus the discussion on other issues or underlying interests.

There are many reasons why it is difficult to refocus the discussion. Sometimes the parties have an interest in keeping the issue narrowly defined for political or other reasons. For example, where union leaders have trouble screening grievances, or fear duty of fair representation suits, mediation can serve the purpose of "chilling out" a troublesome union member. The leadership turns to the mediator to "tell it like it is." In one case, for example, welders were assigned to the "owl shift," and a senior union member grieved because he wanted his day shift job back. The essence of this mediation was to convince this union member that even if there were a provision to bid on a day job, he could not be assured that he would get the job. Hobgood described this grievance as one where his reiteration of the argument lent support to the union representative, who had failed to convince this grievant that he could not win, even if the rule on welders was changed.

The initial framing of the issues as contract violation is reinforced in the ways that parties argue their case. Typically, the parties come to mediation with folders filled with documentation about the grievance. Evidence is introduced, exhibits are shown, and testimony is taken from supervisors, grievant, and witnesses—all activities that would occur in arbitration as well. In certain situations, the representatives on both the union and management sides introduce their cases with prepared statements that they read aloud.

The possibility of arbitration figures prominently in mediation. If the parties do not reach an agreement during the mediation, arbitration is the next formal step. It is always possible that the parties will settle prior to arbitration, in part because they rethink their chances as a result of the mediation. The mediator's expert assessment of the quality of the case the parties can present to an arbitrator may be one of the triggers to this rethinking. Hobgood often begins meetings with one of the parties, typically the union, by discussing its chances in arbitration. He was not always able to predict who would actually win, but was usually able to let the union know what kind of case it would have to make, and the risks of doing so. In making these arguments he would refer to a number of factors, including:

- the uncertainty of an arbitration decision—"you never know which way an arbitration will go";
- trends in arbitration awards relative to a given case—"on welding cases, it is always hard to figure out whether the contract has been violated";
- the quality of the union or management's case—"unless you can show that the out of class assignment is a safety issue, you will have a tough time in arbitration";
- the kind of data that they would need to provide, and management's inherent record-keeping advantage in this regard—"on these kinds of

cases it is always easier for management to argue the case because they have the job assignment data and you would have to find witnesses";

- patterns in arbitral decision making—"arbitrators are reluctant to rule on internal jurisdictional cases unless you can show that the union lost work";

- arbitration would not deal with the *real* problem—"even if the arbitrator decided that senior welders should be on the day shift, you (the grievant) wouldn't necessarily get your job back." (Kolb, 1994)

Hobgood believes that arbitration is essential to grievance mediation for several reasons. One, "the threat of arbitration makes mediation work." If parties think that they will not win in arbitration, then it forces them, he claims, to look at the mediation options more seriously. His predictions of how they will fare in arbitration helps the process along.

In many of Hobgood's cases, the discussion of rights and chances in arbitration dominated the discourse in the mediation session. It was difficult, if not impossible, for the parties to shift the focus to interests or problem solving. Mediation becomes, in this kind of situation, largely a matter of assessing the quality of the case the parties can put before an arbitrator. What we get is a mediation process that resembles arbitration, but without some of its procedural protections (Delgado, Dunn, Brown, Lee, & Hubbert, 1985).

There are, however, other occasions when the mediator is able to shift the discussion away from contractual issues and get the parties to consider ways to deal with the underlying problem that gave rise to the grievance in the first place. One of Hobgood's cases, for example, concerned a coalminer named Rosie who received a disciplinary warning due to her high accident record. The union's position, backed by a previous arbitral decision, was that the company had to prove that the employee was at fault in order to warrant the disciplinary action. The company argued, also on the basis of an arbitration award, that they would take disciplinary action, based solely on the number of accidents. Hobgood tried, and was ultimately successful, in shifting the attention of the parties away from fault to a broader discussion of the issues. Although the warning remained in Rosie's record, the company initiated a new safety training program. Indeed, Hobgood often refers to this case as the best example of how mediation can be used to solve problems in the workplace (Kolb, 1994).

It is clear that the institutional context makes it difficult for parties to shift their focus from contractual issues to a consideration of broader problems. But it may also be that the kind of dual role played by the mediator contributes as well. The mediator is called on to be a facilitator of a problem-solving process as well as an expert forecaster of arbitration outcomes. The parties' expectations, coupled with the mediator's desire to produce a settlement, collude to favor one—the forecaster role—at the expense of the other. Consider some of the ways that this happens in Rosie's case.

Hobgood introduces himself as serving both these roles:

> Mediation is an informal process. It is designed to get the parties, who have the best understanding of the contract and the relationships, involved in finding a solution to the problem. We will have an open and frank discussion about the background of the dispute here in a joint meeting and try to resolve it. I may have to separate the parties and try out different approaches, but all the ideas will stay there. We hope that it can be resolved. If no agreement is reached, as it states in your contract, I will advise you on how I think an arbitrator would rule. If we do not resolve the grievance and you do go on to arbitration, nothing we discuss here will be used at that step. (Kolb, 1994)

Embedded in this opening statement are references to legal documentation (i.e., their contract), the arbitrator and the arbitrator's "rule," and an assurance that nothing discussed during mediation will be used at "the next step." It is thus little wonder that disputants subsequently have difficulty shaking off an arbitration, or right-wrong, frame. This difficulty is probably exacerbated by the fact that the legal rhetoric (Sitkin & Bies, 1993) was made in the mediator's opening remarks, during which the tone, or expectations, of the meeting are likely to be set. In another case, Hobgood began his caucus with the union and management by assessing their chances in arbitration. Thus, mediators' difficulty in shifting parties away from their rights and toward their interests may be due to the fact that they simply attempt this too late (i.e., after they have already made reference to arbitration). Indeed in many of Hobgood's cases, he discussed with at least one of the parties, typically both, their chances in arbitration. What is so interesting is that in the majority of these, he began this discussion within the first few minutes of the caucus with the union. That does not mean he was able to predict the outcome in each instance, but he was usually able to tell not only what kind of arbitration case the union would have to make but also the kind of challenges it would face.

This type of communication is intended to focus the parties on mediation and pressure them into making more conciliatory gestures in order to avoid arbitration (cf. Harris & Carnevale, 1990; Kolb & Kressel, 1994). But telling disputants how they will probably fare in arbitration, and how they should prepare for it to increase their chance of faring better, seems unlikely to shift parties' focus away from a litigious (arbitration-like) frame. Instead, when mediators take the role of forecaster, they create an inextricable link between mediation and arbitration, and cause disputing parties to experience mediation in the shadow of arbitration.

When mediators take the role of facilitator, they are more likely to shift parties' focus toward the joint problem-solving orientation. They do this in a number of ways. In contrast to the language of contracts and arbitration that mark the forecaster role, as facilitators they try to assist the parties to speak in a language that is conducive to mediation (Kolb & Kressel, 1994). As parties provide the background to a dispute, one begins to detect ways in which mediators start framing the issues in a manner that they believe will facilitate forms of solving problems that are more likely to lead to agreements.

In the questions they ask and the instructions they give, mediators try to influence both how the parties talk about their issues and the kinds of language they want the parties to use when they give their version of the story. The mediator tries to get parties to phrase their discussions with a look toward the future—what can be done to solve a particular problem, what it will take for a change to occur—rather than a rehash of past wrongs. Mediators also try to get the parties to put emotions aside so that they do not get caught in an accusatory mode, but rather speak to each other in a calm and reasoned manner, in which the problem is the focus. Finally, they try to get the disputants to talk in ways that legitimate the concerns of the party on the other side of the table and, in Hobgood's words, "meet their interests."

Encouraging parties to speak in the language of mediation is important for several reasons. First, it puts the parties into a different mindset than they typically entered with. It is not emotions, rehashing past grievances, and bashing the other party that will compose the mediation process. Rather, it will be one of future-oriented, rational discussion that recognizes the relationships between the parties.

Second, in the varieties of questions and comments the mediators make, they begin to frame the issues in ways that are more likely to be conducive to their way of dealing with the issues on the table. In Rosie's case, for example, Hobgood wanted to focus the discussion on what could be done about safety generally, at the same time as he wanted to protect Rosie from having a final warning in her file. His questions about the safety training program and how people get warnings were directed at these issues. What is not addressed through his questions and comments is the problem of sexual harassment in the mine (although Rosie spoke of it), and the organization's reward system, which prompts mine superintendents to stress production over safety. Thus when mediators claim that they are neutral and impartial because they leave the substantive decision-making to the parties, they are correct. However, they influence that discussion indirectly through the ways they coach the parties to talk to each other and frame the issues. Indeed, coaching the parties in a language of mediation continues during the entire process. It is a major way in which the mediator contributes to possible resolutions of difference.

In this regard Hobgood used a number of these approaches in Rosie's case. He tried to get the parties to shift their attention from the contract issue regarding warnings and focus them on a discussion of problems with safety and accidents in the mine. He drew Rosie, the grievant, into the case with much sympathy and support and tried to get her to identify what it was she wanted from an agreement. Using a questioning mode, he tried to both learn more about the circumstances surrounding the dispute and also engage the parties in coming up with their own possible solutions. Hobgood summarizes this approach:

> I usually know early on whether I can settle a case or not, but you have to take it step by step. You have to *condition* people. You do that by raising issues with them and getting them to think about it, but always one step at a time. You have to let them know that you have considered all the alternatives—it helps the conditioning. You can't do things too soon, first you have to challenge their thinking. (Kolb, 1994)

In summary, in the role of facilitator, Hobgood focuses the parties on issues that are broader than who is right or wrong. He does this by helping the disputants find new ways other than legal rhetoric (Sitkin and Bies, 1993) to talk about their problem. Although the uncertainties of arbitration lurk in the background for both parties, he uses that to keep them focused and committed to the task at hand. These actions are absent from arbitration. Thus, the relationship that mediation has with arbitration can be either distant or close, depending, in part, on which role (facilitator or forecaster) the mediator emphasizes.

The actions associated with the mediator's facilitator role seem likely to result in two important consequences. First, if the disputants feel that the mediator is genuinely interested in helping them solve a problem, they may be more comfortable talking with each other and with the mediator in a manner that moves them from reiterating claims about a past injustice to a more open dialogue about possibilities. The forecaster role is more likely to shut down discussion because it suggests that a cherished idea may in fact be wrong, at least according to an experienced arbitrator. Second, the mediator's facilitative actions can increase disputants' perception that what they are saying is "being considered." This may explain why the perception of consideration is associated more positively with mediation than arbitration, and why mediation is evaluated as fairer (Shapiro & Brett, in press). In this study and others (Tyler, 1987), disputants' valued the chance to talk only when they believed that the third party was, in fact, considering their expressed views. It thus becomes important for the successful practice of mediation or arbitration, or whenever other dispute resolvers want people to talk about their conflict, to understand what actions enhance speakers' perceptions that their opinions, or evidence, will actually get considered.

Actions Showing That Views Will Get Considered

The perception that one's views will, in fact, be considered is important because it appears to be the critical factor in accounting for differences in whether grievants feel they have been justly treated (Lind, Kanfer, & Earley, 1990; Shapiro & Brett, in press; Tyler, 1987). Managers and eventual managers (MBA students) have identified actions necessary to create this perception (Shapiro, in press). Taken together, these suggest that consideration has several dimensions.

The first dimension that seems to be strongly associated with consideration consists of giving grievants feelings of *potential influence* over an authority's decision, or what Brett (1986) calls "indirect outcome control." Managers in Shapiro's study said they would believe that an authority would consider their views if that person promised to share grievants' expressed opinions with more senior people in the organization; if an authority weighed grievants' opinions into their own decision making; if those in authority exhibited a willingness to reconcile their own versus grievants' opinions; or if that person said that his or her decision (regarding an issue grievants care about) was not yet made. In all of these cases, those in authority assured grievants that their views might influence the ultimate decision. The perception of consideration was absent when feelings of potential influence were lacking, for example, when grievants believed "the decision had already been made," or that "top management's mind was already made up and nothing or no one could reverse their decision."

In court, police, and organizational settings, consideration also seems to involve acting toward grievants with *interpersonal sensitivity*. For example, listening without interruption, nodding to show empathy or understanding (see Shapiro, 1993, for an elaboration), and more generally, treating grievants with respect and dignity (Bies & Tyler, 1993; Tyler & Bies, 1990) are actions associated with the perception of consideration. The importance of such actions have caused some to point to the "interpersonal context" (Tyler & Bies, 1990) or a "relational model" (Bies & Tyler, 1993) as key factors in influencing grievants' perceptions of procedural justice, and others to identify "interactional justice" as an important, distinctive justice perception (Bies & Moag, 1986; Bies & Shapiro, 1987).

In addition to listening in an interpersonally sensitive manner, engaging grievants in a *dialogue* seems to be another critical component of consideration. Bies and his associates found this to be aligned with perceptions of dignity and respect (Bies & Moag, 1986; Bies & Tyler, 1993). An illustration of its importance comes from one manager in Shapiro's (1993), study who said that an authority should:

> [A]sk further questions about my opinion, ask me to be specific, look into my eyes while I am speaking, take notes, avoid interruption of our discussion; not just listen, but enter into a dialogue, repeat or sum up what I have said, and finally, give a specific conclusion of our discussion (e.g., tell me when I can return, not just "you'll hear from us").

Thus, according to this respondent, a dialogue—not merely questions and answers or rebuttals—is necessary for the speaker to believe that his or her expressed opinions will be considered. Similarly, many other respondents said that "discussing" their viewpoints would lead them to believe that their views would be considered. Similarly, Cobb (1992) shows that mediators are more likely to get equal involvement when they use techniques such as circular questioning to help parties create new stories that alter their understandings of the problem and its possible solutions.

In many ways, the dimensions of consideration described above are seen in the actions of mediators when they are in the role of facilitators.

For example, by asking grievants for their help in solving a dispute-related problem and asking them how to proceed, the mediator-as-facilitator demonstrates that no solution (decision) is yet known, and that the eventual solution is the disputants' choice to make. In this way, the facilitative mediator provides disputants with feelings of potential influence over their dispute's resolution. Expressions of empathy, understanding, and the desire to gain more understanding are communications used by mediators in the facilitative role, illustrated by Bill Hobgood, who successfully used this rhetoric to encourage the grievant, Rosie, to become more actively involved in discussing her case. When mediators take the role of facilitator, they actively dissuade disputants from engaging in interpersonally destructive communications (e.g., expressing no empathy, no understanding, nor any desire to understand the other side's viewpoint), and instead coach them to talk to each other in a language more conducive for promoting constructive discussion that will ease disputants' ability to find mutually beneficial ways to resolve their differences.

The rhetoric described above that leads speakers to perceive that their views will be considered is more easily accessible to mediators than arbitrators. Mediators, for example, have more leeway in how they organize the physical space in joint meeting or separate caucus in such a way that discussion, or dialogue, is more possible, and more casual and off-the-record. In contrast, arbitration follows a more rigid structure in terms of seating arrangements and order of the procedure. The structure of the discourse is likewise more pro forma in arbitration. Arbitrators listen to disputants' prepared statements, presentation of evidence, questioning of witnesses, rebuttals, and so on, and then remove themselves from the proceeding to prepare a written decision. Mediation has considerably more room for spontaneous and new discourses to emerge. The arbitrator asks disputants only for the facts leading to the dispute, not for ideas about how to proceed or how to settle. Moreover, disputants know that the arbitrator's interest in the facts is to evaluate them as either right or wrong, making it difficult for them to communicate as openly with the arbitrator as they do with the mediator, who does not evaluate them and who has more leeway to express empathy and understanding.

Thus, grievants may evaluate the mediation procedure to be more satisfying and fair than arbitration because the third party in mediation—but not arbitration—can use facilitative language that encourages employees to openly grieve and, more important, to believe that their expressed grievances will be considered. When the forecasting, or advisory, role of the mediator dominates his or her communications, mediation is likely to be in the shadow of arbitration, and hence less distinguishable from the more costly, adversarial, and litigious alternative it is meant to replace. Managers' tendencies to adopt advisory, or authoritative, approaches when intervening in employees' disputes may partly explain why employees tend to seek people outside of the organization (e.g., attorneys, judges, arbitrators, and mediators) to hear their grievances (Kolb & Sheppard, 1985; see Sheppard, Blumenfeld-Jones, & Roth, 1989, for a review). By adopting behaviors associated with mediators' facilitative role, managers may reduce employees' desire to grieve outside the organization, or to use litigious channels to settle their grievances. Conversely, the behaviors that demonstrate consideration should increase employees' desire to communicate grievances openly inside the organization.

■ Conclusion:
The Merits and Paradoxes of Mediation

Mediation is often touted as the preferred alternative to adversarial and legal dispute resolution procedures. Our analysis of some of the nuances of mediation suggest that not all mediation is equal in this regard. Because mediation is typically located within a hierarchy of other dispute resolution processes and procedures, the boundaries between it and its alternative are blurred.

We have seen that in the case of grievance mediation, there are occasions when it resembles more of an arbitral procedure than it does the kind of problem solving one tends to associate with mediation (Kolb, 1989). This blurring occurs because of the kinds of expectations the parties bring to the process, and the kinds of language and contractual arguments they use to support their case. But it also arises from the very real pressures on the mediator to get agreements. Forecasting the outcome in arbitration can be the incentive to keep parties committed to finding a solution to their issues, or it can inhibit that kind of process.

But there is an alternative language that mediators use, one which is future-oriented, conveys legitimacy and concern, and signals to the parties that their views are being considered. It is that kind of process that people are referring to when they claim that mediation offers us a better way to resolve disputes in organizations. While the potential exists, it is not at all clear that in practice the benefits are as positive. For the practice of mediation in organizations contains a number of paradoxes that limit the possible claims that it contributes to a diminution of litigious behavior. Consider the following paradoxes.

Mediation Is Positively Evaluated, yet Underutilized

One paradox about mediation concerns the finding across many domains that mediation is positively evaluated, yet underutilized. In the management context, disputants have shown a preference for mediation over arbitration (Karambayya & Brett, 1989; Shapiro & Brett, in press; see Brett, 1986, for a review). Yet, managers generally resist approaches to managing conflict that require the use of process skills. Instead, they opt for approaches that allow them to provide just an ear and a decision. A common explanation for this is that managers see authoritative approaches, which require less in the way of process skills, as more timesaving and consistent with their vision of the manager's role (Kolb & Sheppard, 1985; see Sheppard et al., 1989, for a review).

Mediation may be underutilized for other reasons. A mediated approach is often identified as feminine, or the approach of those without influence, and hence devalued on that score (Kolb, 1992). Bill Hobgood noted that even in the face of successful outcomes, mediation is abandoned in favor of arbitration: "[Mediation is] cooperation and compromise. It's not viewed as aggressive enough, it's not manly. It's a soft process."

It may also be that by the time people are ready to go public with a claim, it is justice, not process, that they want. The right-wrong language that disputing parties initially speak in their quest for justice may prohibit managers from (at least easily) invoking mediation, which requires the elimination of this litigious frame.

Mediation May Increase, Instead of Decrease, Disputes

Earlier we argued that employees should be more willing to express grievances inside, instead of outside, the organization when managers behave in ways akin to the facilitative mediator. If this is so, then mediation may increase, rather than decrease, the number of employee disputes.

There is another paradox here as well. The very notion of litigiousness suggests that we have too many conflicts and disputes in our organizations. Indeed, the data used to support the litigiousness argument typically draws on large caseloads in the courts, or the explanations of lawyers, or the number of organizational cases. This data is challenged by numerous studies, which suggest that most conflicts in organizations, as well as other settings such as families, communities, and informal groups, never get publicly expressed as disputes. When probed, people reveal all sorts of grievances, complaints, and differences that could be—but rarely are—voiced. Sometimes people fear retribution or loss of social acceptance; others avoid entrapment in complex or bureaucratic processes; others believe that they lack sufficient resources to pursue their grievance; while yet others see complaining and confrontation as evidence of moral laxity or lack of independence (e.g., Bies & Tyler, 1993; Greenhouse, 1986; Miller & Sarat, 1980-81; Merry & Silbey, 1984). For example, in a study of professional accounting firms, Morrill (1992) reports that 73% of conflict episodes among partners are never expressed directly. Avoidance and toleration are the modal forms of conflict management, rather than confrontation or litigious action.

Given the negative organizational consequences of suppressed conflict, which include lost opportunities for innovation and change, *our problem may not be too many cases, but too few.* Consequently, our goals must be to enhance the capacity of organizations to deal with differences (Kolb & Silbey, 1990). Mediation as part of formal systems and informally part of managerial practice is one avenue to this end, especially when it is practiced in a facilitative manner, with consideration in mind. Practiced this way, mediation offers the possibility of providing employees the certainty they want in knowing that a procedure exists for addressing their conflict, and the flexibility they want in seeing their grievances personally and considerately, not bureaucratically, handled. Mediation thus promises to reconcile the dilemma of maintaining employees' trust in the face of increased reliance on organizational procedures (Bies & Tyler, 1993). This, in turn, should enhance employees' trust in management to deal with conflicts fairly and flexibly, and consequently, their willingness to express more, not fewer, grievances. Thus, it may be more accurate to surmise that the availability of mediation, in contrast to more litigious dispute-resolution procedures, may increase the number of voiced employee disputes.

Mediation Resolves Individual Problems
but Masks Institutional Issues

To the degree that mediation is practiced facilitatively by managers and others, several positive consequences are likely for the organization. First, disputes will be resolved close to the source, precluding the need for outsiders—including lawyers, arbitrators, and news reporters—to get involved. Second, the disposition of disputes can be handled with greater flexibility and responsiveness when they are addressed within the organization; this is less likely in litigious (court) settings, where the communication as well as the fate of disputes is guided by formal rules and procedures (Sitkin & Bies, 1993). Third, the process skills the mediator uses to encourage disputants to speak constructively to each other, and to frame issues with a problem-solving (interest-based) rather than a right-wrong (accusatory) orientation, are skills that benefit the participants and their organizations (and departments, teams, and the like) in the long term. This is because such skills, if applied in future disputes, enhance the possibility that disputing employees will be able to settle their differences without calling for third-party assistance.

Mediation is not an unequivocal good, however. In part it depends on how it is practiced. We have argued that if it is practiced in a facilitative manner, with consideration in mind, all of the above merits can be realized. But we, too, have argued that a probable consequence of practicing mediation facilitatively is that it will lead to more, not fewer, expressions of disputes. Although we have argued that organizations can benefit from enhancing, rather than reducing, the number of employee disputes, it is possible that organizations may reach a state of excessive capacity. Mediators-as-facilitators who are overwhelmed by employee grievances may then do as the initial arbitrators-as-physicians did: redefine their role more narrowly as forecasters in order to process disputes in a more timely and efficient fashion.

But there is a more serious problem as well. Mediators have considerable discretion in how they define what dispute is to be resolved. In Rosie's case, Hobgood had several choices. He could have dealt just with the warning and persuaded the company, based on the uncertainty of arbitration, to drop it. His focus was broader—a package that coupled safety training with the warning. In other words, he kept the focus on the individual grievant and chose not to engage the institutional problems in the mine—the treatment of women and the pressures for production over safety. Mediation has been criticized for its tendency to individualize problems that are collective (Abel, 1982). But there is a further issue as well. Hobgood justified his actions on the basis of what was possible. Given, he argued, that the union had not explicitly raised the harrassment issue or the production pressures, he felt that he could not make them the focus of his efforts. Indeed, there is other evidence that mediators define disputes in such a way that they can succeed in resolving them (Kolb, 1987). These tend to be at the level of the individual, an outcome that gives rise to the criticism of mediation as a process that preserves rather than alters the status quo (Abel, 1982).

It is clear that mediation, when practiced in a facilitative manner, can help individual grievants resolve some of their conflicts in the organization. To the degree, however, that institutional problems are not addressed, and that the organization has become more open to the expression of differences more generally, then it is possible that mediation can indirectly contribute to more litigation, not less. Indeed, barring other forms of organizational development and change, existing dispute-resolution procedures are rarely equipped to handle collective issues, and so parties must go outside the organization to the courts, either as individuals or as part of a class action. Thus, a return, not a reduction, in a litigious mentality on the part of employees may paradoxically be the result of mediation (even when practiced in a facilitative manner), whose aim it is to preclude the need for legal intervention in the first place.

■ Note

1. It should be noted that in laboratory settings, disputants have rated arbitration to be more satisfying and fair than mediation (Thibaut & Walker, 1975; see Lind & Tyler, 1988, for a review). Brett and Shapiro (1985) have pointed out that the operationalization of mediation in these laboratory experiments was contrary to the way they saw mediation practiced in the field. In their laboratory experiment, Brett and Shapiro operationalized two kinds of mediation procedures in addition to arbitration. First, they used a field-like operationalization, in which disputants had the opportunity to help develop the solution to their dispute with the assistance of the mediator; and second, they used the typical laboratory-like operationalization, in which disputants lacked involvement in the development of the settlement and merely had the opportunity to reject the settlement recommended by the mediator. Consistent with the findings of field researchers, Brett and Shapiro found that disputants preferred the field operationalization of mediation over arbitration.

■ References

Abel, R. (1982). *The politics of informal justice.* New York: Academic Press.

Administrative Conference of the United States. (1987). *Sourcebook: Federal agency use of alternative means of dispute resolution.* Washington, DC: Author.

Bercovitch, J., & Rubin, J. (1992). *Mediation in international relations.* New York: St. Martin's Press.

Bies, R. J., & Moag, J. S. (1986). Interactional justice: Communication criteria of fairness. In R. J. Lewicki, B. H. Sheppard, & M. H. Bazerman (Eds.), *Research on negotiations in organizations* (Vol. 1, pp. 43-55). Greenwich, CT: JAI Press.

Bies, R. J., & Shapiro, D. L. (1987). Interactional fairness judgments: The influence of causal accounts. *Social Justice Research, 1,* 199-218.

Bies, R. J., & Tyler, T. R. (1993). The "litigation mentality" in organizations: A test of alternative psychological explanations. *Organization Science, 4*(3).

Brett, J. M. (1986). Commentary on procedural justice papers. In R. J. Lewicki, B. H. Sheppard, & M. H. Bazerman (Eds.), *Research on negotiations in organizations* (Vol. 1, pp. 81-92). Greenwich, CT: JAI Press.

Brett, J. M., & Goldberg, S. B. (1983a). Mediator-advisors: A new third party role. In M. Bazerman & R. J. Lewicki (Eds.), *Negotiating in organizations.* Beverly Hills CA: Sage.

Brett, J. M., & Goldberg, S. B. (1983b). Grievance mediation in the coal industry: A field experiment. *Industrial and Labor Relations Review, 37*(1), 49-70.

Brett, J. M., & Shapiro, D. L. (1985). *Procedural justice: A test of competing theories.* Unpublished manuscript, Northwestern University.

Cobb, S. (1992). *Politics of discourse in mediation.* Video, Program on Negotiation, Harvard Law School.

Delgado, R., Dunn, C., Brown, P., Lee, H., & Hubbert, D. (1985). Fairness and formality: Minimizing the risk of prejudice in alternative dispute resolution. *Wisconsin Law Review,* 1359.

Edelman, L. (1990). Legal environments and organizational governance. *American Journal of Sociology, 95,* 1401-1441.

Ewing, D. W. (1989). *Justice on the job: Resolving grievances in the nonunion workplace.* Cambridge, MA: Harvard Business School Press.

Felstiner, W., Abel, R., & Sarat, A. (1980-81). The emergence and transformation of disputes: Naming, blaming and claiming. *Law and Society Review, 15,* 631-654.

Fuller, L. (1971). Mediation: Its forms and functions. *Southern California Law Review, 44,* 305.

Galanter, M. (1983). Reading the landscape of disputes. *UCLA Law Review, 31,* 4.

Goldberg, S. B., Green, E., & Rogers, N. (1992). *Dispute resolution* (2nd ed.). Boston: Little, Brown.

Goldberg, S. B., Green, E., & Sander, F. (1985). *Dispute resolution.* Boston: Little, Brown.

Greenhouse, C. (1986). *Praying for justice: Faith, order and community in an American town.* Ithaca, NY: Cornell University Press.

Harris, K. L., & Carnevale, P. (1990). Chilling and hastening: The influence of third-party power and interests on negotiation. *Organizational Behavior and Human Decision Processes, 47,* 138-160.

Karambayya, R., & Brett, J. M. (1989). Managers handling disputes: Third party roles and perceptions of fairness. *Academy of Management Journal, 32*, 687-705.

Kochan, T. (1980). *Collective bargaining and industrial relations.* Homewood, IL: Irwin.

Kolb, D. M. (1987). Corporate ombudsman and organization conflict resolution. *Journal of Conflict Resolution, 31*(4), 673-691.

Kolb, D. M. (1989). How existing procedures shape alternatives: The case of grievance mediation. *Journal of Dispute Resolution,* 59-87.

Kolb, D. M. (1992). Women's work: Peacemaking in organizations. In D. Kolb & J. Bartunek (Eds.), *Hidden conflict in organizations: Uncovering behind the scenes disputes.* Newbury Park, CA: Sage.

Kolb, D. M. (1994). Conditioning parties to settle their labor grievances: Profile of William Hobgood. In D. Kolb (Ed.), *When talk works: Profiles of master mediators.* San Francisco: Jossey-Bass.

Kolb, D. M., & Kressel, K. (1994). Making talk work: Struggle in professional practice. In D. Kolb (Ed.), *When talk works: Profiles of master mediators.* San Francisco: Jossey-Bass.

Kolb, D. M., & Putnam, L. L. (1992). The dialectics of disputing. In D. Kolb & J. Bartunek (Eds.), *Hidden conflict in organizations: Uncovering behind the scenes disputes.* Newbury Park, CA: Sage.

Kolb, D. M., & Sheppard, B. H. (1985). Do managers mediate or even arbitrate? *Negotiation Journal, 1,* 379.

Kolb, D. M., & Silbey, S. S. (1990). Enhancing the capacity of organizations to deal with difference. In J. W. Breslin & J. Z. Rubin (Eds.), *Negotiation theory and practice.* Cambridge, MA: Program on Negotiation.

Lewicki, R. J., & Sheppard, B. H. (1985). Choosing how to intervene: Factors affecting the use of process and outcome control in third party dispute resolution. *Journal of Occupational Behaviour, 6,* 49-64.

Lind, E. A., Kanfer, R., & Earley, P. C. (1990). Voice, control, and procedural justice: Instrumental and noninstrumental concerns in fairness judgments. *Journal of Personality and Social Psychology, 59*(5), 952-959.

Lind, E. A., & Tyler, T. R. (1988). *The social psychology of procedural justice.* New York: Plenum.

McEwen, C. A., & Maiman, R. J. (1984). Mediation in small claims court: consensual processes and outcomes. In K. Kressel & D. G. Pruitt (Eds.), *Mediation research: The process and effectiveness of third-party intervention.* San Francisco: Jossey-Bass.

Merry, S. (1990). *Getting justice and getting even.* Chicago: University of Chicago Press.

Merry, S. E., & Silbey, S. S. (1984). What do plaintiffs want?: Reexamining the concept of dispute. *Justice System Journal, 9,* 151-179.

Miller, R., & Sarat, A. (1980-81). Grievances, claims, and disputes: Assessing the adversary culture. *Law and Society Review, 15,* 525-566.

Milner, N., Lavaas, K., & Adler, P. (1987). *The public and the private in mediation: The movement's own story.* Working paper, Program on Conflict Resolution, University of Hawaii.

Morrill, C. (1992). The private ordering of professional relations. In D. Kolb & J. Bartunek (Eds.), *Hidden conflict in organizations: Uncovering behind the scenes disputes.* Newbury Park, CA: Sage.

Near, J. P., Dworkin, T. M., & Miceli, M. P. (1993). Explaining the whistle-blowing process: Suggestions for power theory and justice theory. *Organization Science, 4*(3).

Peach, D., & Livernash, R. (1974). *Grievance initiation and resolution: A study in basic steel.* Working paper, Harvard Business School.

Pearson, J., & Thoennes, N. (1989). Divorce mediation: Reflections on a decade of research. In K. Kressel & D. Pruitt (Eds.), *Mediation research: The process and effectiveness of third-party intervention.* San Francisco: Jossey-Bass.

Rowe, M. (1987). The corporate ombudsman. *Negotiation Journal, 3,* 127.

Shapiro, D. L. (in press). Reconciling theoretical differences among procedural justice researchers by re-evaluating what it means to have one's views "considered": Implications for third-party managers. In R. Cropanzano (Ed.), *Justice in the workplace: Approaching fairness in human resource management.* Hillsdale, NJ: Lawrence Erlbaum.

Shapiro, D. L., & Brett, J. M. (1991). *Comparing the instrumental and value-expressive models of procedural justice under conditions of high and low decision control.* Paper presented at the national meeting of the Academy of Management, Miami, Florida.

Shapiro, D. L., & Brett, J. M. (in press). Comparing three processes underlying judgments of procedural justice: A field study of mediation and arbitration. *Journal of Personality and Social Psychology.*

Sheppard, B. H., Blumenfeld-Jones, K., & Roth, J. (1989). Informal third partyship: Studies of everyday conflict intervention. In K. Kressel & D. G. Pruitt (Eds.), *Mediation research: The process and effectiveness of third-party intervention.* San Francisco: Jossey-Bass.

Sitkin, S. B, & Bies, R. J. (1993). The legalistic organization: Definitions, dimensions, and dilemmas. *Organization Science, 4*(3).

Silbey, S., & Merry, S. (1986). Mediator settlement strategies. *Law and Policy, 8,* 7.

Slichter, S., Healy, J., & Livernash, R. (1960). *The impact of collective bargaining on management.* Washington, DC: Brookings Institution.

Thibaut, J., & Walker, L. (1975). *Procedural justice: A psychological analysis.* Hillsdale, NJ: Lawrence Erlbaum.

Thomson, A. (1974). *The grievance procedure in the private sector.* New York: State School of Industrial and Labor Relations.

Tyler, T. R. (1987). Conditions leading to value expressive effects in judgments of procedural justice: A test of four models. *Journal of Personality and Social Psychology, 52,* 333-344.

Tyler, T. R., & Bies, R. J. (1990). Beyond formal procedures: The interpersonal context of procedural justice. In J. S. Carroll (Ed.), *Applied social psychology and organizational settings* (pp. 77-98). Hillsdale, NJ: Lawrence Erlbaum.

Ury, W. L., Brett, J. M., & Goldberg, S.B. (1989). Getting disputes resolved: Designing systems to cut the costs of conflict. San Francisco: Jossey-Bass Publishers.

Westin, A. F. & Feliu, A. G. (1988). Resolving employment disputes without litigation. Washington, DC: Bureau of National Affairs.

Ziegenfuss, J. T. (1988). *Organizational troubleshooters: Resolving problems with customers and employees.* San Francisco: Jossey-Bass.

Reflections on the Legalistic Organization

13

The Costs of Legalization:
The Hidden Dangers of Increasingly Formalized Control

Jeffrey Pfeffer

S itkin and Bies (this volume) have noted that a legalistic mentality is on the ascendancy in American organizations. They note that this creates an emphasis on what is "legally defensible (versus that which is organizationally or interpersonally sensible)." They go on to note that increased legalization entails greater reliance on formal rules and standardized procedures; use of litigation or other adversarial, formal modes of conflict resolution; and an increasing emphasis on uniformity and standardization.

Why this trend is occurring is a matter open to multiple interpretations. Certainly, a part of the story is the vast number of lawyers in the United States (one estimate is that one-third of all lawyers in the world practice in the United States). Another part of the explanation involves the breakdown of trust in an increasingly demographically heterogeneous society. Zucker (1986) has noted that in the past, immigration and the growth in the scope and impersonality of economic relations necessitated the development of formal institutions and mechanisms to substitute for trust based on personal knowledge, familial connections, or social similarity. The problem is that as Roth, Sitkin, and House (this volume) noted, "trust violations can be halted by legalistic interventions, but distrust is escalated both by increasing perceived interpersonal distance and by failing to address the tendency of perceptions of value incongruence to generalize." Thus, a legalistic response to problems of distrust or violations of trust sets in motion a self-fulfilling cycle of behavior, as trust is further eroded by the very application of legalistic remedies.

Whatever the causes, it is clear that this increasing legalization creates vast costs of numerous types for both the economy and the society. This chapter briefly reviews some of these costs. Other costs have already been treated in earlier chapters in this volume—for instance, Van Maanen and Pentland's descriptions of how the records of both police and auditors are developed with the goal of impression management, with the potential loss of accuracy and data as a result; Browning and Folger's description of how the search for plausible deniability in the Iran-Contra scandal (and more generally when subordinates are asked to do things by their superiors that their superiors don't want to be associated with) leads to a loss of control and the likelihood of general lapses in ethics; and Randall and Baker's documentation of how the development of legalistic fetal protection policies at the Bunker Hill Company actually produced additional litigation from nonprotected male employees concerned about reproductive risks. Our concern here is with costs of two general types: direct, economic costs, and efficiency loss in organizations that result from a climate of distrust and excessive control.

The substantive focus of this chapter is the employment relation. It is somewhat ironic that just at the time there is increasing emphasis on employee involvement, working in teams, decentralization of decision making, and total quality efforts that rely importantly on employee initiative and cooperation, the employment relation itself has suffered the same trend toward legalization as other aspects of organizations. The chapter first discusses the more direct and apparent costs of this move toward legalization and then considers other, more subtle and perhaps deeper costs on the management process and the development of trust in organizations.

■ The Legalization of the Employment Relation

In the beginning, so to speak, there were no employees. Clawson (1980) has documented the dramatic change in the organization of work between 1860, when most people worked for themselves or for fairly small enterprises, and 1920, by which time the majority of people worked in an employment relation for increasingly large organizations. Prior to the employment relation becoming so extensive, production was organized first in a so-called putting out system, and subsequently in a system of inside contracting. In both instances, the merchant furnished materials and perhaps capital equipment, but the laborers worked either for themselves or for inside contractors and were generally paid by the merchant, according to what was produced. There is evidence that a system of contracting or relying on contingent, nonemployee labor is again becoming popular (Pfeffer & Baron, 1988) for various reasons, including the increasing litigation costs and regulations that are associated with the employment relation.

When workers were brought inside the firm as employees, the problem of management control was created (Braverman, 1974). As Braverman (p. 57) noted, "what the worker sells, and what the capitalist buys, is *not an agreed amount of labor, but the power to labor over an agreed period of time*. What he buys is infinite in *potential* but in its *realization* it is limited by the subjective state of the workers." The employment relation makes issues of management and control important—"there aren't 'managers' in markets" (Pfeffer, in press, p. 139). At first, control was exercised by the owner-manager directly supervising the employees. This personal control (Edwards, 1979) was based on a set of personal interactions and relationships between ownership and labor, and as such, was apparently much more palatable to the employees. For instance, histories of the Ford Motor Company (e.g., Lacey, 1986) maintain that Henry Ford worked with his engineers in designing cars, with his manufacturing executives in laying out production systems, and in general was visible in the plant, even as the company grew substantially. This and early versions of managing by walking around provided employees with a visible, tangible connection to ownership, and there was little separation of ownership from the management function.

The growth of enterprises and the rise of foremen, supervisors, and professional managers was accompanied by a reign of industrial despotism that resulted in frequently bloody strikes, industrial sabotage, and levels of turnover so high as to make organizations essentially spot labor markets (e.g., Jacoby, 1985, 1991). For instance, in 1913, Ford Motor Company experienced a turnover rate of 380% at its Highland Park plant (Lacey, 1986, p. 130). As documented by Edwards, (1979), Jacoby (1985), and others, this regime of control ended under pressure from reformers and social activists, trade unions, and business requirements to manage labor more effectively to take advantage of the increasingly sophisticated and expensive capital equipment that was modernizing and enhancing the production process in numerous industries—and that made sabotage and strikes much more costly. It was replaced by what some have called bureaucratic control (Edwards, 1979), a system of rules and procedures that substituted due process and formal procedure for the arbitrary exercise of power by foremen and other managers. One of the effects of bureaucratic control was to make power relations in the workplace less visible, because the exercise of personal power was curbed by the formal systems and practices instituted. In this administration of industrial due process, the personnel department came to play a central role.

The formalization of the management of the employment relation, and the growth of the personnel function, were both helped along by the Second World War (Baron, Dobbin, & Jennings, 1986). The government needed to be able to manage the nation's human resources and allocate them to the war effort, and consequently instituted reporting requirements and facilitated the growth of a stronger personnel management function. Of course, once in place, these activities persisted even after the war was over.

The development of some internal mechanisms for curbing the arbitrary and capricious exercise of power by foremen, often for their own benefit rather than the corporation's, was an inevitable development. Foremen often hired people who bribed them for the jobs, and set wages in a similar fashion. Although this arrangement benefited the foremen, it did not necessarily produce the most skilled or motivated work force and thus came to be disliked by owners. Certainly, providing both procedural and substantive justice in the work place was and is important for building a committed work force, for avoiding unionization (one of the aims of instituting regimes of bureaucratic control), and for managing the organization's people more effectively. Indeed, most people would view the development of internal procedures to ensure justice as positive. What was not inevitable and needs explanation is how and why bureaucratic control continued its evolution to become increasingly legalistic and concerned with formalism, and why outside litigation came to increasingly be a substitute for internal grievance or other mechanisms for redressing workplace problems. The irony is that these increasingly legalistic procedures often substitute "law" for justice, "as managerial decisions are dominated increasingly by a concern for what is 'legal' at the expense of humanistic and social considerations" (Sitkin & Bies, 1993, p. 349).

There are a number of possible answers to this question. Perhaps the most fundamental insight is that "trust offers an effective substitute to law" (Smitka, this volume) or, for that matter, to formal legalisms.

Thus, legalization arises in the absence of trust (Sitkin & Roth, 1993). Formal procedures and recourse to external authorities for dispute resolution signal that the parties involved do not trust each other and cannot rely on mutual goodwill and the relationship between them to solve their problems. The history of adversarial relations between management and the work force in the United States has produced a legacy of distrust. Taft and Ross (1969), for instance, have reviewed evidence indicating that the United States has experienced a level of actual physical violence toward labor that is quite unprecedented in other industrial countries. The tendency of the government to actively take the side of employers against employees—another feature unique to the United States—produces a power imbalance and the sense that firms can win the battle. Much as the prospect of mutually assured destruction—nuclear deterrence—prevented war by creating a situation in which there were likely to be no winners, so a more balanced power distribution between management and the work force would be likely to produce, once the inevitability of the balance was recognized, a stance toward accommodation and learning how to get along cooperatively. By contrast, a power imbalance tends to produce continuing conflict and the absence of a relationship of trust and mutual respect.

The dominance of finance and the comparatively limited power of the human resources or personnel function in most U.S. firms have also contributed to the legalization of employment. The dominance of finance and strategic considerations led to the deemphasis on effective management of the work force. The limited power of human resources meant that personnel practitioners were often more than ready to form alliances with both internal and external lawyers as a way of buttressing their own power. I have often heard personnel people admit that external legal problems such as age, race, or gender discrimination, or problems with wrongful termination suits, provided a benefit—in that it gave them leverage within the organization, more visibility, and more importance. Thus, somewhat ironically, those responsible for keeping the organization out of trouble and managing its human resources effectively frequently have limited influence to do their job effectively, except when the organization is caught up in a legal crisis or industrial dispute of some importance.

The erosion of union power, as the proportion of the work force covered by collective bargaining has declined and the power of unions has correspondingly decreased, provides another part of the answer. On the one hand, one might argue that formal grievance and arbitration

mechanisms, inevitably part of collective bargaining agreements themselves, constitute a formalization and legalization of work relations.
But the real question is, compared to what? Grievance and arbitration
are often not used when unions and companies have developed sound
working relationships—note the tremendous decrease in labor disputes when New United Motor Manufacturing took over the Fremont
plant formerly operated by General Motors (Adler, in press). And,
grievance processes are still less legalistic than reliance on a civil
litigation system, which is what often replaces the dispute-resolution
processes provided through collective bargaining.

For whatever reasons, employment law is one of the booming legal
specialties, and labor litigation has grown rapidly over the past
decades. Moreover, this litigation has caused organizations to become
increasingly legalistic in their internal dealings with employees. For
instance, it is now difficult to get a reference on someone from the
person's former employer because of the fear of being sued for libel
or defamation. It is difficult to obtain personnel data for research
purposes because organizations are concerned about the ability of
such data to reveal race or gender discrimination. Organizations have
rewritten their personnel policies and employment manuals, often
with an eye to the potential for litigation, rather than on a basis of
what will make them effective in attracting and retaining a work
force. Although the precise scope of the increase in the legalization
of the employment relationship is difficult to assess, there is general
agreement that these things, and others, all point to a more legalistic
environment for managing the employment relation.

■ The Economic Costs of Legalization

The direct economic costs of the legalization of the employment
relation are staggering, and moreover, there is evidence that this system
produces neither a set of equitable outcomes nor economic benefit
to those employees who are injured. Rather, the system seems to primarily benefit lawyers and others associated with the legal process.

In the United States each year there are approximately 3 million
employees terminated for noneconomic reasons (Pfeffer, in press).
Under the doctrine of employment-at-will, employees can be dismissed for any cause or for no cause at all. The United States is the
only major industrial country that adheres to at-will employment to
even a limited extent (Hill, 1987). Although exceptions to the at-will

doctrine have developed—for instance, one cannot dismiss someone because of that person's race, gender, age, or physical handicap, and people cannot be dismissed for their union activities—litigation over the issue of wrongful discharge has proliferated. A study of case filings in Los Angeles County Superior Court observed an almost 700% increase between 1980 and 1986 (Dertouzos, Holland, & Ebener, 1988). By 1989, one report estimated that there were some 25,000 wrongful discharge cases pending in the state and federal courts and that between 1982 and 1987, wrongful discharge cases doubled (Geyelin, 1989).

The RAND Corporation's comprehensive study of 120 jury trials decided in Los Angeles County between 1980 and 1986 provides the most comprehensive data on the costs of litigation (Dertouzos et al., 1988). This study found the following: (1) It took on average more than 3 years for the cases to come to trial; (2) even for cases that were closed by the time of study, it took almost another half year after trial for final disposition; (3) the plaintiffs won about two-thirds of the cases, with the average award of about $650,000; (4) the largest award was $8 million, and the smallest was $7,000; (5) the average legal fee expended defending one of these cases was more than $80,000, with the largest defense fee being $650,000; and (6) considering the time to trial and median award compared to the plaintiff's salary, the evidence was that "the typical plaintiff receives the equivalent of one-half year's severance pay. By inducing terminated employees to accept such a severance, employers could save $84,000 in defense fees" (Dertouzos, et al., 1988, p. 39). The study found that plaintiff's and defense legal fees were, on the average, larger than the amount actually received by the injured party.

But there is one aspect to the RAND study that is even more troubling. The study attempted to predict the size of the final award, using factors such as the plaintiff's age, earnings, gender, position, size of employer, and so forth. The analysis was able to account for less than one third of the variation. So much unexplained variation in award size leads one to conclude that there is substantial randomness in the process. The fact that litigation over wrongful discharge is costly; recovers less for the plaintiff, even when successful, than on average is spent on attorneys; and has a large element of chance involved leads one inexorably to the conclusion that the process is not very effective or equitable.

Nor is the problem of litigation costs confined to the domain of wrongful discharge and employment-at-will. The National Labor

Relations Board (NLRB) is charged with the task of supervising unionization elections and investigating and adjudicating charges of unfair labor practices. Although the proportion of the work force that is unionized has declined significantly in the period after World War II, there has been substantial increases in litigation. For instance, just between 1970 and 1980, the number of unfair labor practice cases filed more than doubled (Flanagan, 1987). By 1983 the budget of the NLRB was larger by more than 50% than the budget of either the Securities and Exchange Commission or the Federal Communications Commission (Flanagan, p. 22). This seems like a disproportionate expenditure of regulatory resources, given the declining role of unions in the economy—but it is an expenditure required by the adversarial, litigious atmosphere that characterizes relations between employers and unions.

Meanwhile, enforcement of laws forbidding discrimination on the basis of race, gender, national origin, age, or physical handicap has languished in recent years. Even when the Equal Employment Opportunity Commission (EEOC) pursues and wins judgments, the amount of economic benefit to those harmed by discrimination is minuscule. In 1977 the average dollars received per person benefited in the cases actually settled by the EEOC was just $1,170, an amount that by 1985 had increased only to $5,848 (Pfeffer, in press). It is difficult to reconcile the differences in damages received from wrongful discharge compared to discrimination cases, and to make sense of the difference in the resources spent enforcing labor laws versus anti-discrimination laws. The preponderance of evidence is that not only does the legalistic approach to employment expend tremendous resources, it also produces results in which punishment is not proportional to the severity of the offense, and the amount of recovery by injured parties is poorly related to the damage these individuals suffered.

■ The Systemic Costs of Legalization

The direct economic costs—expenditures on lawyers and legalistic proceedings—represent just the tip of the iceberg. It is difficult to fully account for the costs of managerial time spent in depositions, in hearings, or worrying about pending disputes. It is not only time, but also attention and focus that get diverted by these formal, legalistic procedures—and attention focused on employment law issues is attention diverted from other aspects of the business. Sitkin and Bies

(1993, p. 547) have noted that too much attention to only the legal ramifications of decisions can lead to ignoring other relevant factors.

And, there are even more significant costs. In response to the potential for suit, firms adopt policies that may be appropriate, given a goal of avoiding legal liability, but which are certainly questionable, given a goal of managing an organization effectively. For instance, the Bureau of National Affairs studied the wrongful discharge law and cases and recommended the following:

> Do not make any statement concerning the length of employment. . . . Avoid statements that employment at the company should be viewed as a long term career. . . . Avoid references to job security, longevity, or career paths that employees will take. Avoid discussion of the policies and practices for layoffs and terminations. Interviewers should not describe probationary periods of employment. (Shepard, Heylman, & Duston, 1989, pp. 21-22)

Consider the task of attracting, retaining, and motivating a work force if an organization were to fully implement these recommendations. One could not talk about future career prospects and potential career paths; one could not have an employment security policy; one could not even talk about future staffing prospects; and in general, one would need to behave as if the employment relation were more like a spot market transaction—which is, after all, what at-will employment implies.

Organizations do act on these recommendations. A graduating Stanford MBA student declined an offer at a firm, when, late in the recruitment process, he was given a statement to sign, acknowledging that he would be an at-will employee. He noted that this statement was inconsistent with the organization's talk about people as a source of advantage. And even though he was told this was only a legal formality (required by personnel and the company's labor lawyers), this "formality" was quite distressing to him, as I am sure it would be to potential applicants. Even those who signed on entered the organization with some skepticism about the sincerity of its commitments and the purity of its motives and intentions.

The legal process is, at its core, adversarial. In a similar fashion, the legalization of the employment relationship inside organizations institutionalizes and legitimates conflict. Instead of seeking to find common ground and common interests, working to resolve differences, a legalistic approach fosters an attempt to see who is right and a win-lose dynamic, which tend to exacerbate rather than solve problems. The dynamic established is one that creates rather than resolves differences, and in this sense nicely produces more fodder for the legalistic mechanisms. But such an approach fails to produce an environment of trust and one in which effective interaction or problem resolution is encouraged.

For instance, consider the case of gender discrimination at the Stanford University Medical School. Brought into focus as well as national attention by the resignation of neurosurgeon Frances Conley, the school's initial response was to appoint a committee, headed by a respected senior cardiac pathologist, Margaret Billingham. When confronted with systematic complaints by women working in the radiology department, Billingham brought the situation to the attention of the dean in the form of a letter detailing the problems. The school's response, however, was to demand "data," and by that they did not mean an individual's perceptions or feelings but numbers, hard evidence. Documenting discriminatory behavior is not always easy. What the demand for data, for evidence, did, of course, was provoke two responses: Some saw this as an attempt to stonewall the problem, and many women resigned from the radiology department; others took the challenge literally, and the medical school was soon filled with individuals trying to document (or undocument, depending on their position), the problem. Certainly, this search for hard data, neglecting all other aspects of the process, wastes a lot of effort but, most important, institutionalizes an atmosphere of conflict. Each side tries to obtain facts to support its position, and each attempts to discredit the facts brought forward by the other side. In all of this, there is little attention to either building more harmonious working relationships or even to solving the fundamental underlying issues. In this sense, a legalistic response is often diversionary. Although this diversion may be desired by those seeking to escape reprobation, it also diverts time and attention away from fundamental issues and problem solving to efforts at problem proving.

The medical school example nicely illustrates two of the paradoxes of legalization noted by Sitkin and Bies (1993). They note that there is a power paradox, in which legalistic procedures installed to protect disadvantaged groups often work to their detriment. This was certainly the case here, in which the very requirements of legal formalism imposed costs on those who complained, and in which the trappings of the legal process—including having court reporters in what otherwise might have been informal hearings—served to create an atmosphere of intimidation. The situation also nicely illustrates the formalization paradox—in which attempts to minimize conflict through formalization of the process can "actually contribute to a growing adversarial climate in which the organization is undermined anyway" (Sitkin & Bies, 1993, p. 349).

By forcing people to take sides—for in a legalistic process, one must bear witness for one side or the other—the formalization of internal dispute resolution can create diversions or deepen preexisting differences. In this sense the very act of mustering and presenting one's case creates a commitment to one's position. After all, the expenditure of effort is one of the most committing of activities (e.g., Salancik, 1977). Having devoted time to assembling one's case, the individual will certainly have convinced himself or herself by the effort. Thus, the person's position will be hardened, the sense of wrong or injustice increased, and in the process, the person will have probably called on others to provide corroborating evidence, thereby widening the dispute and causing further divisions and unhappiness. Social information and diffusion processes are potent in organizations (Ibarra & Andrews, 1993), and the act of putting together a case for a legalistic procedure inevitably activates social networks in ways that increase conflict and produce more disaffection.

The emphasis on gathering data to buttress legal actions, and the absence of trust created by a legalistic approach to one's employees, have yet another cost—the cost of surveillance. The Office of Technology Assessment estimated that in 1988 more than 10 million workers were subject to concealed telephone and computer observation. This congressional research arm reported that the number of surveillance systems sold to businesses increased by almost 300% just from 1985 to 1988 (Lopez, 1990). These systems themselves cost money to install, maintain, and operate. Moreover, they produce costly effects on the work force. For instance, video display workers who are monitored suffer substantially higher levels of stress-related medical problems, such as ulcers, heart disease, fatigue, and depression, compared to unmonitored workers doing the same jobs (Lopez, 1990).

■ Why the Costs Continue

The preceding discussion poses a fundamental paradox: Why would organizations continue to incur these costs if they were behaving rationally and were interested in enhancing their profits and effectiveness? Those who believe in the moment-by-moment efficiency of organizations in fact wonder if all of these costs are so severe, or alternately they search for corresponding benefits that outweigh the costs and thereby make sense of the behavior. Why organizations behave in ways that are seemingly inconsistent with their long-run economic interests is an important issue, but it is essential to note that in other areas as well—such as capital investment and investment in research and development—there are examples of firms behaving in ways that do not make long-run sense.

In the present case, the emphasis on legalistic remedies for problems of trust comes, in part, from a view of human behavior that is articulated in most of the prominent economic theories of the employment relationship, such as agency theory and transaction costs, and that is, in any event, quite consistent with the cultural emphasis on control so prominent in the United States. Theories of behavior are important because, as Robert Frank has argued, "Views about human nature have important practical consequences. . . . They dictate corporate strategies for preventing workers from shirking, for bargaining with unions . . . our beliefs about human nature help shape human nature itself" (1988, p. 237).

Transaction cost economics presumes that individuals exercise a vigorous form of self-interest seeking behavior, opportunism, which may involve actual guile and deception. Oliver Williamson defined opportunism as "self-interest seeking with guile. This includes, but is scarcely limited to, more blatant forms such as lying, stealing, and cheating. Opportunism more often involves subtle forms of deceit" (1985, p. 47). Because of the presence of opportunism, one cannot rely on the goodwill of others to deal with issues involved in contracting relationships as they emerge. And because of the uncertainty and limited information-processing capacity, all future contingencies cannot be anticipated at the time agreements are reached. This leads to the efficiency of hierarchy—internalizing transactions in a governance structure that can accommodate future contingencies as they arise, and which provides the monitoring necessary to prevent opportunism from running rampant.

The view of human behavior articulated by agency theory is scarcely more flattering. Agency models emphasize the conflict of interest that is inevitable between principals and their agents. Eisenhardt noted that agency problems arise when "(a) the desires or goals of the principal and agent conflict and (b) it is difficult or expensive for the principal to verify what the agent is actually doing" (1989, p. 58). Since economic models, including agency theory, proceed from the presumption that people are effort averse, or simply put, don't like to work, agency problems in the employment relationship must be ubiquitous because the desires of effort-averse workers conflict with the needs of employers to have their employees work. Agency theory emphasizes the development of either optimal contracts to align incentives between agents and principals, or else ways of monitoring and controlling behavior to preclude shirking.

The portrayal of people in these economic models is virtually Newtonian:

> [E]mployees remain in a state of rest unless compelled to change that state by a stronger force impressed upon them—namely, an optimal labor contract. Various incentive features of internal labor markets are claimed to provide forms of insurance that overcome worker's reluctance to work. (Baron, 1988, p. 494)

If one believes that people are effort-averse and prone to shirking, are opportunistic and therefore are likely to engage in subtle or perhaps not so subtle forms of deceit, and that it is management's job to preclude this from happening, there is little surprise that there is so much emphasis on surveillance and control, and so little attention paid to developing collaborative relationships. Trust is virtually precluded by these formulations of human behavior.

But certainly this account must give too much credit to economic theories that few actual managers learned in school or read about elsewhere. There are two responses to this objection. First, the implicit theories of human behavior represented in these perspectives dominate (and have dominated) business education for a long time. One need not know the niceties of Williamson (1985) or Jensen and Meckling (1976) to be influenced by their implicit conceptions of the world and human behavior. Second, one could argue that these economic approaches and managerial behavior are both related to underlying social values pervasive in the United States—a country that has a social Darwinist legacy, an almost religious belief in the prepotency of markets, and a tradition of laissez faire that emphasizes the ability of narrowly self-interested behavior to produce optimal system-level results as long as there is open competition and plenty of information. For whatever reason, trust is noticeably absent from the implicit theories of behavior that guide things, ranging from the design of compensation and control systems in organizations to the reform of health care in the United States—a movement that proceeds as if the main problem is controlling the greedy rapacity of doctors and the desire of patients to consume as much medical care as they can.

Nor is it the case that erroneous assumptions about human motivation and behavior will necessarily be readily corrected when confronted with disconfirming evidence. In the first place, processes of selective perception act to ensure that contrary data are not noticed. We see what we expect to see. In the second place, as Kuhn (1970) argued in the case of science, it takes an alternative theory to replace one that is under attack because of inconsistent data—the data alone are insufficient. Although there are a number of alternative theoretical conceptions of behavior that could conceivably replace those prominent in agency and transactions cost theories—including self-perception and cognitive dissonance, reactance theory, and the self-fulfilling prophecy—none has yet done so. But perhaps the biggest factor accounting for the persistence of these models of human behavior that foster distrust and a legalistic approach to the employment relation is that theories of human behavior create the very behavior they are supposed to explain. By acting on the basis of our perspectives, we produce in the behavior of others actions that confirm the theories we began with.

In the domain of trust and cooperation, this is nicely illustrated by the classic experiment reported by Strickland (1958). Subjects were placed in a situation in which they observed one subordinate more closely than another, with the assignment of whom they would monitor more closely being random. Both subordinates were, in fact, confederates of the experimenter and in fact behaved and performed similarly. Subjects, however, came to believe that the subordinate monitored more closely did in fact require more supervision and was less trustworthy. Strickland noted that the supervisors confronted a fundamental dilemma:

> The supervisor . . . may become victimized by his own previous . . . behavior. If his interactions with the subordinates have been largely confined to frequent monitoring of the subordinates' work . . . then the supervisor has, in effect, denied himself the opportunity to obtain relevant information concerning their unsupervised work efforts . . . he will tend to perceive the causal locus for the work efforts . . . as being "outside" them. . . . Such an inference will obviously have consequences for his future interaction . . . and something like a self-perpetuating information loss may be the result (p. 201).

A study by Lingle, Brock, and Cialdini (1977) demonstrated that the effects were even more pernicious. Giving someone the job of surveillance furnishes that person with a reason—justifying his or her own activity—not only for discovering a need for surveillance, but even for provoking or manufacturing the forbidden activities. Their experimental study of entrapment discovered that surveillance did produce distrust and alienation, but also actually increased the frequency of the undesired behaviors by stimulating entrapment activities.

There is no reason to believe that, in the domain of monitoring, surveillance, and control, we would observe any less effect for behavior to create self-reinforcing cycles of response on the part of others than has been observed in interviewing situations or male-female interactions (Snyder, 1982). Thus, in addition to all of the commitment effects and self-perception reasons that would preclude changing the perception of workers as opportunistic, effort-averse, and untrustworthy, the behavior that managers enact, based on such assumptions, tends to actually produce workers who exhibit those undesired characteristics—and a self-perpetuating cycle of distrust and misbehavior is created.

■ Conclusion

Considering the various costs and consequences of the legalization of the employment relation leads to a set of fairly simple conclusions. First, because these costs are significant, understanding the process of legalization, and how what often begins as a sensible attempt to provide due process and procedural justice can go awry with more emphasis on the procedure than on justice, is an important research task. What this volume asks the reader to do is not take legalization for granted, but to explore why and how it has advanced more in some domains and in some settings than others. It is particularly important to find and study settings in which what often seems to be an inexorable trend toward formalization and legalization is reversed. We desperately need to know more about what produces change in this process.

Second, better information on the full costs of legalization in different settings, and even in different countries, would be quite useful. There is evidence that legalization hinders the delivery of medical care in the United States—witness the furor over the practice of defensive medicine and the claims about malpractice insurance driving up the cost of medical care. There is evidence presented in this chapter that legalization drives up the cost of the employment relation, and somewhat ironically leads organizations to want to avoid employees by using temporary help and outside contractors. But the full range of settings and the full range of costs remain to be thoroughly documented.

Finally, the hidden, and not so hidden, costs of the legalization of the employment relationship, even under competitive pressure to become more efficient and productive, suggest that analysis based on the presumption of some inexorable efficiency logic is almost certainly flawed. Organizations persist in expending resources in ways that not only do not provide proportional economic benefit, but also often increase the very problems they were supposed to solve. The ability of such behavior to persist suggests that the internal self-perpetuating dynamics of distrust and conflict are difficult to overcome, in large measure because distrust and conflict produce behavior that justifies distrust and further conflict.

The positive feedback inherent in these processes means that change is difficult to accomplish. The dynamics described in this chapter, and the process of legalization covered throughout this volume, can provide a partial answer to the perplexing question of why firms continue to behave toward their work force in ways that are inconsistent with what we know good management practice to be, that are incompatible with what they are trying to accomplish with that work force, and that are often quite costly. Once started down the process, it is as if the organizations are unable to extricate themselves, or even at times to see clearly both the course they are on and the possibility of any alternatives.

■ References

Adler, P. S. (in press). The "learning bureaucracy": New United Motor Manufacturing, Inc. In B. M. Staw & L. L. Cummings (Eds.), *Research in Organizational Behavior*. Greenwich, CT: JAI Press.

Baron, J. N. (1988). The employment relation as a social relation. *Journal of the Japanese and International Economies, 2*, 492-525.

Baron, J. N., Dobbin, F., & Jennings, P. D. (1986). War and peace: The evolution of modern personnel administration in U.S. industry. *American Journal of Sociology, 92*, 350-383.

Braverman, H. (1974). *Labor and monopoly capital*. New York: Monthly Review Press.

Clawson, D. (1980). *Bureaucracy and the labor process: The transformation of U.S. industry, 1860-1920*. New York: Monthly Review Press.

Dertouzos, J. N., Holland, E., & Ebener, P. (1988). *The legal and economic consequences of wrongful termination*. Santa Monica, CA: RAND.

Edwards, R. (1979). *Contested terrain: The transformation of the workplace in the twentieth century*. New York: Basic Books.

Eisenhardt, K. M. (1989). Agency theory: An assessment and review. *Academy of Management Review, 14*, 57-74.

Flanagan, R. J. (1987). *Labor relations and the litigation explosion*. Washington, DC: Brookings Institution.

Frank, R. H. (1988). *Passions within reason: The strategic role of the emotions*. New York: Norton.

Geyelein, M. (1989, September 7). Fired managers winning more. *Wall Street Journal*, p. B1.

Hill, A. D. (1987). *"Wrongful discharge" and the derogation of the at-will employment doctrine* (Labor Relations and Public Policy Series No. 31). Philadelphia: Industrial Research Unit, Wharton School, University of Pennsylvania.

Ibarra, H., & Andrews, S. B. (1993). Power, social influence, and sense making: Effects of network centrality and proximity on employee perceptions. *Administrative Science Quarterly, 38*, 277-303.

Jacoby, S. M. (1985). *Employing bureaucracy: Managers, unions, and the transformation of work in American industry, 1900-1945*. New York: Columbia University Press.

Jacoby, S. M. (1991). American exceptionalism revisited: The importance of management. In S. M. Jacoby (Ed.), *Masters to managers: Historical and comparative perspectives on American employers* (pp. 173-200). New York: Columbia University Press.

Jensen, M. C., & Meckling, W. H. (1976). Theory of the firm: Managerial behavior, agency costs and ownership structure. *Journal of Financial Economics, 3*, 305-360.

Kuhn, T. S. (1970). *The structure of scientific revolutions* (2nd ed.). Chicago: University of Chicago Press.

Lacey, R. (1986). *Ford: The man and the machine*. New York: Ballantine.

Lingle, J. H., Brock, T. C., & Cialdini, R. B. (1977). Surveillance instigates entrapment when violations are observed, when personal involvement is high, and when sanctions are severe. *Journal of Personality and Social Psychology, 35*, 419-429.

Lopez, J. A. (1990, October 5). When "big brother" watches, workers face health risks. *Wall Street Journal*, p. C9.

Pfeffer, J. (in press). *Competitive advantage through people: Unleashing the power of the work force*. Boston: Harvard Business School Press.

Pfeffer, J., & Baron, J. N. (1988). Taking the workers back out: Recent trends in the structuring of employment. In B. M. Staw & L. L. Cummings (Eds.), *Research in organizational behavior* (Vol. 10, pp. 257-303). Greenwich, CT: JAI Press.

Salancik, G. R. (1977). Commitment and the control of organizational behavior and belief. In B. M. Staw & G. R. Salancik (Eds.), *New directions in organizational behavior* (pp. 1-54). Chicago: St. Clair Press.

Shepard, I. M., Heylman, P., & Duston, R. L. (1989). *Without just cause: An employer's practical and legal guide on wrongful discharge*. Washington, DC: Bureau of National Affairs.

Sitkin, S. B, & Bies, R. J. (1993). The legalistic organization: Definitions, dimensions, and dilemmas. *Organization Science, 4*(3), 345-351.

Sitkin, S. B, & Roth, N. L. (1993). Explaining the limited effectiveness of legalistic remedies for trust/distrust. *Organization Science, 4*(3), 367-392.

Snyder, M. (1982, July). Self-fulfilling stereotypes. *Psychology Today, 16*, pp. 60-68.

Strickland, L. H. (1958). Surveillance and trust. *Journal of Personality, 26*: 200-215.

Taft, P., & Ross, P. (1969). American labor violence: Its causes, character, and outcome. In H. D. Graham & T. R. Gurr (Eds.), *Violence in America: Historical and comparative perspectives* (Vol. 1, pp. 221-301). Washington DC: Government Printing Office.

Williamson, O. E. (1985). *The economic institutions of capitalism.* New York: Free Press.

Zucker, L. G. (1986). Production of trust: Institutional sources of economic structure, 1840-1920. In B. M. Staw & L. L. Cummings (Eds.), *Research in Organizational Behavior* (Vol. 8, pp. 53-111). Greenwich, CT: JAI Press.

14

Litigation Mentality
and Organizational Learning

Chris Argyris

A central thrust of my comments will be concerned with the actionability of the research illustrated in this volume. Social scientists have, for years, been concerned with knowledge that has external validity. Such knowledge is applicable in the sense that it is relevant to real world problems. The concept of litigation mentality is clearly relevant and applicable.

But there can be a wide gap between being applicable and being actionable. By actionable, I mean knowledge that specifies the actual face-to-face behaviors that are required to implement the applicable insights (Argyris 1993).

I believe the gap between applicability and actionability is illustrated, in varying degrees, by most of the chapters in this book. I will try to illustrate this claim by focusing upon several of the chapters, but doing so in some depth.

One of the fundamental theses of this interesting and provocative book is that there is an increasing emphasis within organizations upon a litigation mentality (Bies & Tyler, 1993). The editors differentiate two distinct but interrelated litigation mentalities. I will label the first mentality as *legal-legalistic*. This type of legal mentality is characterized by (a) decisions being increasingly dominated by a concern for enforcing what is mandated by law and (b) infusing organizational governance activities with the aspirations and constraints of the legal order.

The causal connection between the legal laws and the behavior within the system is relatively straightforward. Organizational policies and rules regarding sexual harassment or racial discrimination are "caused" by the laws of the land. The laws are passed with the intention that this causal connection is clear: The requirements of the laws cause the behavior and policies. The causal connection, when implemented correctly, represents a match between intentions of society and the consequential actions of organizations.

I should like to label the second legalistic mentality *administrative-legalistic* mentality. The operational definition of administrative-legalistic mentality that I infer from the cases includes (a) adaptation of excessively cumbersome or inappropriate administrative control processes, (b) magnification of the control procedure, and (c) unnecessarily high levels of formalization and standards of uniformity.

The causality related to administrative legalistic is different from the one described in the legal-legalistic causality. First, the laws do not mandate that the organizations' reactions be excessive, magnified, or unnecessarily rigid. It is the agents of the organization who create these features. Thus, from a legal point of view, there is a mismatch between the intentions of the law and the reactions of the organization.

How do we account for a mismatch that, according to this volume, is massive? Moreover, how do we account for the fact that the mismatch perseveres? Most of the explanations in this book are in the form of generalizations of what is going on, such as excessive bureaucratization or increasing numbers of bypasses and cover-ups. To my knowledge formal managerial theory does not dictate that the production of actions should be excessive, cumbersome, magnified, and unnecessarily rigid. In this sense they are mismatches. Moreover, as I hope to show below, such actions are designed by individuals and protected by organizational structural factors (such as cultural norms). How come mismatches are produced; how come they persevere when they are counterproductive to formal managerial theory?

One possible explanation for the puzzle is that these mismatches are really matches with another set of organizational values and practices. We might hypothesize, for example, that the puzzle is created by agents of organizations striving to prevent the creation of embarrassment or threat if they are caught violating some laws. I intend to argue that this hypothesis is worth serious consideration. Moreover, I plan to argue that all organizations have ways of dealing with embarrassment or threat; that these ways are the underlying causes; and that the fear of being caught violating laws is an explanation that is valid but phenotypic. In order to illustrate this claim, I should like to introduce an organizational perspective, namely, a perspective about organizational learning.

■ Organizational Learning

The perspective to which I refer is learning at all levels of the organization (individual, group, intergroup, and organization).

Learning may be defined as (a) producing a match between intentions and actuality that is new to the actors, or (b) detecting and correcting mismatches. Learning occurs when diagnosis, or insight or understanding, or new ideas are actually implemented. How do you know when you know something? The answer is when you can produce what you say you know. From this perspective, learning is evidenced, in the final analysis, through action.

There are at least two generic forms of learning. In single-loop learning an error is detected and corrected by changing the actions of the participants. In double-loop learning the error is corrected by first changing the underlying governing values and policies, which, in turn, leads to new actions and, in turn, to new consequences (Argyris & Schön, 1974).

If human action is designed, then whenever human beings produce what they design, they are producing a match. This is also true where their designs follow the dictates of such factors as others, groups, organizational policies, and culture. This logic would say that whenever individuals produce what they design, they cannot be producing an error. Yet mismatches or errors do occur. How do we explain this puzzle?

One explanation for an error is lack of knowledge. "We did not know." Error due to this kind of ignorance is correctable through education. Indeed, this is the primary function of the educational system within society and within organizations. It could also be corrected by the legal staff in the organizations.

Recall that the authors described the legalistic actions as excessive, cumbersome, magnified, unduly rigid. Such actions are produced by design. But, I just said it was not possible for human beings to design and produce errors.

One explanation of this puzzle is that the individuals are producing cosequences that are consistent with the organizational defensive routines of their organizations.

Organizational defensive routines are any policies and practices that are intended to prevent the participants from experiencing embarrassment or threat and, at the same time, intentionally prevent the participants from getting at the causes of the embarrassment or threat. Organizational defensive routines are therefore antilearning and overprotective (Argyris 1990).

Formal managerial theories of governance do not, to my knowledge, admit to or sanction antilearning and overprotective actions. Therefore, defensive routines are often covered up and the cover-up is covered up. To implement this cover-up, organizational defensive routines are typically not discussable, while they are occurring, in problem-solving and decision-making meetings. Moreover, their undiscussability is also undiscussable. This produces another loop reinforcing the antilearning and overprotective features of defensive routines. The antilearning and overprotective character of these loops assures the development of self-reinforcing, self-fueling processes that are counterproductive to building effective learning organizations (Argyris 1990).

The chapter by Browning and Folger on plausible deniability contains many examples of organizational defensive routines. For example, they cite such rules as: Have vague recollections; use multiple, ambiguous estimations of wrongdoing; place blame on lower-level members; and use conceptual diversions to insulate the leaders from responsibility. The key to the successful implementation of these rules is to act consistently with them and act as if there is nothing being covered up. The actors know that they are withholding the truth about creating conditions for plausible deniability, but they act as if this is not the case. If others know that this is what is happening, the actors expect that the others will act as if this is not happening. The others hold the same defensive strategies as do the actors.

The same is true for the impression management activities of accountants and police described by Van Maanen and Pentland. The accountants are likely to cover up their intention of impression management with their clients. The police, at the local level, may collude openly to protect themselves, but cover up that they are doing so with the authorities above them.

■ Implications: A Different Perspective of Underlying Causes

The first implication, implicit in several chapters, made explicit by an organizational learning perspective, is to suggest that the underlying causes of litigation mentality in the domain of administration and governance are not laws but the organizational defensive routines. The laws activate the organizational defensive routines, which, in turn, produce the responses that many of the authors describe as inappropriate and counterproductive. In this sense the laws are surface causes; the organizational defenses are the underlying causes.

Several authors have asserted that the legalistic mentality is likely to develop at an increasing rate and cannot be explained except by attributions to the developmental perspective, namely "maturity." This assertion is inadequate. What is maturity? Is it age, is it size, is it technological sophistication? Could we find organizations with the same age or size that have varying degrees of litigation mentality? One way to begin addressing some of these questions is to measure the number, depth, and scope of influence of organizational defensive routines. I have found, for example, that some young organizations have more powerful organizational defensive routines than do others that are significantly older. I have also observed the reverse. What I have almost never observed is organizations who make these questions discussable and who give them priority in their education or change programs.

The various operational indices of legalistic mentality provided by the authors appear to me to be valid. The assertion that these will grow is a valid extrapolation from the empirical observation of legalistic mentality. However, this valid empirical generalization requires an explanation. Suggesting that the pattern is caused by increasing bureaucratization leaves unanswered the question of by what organizational mechanisms or processes this development occurs.

I suggest that, in the domain of organizational governance, it is the way actors deal with embarrassment or threat that leads to defensive routines that are self-sealing and counterproductive. (Sitkin & Roth, 1993; Staw, Sandelands, & Dutton, 1981). This is not a play on words. It is a focus of where causal responsibility lies.

For example, Randall and Baker (this volume) present an interesting argument about possible causes of the litigation mentality. The argument is, in effect:

There are limits in the capacity for human cognition.

These limits are dealt with by judgmental heuristic and knowledge structures.

These may eventually escalate into the institutional environment in the form of formal rules.

The argument, in my view, makes sense. The problem is that it is incomplete. The incompleteness, unless acknowledged (and eventually reduced through research), may cause some important misunderstandings. For example, the literature on cognitive limits also speaks of external memories that can be used to overcome the cognitive processing limits. Indeed Donald (1991) has proposed that the creation and use of external memory may be a key differentiating feature between human beings and other organisms. A central dilemma is that human beings use organizational defensive routines as a form of external memory (the defensive routines tell them how to think and act), then they act to exacerbate the counterproductive activities, because whenever actors follow the dictates of the defensive routines, they are reinforcing the counterproductive activities.

A similar conclusion may be drawn about their concept of knowledge structure. Randall and Baker state that "knowledge structures contain preconceptions, beliefs, and ideologies about the environment that help to frame and to anticipate events." This is precisely the core role of organizational defensive routines.

■ The Causes of Paradoxes

Sitkin and Bies (this volume) describe several paradoxes that materialize when organizations develop a strong litigation mentality. For example, there is the power paradox. Legalistic approaches intended to reduce the arbitrary use of power may actually increase it. The editors illustrate the paradox with the strategies to implement "plausible deniability" (Browning & Folger, this volume). If I understand these strategies, they require bypassing embarrassment or threat and covering up that this is going on. Bypass and cover-up strategies, in turn, are undiscussable and their undiscussability is undiscussable. Under these conditions learning cannot occur and dysfunctional features are not likely to be corrected. One result is the paradox that the authors correctly identify.

The same causal explanation may be applied to the rationality paradox. The example used is typically called "going by the book." The emphasis on strict rule adherence may undermine the rationality of organizational actions. I suggest that these consequences are correct as long as the intentions for "going by the book" are undiscussable and their undiscussability is undiscussable and uninfluenceable. (Roth, Sitkin, & House, this volume).

An organizational learning perspective of the kind that I am describing would lead to the conclusion that it is not correct to say that the litigation mentality causes the paradoxes. The way organizations deal with embarrassment and threat is the underlying causal factor. One has to include the operation of organizational defensive routines for a more complete explanation. These distinctions are especially important if one were to attempt to reduce the dysfunctional features of the litigation mentality so richly described in this volume.

■ Implications for Action

There are several unrecognized consequences of the above for scholarly research and for the practitioner.

Although the reader will find in this volume many explicit and tacit examples of defensive routines, there is little attention paid to how to reduce them, and even less to trying to do so through interventions in the settings in which they were discovered. This consequence is consistent with scholarly norms of being descriptive. What also follows is a normative consequence, namely, of indirectly supporting the status quo.

I recently reviewed the literature on organizational defensive routines and found it full of powerful examples. As in the case of this book, there was almost no attention given to interventions that illustrated how to reduce them (Argyris, 1993). I wonder how the perspective on cognitive limits and inferential heuristics would explain this phenomenon. Could it be, for example, that the rules about conducting rigorous descriptive research lead to knowledge structures that are used by scholars to legitimize the dearth of research on reducing the dysfunctional features of the litigation mentality? Or, how would the scholars who write about impression management use that concept to explain the phenomena?

The review of the literature on advice given by scholars (and expert practitioners) also exhibited a powerful pattern. The majority of the advice given about dealing with organizational defensive routines was abstract and not actionable. Moreover, where it approached actionability, if it were followed correctly, it would actually reinforce the very dysfunctional defenses that the advisers were trying to reduce (Argyris, 1990, 1993; Sitkin, 1992).

An example from this volume is Feldman and Levy, who suggest that, at times, actions that may appear to be failures may be sensible.

Gossip may keep channels open. Being hypocritical may promote useful changes. Information not used for making decisions may be useful for legitimating them. All these conclusions are valid. But their existence depends upon a cover-up. For example, the fact that channels are kept open by gossip is covered up—or it would not have to be gossip. Being hypocritical to promote useful change may achieve the change, and strengthen hypocrisy. Information used to legitimating decisions, which was not used in making the decisions, will reinforce the necessity for diplomacy and cover-up that such was the strategy used by the actors.

There is an even more profound normative impact of descriptive research on organizational defensive routines. Let us say that practitioners read the literature and find it full of compelling examples. They find few or no studies on how to reduce the defensive routines. They may then conclude, as do the researchers, that defensive routines are an integral part of everyday life. This is descriptively accurate—but dysfunctionally misleading. Because of the lack of research on how to reduce organizational defensive routines, the practitioners may understandably conclude that the defenses are not reducible. Many of them may conclude that it would be dangerous to try doing so. Indeed, scholars maintain this position explicitly (Schein, personal communication). More frequently, this position is maintained by scholars, perhaps unintentionally, by conducting years of research that illustrates defensive routines, and not including in their research programs research on how to overcome them (Argyris 1993).

The reasoning behind these consequences is not healthy for science or for practice. Conducting research on changing defensive routines would provide a more complete description of the universe as is. The research would produce descriptive generalizations about how organizations react when attempts are made to reduce their defensive routines. Moreover, the development of field experiments or interventions to change defensive routines would provide more rigorous tests of the existing empirical generalizations.

There is another consequence of descriptive research that most scholars would label, I believe, as unintended and undesirable. For example there are several chapters that focus upon the finite information-processing capacity of the human mind and the use of inferential heuristics by human beings. These two descriptive generalizations are among the best documented in the field of cognitive science and organizational behavior.

Randall and Baker use such knowledge to explain what happened in their case. For example: The policy was adopted without extensive consideration of alternatives. Yet other options were available. Despite numerous and various complaints, the Bunker Hill managers did not review any of the other plausible options, nor did they reconsider or revise the fetal protection policy.

The authors' explanation for what they observed included:

- Managers have limited information-processing capacity.
- Managers' attentiveness was focused on the vivid cues of legal liability.
- Knowledge structure about the role of women was not questioned (because) the knowledge structures' function, to tell human beings what to think and believe, was accepted, and the acceptance was taken for granted.

The unintended consequence of these explanations is that they can be used by the actors to explain away their lack of personal causal responsibility. They could say, in effect:

- We are limited information-processors and, given all the pressures on us, we did our best.
- We focused on the vivid cues, just as social scientists say our mind works.
- We took the powerful knowledge structures for granted, just as social scientists find that human beings do when they take action under the pressures of everyday life.

In other words, without research on how to overcome the potential dysfunctional features of cognitive limits, inferential heuristics, and knowledge structures, the practitioners could legitimately distance themselves from their causal responsibility. Like Van Maanen and Pentland, I, too, have witnessed accountants and police, when "caught," attempting to protect themselves by claiming that everyone does it; that it is a part of organizational life. The argument above could be used by some to give their defensive reactions scientific respectability. Thus, the descriptive generalizations become normative propositions in a way that is unintended by scholars.

Scholars may wish to distance themselves from their causal responsibility in facilitating such defensive reasoning on the part of practitioners. I believe that such a strategy is counterproductive.

The concern is that readers could interpret scholarly conclusions in ways that were never intended by the scholars, namely, to permit practitioners to distance themselves from their personal responsibility in creating problems. One way to minimize the likelihood that this possibility will occur is to produce scholarly research that specifies ways to reduce the dysfunctional features of limited information-processing, inferential heuristic, and organizational defensive routines (knowledge structures).

We, as scholars, have to face up to the fact that the universes we describe are created by human beings. For example, it is human beings who create litigation mentality. Thus, when we describe the litigation mentality, we are describing a phenomenon that is created by human beings, based on their theories of action. Theories of action are normative theories; they are theories about effectiveness (Argyris & Schön, 1974). Scholars who maintain that their primary function is to describe reality are producing generalizations that are created by actors with normative intentions. If we do not examine these normative theories of action, to question inconsistencies or gaps, we are likely to be colluding in maintaining the status quo. Ironically, such collusion is normative.

For example, there are several core relational concepts in the behavioral theory of the firm (Cyert & March, 1963). They include premises about limited learning, coalition groups, and organizational politics. These phenomena are assumed to be basic to the nature of organizations and not likely to be changeable. Early practical management theorists, who advised the use of hierarchical organizations and scientific management, made the same assumptions (Argyris, 1957).

Practitioners followed the advice of these managerial gurus, even though, as Simon (1976) has shown, their advice is full of inconsistencies. This results in concepts, such as those just described, that the Behavioral Theory of the Firm defines as part of the nature of the universe. Thus, we have practitioners creating a universe based on shaky assumptions and scholars who describe important features of it as reality and not likely to be altered. I suggest that this will lead to science whose knowledge seeking will be unrealizingly limited (Argyris, forthcoming).

The negative impact on practice is that it will reinforce incorrect managerial assumptions and lead to the strengthening of organizational defensive routines.

There is a final concern. Scholars appear to have a predisposition to stay away from conducting scholarly interventions to reduce the features of the everyday world that they describe as dysfunctional. The argument that I have heard most often is that such research is akin to applied and less to basic research. This argument is reinforced by Cronbach and Suppes (1969), who separate "conclusion-oriented research" (basic research) from "decision-oriented research" (applied). Coleman (1972) makes a similar destinction between "discipline research" and "policy research."

Lewin, in my opinion, would not agree with this distinction. I believe that his genius was to conduct basic research, for example, on small groups and on authoritarian and democratic climates that greatly informed social psychological theory as well as decisions, policies, educational activities, buying bonds, and feeding children nutritious foods. (Argyris, 1993).

I suggest the basis for these distinctions between basic and applied research is that they are consistent with the present norms of the scholarly community. Such norms are powerful (Kuhn, 1970). They provide scholars with the legalistic mentality that can lead to the same defensive routines, such as impression management.

My first experience that illustrates this possibility came several decades ago, when I was a member of a board of scholars advising the Ford Foundation on how to spend its money to support behavioral research. The representatives of the foundation with whom we talked were all world-class scholars. To my surprise every one of them expressed a deep mistrust of the idea that scholars are genuinely concerned about helping to create a better world. Several even said that they would expect scholars to lie in their proposals about their concern for actionability of knowledge because the foundation indicated that this was an increasing concern of its top officials and directors. When I asked if they could cite examples, they did so easily. Moreover they began with themselves. Although, I do not have any systematic evidence, my hypothesis is that one reason the Ford Foundation became more activist is that it gave up on the best and brightest in the scholarly community.

Recently, some evidence has appeared that is consistent with this hypothesis. In a recent article Johnson (1993) describes the increasing frustration and disenchantment of friends of science in Congress with the promises made by scholars that have not been kept. Representative George E. Brown, who is described by Johnson as a great champion for science, recently wrote a report that warned about the credibility of scholars with some of their closest allies and supporters, because of the increasing breach between the generators of and users of knowledge. Apparently, scientists promised nearly 30 years ago to strive to reduce this breach. The conclusion today, to put it mildly, is that the promises are seen as part of a deliberate impression management by scientists in order to get money to do what they please.

I believe this inference has more validity than we as scholars care to admit. I also believe that, due to individual and scholarly community defenses, it is unlikely the senior members will take much corrective action. And finally, I believe that all we are doing is sacrificing the opportunities for younger scholars to get future funding. Foundations and Congress will act in ways to create their own policies and "laws" that will be reminiscent of the litigation mentality described in this book. What I am suggesting is that, if our research on organizational litigation does not address the issues described above, then we as scholars will be recreating and maintaining the very phenomena that we study.

■ References

Argyris, C. (1957). *Personality & Organization*. New York: Harper & Row.

Argyris, C. (1990). *Overcoming organizational defenses*. Needham, MA: Allyn & Bacon.

Argyris, C. (1993). *Knowledge for action*. San Francisco: Jossey-Bass.

Argyris, C. (forthcoming). Unrecognized defenses of scholars: Impact on theory and research.

Argyris, C., & Schön, D. (1974). *Theory in practice*. San Francisco: Jossey-Bass.

Bies, R. J., & Tyler, T. R. (1993). The "litigation mentality" in organizations: A test of alternative psychological explanations. *Organization Science, 4*(3).

Coleman, J. S. (1972). *Policy research in the social sciences*. Morristown, NJ: General Learning Press.

Cyert, R. M., & March, J. G. (1963). *A behavioral theory of the firm*. Englewood Cliffs, NJ: Prentice-Hall.

Cronbach, L. J., & Suppes, P. (Eds.). (1969). *Research for tomorrow's schools*. London: Macmillan.

Donald, M. (1991). *Origins of the modern mind*. Cambridge, UK: Cambridge University Press.

Johnson, D. (1993). Psychology in Washington: Measurement to improve scientific productivity: A reflection on the Brown report. *Psychological Science, 4*(2), 67-69.

Kuhn, T. S. (1970). *The structure of scientific revolutions* (2nd ed.). Chicago: University of Chicago Press.

Simon, H. A. (1976). *Administrative behavior* (2nd ed.). New York: Macmillan. (Original work published 1946)

Sitkin, S. B. (1992). Learning through failure: The strategy of small losses. *Research in Organizational Behavior, 14*, 231-266.

Sitkin, S. B, & Roth, N. L. (1993). Explaining the limited effectiveness of legalistic remedies for trust/distrust. *Organization Science, 4*(3), 345-351.

Staw, B. M., Sandelands, L. E., & Dutton, J. E. (1981). Threat-rigidity effects in organizational behavior: A multilevel analysis. *Administrative Science Quarterly, 26*(4), 501-524.

Author Index

Subject Index

About the Contributors

Chris Argyris is the James Bryant Conant Professor of Organizational Behavior and Education at the Schools of Business and Education at Harvard University. He received his A.B. from Clark University, his M.A. from Kansas University, his Ph.D. from Cornell University, and honorary doctorates from McGill University, University of Leuven, DePaul University, Stockholm School of Economics, and IMCB. From 1951 to 1971 he was a faculty member at Yale University, serving as chair of the Administrative Sciences Department during the latter part of this period. His present research focuses on organizational learning, intervention, and organizational change. Some of his more recent books are *Knowledge for Action, Organizational Learning, Overcoming Organizational Defenses*, and *Action Science* (with Robert Putnam and Dianna Smith).

Douglas D. Baker is an associate professor in the Management and Systems Department at Washington State University. His research interests lie at both the individual and organization level and include change in organizational structure, decision making, goal setting, sexual harassment, and theory construction. His work has been published in *Academy of Management Journal, Basic and Applied Social Psychology, Decision Sciences, Group and Organization Studies, Human Performance, Journal of Applied Psychology, Journal of Organizational Behavior, Motivation and Emotion*, and *Sex Roles*. He has consulted with a number of corporations in the United States and Australia and has received four teaching awards from graduate and undergraduate students. The work on his Ph.D. was done at the University of Nebraska-Lincoln. Prior to his doctoral work, he attended Colorado State University and The Ohio State University.

Robert J. Bies is an associate professor of management in the School of Business Administration at Georgetown University. His research interests include the delivery of bad news, the "litigation mentality," privacy, and procedural justice in organizations. He has published articles on these topics in the *Academy of Management Journal, Organization Science, Academy of Management Review, Organizational Behavior and Human Decision Processes, Human Relations, Research in Organizational Behavior, Research on Negotiation in Organizations, The Employee Responsibilities and Rights Journal, Social Justice Research,* and *Communication Research.* He received his B.A. and M.B.A. from the University of Washington, and his Ph.D. from Stanford University.

Larry D. Browning is an associate professor of organizational communication in the Department of Speech Communication at The University of Texas at Austin, and director of research for Partnerwerks, an Austin-based research and training firm that focuses on cooperation in competitive environments. In addition to studying communication under conditions of risk, he does research on cross-functional teamwork at Motorola, and cooperation among competitors at SEMATECH. He received his Ph.D. from The Ohio State University in communication and organizational psychology.

Mary J. Culnan is an associate professor in the School of Business Administration, Georgetown University. Her research interests include information privacy, organizational information processing, and the social and public policy impacts of information technology. Her work has been published in the *MIS Quarterly, Management Science, Organization Science, Decision Sciences,* and the *Journal of the American Society for Information Science.* Her research on constituent mail processing in U.S. Senate offices was funded by the National Science Foundation. She has also testified before Congress on consumer privacy. Dr. Culnan received her Ph.D. from the Graduate School of Management at the University of California, Los Angeles.

Martha S. Feldman is an associate professor of political science and public policy at the University of Michigan, Ann Arbor. Her research interests involve how people construct their social reality and how they act in a social context. Her particular focus has been on organizational decision making and how various forms of information and communication are involved in that process. She is currently studying organizational routines as a form of intelligence that is organizational rather than individual. Her publications include *Order Without Design: Information Production and Policy Making, Reconstructing Reality in the Courtroom* (co-authored with W. Lance Bennett), and "Information in Organizations as Signal and Symbol" (coauthored with James G. March).

Robert Folger is professor of organizational behavior at the A. B. Freeman School of Business, Tulane University. He has been on the editorial board of the *Journal of Management* and has published in such journals as the *Academy of Management Journal, Journal of Applied Psychology, Journal of Personality and Social Psychology, Psychological Bulletin,* and *Psychological Review.* He also coauthored *Controversial Issues in Social Research Methods* and edited *The Sense of Injustice.* His interests include work motivation, procedural justice, business ethics, and entrepreneurship.

Ann House is an assistant professor of communication arts and sciences at Western Illinois University. She received her Ph.D. from The University of Texas and is currently working on the relationship between knowledge and communication.

Jeffrey B. Kaufmann is currently a doctoral candidate in corporate strategy at the University of North Carolina-Chapel Hill. His research interests include organizational responses to crisis situations, corporate governance, and the use of hybrid organizational structures to cope with environmental and technological uncertainty. Kaufmann received his J.D. from the College of William and Mary, where he was the managing editor of the *Administrative Law Review.*

Idalene F. Kesner is a professor at the Kenan-Flagler School of Business of the University of North Carolina-Chapel Hill. Much of her work is concentrated in the areas of CEO succession, corporate boards, and mergers and acquisitions. She has been published in numerous journals, including *Academy of Management Journal, Strategic Management Journal,* and *Organization Science.* She has also been active in teaching and consulting on the subject of corporate boards of directors. Kesner received her B.B.A. from Southern Methodist University, her M.B.A. and Ph.D. from Indiana University.

Deborah M. Kolb is a professor of management at the Simmons College Graduate School of Management, and executive director of the Program on Negotiation at Harvard Law School. She is the author of *The Mediators,* coeditor of *Hidden Conflict in Organizations: Uncovering Behind-the-Scenes Disputes,* and the editor of *Making Talk Work: Profiles of Mediators at Work.* She is currently carrying out field research on gender issues in negotiations, dispute resolution and diversity, and work/family practices and their gender equity in corporations. She received her B.A. from Vassar College, M.B.A. from the University of Colorado, and Ph.D. from the Massachusetts Institute of Technology's Sloan School of Management.

Alan J. Levy is the director of public affairs for the University of Michigan Housing Division, one of the largest campus housing systems in the United States. He is responsible for media relations, internal and external communications, crisis management, and publications. He has a B.A. in political science from Middlebury College and did graduate work in international politics at the University of Michigan.

Brian T. Pentland is an assistant professor at the Anderson Graduate School of Management at the University of California, Los Angeles. He is currently doing research on generative models of organizational routines, classification of organizational processes, and technical service work. He received his Ph.D. in organization studies from the Massachusetts Institute of Technology.

Jeffrey Pfeffer is the Thomas D. Dee II Professor of Organizational Behavior at the Graduate School of Business, Stanford University. He received his B.S. and M.S. degrees from Carnegie-Mellon University, and his Ph.D. from Stanford Business School. He has served on the faculties of the University of Illinois; the University of California, Berkeley; and as a visiting professor at the Harvard Business School. He is the author of five books and more than 80 articles and book chapters. His book, *Organizations and Organization Theory,* won the George R. Terry Book Award from the Academy of Management, and he has won the Irwin Award for scholarly contributions to management.

Linda L. Putnam is professor and head of the Speech Communication and Theater Arts Department at Texas A&M University. Her current research interests include communication strategies in negotiation, organizational conflict, contradictory and paradoxical messages, and language analysis in conflict. She serves on the editorial boards of seven journals and has edited special issues on dispute resolution for *Communication Research* and *Management Communication Quarterly*. She is the co-editor of four books, including *Communication and Organization: An Interpretive Approach, Handbook of Organizational Communication,* and *Communication Perspectives on Negotiation,* a volume in the Sage Annual Reviews of Communication Research. Three of her articles and books have received best publication awards from the Organizational Communication Division of the Speech Communication Association. Putnam received her M.A. from the University of Wisconsin and her Ph.D. from the University of Minnesota.

Donna M. Randall is an associate professor and chair in the Department of Management and Systems at Washington State University. Her research interests lie in the areas of organizational behavior, reproductive risk in the workplace, and the study of organizational commitment. Her interest in business ethics has also been reflected in research on media coverage of elite crime, ethical decision-making models, and methodological problems in the study of business ethics. Her publications have appeared in such journals as *Decision Sciences, Academy of Management Review, Journal of Business Ethics, Proceedings of the Academy of Management, Journal of Vocational Behavior,* and *Journal of Business Research.* She has received a number of teaching awards from undergraduate and graduate students. She received her M.B.A. and Ph.D. in sociology from Washington State University.

Nancy L. Roth is assistant professor of communication at the School of Communication, Information and Library Studies, Rutgers University. Her research focuses on communication about uncomfortable topics, particularly in organizational settings. During the 1992-1993 academic year she was a Visiting Research Fellow at the National Centre for HIV Social Research, University of New South Wales, Australia. She received her Ph.D. in Speech Communication from The University of Texas.

W. Richard Scott is professor of sociology at Stanford University, with courtesy appointments in the Graduate School of Business, the School of Education, and the School of Medicine. He serves as director of the Stanford Center for Organizations Research. He is the author of *Organizations: Rational, Natural and Open Systems* and, together with John W. Meyer, he is compiling a second volume of essays and articles on institutional approaches to organizational environments.

Debra L. Shapiro is an associate professor of management at the Kenan-Flagler Business School at the University of North Carolina-Chapel Hill. Her research centers on actions managers take to manage conflict in organizations, including communication tactics designed to soften bad news, dispute intervention strategies, negotiation strategies, and grievance resolution procedures. Using laboratory, simulation, and field methodologies, she has examined factors that influence when, and to what extent, these conflict management strategies are successful. An author of more than 20 articles, she has been published in many scholarly and professional journals, including *Administrative Science Quarterly, Academy of Management Journal, Organizational Behavior and Human Decision Processes,* and *The Negotiation Journal.* Shapiro received her Ph.D. from the J. L. Kellogg Graduate School of Management, Northwestern University.

Sim B Sitkin is currently an assistant professor of management at the Graduate School of Business, The University of Texas. His primary research interests focus on the effect of legalistic influences and organizational control systems on organizational risk taking, learning, and adaptability. His research appears in edited collections and academic and professional journals, including *Administrative Science Quarterly, Academy of Management Review, Organization Science, Harvard Business Review, Human Communication Research,* and *Research in Organizational Behavior.* He currently serves on the editorial boards of *Organization Science* and the *Academy of Management Review.* Sitkin received his B.A. from Clark University, Ed.M. from Harvard University, and Ph.D. from Stanford University.

H. Jeff Smith is an assistant professor in the School of Business Administration at Georgetown University. His research focuses on societal reactions to strategic uses of information technology. In particular, he has studied the concerns related to personal privacy that often develop when new information technologies are introduced in the marketplace. He received his doctorate from Harvard Business School. From 1982 to 1987, he worked for the IBM Corporation, where his duties included the management of software development.

Michael J. Smitka is an associate professor of economics at Washington and Lee University. A specialist on the Japanese economy, he has written one book, *Competitive Ties: Subcontracting in the Japanese Automotive Industry.* During 1991-1992 he was a Japan Foundation Fellow and Visiting Scholar at the Faculty of Law, Rikkyo University, in Tokyo. He has also been a Fulbright Research Fellow at Hitotsubashi University. His current interests include law and economics, Japanese real estate markets, and the automotive industry, where he is conducting research in conjunction with the MIT International Motor Vehicle Program. He is a graduate of Harvard College and has his Ph.D. from Yale University.

Randall K. Stutman is an associate professor and director of applied communication in the Department of Rhetoric and Communication at Temple University in Philadelphia. His current research examines social influence and conflict processes in organizations. He is the author of two books on communication theory and maintains an active consulting practice in applied communication.

John Van Maanen is the Erwin Schell Professor of Organization Studies at the Sloan School of Management at the Massachusetts Institute of Technology. He publishes in the general area of occupational sociology. Cultural descriptions figure prominently in his studies of the work worlds of patrol officers on city streets in the United States; police detectives and their gov'nors in London; fishermen in the northeast Atlantic; and currently, ride operators at Disneyland. His latest book is an edited volume on ethnographic narratives, titled tentatively *In Other Wor(l)ds*.

Mark G. Yudof is Dean of the School of Law and holds the John Jeffers Research Chair in Law at The University of Texas at Austin. He received his B.A. in political science and his law degree from the University of Pennsylvania, where he was an editor of the *Pennsylvania Law Review*. He is the author or coauthor of many books and articles on education law, property taxation, and constitutional law, including *When Government Speaks* (for which he received the Scribes Most Meritorious Book Award in 1983) and *Educational Policy and the Law*. He has participated in numerous court cases, including *San Antonio v. Rodriguez* and *Pennzoil v. Texaco*. He has served on the executive committee of the American Association of Law Schools, is a Fellow of the American Bar Foundation and Texas Bar Foundation, and in Texas has served on the Governor's Task Force on Public Education and Task Force on School Finance.

Printed in the United States
By Bookmasters